Copyright © 2024 Linda Stevens

*All rights reserved. No part of this publication may be reproduced, distributed, or transmitted in any form or by any means, including photocopying, recording, or other electronic or mechanical methods, without the prior written permission of the publisher, except in the case of brief quotations embodied in critical reviews and certain other noncommercial uses permitted by copyright law.*

*CMSRN Exam Study Guide 2024-2025: All in One CMSRN Study Guide for the Certified Medical-Surgical Registered Nurse Certification. With CMSRN Exam Prep Review Material and 865 Practice Test Questions.*

*ISBN: 978-1-964079-43-1*

# CMSRN EXAM PREP

Disclaimer: The information contained within this book is intended for educational and informational purposes only. It is not designed to replace or substitute for professional medical advice, diagnosis, or treatment. Always seek the advice of a qualified physician or other healthcare provider with any questions you may have regarding a medical condition or treatment and before undertaking any new healthcare regimen.

The authors, editors, and publisher of this book have made every effort to provide accurate and up-to-date information. However, the medical field is constantly evolving, and information regarding standards of care, medications, dosages, or treatment protocols may change. Always consult the most recent reliable sources, including the latest research literature, drug formularies, and guidelines from relevant medical associations.

The authors, editors, and publisher expressly disclaim responsibility for any adverse effects, losses, or damages arising from your use of or reliance on any information contained within this book. Your use of this book and the information within constitutes your agreement to these terms.

# Table of Contents

Welcome..................................................................................................................4

Chapter 1: Medical-Surgical Nursing Foundations.................................................7

Chapter 2: Test-Taking Strategies and Mindset...................................................12

Chapter 3: Cardiovascular System........................................................................17

Chapter 4: Respiratory System.............................................................................45

Chapter 5: Endocrine System................................................................................54

Chapter 6: Gastrointestinal System......................................................................59

Chapter 7: Renal/Urologic System........................................................................66

Chapter 8: Neurological System...........................................................................70

Chapter 9: Musculoskeletal System......................................................................76

Chapter 10: Hematology/Oncology......................................................................82

Chapter 11: Integumentary System......................................................................88

Chapter 12: Perioperative Care.............................................................................92

Chapter 13: Domains of Nursing Practice.............................................................96

Practice Questions................................................................................................104

# Welcome

Imagine your hands, not smooth and pristine like a surgeon's, but slightly calloused, marked by long shifts and countless IV starts. Those aren't just the hands of a nurse; they're the hands of a healer, a problem-solver, a relentless advocate for those at their most vulnerable. You see things the rest of us don't, or try not to. You notice the subtle signs that tell you a patient is about to take a turn for the worse, the flicker of anxiety in a family member's eyes, the way a confused patient reaches for the familiar even when surrounded by the unfamiliar.

Medical-surgical nursing isn't glamorous. It's hard. It demands that you have an encyclopedic knowledge of the human body, the intuition of a seasoned detective, and the stamina to be on your feet for hours on end. You already know all of this. But what you might not know is that you're not just a nurse – you're poised to be a CMSRN.

That certification isn't another line on your resume. It's a testament. It says you won't settle for 'good enough.' That you're driven to be the absolute best nurse you can be. To see patterns others miss, to save lives others might not have caught in time. It's demanding – of course it is. The things worth having always are.

This book won't give you magic shortcuts. But it will be like having that incredibly knowledgeable senior nurse, the one with the hawk eyes and unflappable demeanor, right there whispering in your ear. We're going to dissect heart failure, not just as a disease, but as something you'll recognize at the bedside before the alarms even start going off. We'll untangle the web of medications, so you know what your patient is getting and why. And we'll walk through the chaos of emergencies, so when your patient's world is upside down, you'll be the steady anchor.

The CMSRN isn't about being a know-it-all. It's about knowing the right things at the right time. It's about having confidence in your gut feeling when things feel off because that 'feeling' is your hard-won experience speaking. This exam is the next step on your path. Let's get started.

Let's now talk about everything you need to know about the CMSRN exam itself – the nuts and bolts of what you'll face on test day and how to best prepare.

**Understanding the CMSRN Blueprint**

Think of the exam blueprint as your treasure map. It outlines every single topic that might appear on the exam and how heavily each area is weighted. Familiarize yourself with this blueprint thoroughly – it's your guide to prioritizing your study time. You can find it directly on the Medical-Surgical Nursing Certification Board (MSNCB) website, but let's break down the major content categories:

- **Cardiovascular (16%):** Heart failure, arrhythmias, myocardial infarctions – the big players in cardiac care.
- **Respiratory (13%):** COPD, asthma, pneumonia, respiratory failure – understanding how the lungs work and when they don't is critical.
- **Endocrine (10%):** Diabetes, thyroid disorders, adrenal insufficiency – metabolic issues that affect multiple body systems.

- **Gastrointestinal (12%):** GI bleeds, liver failure, bowel disease – knowing how the digestive system functions and the things that can go seriously wrong.
- **Renal/Urologic (10%):** Kidney disease, urinary tract infections, fluid and electrolyte imbalances – the delicate balance your body maintains.
- **Neurological (12%):** Stroke, seizures, traumatic brain injury – when the brain is compromised, every body system is at risk.
- **Musculoskeletal (8%):** Fractures, arthritis, compartment syndrome – knowing how movement works and how to support patients when it doesn't.
- **Hematology/Oncology (7%):** Anemias, bleeding disorders, cancers – understanding blood and the devastating things that can happen to it.
- **Integumentary (6%):** Wounds, burns, skin infections – often your first sign of trouble brewing in a patient.
- **Perioperative Care (6%):** Pre-op, intra-op, and post-op – what nurses need to know to support surgical patients through their journeys.

**Exam Logistics**
- **Computer-Based:** The CMSRN is taken at a testing center. You'll have 3 hours to answer 150 multiple-choice questions (125 scored, 25 unscored).
- **Eligibility:** You need a current, unrestricted RN license in the U.S. or its territories. Additionally, you must have practiced as a medical-surgical RN for a minimum amount of hours.
    - Option 1: 2000 hours within the last 3 years.
    - Option 2: 1000 hours within the last 3 years PLUS completion of a formal med-surg continuing education program

Understanding the format, content areas, and eligibility requirements gives you a solid foundation as you start to plan your studies and tackle this mountain.

Now let's shift gears from understanding the exam itself to focus on how to get the most out of this study guide. This isn't just a book to be passively read; it's a tool designed to help you actively learn and retain the crucial information needed to conquer the CMSRN.

Finding Your Starting Point
Self-Assessment: Be honest with yourself. Do you feel strong in some content areas but shaky in others? Is there a system, like respiratory, that totally terrifies you? Taking a practice exam early in your studies can reveal precisely where to focus your efforts.
Customize Your Approach: If you've been a med-surg nurse for years, you may not need to spend as much time on the basic anatomy and physiology as a newer nurse. On the other hand, even the most experienced med-surg nurses can have blind spots that need intensive review.
Engaging with the Material

Active Learning: Don't merely read or highlight passages. After learning a concept, try explaining it out loud as if you were teaching it to a colleague. Draw diagrams to visualize complex processes like the clotting cascade. Create flashcards, make concept maps, or use quizzing apps to test your recall.
Real-World Connection: As you study, think about patients you've actually cared for. Connecting a new piece of knowledge to a patient experience cements it in your mind – you'll remember the patient with severe COPD who looked barrel-chested or the patient who coded because of an unrecognized electrolyte imbalance.
Practice, Practice, Practice!

Practice Questions: This book includes practice questions, but seek out additional resources like online question banks. Practice questions help you apply your knowledge and get used to the question styles of the CMSRN.

Analyze Your Mistakes: Don't just get frustrated if you answer incorrectly. Figure out why you missed the question. Did you misread it? Was it a knowledge gap, or did you fall for a distractor?

Test-Taking Strategies

This guide will teach you not just content, but also strategies to tackle tricky questions confidently and manage your time wisely on exam day. Think of these strategies as extra tools for your toolbox.

Beyond the Book

Study Groups: Find a group of like-minded nurses also preparing for the CMSRN. Sharing knowledge and practicing questions together can offer support and different perspectives.

Online Resources: The MSNCB website offers resources and webinars. There are also online communities designed specifically for nurses pursuing certification.

Remember, this book is designed to be your roadmap, but success depends on how actively you travel the path.

# *Chapter 1: Medical-Surgical Nursing Foundations*

At its core, medical-surgical nursing is the art and science of caring for adult patients (typically 18 years and older) across a vast spectrum of conditions and illnesses. Med-surg nurses are the largest group of practicing nurses in the country, and for a good reason. They work in nearly every inpatient setting imaginable – from bustling hospital units to specialized clinics and rehab facilities.

Why Foundational Knowledge Matters
Think of the human body as a complex, interconnected network. A med-surg nurse must understand how each system works independently, how they affect each other, and how to recognize the often subtle signs that things are starting to go wrong. This foundational knowledge is what separates a nurse who merely performs tasks from a truly exceptional clinician.

Key Concepts We'll Explore
Holistic Assessment: Learning to rapidly assess a patient from head to toe, gathering objective data (vital signs, labs, physical signs) and combining it with the patient's story to form a clinical picture.
Prioritization and Decision-Making: In med-surg, things change rapidly. We'll learn how to distinguish what's immediately critical versus what can wait, and how to make sound judgments under pressure.
Evidence-Based Practice: Knowing not just what to do but why we do it. Understanding the research behind nursing interventions builds confidence and allows you to adapt to new information in this ever-evolving field.
Clinical Reasoning: This is the 'secret sauce' of expert med-surg nurses. It's the ability to connect the dots, recognize patterns, and anticipate complications before they happen. We'll develop this skill together.
Chapter Structure

This chapter will progressively build your understanding. We'll start with the big-picture concepts of a holistic approach to care and then focus on the core components of assessment and nursing interventions that form the base for every system we study throughout the book.

Are you ready to start building that strong foundation?

Now let's talk about the Scope of Practice and the specific role a CMSRN plays within the healthcare team. It's essential to understand the boundaries, expectations, and unique competencies that define this certification to make safe, effective clinical decisions.

CMSRN Scope of Practice
Think of the CMSRN Scope of Practice as your professional territory. It outlines the skills and knowledge you're qualified to use in patient care. Here's how it's defined by the Medical-Surgical Nursing Certification Board (MSNCB):

Assessment and Data Collection: Conducting comprehensive head-to-toe patient assessments, interpreting diagnostic data, and identifying both actual and potential problems or risks.
Planning and Developing a Care Plan: Creating individualized care plans based on evidence-based practice, patient needs and goals, and in collaboration with other healthcare professionals.

Nursing Interventions: Providing a broad range of therapeutic interventions, including medication administration, wound care, patient education, and supporting patients through complex procedures.
Evaluation: Continuously monitoring patients, assessing the effectiveness of interventions, revising the care plan if needed, and documenting the patient's progress meticulously.

Key Responsibilities of the CMSRN
Patient Advocacy: Championing the needs and rights of your patients, actively communicating with them and their families, and ensuring they understand their care options.
Collaboration: Working as an essential part of the interdisciplinary team, including physicians, respiratory therapists, pharmacists, and social workers. Effective communication is vital here.
Leadership: Often serving as charge nurses or mentors for newer nurses, CMSRNs guide and support the professional development of others in the med-surg setting.
Delegation: Appropriately delegating tasks to unlicensed assistive personnel (UAPs) and licensed practical nurses (LPNs), while retaining accountability for the overall care of the patient.
Quality Improvement: Participating in initiatives to improve patient outcomes, safety, and systems within the healthcare facility.

Why the CMSRN Scope Matters for the Exam
The CMSRN exam will absolutely test your understanding of professional boundaries. You'll encounter questions that ask you to determine if a specific task or intervention is something you can:

Do independently as an RN
Delegate to other licensed or unlicensed staff
Requires a physician's order or direct collaboration
Staying within your scope protects your license and keeps your patients safe.

**Mastering the Art of Detective Work: Holistic Assessment and Prioritization**
Imagine yourself as a medical detective, piecing together clues to solve a complex puzzle – the human body in distress. That's the essence of holistic assessment, a core skill for CMSRNs. It's not just about ticking boxes; it's about gathering a complete picture, merging objective data with the patient's story to identify underlying issues and prioritize interventions. Let's break this CSI-style investigation down into manageable steps, using real-world scenarios and a dash of humor (because let's face it, nursing can be intense, but it doesn't have to be devoid of personality!).

The Assessment A-Team: Your Tools of the Trade
Health History: This interview is your goldmine. Ask open-ended questions like "Tell me about your day" or "When did you first notice these symptoms?" Actively listen – verbal and nonverbal cues can be incredibly revealing.
Physical Examination: This is your hands-on detective work. Inspect, palpate, listen, and assess everything from vital signs to skin turgor. Remember, abnormalities are often subtle, so train your eagle eyes (and ears!).
Diagnostic Tests: Labs, X-rays, ultrasounds – these are your high-tech sidekicks, providing objective data to confirm or refine your suspicions.
A Step-by-Step Guide to Cracking the Case (Your Patient's Case, That Is!)

Data Collection: Gather information from the health history, physical exam, and diagnostic tests. Think of it as amassing evidence at the crime scene.

Data Analysis: Don't just collect data – analyze it! Look for patterns, inconsistencies, or anything that throws up red flags. Is the patient's heart rate racing despite a normal temperature? Is their breathing shallow and rapid? These could be vital clues.

Problem Identification: Based on your analysis, identify the actual or potential problems the patient is facing. Is it heart failure, pneumonia, or something else entirely?

Prioritization: Ah, the triage! Not all problems are created equal. Distinguish between immediate life threats (like a collapsing lung) and issues that can wait (like a sprained ankle). Here's a handy mnemonic to remember: ABCDE – Airway, Breathing, Circulation, Disability, Exposure/Environment. Focus on stabilizing the most critical issues first.

Real-World CSI: Putting Your Skills to the Test

Imagine you're admitting a patient complaining of severe abdominal pain. Their temperature is slightly elevated, but their heart rate and blood pressure are normal. During your assessment, you notice they're guarding their abdomen and wincing when you palpate a specific area. Uh oh, this screams potential appendicitis! This would be a high priority because a ruptured appendix can be life-threatening.

Unconventional Examples: Broadening Your Horizons

Think of a car mechanic troubleshooting a complex engine problem. They use a combination of diagnostic tools, their knowledge of the system, and intuition to pinpoint the issue. This parallels the detective work you do as a CMSRN!

Test-Taking Strategies: Conquering the NCLEX-Style Questions

The NCLEX (National Council Licensure Examination) loves to test your assessment and prioritization skills. Here are some tips to ace these questions:

Identify the Most Critical Cues: Focus on the signs and symptoms that point to the most immediate threat.

Beware of Distractor Answers: The exam might present tempting but incorrect options. Stick to your analysis and prioritize the most life-threatening issue.

Think Like a Nurse, Not a Doctor: While physician orders are crucial, some questions might ask about your initial assessment and prioritization independent of a doctor's intervention.

Holistic assessment and prioritization are the foundation of safe and effective nursing care. By mastering these skills, you'll be well on your way to becoming a confident, critical-thinking CMSRN, ready to tackle any medical mystery that comes your way. Now, go forth and assess with the eagle eyes of a true detective!

Picture yourself back on a busy med-surg unit, the air thrumming with activity. Two patients simultaneously ring call bells, one complaining of nausea while the other has a blood pressure that's starting to look a little too low. Your charge nurse is nowhere to be seen. You're on your own. This moment – this chaotic yet oh-so-common moment – is when clinical judgment and decision-making separate good nurses from exceptional ones.

Clinical judgment isn't a textbook definition; it's the invisible thought process that marries knowledge and experience into lightning-fast, high-stakes decisions. It's the difference between merely following orders and knowing when to question them. Let's dive into the inner workings of this essential skill, so you can ace those tricky exam questions and, more importantly, make sound choices that protect your patients.

**How Do We "Think Like a Nurse"?**

- **Pattern Recognition:** Experienced nurses don't treat every piece of data in isolation. They subconsciously compare it against patterns they've seen countless times before. Think of a cluster of subtle symptoms that, when viewed together, scream "early sepsis." That's pattern recognition.
- **Critical Thinking:** This is analyzing information, asking "Why"? questioning assumptions, and considering alternate possibilities. It's the voice in your head saying, "That low blood pressure doesn't make sense with his heart rate..."
- **Context Matters:** Clinical judgment isn't just about the patient in front of you. It's understanding the constraints of your unit – are you short-staffed? Is there a bed available in the ICU? These factors can influence your decision-making.

**Developing Your Clinical Eye**
Building expert clinical judgment takes time. Here's how you can accelerate the process:
- **Be a Sponge:** Don't just follow the care plan – ask your preceptor *why* they're ordering those interventions. Why is this medication given now and not later? Question everything until you understand the rationale.
- **Debriefing is Gold:** After a challenging patient situation, sit down with a seasoned nurse and replay your thought process. What did you consider? What other options were available? This helps rewire your brain.
- **Know Your Resources:** Be familiar with your hospital's policies, rapid response team protocols, and when to involve a physician. Having this knowledge at your fingertips is key during critical moments.

**Exam Tip:** The CMSRN will test your judgment with scenarios where there's no single "right" answer. Your task will be to justify your chosen action or recognize when a situation warrants immediate escalation. Speaking of scenarios, think about it this way: Imagine you're a mountain climber scaling a dangerous peak. You've spent months studying maps, training your body, and packing all the essential gear. But on the mountain, unexpected situations arise – a storm, an injured fellow climber. That's when your judgment truly kicks in. It's about applying knowledge flexibly, making tough choices, and sometimes, knowing when to call for help.

In a world overflowing with medical information, how do we separate the latest hyped-up fad from the truly life-saving interventions? Enter evidence-based practice (EBP), the bedrock of sound clinical decision-making on which the CMSRN exam heavily relies. Think of EBP as a detective tool for nurses – it helps us sift through the mountains of studies and research articles to find the practices that truly improve patient outcomes. Let's ditch the dusty textbooks and unpack EBP so that it makes sense on both the exam and the hospital floor.

Why Does EBP Matter?
Innovation is Constant: New drugs, treatments, and technologies emerge almost daily. EBP helps us separate promising innovations from those that are ineffective or even harmful.
Patient Safety: Relying solely on "that's the way we've always done it" isn't safe. EBP ensures we're always implementing the most up-to-date, research-backed care for our patients.
The CMSRN Exam Wants You to Think Critically: You'll encounter exam questions that test your ability to analyze research findings and apply them to patient scenarios.
The Steps of Putting EBP into Action

Ask a Clinical Question: Start with a specific problem you've encountered in practice. Example: "Does early ambulation after surgery reduce the risk of pneumonia in elderly patients?"
Search for Evidence: Don't just Google it! Utilize reliable sources like PubMed, Cochrane Library, and your hospital's evidence-based practice resources.
Appraise the Evidence: Not all research is created equal. Determine the quality of the study – was it a large randomized controlled trial (very reliable) or a small case study (less so)?
Integrate the Evidence with Your Expertise: Combine the best available research with your clinical judgment, patient preferences, and the unique circumstances of your healthcare setting.
Evaluate the Outcomes: Did implementing the change lead to improved patient outcomes? EBP is an ongoing process. We constantly learn and refine our care.
Real-World Scenario: Imagine a patient with a chronic wound that isn't healing. You could continue using the same dressing that's been standard for years, or you could delve into the research on newer wound care products. This empowers you to advocate for the best possible care for your patient.

Focus on understanding the big picture of EBP. The CMSRN is less likely to quiz you on the finer points of statistical analysis and more likely to test your ability to interpret research findings and understand their implications for practice.

# Chapter 2: Test-Taking Strategies and Mindset

Get ready to unlock the secrets of beating the CMSRN, strategize like a seasoned pro, and conquer your test-day anxiety! Chapter 2 isn't about memorizing facts or practicing calculations; it's about sharpening your mind and crafting an exam-day gameplan to maximize your chances of success.

Why a Winning Mindset Matters

Think of this chapter as the pre-game pep talk that turns knowledge into results. Even the most prepared nurse can crumble under the pressure of a high-stakes exam. We'll learn how to channel that nervous energy into laser-focused determination.

Strategies for Success
Test-taking is a skill, and just like any skill, it can be learned and refined. We'll explore proven techniques to:

Decode Complex Questions: Break down those intimidating, multi-part questions into manageable chunks so you can identify exactly what they're asking.
Manage Your Time: Learn how to pace yourself, avoid getting bogged down on difficult questions, and leave enough time to review your answers.
Second-Guess Smartly: We'll discuss when it's helpful to change your initial answer and when it's best to trust your gut instinct.
Eliminate Distractors: Master the art of zeroing in on the 'best' answer, even when multiple choices could technically be considered correct.
The Emotional Side of the Exam

Let's be honest, the CMSRN is stressful! We'll talk about how to:
Manage Test Anxiety: Learn breathing techniques, visualization exercises, and positive self-talk to calm your nerves and perform at your best.
Build Confidence: Recognize the power of preparation and focus on the knowledge you've already mastered rather than what you fear you don't know.
Embrace the Challenge: Shift your mindset from fear to excitement. This exam is your opportunity to prove just how awesome a nurse you truly are.
Buckle up and get ready to transform yourself from a med-surg expert to a test-taking ninja!

Speaking of mindset – let's address the elephant in the room: test anxiety. Even experienced, highly competent nurses can feel their heart pounding and their mind going blank when faced with a daunting exam. But the good news is, test anxiety doesn't have to control you. Let's dive into actionable strategies to conquer those exam-day jitters and unlock your full potential.

**Understanding Test Anxiety**
- **The Body's Fight or Flight Response:** That rapid heartbeat, nausea, and inability to think clearly? That's your ancient survival system kicking in, mistaking the CMSRN for a saber-toothed tiger. Not super helpful, is it?

- **Negative Thought Loops:** "I'm going to fail," "I don't know anything," – these thoughts spiral and become self-fulfilling prophecies.
- **Perfectionism Trap:** Aiming for a perfect score adds immense pressure and can sabotage your chances of doing well.

**Taking Control: Pre-Exam Strategies**
- **The Power of Preparation:** The more confident you feel about the material, the less intimidating the test becomes. Don't just memorize, seek to truly understand the concepts.
- **Visualization:** Picture yourself calmly taking the exam, answering questions confidently. Your brain can't always tell the difference between imagination and reality – use this to your advantage!
- **Mindfulness Techniques:** Deep breathing exercises, meditation, or simply focusing on the present moment calms the nervous system. Practice these regularly in the weeks leading up to the exam.

**Game Day Tactics**
- **Fuel Your Brain:** Eat a balanced breakfast – but skip the excessive caffeine, which can worsen anxiety.
- **Arrival Logistics:** Give yourself ample time to get to the test center, find the restroom, and settle in. Rushing adds unnecessary stress.
- **Combat Negativity:** If those panicky thoughts arise, counter them with positive affirmations: "I've studied hard, I'm ready for this."

**During the Exam**
- **Pace Yourself:** Start by skimming through the entire exam, noting the easy questions you'll tackle first. This builds momentum and confidence.
- **Breathing Breaks:** If you find yourself panicking, step away for a moment (if permitted), close your eyes, and take a few slow, deep breaths.
- **Trust Your Gut (Often):** That first instinct is usually the right one. Second-guessing yourself can lead to more errors.

Test anxiety is completely normal. By acknowledging it and employing specific strategies, you can redirect that nervous energy into laser-sharp focus. Embrace this exam as an opportunity to prove to yourself just how strong, smart, and capable you are.

Now, let's transition to one of the biggest challenges on the CMSRN: managing that ticking clock. This exam isn't just about knowing your stuff; it's also about knowing how to work quickly, accurately, and strategically. Let's transform you into a time management ninja!

**Why Time Management is Crucial**
- **Avoiding the Rush:** Running out of time forces you to rush through the remaining questions, increasing the chances of careless errors.
- **Maximizing Your Score:** A well-paced exam allows you to showcase your full understanding of the material, not just the answers you happen to finish in time.
- **Reducing Stress:** When you feel in control of your time, it frees up mental space to focus on the questions themselves, improving your critical thinking.

**Pre-Exam Prep**
- **Practice Tests Under Pressure:** Simulate exam conditions as closely as possible. Time yourself and force yourself to finish within the allotted limit. This will condition you to the flow of the real thing.

- **Know Your Weaknesses:** Are there certain topics that always trip you up and make you spend too much time? Devote extra study time to those areas.

**Exam Day Strategies**
- **The First Pass:** Scan the whole exam, quickly answering the easy questions. This builds confidence and reserves your brainpower for the tougher ones.
- **Time Allocation:** Give yourself a time "budget" per question based on the overall time limit. Practice sticking to it ruthlessly.
- **When You Get Stuck:** Don't let one tricky question derail you. Mark it, move on, and come back if you have time.
- **The Art of the Educated Guess:** If you're truly stumped, eliminate any obviously wrong answers and guess strategically.
- **Watch the Clock:** Check periodically to ensure you're on track. Avoid obsessing over every minute, but do make adjustments as needed.

**Exam Tip:** Some questions have longer stems (the setup before the actual question). Read the last sentence first to know exactly what they're asking, then go back and read the rest for details.

Think about it like this: Imagine you're a chef with a complex dish to prepare in a limited time. You don't try to cook everything all at once. You strategize, tackling some tasks simultaneously and saving the most challenging ones for when you can give them full attention. The CMSRN is similar – it's about working mindfully.

Now let's shift gears from managing time to dissecting the CMSRN's trickiest questions. These complex, layered beasts are what separate those who merely pass from those who truly ace the exam. Get ready to think like a detective and uncover the hidden clues within those intimidating blocks of text!

Why Complex Questions Are Tricky
Multiple Layers: They often test several concepts simultaneously, requiring you to juggle different areas of knowledge at once.
Ambiguous Wording: The question might be intentionally vague, forcing you to make inferences and consider different possibilities.
Information Overload: They can bury the real question within a whole backstory about a patient. You need to sift through those details and pinpoint what's crucial.
The Art of Decoding

Breathe: Don't panic when you see a wall of text. Take a deep breath and tell yourself, "I've got this."
The Question Within the Question: Focus on the last sentence. What exactly are they asking you to determine? Is it about prioritization, diagnosis, medication selection?
Highlight Keywords: Look for words like "initial," "most likely," "primary," or "least likely." These words guide your thinking.
The Patient Sketch: As you read, mentally sketch out the patient. What's their main problem? Are there important vital signs or lab values that jump out at you?
Real-World Scenario: Imagine a question describing a post-surgical patient with fever, tachycardia, and a slightly elevated white blood cell count. You need to figure out if it's normal post-op inflammation, the start of an infection, or something else entirely.

Exam Tip: The CMSRN loves to test your understanding of subtle differences between similar conditions. Brush up on those easily confused diagnoses like different types of shock or similar-sounding medications.

Beyond Textbook Knowledge

Complex questions tap into those gray areas of medical practice where there isn't always a single right answer. Here's where your critical thinking skills truly shine:

Play Devil's Advocate: What are the potential arguments against the answer you're leaning towards? By anticipating counterarguments, you strengthen your reasoning.

Think Outside the Box: Have you considered less common complications or alternative possibilities for this presentation?

Let's now talk about those moments on the CMSRN where you get stuck, and you have to resort to the art of the educated guess. It's important to remember that guessing strategically can be the difference between passing and a close fail – so let's make those guesses count!

**When Should You Guess?**
- **Truly Stumped:** If you've re-read the question, eliminated some answers, and are still utterly baffled, don't waste precious time agonizing over it.
- **Running Out of Time:** If you find yourself running low on time, get through the remaining questions quickly. An educated guess is better than a blank answer.

**How to Guess Smartly**
1. **Eliminate the Obvious:** Knock out any answers that you know are definitely wrong. This often narrows down your options significantly.
2. **Look for Patterns:** Sometimes the test makers slip up and create answer choices with similar wording or an obvious outlier. Trust your instincts.
3. **Word Clues:** Look for keywords or root words within the question or answers that link back to your knowledge. Even a vague sense of familiarity can help.
4. **The 'First Instinct' Rule:** Often, your initial hunch is correct. If you're waffling between two answers, it's usually best to stick with your gut feeling.

Sometimes, the longest or most detailed answer choice is the right one. The test makers might be trying to distract you with short, overly simple answers.

**What NOT to Do**
- **Leave Questions Blank:** Always, always guess. You have absolutely nothing to lose and potentially a lot to gain.
- **Get Fixated on One Question:** Don't sacrifice answering several easy questions you know in order to agonize over one difficult one.
- **Change Answers Based on Panic:** Once you've made a reasoned guess, stick with it unless you have a truly compelling reason to switch.

Let's now talk about building the kind of rock-solid confidence that will carry you through the grueling hours of the CMSRN exam. This isn't just about pep talks or positive thinking; it's about cultivating a deep-rooted belief in your knowledge, skills, and ability to succeed under pressure.

**The Power of Preparation**

Honestly, the best way to combat exam nerves is to know you've mastered the material. Don't just memorize facts, strive for genuine understanding. Here's how:
- **Active Recall:** Practice questions, flashcards, and teaching concepts to yourself out loud. This forces your brain to retrieve information, which strengthens those neural pathways.

- **Mock Exams:** Take full-length practice tests under timed conditions. This simulates the exam day experience and helps you identify weak areas.
- **Embrace the Challenge:** Don't shy away from difficult topics. Attack them head-on. Every tough concept you master builds your confidence.

### The Mind-Body Connection

Your mental state significantly impacts your performance. Let's optimize both your brain and body for peak exam day performance:

- **Sleep is Sacred:** Pulling all-nighters cramming throws your body into chaos. Prioritize sleep in the weeks leading up to the exam.
- **Fuel Your Success:** Opt for a nutritious breakfast on exam day – think complex carbs for sustained energy and lean protein for mental alertness.
- **Breathing Breaks:** Remember those calming breaths we talked about for test anxiety? They work for boosting focus and clarity of thought as well.

### Exam Day Mindset

- **Visualize Success:** Imagine yourself confidently tackling questions, leaving the exam feeling accomplished. Your brain has trouble differentiating between visualization and reality – use this to your advantage!
- **Positive Self-Talk:** Counter negative thoughts like "I'm going to bomb this" with "I've prepared diligently, I'm ready to do my best."
- **Focus on the Present:** Don't dwell on past mistakes or worry about questions you haven't gotten to yet. Stay grounded in the task at hand.

The CMSRN is a difficult exam, and moments of self-doubt are normal. Acknowledge them, but don't let them take over. Trust in the hard work you've put in and believe in your ability to rise to the challenge.

# *Chapter 3: Cardiovascular System*

Now, let's get into the intricate workings of the cardiovascular system – the powerhouse that keeps your patients alive. This chapter is foundational to your CMSRN success, as heart-related problems are a significant part of medical-surgical nursing.

**Why It Matters**

Think of the cardiovascular system as an interconnected network that impacts every other organ system. Understanding its normal function, how things go wrong, and how to intervene will make you indispensable on your unit.

**Key Concepts & Anatomy Review**

We'll start by revisiting the basics of cardiac anatomy and physiology:
- **The Pump:** The heart's structure, its chambers, valves, and the all-important electrical conduction system
- **The Vessels:** Arteries, veins, and capillaries — those lifelines carrying oxygen and nutrients throughout the body
- **Blood Flow Dynamics:** Blood pressure, cardiac output, and the factors that influence them

**Common & Critical Conditions**

From heart failure to life-threatening arrhythmias, we'll delve into the pathophysiology, signs & symptoms, and treatment of these key cardiovascular diseases:
- **Heart Failure:** Both systolic vs. diastolic dysfunction, exacerbations, and how to manage them
- **Myocardial Infarctions:** Recognizing the different types, immediate interventions, and crucial ongoing care
- **Arrhythmias:** Interpreting those squiggly EKG lines, recognizing life-threatening rhythms, and understanding different treatments
- **Valvular Diseases:** Stenosis versus regurgitation, and the significance of those heart murmurs to guide your assessment

**Medications & Procedures**
- **Pharmacology Deep Dive:** We'll discuss medications like antiarrhythmics, inotropes, diuretics, and ACE inhibitors – their actions, side effects, and nursing considerations.
- **Cardiac Procedures:** From pacemakers to cardiac catheterizations, we'll explore pre- and post-procedure nursing care for your patients.

The CMSRN loves to test your understanding of how cardiovascular issues impact the whole patient. Be prepared for questions linking cardiac problems to respiratory distress, kidney function changes, and even altered mental status.

Get ready to master the complexities of the cardiovascular system. Your patients' hearts (and your CMSRN score!) will thank you.

## The Heart's Symphony: Chambers, Valves, and Coronary Circulation

The heart, a marvel of muscular engineering, acts as the tireless engine propelling blood throughout our body. To achieve this continuous flow, it relies on a precise interplay between its chambers, valves, and coronary circulation. Let's delve into the intricate details of these structures and how they orchestrate the vital rhythm of life.

### The Chambers: Powerhouse of Pumping

The heart is a four-chambered organ, divided into two upper chambers called atria (singular: atrium) and two lower chambers called ventricles. Each chamber plays a specific role in blood flow:

Right Atrium: This chamber acts as a collection point for deoxygenated blood returning from the body via the superior and inferior vena cavae.
Tricuspid Valve: Also known as the right atrioventricular (AV) valve, this valve safeguards the opening between the right atrium and the right ventricle. It ensures blood flows only forward, preventing backflow into the atrium.
Right Ventricle: Here, the deoxygenated blood receives a boost. The muscular walls of the right ventricle contract, pumping blood through the pulmonary valve.
Pulmonary Valve: Situated between the right ventricle and the pulmonary artery, this valve prevents blood from flowing back into the ventricle after ejection. It channels blood towards the lungs for oxygenation.
The Lungs: A Breath of Fresh Life
The pulmonary artery carries deoxygenated blood to the lungs, where it exchanges carbon dioxide for fresh oxygen. This oxygenated blood then makes its way back to the heart.

Left Atrium: This chamber serves as a temporary resting place for the oxygen-rich blood returning from the lungs via the pulmonary veins.
Mitral Valve (Bicuspid Valve): Located between the left atrium and left ventricle, this valve ensures one-way traffic, preventing oxygenated blood from flowing back into the atrium.
Left Ventricle: This is the heart's strongest chamber. Powerful contractions of the left ventricle propel oxygenated blood throughout the body via the aortic valve.
Aortic Valve: This valve guards the opening between the left ventricle and the aorta, the largest artery in the body. It prevents blood from regurgitating back into the ventricle after it has been ejected.
The Coronary Circulation: Fueling the Engine

Just like any engine, the heart needs its own fuel supply to function optimally. This critical task is accomplished by the coronary circulation system. The coronary arteries branch off from the aorta just above the aortic valve, delivering oxygenated blood directly to the heart muscle itself. The used blood, depleted of oxygen, drains back into the right atrium via the coronary sinus.

Maintaining the Rhythm: A Delicate Balance
The coordinated function of these chambers, valves, and coronary circulation is essential for proper cardiac function. Here's a breakdown of their vital roles:

Chambers: The atria act as receiving chambers, while the ventricles function as powerful pumps. This coordinated contraction and relaxation cycle ensures continuous blood flow.
Valves: These one-way valves prevent backflow, directing blood in the proper direction through the heart chambers. This maintains efficient blood flow and prevents pressure build-up in the wrong areas.
Coronary Circulation: This dedicated system nourishes the heart muscle itself, ensuring it has the oxygen and nutrients required for sustained contractions.
Any malfunction in these structures, whether a faulty valve, a weakened heart muscle, or a blockage in the coronary arteries, can disrupt this delicate balance and lead to various heart conditions.

Understanding the intricate interplay of these components is fundamental to providing optimal care for patients with cardiovascular issues.

By thoroughly comprehending the heart's anatomy and the symphony of its chambers, valves, and coronary circulation, you'll be well-equipped to excel in the CMSRN exam and provide exceptional care for your future patients.

## The Heart's Built-in Orchestra: Understanding the Cardiac Conduction System

Imagine a concert hall bustling with activity. The musicians (heart muscle cells) are all seated, instruments poised, but they wait for the conductor's cue to begin their grand symphony. In the heart, the conductor is the cardiac conduction system, a specialized network of cells responsible for initiating and coordinating the rhythmic contractions that keep blood pumping throughout your body. Understanding this intricate system is crucial for your success on the CMSRN exam, so let's grab our metaphorical stethoscopes and delve into the heart's electrical conduction system!

The Maestro: The Sinoatrial (SA) Node

Think of the SA node, located in the right atrium, as the heart's natural pacemaker. These specialized cells spontaneously generate electrical impulses, setting the tempo for the entire heart. Just like the conductor tapping their baton, the SA node initiates electrical signals that travel through the heart in a precise sequence.

From Atria to Ventricles: The AV Node as the Relay Station

The electrical impulse from the SA node first reaches the atrioventricular (AV) node, located between the atria and ventricles. Unlike the SA node, the AV node acts like a security guard, slowing down the signal before sending it onwards. This delay is vital – it allows the atria to contract completely, squeezing blood into the ventricles before they receive the signal to pump it out.

Imagine this: The sheet music reaches the conductor (SA node) first. They then tap their baton (electrical impulse) to cue the string and wind sections (atria) to play their opening melody (atrial contraction). But before the entire orchestra joins in (ventricular contraction), the conductor waits a beat to ensure the strings and winds are finished (atrial emptying). This ensures a smooth and coordinated performance (blood flow).

Down the Bundle of His: The Electrical Highway

Once the AV node gives the green light, the electrical signal speeds down a specialized pathway called the bundle of His. Think of this bundle as the electrical highway that efficiently transmits the signal to the ventricles. The bundle of His then divides into branches called Purkinje fibers, which fan out like electrical wires throughout the ventricles.

The Grand Finale: Purkinje Fibers and Ventricular Contraction

The Purkinje fibers deliver the electrical impulse directly to the muscle cells of the ventricles. This coordinated electrical stimulation causes the ventricles to contract forcefully, pumping blood out to the lungs and body. And just like that, the concert is in full swing – blood is flowing efficiently throughout the body!

Exam Tip:  The CMSRN exam loves to test your understanding of the sequence of electrical conduction. Remember the order: SA node → AV node → Bundle of His → Purkinje fibers → Ventricular contraction.

Real-World Connections: Beyond the Heart

The concept of electrical conduction systems isn't unique to the heart.  Think about how nerve impulses travel throughout your body, allowing you to move your muscles or feel sensations. Similar specialized cells coordinate these electrical signals, ensuring smooth and coordinated function.

Keeping the Rhythm: When Things Go Wrong

Disruptions in the cardiac conduction system can lead to arrhythmias, irregular heartbeats that can be life-threatening. Understanding the normal electrical conduction pathway will help you recognize abnormal rhythms on an EKG, a crucial skill for nurses.

Gear Up for Success: Mastering the Cardiac Conduction System

To solidify your understanding of this vital system:

Draw and Label: Sketch the cardiac conduction system and label each component.
Mnemonic Magic: Create a catchy mnemonic to remember the sequence (e.g., Silly Athletes Need Help Vaulting Poles).
Practice Makes Perfect: Take practice exams that focus on the cardiac conduction system and ECG interpretation.
By mastering the intricate workings of the cardiac conduction system, you'll not only shine on the CMSRN exam but also gain a deeper appreciation for the remarkable electrical marvel that keeps us alive: the human heart.

Think about the heart's action not as just a single pump, but as a continuous, rhythmic cycle of squeezing and relaxing.  This is the cardiac cycle, and it's the driving force behind blood flow.  Within this cycle, there are two main phases – systole, the period of contraction, and diastole, when the heart refills.  Let's dive deeper into each phase and examine how they work together to make the beautiful symphony of your heartbeat.

Systole: The Heart's Powerhouse Phase

Systole is like the power stroke of the heart.  Picture it squeezing mightily as it delivers life-giving oxygenated blood throughout your body.  There are several key things happening here:

Atrial Systole: This is the warmup act! The atria contract, giving a final little top-up to the ventricles, maximizing the amount of blood ejected with each heartbeat.
Ventricular Systole: The big squeeze! The ventricles contract forcefully, causing a spike in pressure within them. This high pressure slams shut the mitral and tricuspid valves (preventing backflow into the atria) and forces the aortic and pulmonary valves open, propelling blood forward.

Think about this: Imagine squeezing a water balloon. As pressure inside the balloon increases, it forces water out through any openings it can find. Your ventricle works in a similar way!

Diastole: Rest and Refuel

Diastole is when the heart muscle relaxes, allowing its chambers to refill with blood. Here's the breakdown:

Pressure Drop: As the ventricles relax, pressure within them drops below that of the atria and the aorta/pulmonary artery (think about the water balloon deflating).
Valves React: The mitral and tricuspid valves swing open (allowing blood flow from the atria), while the aortic and pulmonary valves snap shut (preventing blood backflow into the ventricles.
Passive Filling: The majority of ventricular filling happens during the initial part of diastole, even before the atria contract. Like water flowing downhill, blood rushes into the relaxed ventricles.

The Dance of Pressure and Volume

It's important to understand that pressure and volume within the heart have an inverse relationship. When pressure increases, volume decreases (think of squeezing that water balloon again) and vice versa. These shifts in pressure and volume are what open and close the heart valves at just the right moment, ensuring blood flows in the correct direction.

Exam Tip: The CMSRN loves to test your understanding of how these pressure changes relate to the opening and closing of valves. Make sure you grasp the concept that it's not just muscle contraction, but specific pressure differences that cause valves to function.

Imagine the heart as a magnificent pump, and its efficiency depends on a delicate interplay between three key factors: preload, afterload, and contractility. Each plays a vital role in determining how much blood the heart pumps out with each beat, a metric known as cardiac output. Let's delve into these factors and how they influence the heart's magnificent performance.

Preload: The Stretch Factor

Think of preload as the initial stretch of the heart muscle fibers before contraction. Just like a stretched rubber band snaps back with more force, a well-filled ventricle can contract more powerfully. Here's the connection:

Increased Preload: More blood in the ventricles at the end of diastole (filling phase) stretches the muscle fibers further.
Frank-Starling Mechanism: This inherent property of the heart muscle allows for stronger contractions with increased preload, up to a certain point. A fuller ventricle has more "oomph" to squeeze blood out.
Real-World Example: Imagine a pitcher winding up before throwing a fastball. The further they wind up (more stretch), the harder they can throw (stronger contraction) – up to a limit, of course!

Afterload: Pumping Against Resistance

Now, picture the heart not just pushing blood out, but doing so against a certain level of resistance. This resistance is called afterload. Here's how it impacts the heart's work:

Higher Afterload: Increased resistance in the arteries (think clogged arteries or high blood pressure) makes it harder for the heart to eject blood. Imagine trying to squeeze water out of a stiff, clogged hose – it requires more effort!

The Afterload Challenge: The heart has to work harder to overcome this resistance, which can decrease cardiac output if not managed effectively.

Contractility: The Inherent Strength

Independent of preload and afterload, contractility refers to the intrinsic strength of the heart muscle itself. Several factors can influence contractility, such as:

Muscle tone: A healthy, well-conditioned heart muscle will contract more forcefully.

Chemical messengers: Calcium and certain hormones play a role in regulating the force of contraction.

The Grand Equation: Cardiac Output and Ejection Fraction

Cardiac output, the amount of blood pumped out by each ventricle per minute, is essentially the product of heart rate and stroke volume (the amount of blood ejected with each beat). Here's where preload, afterload, and contractility come together:

Increased Preload (up to a point) & Enhanced Contractility: These factors generally lead to a higher stroke volume and potentially a greater cardiac output.

Elevated Afterload: This can significantly decrease stroke volume and ultimately cardiac output, even if preload and contractility are normal.

Ejection Fraction: A Window into Heart Function

Ejection fraction (EF) is a valuable measure of how efficiently the heart pumps. It's calculated by dividing the stroke volume by the end-diastolic volume (the amount of blood in the ventricle before contraction). Think of it as a percentage of how much blood the ventricle can eject with each beat.

A healthy heart typically has an EF of 55% or higher. Understanding how preload, afterload, and contractility influence both stroke volume and EF is crucial for assessing cardiac function and potential heart problems.

The Takeaway: A Delicate Balance

The heart thrives on a delicate balance between preload, afterload, and contractility. Various medications and therapeutic interventions can target these factors to optimize cardiac output and improve heart function in patients with cardiovascular issues. By mastering these concepts, you'll not only shine on the CMSRN exam but gain a deeper appreciation for the remarkable interplay that keeps blood flowing and sustains life.

**Heart failure**. It's more than just a failing pump; it's a complex spectrum of dysfunction that can cripple a patient. Understanding the different faces of heart failure is paramount in tackling the CMSRN exam and effectively caring for these challenging patients.

**HFrEF vs. HFpEF: A Tale of Two Hearts**

- **HFrEF (Reduced Ejection Fraction):** Think of a deflated balloon that struggles to pump anything out. In HFrEF, the heart is weakened, dilated, and can't forcefully contract to eject blood. Ejection fraction is significantly reduced (usually below 40%) – like pushing a small amount of water out of a giant water balloon.

- **HFpEF (Preserved Ejection Fraction):** Here's where things get tricky. In HFpEF, the heart muscle becomes stiff and unyielding. While it can still squeeze (EF may be near normal), it struggles to relax and refill properly. Like trying to fill a rigid bottle, the filling volume is drastically reduced.

**Why the Distinction Matters**

While both HFrEF and HFpEF lead to heart failure symptoms, they often have different underlying causes and require tailored treatment approaches. Misdiagnosing the type of heart failure can have serious consequences for your patient!

**NYHA: Functional Classification for Treatment Guidance**

Adding to the complexity is the New York Heart Association (NYHA) classification used to assess heart failure severity based on symptoms. It provides a framework for treatment decisions:

- **Class I:** No limitations on physical activity.
- **Class II:** Slight limitations, comfortable at rest, but ordinary activity causes symptoms (fatigue, shortness of breath, palpitations).
- **Class III:** Marked limitations with physical activity; even minimal activity triggers symptoms.
- **Class IV:** Symptoms even at rest, any physical activity increases discomfort.

**Exam Tip:** The CMSRN loves questions focusing on the relationship between NYHA class and clinical decision-making. Know which NYHA classes warrant which medication classes, diuretics, and even cardiac devices.

**Acute Decompensated Failure: A Medical Emergency**

Both HFrEF and HFpEF patients can experience acute exacerbations, often triggered by infections, medication noncompliance, or arrhythmias. Here's what happens in a nutshell:

- **Fluid Overload:** The failing heart can't keep up, leading to fluid backup in the lungs (crackles, pink frothy sputum) or peripheral edema (leg swelling).
- **Decreased Cardiac Output:** This means less blood reaching vital organs. Patients may exhibit mental status changes, weakness, and cool extremities.

**Management: Think ABCs**

- **Airway/Breathing:** Oxygen, BiPAP, or even intubation may be necessary.
- **Circulation:** IV diuretics to remove excess fluid, inotropes to boost heart contractility (if EF is very low), and careful monitoring.
- **Additional Measures:** Treating the underlying triggers and meticulous hemodynamic assessment play a crucial role.

Understanding heart failure is an ongoing journey - there's always more to learn. But by grasping the distinction between HFrEF and HFpEF, the NYHA framework, and the emergency management of exacerbations, you're laying a formidable foundation for success on the CMSRN and, more importantly, in the care of patients struggling with this complex disease.

## The Acute Coronary Syndrome Drama: A Stage for Three Acts

Imagine the heart as a bustling city, and its coronary arteries as the highways delivering vital oxygen-rich blood. Acute coronary syndrome (ACS) is like a sudden traffic jam on these highways, disrupting blood flow and potentially leading to heart muscle damage. But not all traffic jams are created equal – ACS has three main players, each with its severity and diagnostic nuances.

Act I: ST-elevation Myocardial Infarction (STEMI) – A Complete Blockage

The Scene: A complete blockage of a coronary artery by a blood clot.

The Drama: Imagine a major highway completely shut down. No blood flow reaches the heart muscle downstream, leading to a full-blown heart attack. This is a medical emergency!

The Diagnosis: ECG changes – ST elevations on the electrocardiogram (ECG) are a telltale sign. Think of them as giant red warning signs screaming "complete blockage!"

Act II: Non-ST-elevation Myocardial Infarction (NSTEMI) – A Partial Blockage

The Scene: A partial blockage of a coronary artery, not a complete shutdown.

The Drama: Think of a single lane closed on the highway. Blood flow is still possible, but significantly reduced. Some heart muscle damage might occur, but not necessarily a full-on heart attack.

The Diagnosis: The picture isn't as clear-cut as STEMI. ECG changes might be subtle, and cardiac biomarkers like troponin become crucial. Troponin is a protein released by damaged heart muscle cells. Think of it as debris from the accident scene – elevated troponin levels indicate injury, but not necessarily a complete road closure (STEMI).

Act III: Unstable Angina – A Threatening Blockage

The Scene: A coronary artery with a significant, but not complete, blockage. This blockage can cause chest pain, but usually at rest or with minimal exertion.

The Drama: Imagine rush hour traffic causing stop-and-go situations. The heart muscle isn't getting enough blood flow, especially during exertion, leading to chest pain (angina). Unstable angina is a warning sign of a potential future heart attack, but not a full-blown one – yet.

The Diagnosis: Similar to NSTEMI, the picture can be blurry. Stress tests or imaging techniques might be needed to assess the severity of the blockage.

Time is Muscle: Unclogging the Arteries ASAP

Here's where the saying "time is muscle" takes center stage. In STEMI, where complete blockage is choking the heart muscle, every minute counts. The goal is to quickly reperfuse (reopen) the blocked artery using procedures like angioplasty or thrombolysis (clot-busting drugs). The faster blood flow is restored, the less heart muscle damage occurs.

Cardiac Biomarkers: The Silent Witnesses

Cardiac biomarkers like troponin are like silent witnesses to the heart's struggle. While ECG changes might be subtle in NSTEMI, elevated troponin levels provide crucial evidence of heart muscle injury. By measuring troponin levels over time (serial troponin), healthcare professionals can assess the extent of damage and risk of future complications.

The Final Curtain: Putting it All Together

Understanding the different presentations, diagnostic approaches, and the importance of early reperfusion in ACS is vital for CMSRN success. Remember, STEMI is a clear medical emergency, while NSTEMI and unstable angina require a more nuanced approach, involving cardiac biomarkers and risk stratification to guide treatment decisions. The better you grasp the drama unfolding on the stage of ACS, the more effectively you can advocate for your patients.

Imagine your heart's steady, rhythmic beat thrown into chaos. This is the world of arrhythmias – those pesky deviations from the normal electrical symphony. From the rapid fluttering of the atria to the life-threatening chaos of ventricular tachycardia, arrhythmias can transform a well-functioning heart into a ticking time bomb. Let's delve into the mechanisms behind some of the most common culprits and explore the life-saving algorithms that guide their management in emergent settings.

Atrial Arrhythmias: When the Top Chambers Lose Their Rhythm

Atrial Fibrillation (AFib): Think of this as complete electrical chaos in the atria. Instead of coordinated contractions, the atria quiver ineffectively. This can lead to blood stasis within the heart chambers, increasing the risk of clots and stroke.
Atrial Flutter: While more organized than AFib, atrial flutter involves a rapid, circular electrical signal within the atria, causing them to contract at a rate too fast for the ventricles to keep up with.
Supraventricular Tachycardia (SVT): A catch-all term for tachycardias (fast heart rhythms) that originate above the ventricles. Often, an abnormal loop of electrical activity creates rapid, regular (and sometimes very uncomfortable) heartbeats.
Ventricular Tachycardia (VTach): Dangerous Territory

When this arrhythmia arises, the ventricles, those powerful pumping chambers, start firing off rapid electrical impulses independently. This disorganized rhythm can rapidly deteriorate into life-threatening cardiac arrest, highlighting the urgency of rapid recognition and intervention.

The ACLS Playbook: Tackling Tachycardia

The ACLS (Advanced Cardiac Life Support) Tachycardia Algorithm is like a game plan that clinicians use to manage unstable patients with fast heart rhythms. Here's the basic flow:

Assess the Patient: Is the tachycardia causing hemodynamic instability (low blood pressure, altered mental status)?
Stable vs. Unstable: If the patient is stable, the focus shifts towards identifying the arrhythmia and controlling the heart rate. If the patient is unstable, immediate synchronized cardioversion (a controlled electrical shock to reset the heart rhythm) is often the first line of action.
Identifying the Rhythm: Characteristics on the ECG, such as the presence of P waves or QRS width, help pinpoint the type of tachycardia, further guiding treatment decisions.
Managing Bradyarrhythmias: Sometimes We Need to Speed Things Up

Bradyarrhythmias involve a drastically slowed heart rate, potentially compromising blood flow to vital organs. The ACLS Bradycardia Algorithm provides a framework for intervention:

The Root Cause: It's vital to identify any underlying causes of the slow heart rate, such as medication side effects, electrolyte imbalances, or damage to the heart's conduction system.
Symptomatic vs. Asymptomatic: A patient with a slow heart rate but stable blood pressure and no concerning symptoms might just require close observation. However, a patient with symptomatic bradycardia may need medications like atropine to speed up the heart rate or even temporary pacing with a pacemaker.
Important Note: Algorithms are guides, not rigid rules. Each patient is unique, and clinical judgment is key in determining the most appropriate treatment course.

Understanding the unique mechanisms behind different arrhythmias and the logic guiding their emergent management is essential for CMSRN success and for saving lives on the frontlines of medical care. By mastering these concepts, you equip yourself with the knowledge to identify and manage these rhythm disturbances and restore stability to the chaotic heart.

Imagine the heart's valves as elegant gatekeepers, ensuring a smooth, one-way flow of blood. In valvular heart disease, these gates become faulty. Let's explore how things can go wrong, with valves either becoming too narrow (stenosis) or leaky (regurgitation), and how these defects impact the heart's function.

Stenosis: Obstructed Flow
Think about a rusty gate that barely opens. Valvular stenosis forces the heart to work harder to squeeze blood through the narrowed opening. Over time, this extra strain can thicken and overwork the heart muscle. Key points about stenosis:

Turbulent Blood Flow: Creates those characteristic murmurs that clinicians listen for with their stethoscopes.
Upstream Consequences: The heart chamber before the stenotic valve faces increased pressure and can become enlarged. For example, in aortic stenosis, the left ventricle thickens and becomes less efficient.
Symptoms: Shortness of breath, fatigue, and chest pain often develop as the stenosis worsens.
Regurgitation: Leaky Valves

Now, picture a gate that doesn't close fully, allowing backflow. In valvular regurgitation, blood leaks backward, creating extra volume the heart has to handle. Imagine constantly pumping water uphill, only to have some of it fall back down. The heart dilates to accommodate, but eventually, this compensatory mechanism fails.

Murmurs: Regurgitation also produces telltale murmurs.
Upstream & Downstream Consequences: Both the upstream and downstream chambers become enlarged due to the extra volume load. For example, in mitral regurgitation, both the left atrium and ventricle dilate.
Symptoms: Symptoms can be subtle initially but may include palpitations, fatigue, and fluid buildup in the lungs (in left-sided regurgitation) or legs (in right-sided regurgitation).
Severity Assessment: The Echo's Importance

Echocardiography is the ultimate detective in determining the type and severity of valvular disease. It allows clinicians to visualize valve structure and blood flow patterns. Specific measurements, such as the valve area (narrowing in stenosis) or the regurgitant volume (leakage amount), play a crucial role in deciding when and how to intervene.

The "55/0.6" Rule for Aortic Stenosis

A severely narrowed aortic valve can seriously compromise blood flow out of the heart. The "55/0.6" rule helps identify patients with aortic stenosis who might benefit from surgical intervention before they become profoundly symptomatic. Here's the gist:

Aortic valve area (AVA) < 0.6 cm2/m2: This represents a severely narrowed aortic valve.
Mean gradient > 55 mmHg: This indicates a large pressure difference across the valve, suggesting significant obstruction to blood flow.

Treatment: A Spectrum

Management ranges from watchful waiting (for mild cases) to medications (mainly to control symptoms) to invasive interventions like:

Valve repair: The preferred approach when possible, preserving the patient's native valve.
Valve replacement: A prosthetic valve, mechanical or biological, replaces the faulty valve.
Exam Tip: The CMSRN loves to test your understanding of valvular disease manifestations and how they align with specific heart chambers. Think about the direction of blood flow to identify which chambers would experience enlargement in different scenarios.

The Heart's Resilient Struggle
Valvular heart disease showcases the heart's remarkable ability to compensate for a defect – but for only so long. Understanding the distinct pathophysiologies, how they present, and the tipping points for intervention will allow you to provide optimal care for your patients with these conditions and excel on the CMSRN exam.

Speaking of those rhythmic beats we discussed earlier, let's now shift gears to the electrical symphony within your heart. Understanding how to decipher the squiggly lines of the electrocardiogram (ECG) is a superpower for any med-surg nurse. It's like learning the secret language that reveals vital clues about heart function, rhythm disturbances, and even potential signs of trouble.

The Art of Lead Placement
Think of an ECG as a series of cameras pointed at your heart from different angles. Each lead records electrical activity across a specific axis. Here's the basic layout:

Limb Leads: Like those colorful stickers the tech places on your arms and legs, they form the basis of Einthoven's triangle – it sounds fancy, but it simply provides several different views of your heart.
Chest Leads (Precordial Leads): Those little suction cups across your chest offer even more perspectives, providing an in-depth picture of the front and side portions of the heart.
Decoding the Waves

Now, let's decode those squiggles!
P Wave: This little bump represents atrial depolarization, the electrical impulse that triggers the atria to contract.
QRS complex: This sharp spike is the star of the show! It signifies ventricular depolarization, the powerful electrical surge that makes your ventricles squeeze and pump blood.
T Wave: This final wave represents ventricular repolarization, as the ventricle muscles reset themselves, ready for the next cycle.
ECG Analysis: A Step-by-Step Approach

The CMSRN loves to test your ECG interpretation skills. Let's break it down with the "4-Step Method":

Rate: Is it too fast, too slow, or just right? A normal heart rate is usually between 60-100 beats per minute.
Rhythm: Is it regular or irregular? Think of your heartbeat like music – is there a steady beat, or does it sound like someone's randomly hitting the drums?

Waves and Intervals: Are the P waves, QRS complexes, and T waves present in their expected shape and duration? Any abnormalities here might indicate conduction problems or muscle damage.

Axis: This tells you the general direction of the heart's electrical activity, which can sometimes hint at anatomical problems.

Exam Tip: Master the basics of normal ECG interpretation before tackling complex arrhythmias. Practice, practice, practice!

Beyond Basic Rhythm Analysis

An ECG is a powerful diagnostic tool that goes far beyond just looking at heart rate and rhythm. Here's where things get exciting:

Myocardial Ischemia or Infarction: Specific ECG changes, like ST-segment elevation, can be clues to a heart attack in progress!

Electrolyte Abnormalities: Tall, peaked T waves anyone? ECG changes can hint at electrolyte imbalances like hyperkalemia.

Chamber Enlargement: Patterns on the ECG can reveal which heart chambers might be enlarged due to various types of heart disease.

ECG Interpretation: A Vital Skill

Mastering the fundamentals of ECG interpretation is not just about the CMSRN exam – it's about unlocking a fascinating window into a patient's cardiovascular health. Understanding those squiggly lines empowers you to rapidly recognize potential cardiac emergencies and provide life-altering interventions. Now, let's dive deeper into rhythm disturbances, where ECG analysis truly begins to shine.

Now that we've familiarized ourselves with the basic language of ECGs, let's turn the focus to a time-sensitive situation: ST-elevation myocardial infarction (STEMI), a heart attack caused by a complete blockage in a coronary artery. Every second counts in a STEMI, and a well-interpreted ECG is the key to rapid diagnosis and life-saving interventions.

**The Hallmarks of STEMI on ECG: When Squiggles Scream Trouble**

Our "4-Step Method" from before becomes even more crucial in a suspected STEMI. Here's what we're looking for:

- **ST-segment Elevation:** The big one! In STEMI, the ST segment (that flat line between the QRS complex and the T wave) becomes elevated in specific leads depending on the location of the blockage.
- **The 3-point LAD Occlusion Sign:** Think of the left anterior descending (LAD) artery as the heart's widowmaker. ST elevation in leads aVL, V1, and V2 strongly suggests a blockage in this critical vessel.

**Beyond the Classics: Recognizing Less Common Presentations**

But the ECG story doesn't always follow a neat script. Here are some additional patterns to keep in mind:

- **De Winter T-waves:** Imagine inverted T waves in leads V1-V3 alongside reciprocal ST elevation in leads aVL and I. This pattern can indicate a proximal LAD occlusion (blockage closer to the origin of the artery).
- **STEMI Equivalents:** Not all heart attacks present with textbook ST elevation. Recognize that posterior and right ventricular infarctions can manifest with subtle ST-segment depression or T wave inversions in specific leads. Missing these can lead to disastrous delays in treatment.

**Why Recognizing STEMI Equivalents Matters**

Think of a patient presenting with chest pain and subtle ECG changes not fulfilling the classic STEMI criteria. While the initial ECG might not scream "heart attack," recognizing these "equivalents" allows for further evaluation with cardiac enzymes and imaging studies. Early intervention in any STEMI, regardless of presentation, significantly improves patient outcomes.

When in doubt, consult with a cardiologist! A missed STEMI diagnosis can have devastating consequences. The CMSRN exam loves to test your ability to recognize both classic and less common presentations of STEMI on ECG.

**ECG Interpretation: A Sharpened Tool**

By honing your ECG interpretation skills and recognizing the specific criteria for diagnosing STEMI and its equivalents, you become a guardian at the gate of the cardiac emergency room. Your eagle eyes on that ECG can make the difference between life and death for a patient experiencing a heart attack. In the next section, we'll delve deeper into the fascinating world of arrhythmias – those deviations from the normal heart rhythm that can wreak havoc on the body's electrical symphony.

Let's continue our exploration of the electrical language of the heart and delve into the world of heart blocks – conditions where the electrical impulses get delayed or interrupted on their journey through the heart's conduction system. A keen eye for ECG changes is essential for diagnosing these sometimes subtle abnormalities.

The Conduction Highway: When Traffic Gets Slow

Imagine the heart's conduction system as a superhighway for electrical signals. Normally, these impulses travel smoothly from the atria to the ventricles, coordinating contractions. In heart blocks, there's a glitch in the system, causing delays or complete blockages. Let's explore how this translates to ECG findings:

PR Interval: This interval measures the time it takes for the electrical impulse to travel from the atria (P wave) to the ventricles (QRS complex). It's like a traffic report – a longer PR interval indicates a delay.

Types of Heart Blocks: Decoding the ECG

First-Degree Heart Block: The most common type. Here, there's a slight delay in conduction, but all P waves are eventually followed by QRS complexes, although the PR interval might be prolonged.

Second-Degree Heart Block: Things get a bit more complex here. We have two main subtypes:

Mobitz Type I (Wenckebach): Think of it as a traffic jam with occasional stalls. There's a progressive increase in PR interval until a P wave isn't followed by a QRS complex (dropped beat). Then, the cycle repeats with a slightly longer PR interval before the next dropped beat.

Mobitz Type II: This is more like a complete road closure at the AV node. Some P waves simply don't make it through, resulting in dropped QRS complexes without any change in the PR interval before the dropped beat.

The 3:1 Rule: Cracking the Mobitz Code

The key to differentiating Mobitz I from Mobitz II lies in the pattern of dropped beats. The golden rule:

Mobitz I: Typically shows a 3:1 conduction pattern. This means for every 3 P waves, there are only 2 QRS complexes.
Mobitz II: Shows variable conduction, with dropped QRS complexes not necessarily following a specific pattern.
Third-Degree (Complete) Heart Block: This is the most severe block. There's a complete electrical disconnect between the atria and ventricles. The ECG will show completely independent P wave and QRS complex rates, with no relationship between them.

The rhythm strips on the CMSRN exam might be short. Look for the presence or absence of P waves before QRS complexes and any patterns in PR intervals or dropped beats to identify the type of heart block.

The Silent Blockade vs. The Lifesaving Diagnosis

Some heart blocks are benign, while others can significantly compromise cardiac output. Understanding ECG findings is crucial for distinguishing between these scenarios and guiding treatment decisions. In the next section, we'll explore the fascinating world of arrhythmias – those deviations from the normal heart rhythm that can wreak havoc on the body's electrical symphony.

Imagine being presented with a critically ill patient whose vital signs are precarious. How can you delve deeper to understand the underlying issues and guide your interventions? Hemodynamic monitoring offers a window into the inner workings of the cardiovascular system, revealing hidden pressure gradients and the elusive measure known as cardiac output. Let's unravel the mysteries of these powerful monitoring tools and their significance in caring for your most complex patients.

**Understanding the Pressure Players**

Understanding hemodynamic parameters is like solving a physiological puzzle. Here are the key players and their typical ranges:

- **Central Venous Pressure (CVP):** Think of it as the pressure in the right atrium. Normal range: 2-6 mmHg. It reflects volume status or right-sided heart function. A high CVP suggests fluid overload or right-sided heart issues.
- **Pulmonary Artery Wedge Pressure (PAWP):** Obtained with a Swan-Ganz catheter, this measurement indirectly reflects left heart pressures. Normal range: 6-12 mmHg. An elevated PAWP might indicate left-sided heart failure or overhydration.
- **Cardiac Output (CO):** The star of the show! CO (usually reported in liters/minute) measures how much blood the heart pumps per minute. Normal range: 4-8 L/min. CO is the product of heart rate and stroke volume.
- **Systemic Vascular Resistance (SVR):** A measure of how constricted or relaxed the patient's blood vessels are. Normal range is roughly 800-1200 dynes/sec/cm-5. Elevated SVR represents high afterload (increased resistance to blood flow, commonly seen in hypertension), while low SVR implies vasodilation (like in sepsis).

**Interpretation: A Delicate Balance**

These parameters don't operate in isolation – interpreting them correctly involves a nuanced understanding of the patient's whole clinical picture. Think of an orchestra: A single instrument out of tune might not be readily apparent, but it affects the overall symphony. Here's a real-world example:

- A patient with cardiogenic shock: You might see a low CO, a high PAWP (indicating blood backing up into the lungs), and a high SVR. These findings suggest a failing pump, fluid overload, and a body constricting blood vessels to compensate.

**Beyond Textbook Numbers**
Hemodynamic monitoring is more than just staring at a screen. Remember these points when utilizing these tools for your patients:
- **Trends over time:** Single values are less revealing than changes in parameters over time, especially when observing the patient's response to various interventions.
- **Clinical context:** Always correlate these numbers with the patient's underlying conditions, symptoms, and physical exam findings.

The CMSRN loves scenarios where you must interpret hemodynamic parameters and apply your understanding to treatment decisions. For instance, how might a fluid bolus or diuretic impact CVP and PAWP?

**Mastering Hemodynamics: Your Clinical Compass**
By mastering the language of hemodynamic monitoring, you gain valuable insights into the circulatory health of your critically ill patients. This knowledge empowers you to make targeted interventions, optimizing fluid management, vasopressor use, and even mechanical support therapies. Now, let's transition to the realm of blood gas analysis, another invaluable tool for assessing respiratory and metabolic function.

Shock – it's the cardiovascular system's version of a worst-case scenario, where vital organs become starved of oxygen and nutrients due to inadequate blood flow. Understanding the different forces that can tip a patient into shock is essential for rapid diagnosis and intervention. Enter the "5 Ms of Shock," a mnemonic that helps categorize the diverse causes of this life-threatening state. Let's explore each "M" and its effect on the heart and circulation:

Myocardial Depression:
The Heart Loses Its Pump: Imagine the heart itself weakened due to conditions like a massive myocardial infarction, severe arrhythmias, or myocarditis (inflammation of the heart muscle).
Hemodynamic Impact: Low cardiac output, low blood pressure, and possibly signs of fluid backup (elevated CVP and PAWP) if the weakened pump can't keep up with the body's demand.
Mechanical Obstruction
Blockages in the Circulatory Superhighway: Think of conditions like cardiac tamponade (fluid buildup around the heart), tension pneumothorax (air pocket crushing the lung), or a massive pulmonary embolism (blood clot blocking lung circulation).
Hemodynamic Impact: Variable depending on the cause, but can involve low cardiac output and potentially signs of obstruction, such as elevated CVP and distended neck veins in cardiac tamponade.
Massive Fluid Loss
Low Volume in the Tank: Hemorrhagic shock from significant blood loss (trauma, bleeding GI ulcer) or severe dehydration (prolonged vomiting/diarrhea) are prime examples. Loss of fluid from burns also falls into this category.
Hemodynamic Impact: Low CVP and potentially low PAWP, indicating decreased intravascular volume. The heart might be pumping strongly but has less volume to work with.
Metabolic/Endocrine Derangements
Internal Sabotage: Think of severe acidosis (abnormally low blood pH), profound electrolyte imbalances, or endocrine disorders like adrenal insufficiency affecting the stress response. These disturbances can disrupt cell function and vascular tone.

Hemodynamic Impact: Can be complex and depend on the specific problem. Some scenarios may involve low SVR (systemic vascular resistance) and profound vasodilation (like in anaphylaxis).
Medications/Toxins
The Pharmacological Twist: Certain medications, like overdose of blood pressure meds or sedatives, can depress heart function or cause vasodilation. Exposure to toxins can trigger a similar response.
Hemodynamic Impact: Variable depending on the agent. Could involve low cardiac output and low SVR with certain types of overdose, or present as cardiogenic shock with some poisons.
The Clinical Detective: Putting It All Together

Understanding the "5 Ms" gives you a framework for quickly assessing a patient in shock. By combining the clinical presentation with hemodynamic data (if available) and a thorough history, you can pinpoint the underlying cause. Here's how this knowledge translates to action:

Rapid Identification: The "5 Ms" guide your initial questioning and physical examination. Was there any trauma (blood loss), history of heart disease (myocardial depression), or recent medication changes?
Tailored Treatment: Identifying the root cause allows for targeted interventions (fluids for hemorrhagic shock, inotropes to boost a failing heart, vasopressors in severe vasodilation).
The CMSRN loves to incorporate case studies of patients in shock. Keep the "5 Ms" in mind as you work through these scenarios, systematically considering potential culprits.

Remember, recognizing and treating shock early is crucial! By understanding the diverse mechanisms that can lead to shock and their impact on hemodynamic parameters, you'll be better equipped to save lives through rapid diagnosis and targeted interventions.

Alright, let's now shift gears and delve into the battlefield of sepsis management. Sepsis and septic shock, a life-threatening condition where the body's response to an infection spirals out of control, require swift and decisive action. Here, the Surviving Sepsis Campaign (SSC) guidelines serve as a roadmap to improve patient outcomes.

Imagine a patient in septic shock, their blood pressure plummeting and organs on the brink of failure. The SSC promotes a time-sensitive approach, emphasizing the implementation of specific bundles of care within crucial timeframes. Let's unpack these lifesavers:

The 1-Hour Bundle: A Race Against Time

The first hour after recognizing septic shock is golden. The 1-Hour Bundle focuses on early interventions to stabilize the patient's condition. Here's what this bundle entails:

Blood Culture: This is the foundation for identifying the culprit organism causing the sepsis. Early identification allows for targeted antibiotic therapy.
Broad-Spectrum Antibiotics: Wasting no time, broad-spectrum antibiotics are initiated within that first hour to combat the raging infection.
Fluid Resuscitation: Sepsis often leads to profound fluid loss. Aggressive fluid resuscitation is crucial to restore blood volume and tissue perfusion.
Vasopressors for Hypotension: If blood pressure remains stubbornly low despite fluids, vasopressor medications might be needed to maintain adequate organ perfusion.
The 6-Hour Bundle: Building on the Foundation

The 1-Hour Bundle sets the stage for further interventions within the next 6 hours. Here, the focus remains on optimizing hemodynamic parameters and providing critical support:

Source Control: Identifying and eliminating the source of infection is paramount. This might involve surgical intervention to drain an abscess or remove infected tissue.
Repeat Lactate Measurement: Serial lactate measurements provide a valuable window into the body's response to therapy. A persistently high lactate might indicate inadequate tissue perfusion, prompting adjustments to the resuscitation strategy.
Hitting the Hemodynamic Targets: Keeping the Body in the Game

Now, let's talk about specific hemodynamic goals in sepsis management. Think of these goals as guardrails to ensure adequate blood flow to vital organs. Here's what we're aiming for:

Mean Arterial Pressure (MAP) ≥ 65 mmHg: This ensures sufficient blood pressure to deliver oxygen and nutrients to the body's tissues.
Central Venous Pressure (CVP) of 8-12 mmHg: CVP reflects the filling pressure of the heart. This range helps maintain adequate cardiac output without fluid overload.
The Importance of Early Recognition and Intervention

Remember, sepsis is a time-sensitive illness. The sooner these bundles are implemented, the better the patient's chances of survival. By adhering to the SSC guidelines and closely monitoring hemodynamic parameters, you can significantly improve patient outcomes in this life-threatening condition.

Now let's dive into the world of cardiovascular pharmacology – a complex yet fascinating landscape where drugs can enhance heart function, control blood pressure, and restore rhythm. Understanding the mechanisms and uses of these medications is essential for the CMSRN exam and, more importantly, for optimizing the care of your cardiovascular patients.

**Beta-Blockers: Calming the Overworked Heart**
- **How They Work:** Beta-blockers act like traffic cops, blocking beta receptors in the heart and blood vessels. This results in a decreased heart rate, decreased force of contraction, and relaxation of blood vessels.
- **Indications:** Beta-blockers are used in a wide range of cardiovascular conditions, including hypertension, heart failure, angina, and post-myocardial infarction (heart attack).
- **Side Effects:** Watch out for bradycardia (too slow heart rate), hypotension (low blood pressure), fatigue, and sometimes cold extremities.

**ACE Inhibitors and ARBs: Blocking a Hormonal Culprit**
These two medication classes target the renin-angiotensin-aldosterone system (RAAS) – a key player in blood pressure regulation and fluid balance:
- **ACE Inhibitors (-pril ending):** These block the conversion of angiotensin I to angiotensin II, a potent vasoconstrictor (blood vessel tightener). This leads to vasodilation, decreased blood pressure, and reduced workload on the heart.
- **ARBs (-sartan ending):** ARBs also block the RAAS but at a slightly different point. They block angiotensin II receptors directly, leading to similar effects as ACE inhibitors.
- **Indications:** Both ACE inhibitors and ARBs are used for hypertension, heart failure, diabetic kidney disease, and post-myocardial infarction.

- **Side Effects:** Be wary of hypotension, hyperkalemia (high potassium), and cough (more common with ACE inhibitors).

**Diuretics: Managing Fluid Overload**

Diuretics act like water removal specialists, increasing urine output and reducing fluid volume. There are multiple types, each working on different parts of the kidney:

- **Loop Diuretics (furosemide, bumetanide):** These are strong players, often used in heart failure and severe hypertension.
- **Thiazide Diuretics (hydrochlorothiazide):** Commonly used for hypertension.
- **Potassium-Sparing Diuretics (spironolactone):** Often combined with other diuretics to prevent potassium loss.
- **Side Effects:** Watch for electrolyte imbalances, particularly hypokalemia (low potassium) and hyponatremia (low sodium), as well as hypotension and dehydration.

**Antiarrhythmics: Restoring Rhythm**

Used to treat and prevent various arrhythmias, antiarrhythmics fall into several different classes, each with its own mechanism of action:

- **Sodium Channel Blockers (lidocaine, quinidine):** These primarily slow the conduction of electrical impulses in the heart.
- **Potassium Channel Blockers (amiodarone):** Prolong the duration of the cardiac action potential.
- **Calcium Channel Blockers (diltiazem, verapamil):** Slow conduction and decrease heart rate, particularly at the AV node.

**Side Effects:** Antiarrhythmics can have diverse side effects and potential drug interactions. Be sure to know the specific ones for each drug!

**Real World Tip:** Mastering cardiovascular drug combinations is crucial. Think of it like a chef combining ingredients – some combinations work synergistically, while others can have unwanted side effects.

The CMSRN loves to test your understanding of medication side effects and nursing implications. Always think about what you'll be monitoring for when your patient is on a particular drug.

Remember, understanding the inner workings of these medications is just as important as knowing their indications. By mastering their mechanisms of action and side effects, you'll be empowered to optimize drug therapy and anticipate potential adverse effects in your patients.

Actually, now would be a great time to talk about the MONA mnemonic, a foundational tool for guiding initial management of patients with suspected acute coronary syndrome (ACS). Remember, ACS encompasses a spectrum of conditions – from unstable angina to ST-segment elevation myocardial infarction (STEMI) – all stemming from an acute imbalance between myocardial oxygen supply and demand. Recognizing the signs and symptoms of ACS and initiating prompt interventions is crucial for improving patient outcomes. So, let's delve into each component of MONA and its role in ACS management:

**Morphine:** A cornerstone of pain management in ACS. Morphine works by binding to opioid receptors in the central nervous system, decreasing perception of pain and anxiety associated with the ischemic episode.

**Contraindications and Precautions:** While morphine is a mainstay for pain relief, be aware of these contraindications and proceed with caution:

- **Respiratory depression:** Morphine can suppress respiratory drive, so use it judiciously in patients with pre-existing respiratory issues like COPD or severe asthma.
- **Hypotension:** Morphine can cause vasodilation and a decrease in blood pressure. Use cautiously in hypotensive patients or those with conditions like hypovolemic shock.

- **Head injury:** Morphine might blunt the level of consciousness, making assessment in head injury patients trickier.

**Oxygen:** Think of oxygen as essential fuel for the starved myocardium. In ACS, myocardial ischemia due to plaque rupture or coronary thrombosis leads to oxygen deprivation. Supplemental oxygen aims to increase oxygen delivery to the ischemic tissue, potentially salvaging some myocytes and limiting infarct size.

**Contraindications and Precautions:** While oxygen therapy is generally safe, high concentrations (>60%) in certain situations can be detrimental:

- **Chronic obstructive pulmonary disease (COPD):** High-flow oxygen can worsen CO2 retention in some COPD patients. Aim for pulse oximetry saturation goals of 88-92% in these patients.
- **Free radical formation:** Controversial but worth mentioning – prolonged exposure to high FiO2 might contribute to free radical formation and further tissue injury.

**Nitroglycerin:** This vasodilator comes in handy in ACS by relaxing blood vessels, including the coronary arteries. Improved coronary blood flow can help alleviate ischemia and chest pain.

**Contraindications and Precautions:**

- **Hypotension:** Nitroglycerin can further decrease blood pressure, so use cautiously in hypotensive patients.
- **Head trauma:** Similar to morphine, nitroglycerin can cause hypotension, which might be undesirable in head injury patients.
- **Increased intracranial pressure:** Vasodilation can worsen intracranial pressure, so avoid nitroglycerin in this scenario.
- **Tachycardia:** Nitroglycerin can reflexively increase heart rate, which is not ideal in ACS. Consider alternative antianginal medications if tachycardia is a concern.

**Aspirin:** An antiplatelet agent that plays a crucial role in ACS management. Aspirin irreversibly inhibits platelet aggregation, preventing further clot formation and potential coronary artery occlusion. Timely administration of aspirin can help prevent recurrent ischemic events.

**Contraindications and Precautions:**

- **Active bleeding:** Aspirin can worsen bleeding tendencies, so avoid it in patients with active GI bleeding or suspected intracranial hemorrhage.
- **Peptic ulcer disease:** Aspirin can irritate the gastric lining and exacerbate peptic ulcer disease. Consider alternative antiplatelet medications in such cases.
- **Aspirin allergy:** This is a rare but important contraindication.

**Remember, MONA is a starting point, not a rigid protocol.** The cornerstone of ACS management is a thorough history, physical examination, and ECG findings. This will guide further interventions such as aggressive lipid management, consideration for additional antiplatelet medications, and potential cardiac interventions like percutaneous coronary intervention (PCI) or coronary artery bypass graft (CABG) surgery.

The key takeaway? Mastering the MONA mnemonic equips you with the initial tools to manage ACS while keeping in mind the contraindications and necessary precautions for each medication. By understanding the rationale behind each component of MONA, you'll be better prepared to provide timely and effective care to patients experiencing this life-threatening condition.

### Conquering Heart Failure: A Guide to ACC/AHA Guidelines and GDMT

Imagine your heart, a tireless pump keeping you alive. But what if this pump weakens, struggling to deliver life-giving blood throughout your body? That's the essence of heart failure (HF), a chronic condition where the heart's efficiency diminishes. Fear not, future CMSRNs! The American College of

Cardiology (ACC) and American Heart Association (AHA) have created a roadmap to battle HF – the "ACC/AHA Guidelines" featuring the "GDMT" (Guideline-Directed Medical Therapy) approach. Let's crack the code on managing HF and ace that exam!

Think of GDMT as your personal trainer for the failing heart. It emphasizes a multi-pronged approach, incorporating various medications to strengthen your patient's heart and improve symptoms. Here's a breakdown of the key players in this champion team:

ACE Inhibitors and ARBs (Angiotensin-Converting Enzyme Inhibitors & Angiotensin Receptor Blockers): These medications act like highway tollbooths, regulating a hormone that constricts blood vessels. By opening up these passageways, they ease the workload on the heart and improve blood flow. Consider them as the smooth traffic directors for stressed arteries.

Beta-Blockers: Picture beta receptors as tiny gas pedals on heart muscle cells. Beta-blockers gently step on the brakes, slowing down the heart rate and reducing its workload. This allows the heart to fill with blood more efficiently, ultimately giving it more power with each pump.

Mineralocorticoid Receptor Antagonists (MRAs): Imagine the heart as a leaky faucet, and potassium as precious water. MRAs act like plumbers, plugging those leaks and preventing excessive potassium loss. This is crucial because potassium imbalances can disrupt the heart's electrical rhythm, potentially leading to dangerous arrhythmias.

Remember, GDMT is a personalized approach. Not every patient needs all these medications, and the specific choices will depend on the severity of HF and individual patient factors. Think of it like crafting a unique recipe for each patient's heart health!

Let's break the monotony with a real-world example:

Say you have a patient named Mr. Jones with chronic HF. He experiences shortness of breath and fatigue, classic signs of a struggling heart. An echocardiogram (think of it as an ultrasound for the heart) confirms his diagnosis. Based on the ACC/AHA guidelines and Mr. Jones' specific condition, you might initiate a combination of an ACE inhibitor and a beta-blocker. This personalized GDMT regimen aims to improve Mr. Jones' symptoms, slow disease progression, and hopefully enhance his quality of life.

But wait, there's more! The ACC/AHA guidelines extend beyond just medications. They also emphasize lifestyle modifications – a healthy diet, regular exercise (think moderate walks, not marathons!), and weight management. Imagine these lifestyle changes as complementary exercises alongside the medications, working together to strengthen Mr. Jones' heart and improve his overall health.

Master the mechanisms of action: Understanding how each medication works in GDMT will solidify your knowledge and aid in exam recall.
Think side effects: Be familiar with potential side effects of each medication, like dizziness with beta-blockers or cough with ACE inhibitors.
Practice, Practice, Practice! Work through case studies applying the ACC/AHA guidelines and choosing appropriate GDMT regimens for different HF scenarios.
Visualize success: Imagine yourself confidently explaining GDMT to a patient, empowering them to take charge of their heart health.

By understanding and applying the ACC/AHA Guidelines and GDMT, you'll be well-equipped to combat heart failure and improve patient outcomes. Remember, this knowledge isn't just for the exam – it empowers you to make a real difference in the lives of your future patients. Now go forth, future CMSRNs, and conquer heart failure!

**Unraveling the Mystery: CHA2DS2-VASc Score and Anticoagulation for Atrial Fibrillation**

Atrial fibrillation (AFib) – a quivering arrhythmia where the heart's upper chambers lose their coordinated rhythm. While it might sound chaotic, a crucial aspect of managing AFib is preventing stroke, a potential complication. Enter the **CHA2DS2-VASc Score**, a scoring system that helps guide decisions about anticoagulation therapy – medications that thin the blood and reduce clot formation. Let's decipher this score and explore anticoagulation recommendations based on the American Heart Association (AHA) Atrial Fibrillation Guidelines.

**Imagine CHA2DS2-VASc as a risk calculator for stroke in AFib patients.** Each component of the score represents a risk factor:

- **Congestive Heart Failure (CHF):** 1 point
- **Hypertension (HTN):** 1 point
- **Age ≥ 75 years:** 2 points (doubled due to increased risk)
- **Diabetes Mellitus (DM):** 1 point
- **Stroke (history of):** 2 points (doubled due to increased risk)
- **Vascular Disease (history of):** 1 point
- **Age 65-74 years:** 1 point
- **Sex Category (female):** 1 point (for women without prior stroke or other high-risk features)

**The higher the score, the greater the risk of stroke.** Here's how the AHA uses this score for anticoagulation recommendations:

- **Score 0:** Anticoagulation is generally not recommended unless there are other specific risk factors.
- **Score 1:** The decision for anticoagulation requires careful consideration of individual risk factors and potential bleeding risks.
- **Score ≥ 2:** Anticoagulation is usually recommended to reduce stroke risk.

**An Important Note:** The CHA2DS2-VASc score is a guide, not a strict rulebook. A doctor's judgment plays a crucial role in weighing the individual patient's bleeding risk against their stroke risk when making anticoagulation decisions.

**Let's unpack a real-world scenario:**

Imagine Mrs. Garcia, a 72-year-old woman with a history of hypertension and newly diagnosed AFib. Using the CHA2DS2-VASc score:

- CHF: 0 points
- HTN: 1 point
- Age: 2 points
- DM: 0 points
- Stroke: 0 points
- Vascular Disease: 0 points
- Age group (65-74): 0 points
- Sex: 1 point (female)

Total Score: 4 points

Based on her score and the AHA guidelines, Mrs. Garcia is at high risk for stroke and would likely benefit from anticoagulation therapy. However, her doctor would also consider her individual bleeding risk factors, such as a history of peptic ulcers, before making a final decision.

**Remember:**
- A low CHA2DS2-VASc score doesn't guarantee zero stroke risk.
- The AHA guidelines consider other factors beyond the score, like a patient's overall health and bleeding risk.
- As a future CMSRN, understanding the CHA2DS2-VASc score and its role in anticoagulation decisions empowers you to participate effectively in patient care discussions.

**Bonus Tip:** There's an easy-to-remember mnemonic for the CHA2DS2-VASc score: **"Congestive heart failure, Hypertension, Age, Diabetes, Stroke, Vascular disease, Sex category."** Use it as a memory aid, but remember the full risk factors the score represents.

By mastering the CHA2DS2-VASc score and the AHA Atrial Fibrillation Guidelines, you'll be well on your way to providing optimal care for AFib patients and reducing their risk of stroke.

Now.. Think about a car struggling to start, its engine sputtering and faltering. For some patients, their heart, quite literally their internal engine, can face a similar struggle. Enter the world of pacemakers and implantable cardioverter-defibrillators (ICDs) – tiny life-saving powerhouses that can offer a much-needed jumpstart or even a forceful reset to a malfunctioning cardiac system.

**Pacemakers: The Rhythm Fixers**

Imagine a pacemaker as a gentle coach for a heart that's fallen out of step. These devices specialize in treating slow or irregular heart rhythms (bradyarrhythmias) caused by problems with the heart's natural electrical system. How do they work?

- **Leads:** These insulated wires are threaded through veins into the heart, resting in the right atrium and/or ventricle.
- **Pulse Generator:** This miniature, computer-like unit houses the battery and electronics. It sends tiny electrical signals through the leads to stimulate the heart muscle to contract.
- **Sensing:** Modern pacemakers can "sense" the heart's natural rhythm and only pace when needed, allowing for a more customized approach.

**ICDs: The Vigilant Protector**

Now, think of an ICD as a powerful defense system for a heart prone to dangerous, even life-threatening arrhythmias like ventricular tachycardia or ventricular fibrillation. These devices can act as both a pacemaker (sensing and pacing if needed) AND a defibrillator:

- **Defibrillator Function:** If an ICD detects a dangerously fast or chaotic rhythm, it can deliver a powerful shock to essentially "reset" the heart. This shock might feel startling, but it can interrupt the arrhythmia and restore normal rhythm.

**The Pacemaker Code: Decoding the Secret Language**

You've likely seen codes like 'DDD' or 'VVI' on patient charts. This seemingly cryptic notation actually holds the key to pacemaker functionality. Here's the decoder:

- **Position 1 – Chamber Paced:** V (ventricle), A (atrium), D (both)
- **Position 2 – Chamber Sensed:** V, A, D, O (none)
- **Position 3 – Response to Sensing:** I (inhibited), T (triggered), D (both)
- **Position 4 – Rate-Modulation:** R (Rate-responsive)
- **Position 5 – Multisite Pacing:** V, A, D, O

For example, a DDDR pacemaker:
- Paces both chambers (atrium and ventricle)

- Senses intrinsic activity in both chambers
- Can inhibit or trigger pacing based on sensed activity
- Offers a rate-adaptive feature that adjusts pacing based on the patient's activity level

**Programming: Tailoring the Therapy**

Each pacemaker or ICD is carefully programmed by specialists to align with the patient's specific needs. Think of it like customizing a computer program for the heart. Programmers adjust things like pacing rates, sensitivity settings, and shock therapy thresholds.

Know the common pacemaker and ICD modes for the CMSRN exam. Practice scenarios where you interpret the pacemaker code and think through the implications for a patient's care.

**Real-World Considerations**

Understanding pacemakers and ICDs is both a fascinating and practical aspect of caring for patients with heart disease. Key nursing points:

- **Patient Education:** Be a teacher for your patients with pacemakers/ICDs. Explain their device's function, restrictions (like avoiding strong magnets), and how to identify any potential problems.
- **Device Checks:** Patients with these devices require regular follow-up and monitoring.

By mastering pacemakers, ICDs, and the 'code' behind them, you'll gain a deeper understanding of cardiac electrophysiology and play a vital role in managing patients who rely on these life-altering devices.

Imagine a heart so weakened, it struggles to pump enough blood to keep your body functioning. This is the grim reality of advanced heart failure. But there's a beacon of hope – left ventricular assist devices (LVADs), remarkable mechanical pumps that can take over some of the heart's workload, offering a lifeline to these patients. Let's delve into LVADs, explore the INTERMACS profile for assessing heart failure severity, and understand how these two work together to guide treatment decisions.

**LVADs: The Mechanical Marvels**

Think of an LVAD as a miniaturized marvel of engineering. Surgically implanted, it rests next to the heart and draws blood from the left ventricle (the heart's main pumping chamber). The LVAD then propels this blood forward into the aorta, the body's major highway, ensuring vital organs receive the oxygen-rich blood they desperately need.

**LVADs offer two main advantages in heart failure management:**

- **Bridge to Transplant:** For some patients awaiting a heart transplant, LVADs can act as a bridge, keeping them stable and alive until a donor heart becomes available.
- **Destination Therapy:** For patients not eligible for transplant due to factors like age or other health conditions, LVADs can serve as a long-term solution, significantly improving their quality of life.

**The INTERMACS Profile: Matching Patients with the Right Treatment**

Not every patient with heart failure is a candidate for an LVAD. Here's where the INTERMACS profile comes in. This classification system categorizes heart failure severity based on functional capacity, symptoms, and hemodynamic measurements (blood pressure, cardiac output). Let's break down the INTERMACS levels:

- **Level 1-3 (Critical Condition):** Patients in these levels are the most critically ill, often hospitalized and requiring intensive support. LVAD implantation is a primary consideration for these patients, particularly as a bridge to transplant.
- **Level 4 (Advanced Heart Failure):** These patients experience significant limitations in daily activities due to heart failure symptoms. LVADs are a potential option for both bridge to transplant and destination therapy depending on other factors.

- **Level 5 (Early Stage):** Patients in this category have milder symptoms and may not be candidates for LVADs at this stage. However, their condition might progress, necessitating reevaluation in the future.

**The INTERMACS profile plays a crucial role in guiding LVAD decisions:**
- **Optimizing Patient Selection:** It helps identify patients who will benefit most from LVAD implantation, considering factors beyond just disease severity.
- **Risk Stratification:** The profile allows healthcare professionals to weigh the potential benefits of LVAD therapy against the risks associated with surgery and device complications.

Familiarize yourself with the INTERMACS levels and their corresponding heart failure severity. This will help you anticipate LVAD candidacy for patients in different scenarios on the CMSRN exam.

**The LVAD + INTERMACS Duo: A Powerful Force in Heart Failure Management**

By understanding LVADs and the INTERMACS profile, you'll gain valuable insights into managing advanced heart failure. LVADs offer a technological marvel for these patients, and the INTERMACS profile provides a roadmap for making informed treatment decisions. It's a powerful combination that can significantly improve the lives of those struggling with this debilitating condition.

**Pacemakers** – they're lifesavers for many with heart rhythm problems. But, sometimes, even the best intentions have unintended consequences. Enter "pacemaker syndrome," a somewhat paradoxical condition where the lifesaving pacemaker itself can lead to a new set of problems.

The Problem with Pacing:
Picture this: A patient's heart receives an electrical impulse from their pacemaker to stimulate a contraction. Logically, this blood is pumped out into the circulation. But what if that newly 'pumped' blood runs into a roadblock?

Normally, the atria (the top chambers) contract just before the ventricles. This timing allows for ideal ventricular filling. In certain situations, the pacemaker can disrupt this synchrony, leading to something called "atrioventricular dyssynchrony" – essentially, the atria and ventricles are out of step. When this happens, the atria might try to pump blood against closed ventricular valves, sort of like trying to run uphill while carrying a heavy backpack. This can have consequences.

Symptoms of Pacemaker Syndrome

Think of it this way: the heart becomes less efficient due to this abnormal blood flow pattern. Patients might experience:

Shortness of breath
Fatigue
Dizziness
A feeling of palpitations or forceful heartbeats
Hypotension (low blood pressure)
Who's Vulnerable?

Pacemaker syndrome is more common in certain situations:

Patients heavily reliant on pacing: Think of a patient whose heart rarely beats on its own, relying almost entirely on those electrical impulses from the pacemaker.

Ventricular pacing: Pacing the ventricles directly (such as in some older pacemakers) is more likely to disrupt the heart's natural rhythm pattern.

Management: A Multifaceted Approach

Managing pacemaker syndrome requires a careful assessment of the patient's condition and their pacemaker function. Here are some strategies that might be implemented:

Programming Adjustments: Tweaking the pacemaker settings, such as the timing of atrial and ventricular pacing, can sometimes eliminate or reduce the symptoms.

Upgrade to a Biventricular Pacemaker: In some cases, upgrading to a more advanced type of pacemaker (also known as Cardiac Resynchronization Therapy) that paces both the atria and ventricles in a more coordinated fashion might be the best solution.

Medication Adjustments: Especially if the patient has underlying heart failure, optimizing medication might improve overall cardiac function and reduce symptoms.

Exam Tip: The CMSRN loves scenarios where you have to think about optimizing cardiac function and recognizing potential consequences of interventions. Keep pacemaker syndrome in your mental toolkit when addressing related scenarios.

Pacemaker syndrome serves as a reminder that even the most well-intentioned interventions can, at times, have unintended consequences. Understanding the concept of pacemaker syndrome, its manifestations, and management strategies empowers you to provide top-notch care for patients reliant on these life-saving devices.

Think of cardiac catheterization as an exploratory journey into the depths of the circulatory system. Using thin, flexible tubes called catheters, cardiologists can navigate the highways of your blood vessels, visualizing them through dye injections and taking precise measurements. This procedure has revolutionized heart disease diagnosis and treatment, opening the door for life-altering interventions like coronary angiography and percutaneous coronary intervention (PCI).

**The Voyage Begins: Indications for Cardiac Catheterization**

Here are some key scenarios where cardiac catheterization is your patient's ticket to a comprehensive heart checkup:

- **Suspected Coronary Artery Disease (CAD):** It's the gold standard for diagnosing CAD, revealing blockages and pinpointing their severity.
- **Acute Coronary Syndrome (ACS):** A crucial diagnostic tool for STEMI and other unstable cardiac conditions.
- **Before Heart Surgery:** Provides a detailed map for surgeons, especially before valve replacement or bypass surgery.
- **Evaluating Heart Function:** Offers insights into pressures within the heart chambers and the heart's pumping performance.

**Coronary Angiography: Unmasking Blockages**

During coronary angiography, the catheter is carefully advanced to the openings of the coronary arteries. Dye injected through the catheter illuminates the arteries under X-ray, revealing any narrowing or blockages. Imagine it like a detective inspecting crime scene clues to identify the culprit in a patient's chest pain.

**Percutaneous Coronary Intervention (PCI): When Diagnosis Meets Treatment**

Now imagine the catheter as not just a diagnostic tool, but also a means of fixing the problem. PCI, often called angioplasty, involves reopening those narrow vessels using a tiny balloon at the tip of the catheter.

In some cases, a stent (a miniature mesh scaffold) is placed to prop the artery open long-term. It's like calling in a skilled plumber to unclog a pipe in the heart's plumbing system.

**Complications: The Price of the Journey**

While cardiac catheterization is generally safe, it's important to be aware of potential risks:

- Bleeding or hematoma at the insertion site (often the groin area)
- Contrast dye reaction (possible allergic reaction)
- Kidney damage from the contrast dye (especially a concern for those with preexisting kidney issues)
- Damage to blood vessels
- Arrhythmias (due to catheter irritation within the heart)

**Door-to-Balloon Time: When Minutes Matter**

In a STEMI, every second counts! Door-to-balloon (DTB) time is a critical quality metric measuring the time from the patient's arrival at the hospital to the moment the angioplasty balloon inflates to open the blocked artery. The goal: Less than 90 minutes! Think of it as the cardiac equivalent of the ambulance's siren, reminding everyone that speed is essential in salvaging heart muscle.

Know the DTB target time and why it's crucial. Expect STEMI scenarios on the CMSRN exam where knowledge of cardiac catheterization procedures and DTB time will play a vital role in answering questions about optimal patient management.

By mastering the concepts of cardiac catheterization, coronary angiography, and PCI, you'll be equipped to navigate the complex world of heart disease diagnosis and intervention. Just remember, even the most sophisticated journeys come with risks. Understanding these risks allows you to provide comprehensive care, anticipating potential complications and ensuring patient safety.

Picture the heart enveloped in a protective sac, the pericardium. This sac normally contains a small amount of fluid. However, imagine that fluid steadily accumulating – a situation known as pericardial effusion. If this fluid buildup becomes excessive and rapid, it can lead to a life-threatening emergency: cardiac tamponade. Think of a vise squeezing the heart, restricting its ability to expand and fill properly. This can send your patient into a downward spiral of low blood pressure, potentially leading to cardiogenic shock.

**Enter... Pericardiocentesis: Emergency Relief**

Pericardiocentesis is like a pressure-release valve for the suffocating heart. Using a needle, guided by ultrasound or fluoroscopy (a type of real-time X-ray), the cardiologist carefully punctures the pericardium and drains the excess fluid. This reduces the pressure on the heart, allowing it to pump more effectively. It's a procedure often performed at the bedside in crisis.

**Beck's Triad: Warning Signs of Impending Doom**

Before a patient even reaches the cardiac cath lab for pericardiocentesis, there are often tell-tale signs of potential tamponade – the classic triad of symptoms described by Dr. Claude Beck:

1. **Hypotension:** As the heart struggles to pump against the external pressure, blood pressure drops – sometimes precipitously.
2. **Muffled Heart Sounds:** The buildup of fluid can make those heartbeats sound distant and muffled on auscultation, like listening to someone speaking underwater.
3. **Jugular Venous Distention (JVD):** As venous blood return backs up due to the failing heart, the jugular veins in the neck might appear engorged and bulging.

**The Importance of Early Recognition**

Think of Beck's triad as flashing warning lights on the dashboard of a critically ill patient. Recognizing these signs early and understanding their link to cardiac tamponade is crucial. It alerts healthcare providers to the potential need for urgent pericardiocentesis, which could be life-saving.

Expect scenarios on the CMSRN where you must identify the urgency of a patient's clinical presentation. Understand how Beck's triad and other clues point towards cardiac tamponade and the need for immediate action.

**Beyond Emergency Relief**

While pericardiocentesis offers immediate pressure relief, it's important to remember the bigger picture:
- **Discovering the Cause:** Why did the pericardial effusion develop in the first place? Potential causes range from infection to autoimmune conditions to trauma.
- **Further Treatment:** Sometimes, pericardiocentesis needs to be combined with other treatments like surgery, especially in cases of recurrent tamponade.

Cardiac tamponade is a high-stakes emergency. Understanding Beck's Triad and the life-saving role of pericardiocentesis empowers you to quickly recognize these critically ill patients and advocate for interventions that could make all the difference. Remember, early recognition and swift action are key when it comes to battling this dramatic and potentially fatal condition.

Actually, now that we've explored the world of arrhythmias, it's time to discuss the potential need for a powerful intervention – cardioversion. Think of it as a controlled "reset" for a heart that has veered off its rhythmic course. This procedure involves delivering a precisely timed electrical shock to restore a normal heart rhythm. Let's delve into when cardioversion is indicated, the specific techniques used, and their importance in preventing life-threatening arrhythmias.

Indications: When Cardioversion Is the Answer

Cardioversion plays a crucial role in managing various tachyarrhythmias (rapid heart rhythms) including:

Atrial fibrillation and atrial flutter: Often the first-line treatment, especially in patients with hemodynamic instability or troublesome symptoms.
Supraventricular tachycardias (SVT): For certain SVTs, cardioversion might be the quickest way to restore sinus rhythm.
Ventricular tachycardia with a pulse: While unstable VT usually calls for immediate synchronized cardioversion, sometimes it's used electively if medications prove ineffective.
Types of Cardioversion

There are two main flavors of cardioversion:
Chemical cardioversion: Involves administering antiarrhythmic medications to convert the rhythm. Think of it as using medicine to nudge the heart back in line.
Electrical cardioversion: This is where the classic "paddles" often come to mind. It involves delivering a controlled electrical shock synchronized with the patient's heart rhythm.
Synchronized Cardioversion: Keeping Things in Sync

Synchronized cardioversion is crucial for tachyarrhythmias where there's still some organized electrical activity in the heart (think atrial flutter, SVT, VT with a pulse). Why the synchronization?

Timing is everything! Delivering a shock at the wrong moment during the cardiac cycle could accidentally induce a dangerous arrhythmia like ventricular fibrillation (chaotic quivering of the ventricles).

Synchronization allows the shock to be delivered during a safe window, specifically, at the peak of the QRS complex on the ECG.

Preparing for the Shock

Electrical cardioversion is usually performed under sedation to ensure patient comfort. Here's the basic rundown:

Pads/Paddles on! Electrodes are placed on the patient's chest to deliver the shock.
Sync Mode Activated: The defibrillator is switched to synchronized mode.
Shock Delivered: The machine detects the QRS complex and delivers a precisely timed shock.
Exam Tip: Know the key differences between synchronized and unsynchronized (defibrillation) modes. The CMSRN loves scenarios where you must critically assess a patient's rhythm and determine the appropriate type of electrical therapy.

Cardioversion offers a potent tool for managing tachyarrhythmias and restoring normal heart rhythm. Understanding the indications, different types (chemical vs. electrical), and the importance of synchronization empowers you to anticipate and manage these interventions effectively. Remember, sometimes it takes a jolt to get a heart back on track!

# Chapter 4: Respiratory System

Take a deep breath... and another one. Notice the effortless expansion of your chest, feel the cool air rushing in, and then the slow, satisfying exhale. We take breathing for granted, but imagine if each breath felt like a struggle. For patients with respiratory diseases, this struggle is a stark reality.

Chapter 4 invites us to embark on a journey through the intricate network of airways and air sacs that form the respiratory system. We'll unravel the mechanics of breathing, explore life-sustaining gas exchange processes, and delve into the complex pathophysiology of common respiratory disorders – from the familiar coughs and wheezes of asthma to the devastating effects of chronic obstructive pulmonary disease (COPD).

Think of this chapter as your field guide to understanding how respiratory diseases compromise normal function and impact patients' lives. We'll arm you with the knowledge to recognize abnormal breath sounds, interpret key diagnostic tests, and grasp the rationale behind various treatments. Whether it's a patient struggling with an asthma exacerbation or a COPD patient on supplemental oxygen, your mastery of the respiratory system will empower you to provide informed, compassionate care.

So, as we dive into Chapter 4, hold onto a sense of awe and appreciation for the remarkable respiratory system. Remember, with every breath we take, we celebrate its intricate design and the life it sustains.

**The respiratory system**. Imagine it as a complex network of passageways and delicate air sacs, responsible for the vital exchange of oxygen and carbon dioxide. Understanding the anatomy and physiology of this system holds the key to caring for patients with a wide array of respiratory illnesses.

**The Upper Respiratory Tract: Where the Journey Begins**
Our respiratory adventure starts with the upper airway:
- **The Nose:** The main entry point for air. Tiny hairs in the nasal passages perform the first line of defense, filtering out some dust and particles.
- **The Mouth:** An alternate entry point, especially during exercise or when our nasal passages are clogged.
- **The Pharynx (Throat):** Serves as a shared passageway for both air and food. Think of it as the intersection where the respiratory and digestive pathways briefly intertwine.
- **The Larynx (Voice Box):** Contains the vocal cords, allowing us to speak and generate sounds.

**The Lower Respiratory Tract: Diving Deeper**
As we travel downstream, the airways continue to divide and branch:
- **Trachea (Windpipe):** A sturdy tube supported by rings of cartilage, transporting air towards the lungs.
- **Bronchi:** Think of them as the main branches off the trachea, guiding air into the right and left lungs.
- **Bronchioles:** Smaller subdivisions of the bronchi, resembling twigs on a tree. These tiny airways control airflow into the deepest part of the lungs.
- **Alveoli:** The real stars of the show! Tiny, grape-like air sacs where the crucial gas exchange occurs. Imagine a network of super thin blood vessels wrapped around them – it's the perfect setup for diffusion!

**The Working Muscle: The Diaphragm**

Breathing isn't just about tubes and air sacs; a powerful muscle makes it happen! The diaphragm, a dome-shaped muscle below the lungs, plays a starring role in respiration:

- **Inspiration:** When the diaphragm contracts and flattens out, it expands the chest cavity. This creates negative pressure, sucking air into the lungs.
- **Expiration:** The diaphragm relaxes, the chest cavity recoils, and air is passively pushed out.

**Exam Tip:** Know your respiratory anatomy landmarks! CMSRN questions might ask you to identify the site of a respiratory obstruction or the location where specific breath sounds are best heard. Visual aids are key!

**Gas Exchange: It's All About Diffusion**

Remember, the ultimate goal of the respiratory system is to bring oxygen into the body and remove carbon dioxide. This magical exchange happens in the alveoli, where capillaries (the smallest blood vessels) hug them tightly. Oxygen diffuses across the thin alveolar-capillary membrane into the blood, while carbon dioxide moves in the opposite direction, ready to be exhaled.

**Beyond Mechanics: The Respiratory System's Other Roles**

- **Protection:** From nose hairs to mucus, your respiratory system has defenses against dust, microbes, and irritants.
- **Voice Production:** Airflow passing through the vocal cords creates vibrations – the basis of speech.
- **Sense of Smell:** Olfactory receptors in the nose allow us to detect odors!

By understanding the intricate anatomy and physiology of the respiratory system, you'll gain a deeper appreciation for the complexities of breathing and gas exchange. From the bustling passageways of the upper airway to the delicate network of alveoli, each component plays a vital role in sustaining life. As we delve into respiratory diseases in upcoming sections, this foundational knowledge will be your compass, guiding your understanding of what can go wrong and how to intervene.

Speaking of delicate balances within the body, let's explore common respiratory conditions that can disrupt the vital exchange of gases and make each breath a challenge for patients. These diseases impact millions, ranging from the familiar wheeze of asthma to the devastating effects of life-threatening conditions like ARDS and pulmonary embolism (PE).

**Chronic Obstructive Pulmonary Disease (COPD)**

Think of COPD as a slow, progressive decline in lung function. It's a destructive process often fueled by long-term smoking:

- **Chronic Bronchitis:** Inflammation and mucus overload in the airways, leading to a persistent cough.
- **Emphysema:** Damage to the delicate alveoli, making it hard to fully exhale and trapping air in the lungs.

**Clinical Picture:** Patients with COPD often experience shortness of breath, especially with exertion, chronic cough, and sometimes sputum production. Think of them as breathing through a narrow straw!

**Long-Term Consequences:** COPD can lead to a decreased quality of life, frequent exacerbations (worsening of symptoms), and even respiratory failure.

**Asthma: When Airways Get Reactive**

Asthma is characterized by episodic, reversible airway narrowing due to inflammation and bronchoconstriction. Imagine the airways becoming hypersensitive to triggers:

- **Extrinsic (Allergic):** Triggered by allergens like dust, pollen, pet dander.
- **Intrinsic (Non-Allergic):** Can be set off by exercise, cold air, viral infections, etc.

**What It's Like:** During an asthma flare-up, patients might experience wheezing, chest tightness, shortness of breath, and cough. Think of it as inflammation temporarily closing in those airways.

**Asthma Management: A Multi-pronged Approach**
- Avoiding triggers (when possible)
- Controller medications (inhaled corticosteroids, long-acting bronchodilators) to prevent attacks
- Rescue inhalers (short-acting bronchodilators) for acute symptom relief

**Pneumonia: Infection Attacks the Lungs**
Pneumonia is an infection within the lung tissue itself, often causing inflammation and fluid buildup in the alveoli. This disrupts gas exchange, leading to:
- Fever, chills, productive cough
- Shortness of breath
- Chest pain

**Common Culprits:** Bacteria, viruses, and fungi can all cause pneumonia. It's important to identify the type of organism, as treatment can differ.

**ARDS: When Lungs Fail**
Acute Respiratory Distress Syndrome (ARDS) is a life-threatening condition characterized by widespread inflammation and damage within the lungs, leading to severe respiratory failure. Think of it as a catastrophic inflammatory reaction that floods the alveoli.

**Triggers:** ARDS often occurs as a complication of other severe illnesses or conditions, such as sepsis, major trauma, aspiration, or severe pneumonia.

**Grim Reality:** ARDS carries a high mortality rate. Patients require critical care support, often including mechanical ventilation to take over the work of breathing.

**Pulmonary Embolism (PE): Clot on the Move**
While different from other respiratory conditions, a PE can have devastating impacts on respiratory function. Here's the scenario:
- A blood clot (often from the legs) travels to the lungs, blocking an artery.
- This blockage impairs blood flow and gas exchange, starving parts of the lungs of oxygen.

**Presentation:** Sudden onset of shortness of breath, chest pain, and sometimes coughing up blood (hemoptysis) are key signs. Large PEs can be life-threatening.

**Exam Tip:** The CMSRN loves to test your recognition of these respiratory emergencies. Know the classic presentations of each condition!

From the insidious damage of COPD to the severe derangements of ARDS, respiratory conditions pose a significant challenge to patients and healthcare providers alike. Understanding the unique pathophysiology, clinical presentations, and management strategies of these common diseases will equip you to provide expert care. Remember, when patients struggle to breathe, your knowledge and swift interventions could mean the difference between life and death.

Now, let's explore two invaluable tools that provide a peek into a patient's respiratory status and oxygenation – arterial blood gases (ABGs) and pulse oximetry. Understanding how to interpret these tests is a vital skill for all healthcare providers, especially when caring for critically ill patients.

**Arterial Blood Gases (ABGs): The Gold Standard**
ABGs give us a snapshot of a person's oxygenation, ventilation, and acid-base balance. Think of them as a detailed lab report drawn directly from an artery (radial, femoral, brachial). Key ABG components include:
- **pH:** Reflects blood acidity or alkalinity.
- **PaO2:** Partial pressure of oxygen in arterial blood, indicating how well oxygen moves from the lungs into the bloodstream.

- **PaCO2:** Partial pressure of carbon dioxide in arterial blood, providing insights into ventilation (how well a person is removing carbon dioxide).
- **HCO3:** Bicarbonate level, which plays a role in the body's acid-base balance.

**Interpreting ABGs: Unraveling the Clues**

Analyzing ABGs requires methodical assessment:
1. **Is there an acidosis (low pH) or alkalosis (high pH)?**
2. **Is the primary problem respiratory (look at the PaCO2) or metabolic (look at the HCO3)?**
3. **Compensation:** Does the body's natural buffering system try to compensate for the primary problem?

**Pulse Oximetry: The Non-invasive Option**

Pulse oximeters offer a quick, non-invasive way to estimate oxygen saturation levels (SpO2). That little clip on the finger (or earlobe) shines a light through the tissue and measures the percentage of hemoglobin molecules carrying oxygen.

**Limitations:** While incredibly useful, pulse oximetry has limitations:
- **Inaccuracy:** Factors like poor peripheral circulation, dark nail polish, and even certain types of anemia can affect readings.
- **Doesn't tell the whole story:** A patient might have a normal SpO2 but still have a severe respiratory problem with CO2 retention – a detail only an ABG would catch.

**The Clinical Picture: When to Use Each**
- **ABGs:** Often indicated for critically ill patients, those with suspected acid-base disorders, or when precise measurements of oxygenation and ventilation are needed.
- **Pulse Oximetry:** Used routinely to monitor oxygen saturation in a variety of settings, from the post-op patient to someone with chronic lung disease.

The CMSRN loves ABG interpretation! Practice analyzing various scenarios and identifying respiratory vs. metabolic acidosis/alkalosis, along with compensation mechanisms.

Imagine a COPD patient admitted for an acute exacerbation. An ABG might reveal hypoxemia (low PaO2), hypercapnia (high PaCO2), and a low pH (respiratory acidosis). Meanwhile, continuous pulse oximetry monitoring allows you to quickly track their response to interventions, such as supplemental oxygen or bronchodilator therapy.

- **ABGs and pulse oximetry complement each other:** ABGs provide a comprehensive picture, while pulse ox offers continuous, real-time monitoring.
- **Context matters:** Always interpret ABGs and pulse ox findings in the context of the patient's overall clinical condition. Remember, numbers are just one piece of the puzzle!

By mastering the interpretation of ABGs and pulse oximetry, you'll gain a powerful tool for assessing respiratory status and guiding interventions, allowing you to provide better, more informed care for your patients.

Let's now talk about respiratory assessment – a cornerstone of evaluating patients with respiratory complaints or suspected respiratory disease. Think of respiratory assessment as a multidisciplinary investigation, pulling together clues from the patient's history, physical exam, and diagnostic tests.

Taking a Patient's History: Where the Story Begins
A thorough history lays the foundation, unveiling hints about your patient's respiratory health:

Symptoms: Ask about shortness of breath, cough (productive or not), wheezing, chest pain, etc. Inquire about the timing, duration, and any aggravating or relieving factors.

Smoking History: A major risk factor! Document pack-years for current and former smokers.
Environmental Exposures: Does their work or hobbies involve dust, fumes, or chemicals that could irritate their lungs?
Past Medical History: Conditions like asthma, COPD, allergies, or recent illnesses play a role.
Physical Examination: Piecing Together the Puzzle

Now for the hands-on portion. Let's explore key elements:
Vital Signs: Check for fever, tachycardia (rapid heart rate), tachypnea (fast breathing), hypoxemia (low oxygen on pulse oximetry).
General Inspection: Look for signs of respiratory distress – use of accessory muscles, pursed-lip breathing, cyanosis (bluish skin), or signs of clubbing in finger nails.
Chest Examination:
Inspection: Look at the chest shape and symmetry, and any retractions.
Palpation: Feel for tracheal deviation, areas of tenderness, and tactile fremitus (vibration felt on the chest wall when the patient speaks).
Percussion: Listen to the resonance over the lung fields. Dullness might indicate fluid or consolidation, while hyper-resonance could point towards trapped air.
Auscultation: This is where the stethoscope magic happens! Systematically listen to lung sounds.
Recognize normal breath sounds (vesicular, bronchial), and abnormal ones like crackles, wheezes, rhonchi (think of these as clues to the underlying problem).
Diagnostic Studies: Illuminating Hidden Clues

Chest X-ray: A go-to imaging test to visualize lung fields, look for infiltrates, masses, air trapping, or fluid accumulation.
Pulmonary Function Tests (PFTs): Offer in-depth analysis of lung volumes, airflow, and diffusion capacity. Helps diagnose obstructive vs. restrictive lung diseases.
Lab Tests: May include a CBC (for signs of infection), basic metabolic panel (assessing electrolyte and acid-base status), or more specialized tests when indicated.
Know your normal breath sounds and abnormal ones! Practice with audio recordings or videos to train your ear.

Putting it All Together: The Clinical Picture
A comprehensive respiratory assessment doesn't just involve checking boxes. Instead, it requires integrating findings from multiple sources, weaving them into a likely diagnosis or differential diagnosis. Here's where your critical thinking comes into play, helping guide further diagnostic tests or initiating the most appropriate treatment plan.

Let's get into the world of oxygen therapy, a cornerstone intervention for patients with hypoxemia (low oxygen levels) or respiratory distress. It's the difference between merely surviving and actually thriving for many patients. Knowing the various delivery devices, indications, and potential complications is crucial in ensuring safe and effective oxygen administration.

Oxygen Delivery Devices: A Toolkit for Improved Oxygenation
Nasal Cannula: The workhorse! Two prongs rest in the nostrils, delivering low-flow oxygen (typically 1-6 liters/minute). It's well-tolerated and allows the patient to eat and talk.
Simple Face Mask: Covers the nose and mouth, providing higher oxygen concentrations than a nasal cannula (around 5-10 liters/minute).

Venturi Mask: The most precise! Delivers a fixed, predictable oxygen concentration. Great for patients with COPD where too much oxygen might be a concern.
Non-Rebreather Mask: Features a reservoir bag and delivers the highest possible concentration of oxygen from a non-invasive device. Often used in emergencies.
Beyond Low Flow Systems...

Humidified High-Flow Nasal Cannula: A newer option that delivers warmed, humidified oxygen at high flow rates. Useful for patients needing more oxygen support than a standard nasal cannula provides.
CPAP/BiPAP: "Positive airway pressure" devices use pressurized air to keep airways open. Especially helpful for sleep apnea and sometimes used for acute respiratory failure.
Indications for Oxygen Therapy

Confirmed hypoxemia: Aim to maintain SpO2 (oxygen saturation) within a target range, often 92-94% for most patients, and higher for some specific situations.
Respiratory Distress: Even if a patient's SpO2 is within normal limits, oxygen therapy might be indicated if they show signs of significant work of breathing.
Specific Conditions: COPD, acute pulmonary edema, myocardial infarction, and many other illnesses can warrant oxygen therapy.
Potential Complications: Watching for the Downside

Oxygen Toxicity: Prolonged exposure to high oxygen concentrations can damage the lungs. Be mindful of this, especially in patients with COPD.
Absorption Atelectasis: High oxygen concentrations can displace nitrogen in the alveoli, leading to collapse of air sacs.
Drying of Mucous Membranes: Oxygen therapy can dry out the nasal passages and mouth. Humidification can mitigate this.
Know the oxygen flow rates associated with different delivery devices and their approximate oxygen concentrations. Expect scenarios where you need to choose the appropriate oxygen delivery method.

Nursing Considerations: Your Role Matters
Close Monitoring: Check oxygen saturation regularly and watch for signs of clinical improvement or deterioration.
Patient Education: Explain why oxygen is needed, and ensure they understand how to use the device correctly.
Skin Care: Especially with masks, assess skin integrity and reposition devices periodically to prevent pressure injuries.

Oxygen therapy may seem simple, but there's an art and science to it. It's a life-saving intervention, when used judiciously. Understanding the various oxygen delivery systems, indications, and potential complications allow you to provide the best possible care to your patients, helping them breathe a little easier.

**Mastering the Art of Airway Management:**
Imagine you're a party host, but your guests (oxygen and carbon dioxide) can't get through the door (airway) to mingle. That's the essence of airway management – ensuring a patent (open) airway for proper gas exchange. As a future CMSRN, this skill is your golden ticket to keeping patients breathing comfortably and acing the exam. Buckle up, because we're about to dive deep into this crucial concept!

Airway Assessment: Unveiling the Mystery

Think of airway assessment as detective work. You need to gather clues to identify any potential problems. Here's your toolkit:

Look: Is the airway clear of obstructions? Is there facial trauma or swelling? (Think of a character from a horror movie – any signs of something blocking the airway?)
Listen: Can you hear breath sounds equally on both sides of the chest? Are there any wheezing or stridor sounds (like a musical instrument struggling to play) that might indicate airway narrowing?
Feel: Can you feel air movement from the nose or mouth? Is there any tenderness or crepitus (crackling sensation) in the neck, which could suggest a fracture?
Maintaining a Patent Airway: From Simple to Advanced

Okay, so you've assessed the airway. Now what? Here's your arsenal of interventions, depending on the situation:

Basic Maneuvers: Head tilt-chin lift (think of tilting your head back to sing a high note) and jaw thrust (like you're pushing out a double chin) can open the airway in an unconscious patient.
Airway Adjuncts: Oropharyngeal (placed in the mouth) and nasopharyngeal (inserted through the nose) airways are simple plastic tubes that help maintain an open airway. Imagine them as little splints to keep the airway propped open.
Advanced Airway Management: Stepping Up Your Game

For more critical situations, advanced airway management techniques might be needed. Here's where things get exciting (and a little more complex):

Laryngeal Mask Airway (LMA): This mask is a temporary alternative to endotracheal intubation (placing a tube through the vocal cords into the trachea). Think of it as a more advanced sealing device to ensure proper oxygen flow.
Endotracheal Intubation: The gold standard for advanced airway management, a breathing tube is inserted through the vocal cords and secured in the trachea. Imagine it as a direct highway for oxygen to get straight to the lungs. Exam Tip: Be familiar with the steps involved in endotracheal intubation – it's a high-yield topic!
Remember: Mastering these techniques requires practice, so don't hesitate to ask instructors for demonstrations and hands-on experience in a simulated setting.

The Interconnectedness of Airway Management: A Symphony of Skills

Airway management isn't an isolated skill. It works in beautiful harmony with other aspects of patient care:

Pharmacology: Medications like sedatives and paralytics might be used to facilitate airway maneuvers.
Critical Thinking: You'll need to assess the situation quickly and choose the most appropriate intervention.
Communication: Collaboration with physicians, respiratory therapists, and other healthcare providers is essential.
Beyond the Exam: Why Airway Management Matters

Airway management isn't just about ticking a box on the exam. It's about saving lives. Every breath a patient takes is a testament to the critical role you play. Here's a real-world example:

Imagine you're working in the emergency department and a patient arrives in a choking fit. Your quick assessment, use of basic airway maneuvers, and clear communication with the doctor might be the difference between life and death. Pretty empowering, right?

Remember: This is just the first step in your airway management journey. As you progress in your career, you'll gain experience and confidence in handling even the most challenging situations.

Bonus: Fun Facts and Mnemonics to Spice Up Your Studies!

Did you know the epiglottis, a tiny flap in the throat, acts like a security guard, preventing food from entering the airway? Here's a mnemonic to remember the order of airway assessment: AMPLE – Allusion (look for facial swelling), Movement (check for chest rise and fall), Palpation (feel for air movement), Listen (for breath sounds), Environment (consider potential hazards).

Airway management may seem daunting, but with dedication, practice, and the knowledge you've gained here, you'll

Picture a patient struggling to breathe, each gasp a desperate battle for oxygen. It's in moments like these that mechanical ventilation steps into the spotlight. These machines aren't just a piece of advanced medical equipment; they're a bridge to survival when the lungs themselves falter. Let's delve into the world of mechanical ventilation, its modes, indications, and the potential complications that come with this life-saving intervention.

Ventilator Basics: A Refresher
Think of a mechanical ventilator as a sophisticated bellows, designed to mimic the natural mechanics of breathing. At their core, these machines deliver a controlled mixture of oxygen and air into the lungs under positive pressure. This positive pressure helps overcome resistance within the airways and expands the alveoli (those tiny air sacs), optimizing gas exchange.

Modes of Ventilation: Choices Matter
Mechanical ventilators aren't one-size-fits-all. They offer various modes of operation, each with unique settings and clinical applications. Here's a simplified breakdown:

Volume Control: Delivers a set volume of air with each breath. Think of it as filling a balloon to a specific size.
Pressure Control: Deliver breaths up to a set pressure limit. Imagine a gentle breeze versus a powerful gust of wind.
Synchronized Intermittent Mandatory Ventilation (SIMV): This mode combines patient-initiated breaths with a set number of ventilator-delivered breaths. It's a bit like teamwork between the patient and the machine.
When to Use Mechanical Ventilation

Mechanical ventilation isn't a casual intervention. It's often reserved for critical situations, including:

Acute Respiratory Failure: When the lungs cannot effectively oxygenate the blood or get rid of carbon dioxide, the ventilator can take over the work of respiration temporarily.
Severe Pneumonia: Inflamed, fluid-filled lungs sometimes need assistance from the ventilator.
Trauma or Surgery Recovery: If a patient's breathing is compromised due to injury or anesthesia, mechanical ventilation can provide support.
Beyond Settings: Patient Considerations

Initiating mechanical ventilation involves more than just choosing a mode and turning on the machine. Here's where your nursing skills truly shine:

Monitoring: Observe ventilator readings (pressures, volumes, respiratory rate), oxygenation status (pulse oximetry and ABGs), and the patient's overall clinical picture.
Alarms: Respond quickly and appropriately to ventilator alarms, identifying potential causes and intervening in time.
Comfort: Ensure proper sedation and pain management. Imagine the anxiety of breathing with machine assistance!
Oral Care: Meticulous oral care helps prevent complications like ventilator-associated pneumonia (VAP).
Exam Tip: Know the key differences between volume control and pressure control modes. Practice scenarios where you need to select the most appropriate mode and settings based on a patient's condition.

Complications: The Price of Intervention
While life-saving, mechanical ventilation isn't without its risks. Be watchful for:

Ventilator-Associated Pneumonia (VAP): A serious infection that can develop with prolonged mechanical ventilation. Prevention is key!
Barotrauma: High airway pressures can damage delicate lung tissues leading to complications like a pneumothorax (collapsed lung).
Ventilator Dependence: Some patients can develop difficulty breathing independently after prolonged mechanical ventilation.
Real-World Application

Imagine a patient with severe respiratory failure due to COVID-19. Their oxygen levels are dangerously low despite non-invasive support. You assist with endotracheal intubation and initiation of mechanical ventilation utilizing volume control mode. Careful monitoring, vigilant care, and collaborative efforts with the respiratory therapist and physician ultimately help the patient wean off the ventilator and regain their ability to breathe on their own.

Mechanical ventilation is a powerful intervention that walks a fine line – supporting life while also carrying potential risks. Understanding the mechanics, modes, indications, and complications of this technology will equip you to confidently care for some of healthcare's sickest patients. And as your skills grow, know this – you are part of the team that gives these patients a fighting chance.

# *Chapter 5: Endocrine System*

Get ready to unlock the secrets of the body's ingenious communication network – the endocrine system. In Chapter 5, we'll venture behind the scenes, exploring the powerful chemical messengers known as hormones. You may think of hormones as the teenagers of the body – often misunderstood, sometimes causing drama, but absolutely essential for development and function!

Picture these hormones as tiny couriers traveling through the bloodstream, carrying vital messages to target cells throughout the body. They regulate everything from growth and metabolism to sleep-wake cycles and our response to stress. It's a delicate balancing act, and any deviation from the norm can have a ripple effect on a person's health.

From those intense growth spurts during puberty to the complex interplay of blood sugar regulation, the endocrine system holds the key to many physiological processes. We'll delve into common disorders like diabetes, hyper- and hypothyroidism, and explore their impact on patients' lives.

So, prepare to be amazed by the intricate connections between these tiny glands, their potent hormones, and the far-reaching consequences of even slight imbalances. By the end of this chapter, you'll have a newfound appreciation for this complex and fascinating system that keeps the body in harmony.

Let's start by mapping out the endocrine landscape! Think of your body as a sprawling kingdom, and the endocrine system as its network of messengers. Glands scattered throughout this kingdom each have a unique task – producing hormones that serve as potent chemical signals. Now, let's identify these key locations and explore their specialized roles:

The Brain's Command Centers
Hypothalamus: The true master regulator. It links the nervous and endocrine systems and controls the pituitary gland, often called the "master gland."
Pituitary Gland: This pea-sized gland sits nestled at the base of the brain and has mighty effects. It secretes hormones governing a multitude of functions, from growth to reproduction and stress response.
Pineal Gland: Tucked within the brain, this gland produces melatonin, the hormone that helps regulate your sleep-wake cycles. Think of it as the body's internal clock.
Glands of the Neck and Chest

Thyroid Gland: This butterfly-shaped gland sits in your neck and is a metabolic powerhouse. It produces thyroid hormones that regulate everything from metabolism to heart rate and body temperature.
Parathyroid Glands: Four tiny glands embedded in the thyroid, they play a vital role in calcium balance.
Thymus: Located in the chest, it's part of the immune system and helps develop specialized white blood cells.
The Abdominal Powerhouses
Adrenal Glands: Sitting atop your kidneys, these glands are your stress-response center. They produce cortisol, adrenaline (think fight-or-flight response), and other hormones.
Pancreas: This multitasking organ plays a role in both digestion and endocrine function. It produces insulin and glucagon, the key hormones in blood sugar regulation.

The Reproductive System's Hormonal Harmonizers

Ovaries (in females): They produce estrogen and progesterone, playing a critical role in the female reproductive cycle and beyond.
Testes (in males): The main source of testosterone, essential for male reproductive development and function.
Hormone Action: How They Exert Their Influence

Think of hormones as keys that fit into specific locks (receptors) on target cells. Once they bind, they trigger a cascade of events within the cell, influencing various processes such as growth, metabolism, or even mood.

The Delicate Feedback Loops
The endocrine system excels at maintaining balance. It uses feedback mechanisms, often employing the hypothalamus and pituitary gland, to keep hormone levels in check. For example, if thyroid hormone levels drop too low, the hypothalamus and pituitary sense this and ramp up thyroid hormone production.

Know your major endocrine glands, their primary hormone products, and the general functions of those hormones. Visual aids can be incredibly helpful!

The endocrine system may seem like a complex web of glands and hormones, but remember – it's about communication and maintaining the delicate balance the body needs to thrive. Understanding the anatomical players and their interplay is the first step to unraveling the intricate world of endocrine disorders, a journey we'll continue on in upcoming sections.

Speaking of intricate balances within the body, let's now explore the realm of endocrine disorders where a slight hormonal imbalance can have cascading effects on a patient's health. We'll delve into the complexities of diabetes, thyroid diseases, and adrenal disorders – conditions that you'll undoubtedly encounter in your clinical practice.

Diabetes Mellitus: When Blood Sugar Goes Awry
Diabetes is a metabolic disorder characterized by persistent hyperglycemia (high blood sugar). Think of it as a breakdown in how the body uses insulin, the hormone central to glucose regulation. It comes in a few varieties:

Type 1 Diabetes: The pancreas can't make enough insulin due to an autoimmune attack on the insulin-producing cells. Often develops during childhood or young adulthood.
Type 2 Diabetes: The body becomes resistant to insulin's effects and might also have inadequate insulin production. This type is closely linked to lifestyle factors like obesity and inactivity.
Gestational Diabetes: This form occurs during pregnancy and usually resolves afterward, but increases the mother and child's risk of developing type 2 diabetes later in life.
Clinical Picture: Patients with diabetes might present with classic symptoms of increased thirst, frequent urination, blurry vision, and sometimes unexplained weight loss. Untreated, it can lead to serious complications like heart disease, stroke, kidney damage, and even blindness.

Exam Tip: Know the diagnostic criteria for diabetes (fasting glucose, A1C, oral glucose tolerance test) and the differences between type 1 and type 2.

## Thyroid Disorders: Metabolic Regulators Gone Haywire

The thyroid gland, our metabolic maestro, can malfunction in a couple of ways:

**Hyperthyroidism:** The thyroid is overactive, churning out too much thyroid hormone. Imagine your metabolism revved up all the time – patients might experience weight loss, nervousness, heat intolerance, and heart palpitations.

**Hypothyroidism:** The thyroid becomes sluggish, causing insufficient thyroid hormone. Think of a metabolism slowed to a crawl – fatigue, weight gain, cold intolerance, and constipation become common complaints.

**Causes:** These disorders can stem from autoimmune diseases (like Graves' disease for hyperthyroidism or Hashimoto's thyroiditis for hypothyroidism), nodules, or inflammation of the thyroid gland.

## Adrenal Disorders: Stress Hormones in Disarray

The adrenal glands, perched atop our kidneys, are crucial players in our stress response and beyond. Disruptions within these glands can lead to:

**Cushing's Syndrome:** Excess cortisol, either from long-term steroid use or a tumor. Think of distinctive features like weight gain in the trunk with thin extremities, a round "moon face", and easy bruising.

**Addison's Disease:** Adrenal insufficiency, meaning not enough cortisol. Patients might experience fatigue, weakness, low blood pressure, and sometimes, a darkening of the skin.

### Real-World Scenario

Imagine a patient with unexplained weight gain, fatigue, and hair loss. They also feel cold all the time. Lab tests reveal elevated TSH (thyroid stimulating hormone) and low T4 (thyroid hormone) levels. You suspect hypothyroidism – a condition that significantly impacts their quality of life, but fortunately, can be effectively managed with medication.

Endocrine disorders are a testament to how a small hormonal imbalance can have far-reaching effects on a patient's well-being. Understanding the presentation, diagnosis, and management of these common conditions is essential to providing comprehensive care, whether it's managing diabetic complications, fine-tuning thyroid medication, or recognizing the signs of an adrenal crisis.

Think of lab tests and diagnostic imaging as your crystal ball into a patient's internal world. These investigations hold clues about underlying diseases, confirm diagnoses, and help you monitor the effectiveness of your treatment plans. Now, let's explore some key lab values and diagnostic tools commonly encountered in clinical practice.

**Key Lab Values: Decoding the Numbers**

- **Complete Blood Count (CBC):** Think of this as an essential snapshot of overall health. It checks for anemia (low red blood cells), signs of infection (high white blood cells), and platelet abnormalities (involved in clotting).
- **Basic Metabolic Panel (BMP):** Assesses electrolytes (like sodium, potassium, vital for muscle and nerve function), kidney function (creatinine, BUN), and blood glucose levels.
- **Lipid Panel:** Breaks down cholesterol levels. It includes total cholesterol, HDL (the "good" cholesterol,) LDL (the "bad" cholesterol,) and triglycerides (a type of fat in the blood).
- **Hemoglobin A1c (HbA1c):** This is your go-to for long-term blood sugar control in diabetic patients. It gives you an average blood sugar level over the past 2-3 months.

- **Thyroid Panel:** Usually includes TSH (thyroid-stimulating hormone) along with T4 and sometimes T3 to evaluate thyroid gland function.

Know the normal ranges for these common lab values! CMSRN questions often involve interpreting abnormal lab findings.

**Diagnostic Imaging: Visualizing the Unseen**
- **X-rays:** A classic tool for visualizing bones (think fractures), and sometimes lungs (looking for pneumonia or masses).
- **CT scans:** Offers detailed cross-sectional images of organs and tissues. Useful for identifying internal bleeding, tumors, and various other abnormalities.
- **Ultrasound:** Utilizes sound waves to create real-time images of internal structures. It's helpful for assessing organs, blood flow, and even guiding procedures.
- **MRI:** Employs powerful magnets and radio waves to generate exceptionally detailed images. Great for visualizing soft tissues like the brain, spinal cord, and joints.

A patient presents with chronic fatigue, weight loss, and tremors. You order a thyroid panel and find an elevated TSH and a low T4. This points you towards hypothyroidism. An ultrasound might be the next step to evaluate the thyroid gland itself, looking for potential nodules or inflammation.

**Beyond Just Numbers and Images**

Remember, lab values and diagnostics are only pieces of the puzzle! Always consider the full clinical picture. Here's where your synthesis skills truly shine – combining patient history, physical exam findings, and test results to arrive at a diagnosis.

**Thinking Critically: Lab Limitations**
- Lab values can sometimes be affected by medications, hydration status, or recent illnesses. Don't always jump to conclusions based on a single abnormal result.
- Imaging isn't foolproof either. Incidental findings (something seen but not related to the patient's symptoms) can sometimes lead to additional testing and unnecessary anxiety.

Lab values and diagnostic imaging are indispensable tools in your clinical arsenal. Mastering their interpretation and understanding their limitations empowers you to provide informed, evidence-based care to your patients. Think of yourself as a skilled detective, piecing together clues from various sources to solve the medical mysteries that come your way.

Let's now talk about patient education and self-management – empowering patients to take charge of their own health. Remember, patients aren't just passive recipients of care. They have the potential to be active partners in their health journey, and your guidance can make all the difference!

**The Why: Benefits of Patient Education**

Think of patient education as an investment in better health outcomes. Here's why it matters:
- Improved adherence to treatment plans. Informed patients are more likely to understand their treatment goals and stick to medication regimes or lifestyle changes.
- Enhanced self-care skills. Teaching patients about disease management, symptom recognition, and when to seek help can prevent complications.
- Increased patient satisfaction. When patients feel understood and involved, it builds trust and strengthens your therapeutic relationship.

**Key Principles of Effective Education**
- **Tailor it to the individual:** Consider the patient's health literacy level, learning style, and unique concerns. Avoid a one-size-fits-all approach.
- **Use clear, plain language:** Steer clear of too much medical jargon, opt for simple explanations, and analogies they can relate to.

- **Assess understanding:** Don't just talk AT patients, invite questions, and ensure they grasp the information. The "teach-back" method (asking them to explain it back to you) can be very helpful.
- **Provide written materials:** Reinforce your verbal instructions with handouts, pamphlets, or reputable online resources they can refer to later.
- **Involve family and caregivers:** When appropriate, include them in the education process for additional support at home.

**Techniques for Specific Situations**
- **Newly Diagnosed Chronic Illness:** Break down the information into digestible sessions over time, address their emotional response to the diagnosis, and emphasize the steps they can take for self-management.
- **Medication Teaching:** Explain not only how to take the medication, but also why it's important, potential side effects, and any drug interactions to watch out for.
- **Preparing for Procedures:** Clear instructions about what to expect, any necessary prep (for example fasting before a test), and post-procedure care can reduce patient anxiety.

Know common patient education topics and be prepared to answer scenario-based questions where you demonstrate your ability to communicate effectively, assess understanding, and provide appropriate resources.

Imagine a newly diagnosed diabetic learning how to give themselves insulin injections. Take time to demonstrate the technique, allow them to practice with a saline-filled syringe, and provide resources about insulin storage and disposal.

Patient education isn't a task to check off a list. It's about fostering informed decision-making, building self-efficacy, and ultimately improving quality of life for your patients. Empowered patients often become your greatest allies in their journey toward better health!

# *Chapter 6: Gastrointestinal System*

Think of this chapter as your personal tour guide through the organs, enzymes, and processes involved in breaking down food and absorbing essential nutrients.

From the first bite you take to the final, ahem... exit strategy, your GI system is a marvel of biological engineering. It has to not only extract what your body needs from food but also defend against harmful invaders like bacteria and viruses. And trust me, things can get messy down there! Imagine a chaotic food fight mixed with an intense battle against potential intruders.

We'll venture through the mouth, esophagus, stomach, small intestine, large intestine, and all the specialized organs in between. Get ready to understand the key players like digestive enzymes, gut bacteria, and the intricate interplay between digestion and overall health.

Buckle up and prepare to be amazed! Because understanding the GI system doesn't just equip you to tackle exam questions. It unlocks the secrets to common digestive woes like heartburn, constipation, and inflammatory bowel diseases – knowledge that will empower you to guide patients towards better gut health and well-being.

Think of it as your body's internal disassembly line, breaking down food into usable nutrients and expelling waste products. Let's start our journey down this complex but fascinating system!

**The Upper GI Tract**
- **Mouth:** It's where it all begins! Mechanical digestion starts with chewing, while salivary amylase initiates the breakdown of carbohydrates.
- **Pharynx:** This muscular passageway shared with the respiratory system is crucial for swallowing.
- **Esophagus:** A muscular tube propelling food towards the stomach through peristalsis (wave-like contractions). Remember the lower esophageal sphincter (LES), a crucial valve preventing reflux of stomach contents.
- **Stomach:** Think of this highly acidic muscular sac as a churning chemical vat. Pepsin begins protein digestion, while powerful gastric juices break down food.

**The Lower GI Tract**
- **Small Intestine:** The real MVP of digestion and absorption! It's divided into the duodenum, jejunum, and ileum. Villi and microvilli lining its walls dramatically increase surface area for nutrient absorption.
- **Large Intestine (Colon):** Primary functions include water absorption, waste compaction, and housing our gut microbiome (the trillions of bacteria residing within our intestines).
- **Rectum and Anus:** The final stretch, responsible for storing and expelling stool (waste products).

**Accessory Organs: Working Behind the Scenes**
- **Liver:** A metabolic powerhouse! It produces bile (vital for fat emulsification), processes nutrients, detoxifies substances, and synthesizes various proteins.
- **Gallbladder:** Stores and releases bile into the small intestine, aiding fat digestion.

- **Pancreas:** A double agent! It has endocrine functions (producing insulin and glucagon) and exocrine roles, secreting pancreatic enzymes (amylase, lipase, proteases) into the small intestine for further breakdown of nutrients.

**Physiological Processes: It's Not Just About Organs**
- **Digestion:** The enzymatic breakdown of complex macromolecules (carbs, proteins, fats) into smaller absorbable units.
- **Absorption:** Nutrients, water, and electrolytes move from the intestinal lumen into the bloodstream or lymphatic system.
- **Motility:** Coordinated muscle contractions propel food along the GI tract, crucial for proper digestion and elimination.
- **Secretion:** Production and release of digestive enzymes, bile, gastric acid, and mucus throughout the GI system.

Know the major anatomical structures of the GI tract, their functions, and the key enzymes involved in digestion!

Let's not forget the unsung heroes of the GI tract – the gut microbiota. These trillions of bacteria play crucial roles in digestion, immune function, and even mental health. Any disturbance in their balance can have far-reaching health consequences.

Get ready to rumble through the GI tract, but this time, we're encountering roadblocks! This section tackles some of the most frequently tested GI conditions on the CMSRN exam: Inflammatory Bowel Disease (IBD), Liver Disease, GI Bleeding, and Obstruction. Consider this your personal roadmap to navigating these tricky topics with confidence.

Inflammatory Bowel Disease (IBD): When Your Gut Goes Rogue

Imagine your intestines waging a full-scale war against themselves! That's essentially what happens in IBD, a chronic inflammatory condition. The two main players are:

Ulcerative Colitis: Think of this as inflammation confined to the inner lining of the large intestine (colon), causing frequent bloody diarrhea, abdominal cramping, and urgency.

Crohn's Disease: This inflammatory rebel can attack anywhere along the GI tract, from mouth to anus. Symptoms can vary but often include abdominal pain, weight loss, fatigue, and malabsorption (difficulty absorbing nutrients).

Exam Tip: Remember the key differences between Ulcerative Colitis and Crohn's Disease – location, symptoms, and potential complications. A handy mnemonic? "UC: Keeps it Confined (to the Colon), while Crohn's Can Cause Complementary problems Anywhere."

Liver Disease: When Your Body's Filter Gets Clogged

The liver is your body's detox center, processing nutrients, filtering toxins, and producing essential proteins. But when things go south, you get liver disease. Here are two common culprits:

Hepatitis: Viral infections (A, B, C) that inflame the liver. Symptoms can range from fatigue to jaundice (yellowing of the skin) to liver failure.

Cirrhosis: Think of it as scar tissue replacing healthy liver tissue, hindering its function. It can be caused by chronic alcohol abuse, hepatitis, or fatty liver disease. Symptoms often appear late and include fluid retention, easy bleeding, and confusion.
Exam Tip: Know the modes of transmission for different types of hepatitis (A – fecal-oral, B – bodily fluids, C – blood-borne) and the potential complications of cirrhosis.

GI Bleeding: Uh Oh, There's Blood in My Stool!
Blood in your stool (hematochezia) is a red flag for GI bleeding, and the source can be anywhere along the digestive tract. Common culprits include:

Peptic Ulcers: Open sores in the stomach lining or duodenum, often caused by H. pylori infection or NSAID use.
Diverticulosis: Small pouches in the colon that can bleed if they become inflamed (diverticulitis).
Esophageal Varices: Swollen veins in the esophagus that can rupture and cause life-threatening bleeding, often seen in patients with cirrhosis.
Exam Tip: Be familiar with the clinical presentations and risk factors associated with these common causes of GI bleeding.

GI Obstruction: When the Pipeline Gets Blocked
Imagine a traffic jam in your intestines! A GI obstruction occurs when something blocks the passage of food and waste. The culprits can be:

Adhesions: Scar tissue bands from previous surgeries that can cause adhesions.
Hernias: Organs pushing through weak spots in the abdominal wall.
Tumors: Cancerous or benign growths that can obstruct the passage.
Exam Tip: Recognize the signs and symptoms of GI obstruction, such as severe abdominal pain, constipation, vomiting, and abdominal distention (swelling).

A 25-year-old male presents with frequent bloody diarrhea, urgency to have a bowel movement, and abdominal cramping. He denies fever, recent antibiotic use, or travel abroad. What's the most likely culprit? (Answer: Ulcerative Colitis).

This case highlights the importance of recognizing characteristic symptoms for different GI conditions. This whirlwind tour has equipped you with the essentials for tackling GI conditions on the CMSRN exam. Remember, mastering these concepts goes beyond memorization. Think about the underlying pathophysiology, visualize the processes occurring within the body, and connect the dots between signs, symptoms, and potential causes. By understanding the "why" behind the "what," you'll be well on your way to becoming a GI whiz!

**Fueling the Body and the Fight: Mastering Nutritional Support**
Imagine a critically ill patient – their body is battling illness or injury, but their internal fuel tank is running low. Nutritional support steps in, becoming a crucial weapon in their arsenal for recovery. This section will equip you to understand the different forms of nutritional support, identify assessment techniques, and navigate the complexities of this essential therapy.
**Why Nutritional Support Matters**

Think of the body as a high-performance engine. When illness strikes, its metabolic needs change. Nutritional support ensures patients receive the essential nutrients they can't meet through oral intake alone to:

- **Promote healing:** Protein is the building block for tissue repair, and adequate calories fuel the body's fight against infection.
- **Maintain muscle mass:** During illness, muscle breakdown can occur. Nutritional support helps preserve muscle function and strength.
- **Support immune function:** A well-nourished body is better equipped to combat infections and promote overall well-being.

**Types of Nutritional Support: Tube Feeding or IV Drip?**

The route of nutritional support depends on the patient's specific needs and ability to tolerate oral intake. Here are the main players:

- **Enteral Nutrition (Tube Feeding):** Nutrients are delivered directly into the stomach or small intestine via a feeding tube. This can be short-term (nasogastric tube) or long-term (gastrostomy tube).
- **Parenteral Nutrition (IV Drip):** Nutrients are delivered directly into the bloodstream through a central venous catheter, bypassing the GI tract altogether.

**Exam Tip:** Know the different types of enteral and parenteral feeding formulas, their indications, and potential complications. A handy mnemonic for enteral access sites? **"NG"** (nasogastric) goes in the **N**ose, and a **"G"**-tube goes in the belly (gastrostomy).

**Assessing Nutritional Needs: It's All About Balance**

Just like with medication, the right dose of nutrients is crucial. Here's how we assess a patient's needs:

- **Anthropometric measurements:** Height, weight, and body mass index (BMI) provide a baseline assessment of nutritional status.
- **Biochemical markers:** Blood tests like serum albumin and prealbumin can reflect protein stores and overall nutritional status.
- **Calorie and protein requirements:** These are calculated based on the patient's individual factors like weight, illness severity, and activity level.

**Real-World Scenario: A Case of Picky Eating**

A young child with cystic fibrosis has a history of picky eating and struggles to maintain weight. Enteral feeding may be recommended to ensure they receive the essential nutrients for growth and development.

**The Art and Science of Monitoring: Keeping an Eye on Progress**

Once nutritional support is initiated, close monitoring is essential. We track:

- **Electrolytes and blood sugar levels:** These can be imbalanced with nutritional support and require adjustments.
- **Fluid balance:** Too much or too little fluid intake can have serious consequences.
- **Gastrointestinal tolerance:** We monitor for signs of intolerance like nausea, vomiting, or diarrhea.

Nutritional support isn't just about giving patients nutrients. It's about understanding their specific needs, choosing the right approach, and closely monitoring their progress. Think of yourself as a detective, piecing together the clues from assessments, lab values, and patient responses to optimize their nutritional care.

Be familiar with common complications associated with nutritional support and how to manage them.

**The Future of Nutritional Support: A Personalized Approach**

The field of nutritional support is constantly evolving. Personalized nutrition, tailored to a patient's unique genetic makeup and metabolic needs, is a promising area of research.

By grasping the core principles of nutritional support, understanding the different routes and assessment techniques, you'll be well on your way to conquering this section of the CMSRN exam. Remember, nutritional support is a powerful tool – use your knowledge to ensure your patients receive the fuel they need to heal, fight back, and thrive.

Think back to those lab values and diagnostic tests we discussed previously. They're not just random numbers or images on a screen. They hold clues, whispers of what's happening within the patient's body. Now, it's time to translate those findings into action – deciphering the mystery and determining the best interventions to manage the patient's condition.

**Pharmacological Interventions: Medications as Tools**

Medication plays a central role in treating many medical conditions. Think of them as targeted weapons in your healthcare arsenal:

- **Antibiotics – Battling Bacterial Infections:** Choosing the right antibiotic based on suspected organism and sensitivities is vital in treating infections like pneumonia or cellulitis.
- **Antihypertensives – Taming High Blood Pressure:** From diuretics to beta-blockers, these medications have varying mechanisms for lowering blood pressure.
- **Pain Management – Offering Relief:** NSAIDs, acetaminophen, and sometimes opioids offer different strategies for pain control. Each has its unique uses and risks.
- **Gastrointestinal Medications:** Think of these as peacekeepers for your gut! Antacids for heartburn, antiemetics for nausea, and antidiarrheal for loose stools are common examples.

Know the drug classifications, mechanisms of action, side effects, contraindications, and nursing considerations for the most commonly used medications in your practice area. This knowledge empowers you to make informed decisions for safe and effective medication administration.

**Beyond Medications: Non-Pharmacological Interventions**

Medicine isn't always the sole answer. There's a diverse toolkit of strategies for managing many conditions:

- **Lifestyle modifications – The Backbone of Health:** Often the first line of defense, these include dietary changes, exercise, and managing stress – all crucial factors in conditions like type 2 diabetes, heart disease, and sleep disorders.
- **Oxygen Therapy – When Breathing Needs a Boost:** We discussed this earlier, but remember, it's a key intervention for patients with respiratory distress or hypoxemia.
- **Wound Care – Promoting Healing:** Proper cleaning, dressings, and sometimes specialized treatments are vital in managing wounds and preventing complications.
- **Physical Therapy – Restoring Function:** After an injury, surgery, or stroke, PT helps patients regain strength, range of motion, and independence.

**Interventional Procedures: For Targeted Therapies**

Sometimes, more specialized interventions are indicated. Think of these as minimally invasive techniques with big impact:

- **Cardiac Catheterization:** Provides detailed information about coronary artery disease and can sometimes be paired with therapeutic interventions like angioplasty or stent placement.
- **Endoscopy:** Allows visualization of the upper GI tract, useful in diagnosing conditions like ulcers and taking biopsies if needed.
- **Bronchoscopy:** Similar to endoscopy, but examines the lower respiratory airways aiding in diagnosis and even removal of foreign objects in some cases.

**Nursing Interventions: The Glue Holding It All Together**

Now let's not forget the power of nursing care! Your interventions can make a major difference in a patient's outcome:

- **Close Monitoring:** Vigilant assessment for changes in a patient's status is pivotal. Think of it as detective work, spotting subtle signs of deterioration or treatment response.
- **Patient Education:** We discussed this crucial component earlier – empowering patients to participate actively in their care.
- **Coordinating Care:** You're the hub of the wheel, collaborating with physicians, specialists, and other healthcare team members to ensure cohesive and effective patient management.

Every intervention, from a simple pill to a complex procedure, carries both potential benefits and risks. As a CMSRN, your expertise lies in understanding these, individualizing therapy, and closely monitoring patients for safety and efficacy. Remember, it's not about mindlessly following protocols; it's about applying your knowledge with critical thinking to make the best choices for each unique patient.

Let's imagine your patient is about to undergo major GI surgery – perhaps a colon resection for cancer or a gastric bypass for weight loss management. Their journey doesn't begin and end in the operating room. Pre-operative preparation and meticulous post-operative care are paramount in ensuring a successful outcome and minimizing potential complications.

Pre-Operative Prep: Laying a Strong Foundation

Optimization is the name of the game! The goal is to get your patient in the best possible shape to withstand the stress of surgery. Here's where you step in:

Thorough Assessment: Identify any underlying conditions that could increase surgical risk, such as uncontrolled diabetes, malnutrition, or heart problems.
Medications: Optimize management of existing conditions and review any medications that may need to be temporarily discontinued prior to surgery (think blood thinners).
Patient Education: Explain the procedure, post-operative pain management, and expected recovery plan. Address their fears and emphasize their role in promoting a smooth recovery.
Preventive Measures: Prophylactic antibiotics to reduce surgical site infection risk may be indicated, along with deep breathing exercises to prevent post-operative respiratory complications.
Post-Operative Vigilance: Navigating the Road to Recovery

The surgery is over, but your work isn't done! As your patient awakens, these become your core focuses:

Monitoring Vital Signs: Watch closely for any signs of instability – blood pressure changes, increased heart rate, or respiratory distress.
Pain Management: A delicate balance! Offer adequate pain control to promote comfort and early mobilization but avoid oversedation that can mask complications.
Wound Care: Regular assessment for signs of infection, meticulous dressing changes when needed, and promoting proper incision healing.
Managing Drains and Tubes: Whether it's a nasogastric tube for decompression, surgical drains, or a urinary catheter, knowing proper care and troubleshooting is essential.
Early Mobilization: Encourage movement and deep breathing exercises to prevent post-operative complications like pneumonia and blood clots.

Gradual Advancement of Diet: Progress from clear liquids to solids as tolerated, closely monitoring for nausea, vomiting, and return of bowel function.

Know the potential complications specific to different GI surgeries (such as anastomotic leak after colon resection, for example) and the signs to look out for.

Real-World Scenario

Imagine a patient who underwent a bowel resection with ileostomy creation. Post-operatively, you'd focus on stoma care education, monitoring for high output, and ensuring skin integrity around the stoma.

Remember, post-operative care is a collaborative effort involving the surgeon, nurses, dietitians, and sometimes specialized wound care teams. Effective communication and a clear plan for patient progression are vital.

Your pre-operative assessment and meticulous post-operative care can make a world of difference in a GI surgery patient's recovery journey. Think of yourself as their guide through this challenging period, minimizing risk, optimizing outcomes, and empowering them to embark on the path to healing.

# Chapter 7: Renal/Urologic System

This chapter is a bit like your backstage pass to the body's filtration plant, waste disposal system, and all the plumbing that goes along with it.

Our kidneys - those bean-shaped powerhouses – work tirelessly to filter our blood, removing waste products and toxins while maintaining a delicate balance of fluids and electrolytes. They play a crucial role in blood pressure regulation and even produce hormones that stimulate red blood cell production. Mess with the kidneys at your own peril!

And then we have the urologic system – the network of organs responsible for storing and transporting urine. We'll talk about the bladder, the urethra, and, in males, the prostate (a gland that often causes mischief later in life). Urinary tract infections, a common nemesis to many, will definitely be on the agenda.

Get ready for a deep dive into anatomy, physiology, common disorders like kidney stones and kidney failure, and the treatments we offer to keep these systems running smoothly. This chapter might not be the most glamorous, but trust me, you'll gain a newfound appreciation for how your body silently handles some messy jobs to keep you healthy.

And who knows, understanding the complexities of the renal and urologic system might even come in handy the next time you encounter a mysteriously long bathroom line – you'll have the insider knowledge!

Picture these systems as your body's internal purification network, working in tandem to maintain fluid balance and expel waste products from your bloodstream.

**The Kidney Superstars**
- **Location, location:** These bean-shaped organs reside in the retroperitoneal space, tucked behind your abdominal organs for protection.
- **Key Functions:** Think of the kidneys as filtering machines! They remove toxins, maintain electrolyte and acid-base balance, regulate blood pressure, and even play a role in red blood cell production.

**The Nephron: Where the Filtering Magic Happens**
Each kidney houses about a million tiny functional units called nephrons. Here's the breakdown:
- **Glomerulus:** A tiny network of capillaries where initial filtration occurs.
- **Renal Tubule:** Where the filtrate (fluid from the glomerulus) travels. Vital substances (water, glucose, electrolytes) are reabsorbed back into the blood, while waste products continue their journey.

**The Urinary Tract: Waste Disposal in Action**
Think of the urinary tract as the waste pipeline:
- **Ureters:** Muscular tubes that transport urine from the kidneys to the bladder.
- **Bladder:** A storage tank for urine. It expands as it fills and sends those "gotta-go" signals to your brain.

- **Urethra:** The exit pathway! In males, it passes through the prostate gland, while in females, it's a shorter, separate channel.

**The Supporting Cast: Additional Key Players**
- **Renal Arteries and Veins:** These major blood vessels supply and drain the kidneys.
- **Hormones:** The kidneys secrete renin (involved in blood pressure regulation), erythropoietin (stimulates RBC production), and they activate vitamin D!

Know the basic anatomy – kidney structure and blood flow pathway through the nephron – it's the foundation for understanding renal disorders and treatments.

The renal and urologic systems are intricate and interconnected. Understanding their anatomy and functions empowers you to identify potential problems, interpret lab findings, and provide informed nursing care to patients with renal and urologic dysfunction.

Now let's dive into the realm of common renal and urologic disorders. Think of these conditions as roadblocks disrupting your body's finely-tuned filtration and waste removal system – and unfortunately, they're all too frequent in clinical practice!

**Acute Kidney Injury (AKI): When Kidneys Hit the Brakes**
AKI is a sudden decline in kidney function. Imagine your kidneys slamming on the brakes, causing waste products and toxins to build up in the blood. Causes can be:
- **Pre-Renal:** Think "decreased blood flow" to the kidneys. Can be caused by dehydration, heart failure, or sepsis.
- **Intrinsic:** Something's damaging the kidneys themselves. Drugs, infections, or inflammation can be culprits.
- **Post-Renal:** Think "obstruction." Conditions like kidney stones or an enlarged prostate can block urine flow, causing backup damage.

**Clinical Picture:** Decreased urine output, rising creatinine (a marker of kidney function), and swelling due to fluid retention are common signs.

Know the different classifications of AKI (pre-renal, intrinsic, post-renal) and the potential causes of each.

**Chronic Kidney Disease (CKD): Silent but Serious**
Unlike AKI's sudden onset, CKD is a gradual, progressive loss of kidney function. Leading causes include diabetes and high blood pressure. It's often symptomless in early stages, making it a sneaky adversary.
- **CKD Stages:** Based on glomerular filtration rate (GFR), a measure of kidney function, CKD is classified into 5 stages, with stage 5 representing kidney failure.
- **Complications:** As CKD progresses, complications like anemia, electrolyte imbalances, high blood pressure, metabolic acidosis, and weakened bones arise.

**UTIs (Urinary Tract Infections): Unwelcome Invaders**
These troublesome infections occur anywhere in the urinary tract and are overwhelmingly caused by bacteria that sneak in through the urethra. Classic symptoms include:
- **Burning with urination**
- **Urinary frequency and urgency**
- **Cloudy or foul-smelling urine**
- **Lower abdominal or back pain**

**UTI Types:**
- **Cystitis:** Bladder infection
- **Pyelonephritis:** Kidney infection – more severe, can cause fever, chills, and flank pain

**Kidney Stones (Calculi): When Minerals Go Rogue**

Think of kidney stones as tiny, but mighty crystals that form in the urinary tract. As they try to pass, oh the agony! Symptoms include:
- **Severe pain (renal colic):** Often in the back or flank, radiating to groin.
- **Nausea and vomiting**
- **Blood in the urine**

A patient presents with sudden onset of flank pain, nausea, vomiting, and blood in the urine. You suspect kidney stones. Imaging studies like an ultrasound or CT scan would likely be ordered to confirm the diagnosis.

Disruptions within the renal or urologic systems can range from the uncomfortable (hello, UTIs!) to the life-threatening (as in severe AKI or CKD). Understanding their underlying causes, clinical presentations, and potential complications empowers you to provide timely diagnosis, effective treatment, and education to prevent recurrence.

Now, let's talk about the delicate dance of fluid and electrolytes within the body. Imagine these essential substances as the ingredients in your body's internal soup, and any shift in their balance can throw your entire system out of whack!

**Fluids: The Importance of Hydration**
- **Intracellular vs. Extracellular:** Think of your cells as tiny balloons filled with fluid (intracellular fluid). Outside those cells, fluid resides within blood vessels (intravascular) and the spaces between cells (interstitial).
- **Fluid Shifts:** Fluid can move between compartments based on osmotic forces. Too much salt? Fluid can get pulled out of your cells. Not drinking enough water? Plasma volume can decrease making your blood thicker.
- **Signs of Imbalance:** Too little fluid (dehydration) can cause sunken eyes, dry mucous membranes, low blood pressure, and decreased urine output. Excess fluid (edema) manifests as swelling, particularly in the legs.

**Electrolytes: Little Ions, Big Impact**

These small charged particles play vital roles throughout the body:
- **Sodium (Na+):** Key for maintaining fluid balance and nerve and muscle function.
- **Potassium (K+):** Crucial for heart function, muscle contractions, and nerve impulse transmission.
- **Chloride (Cl-):** Works with sodium and potassium, often following sodium shifts. Think about how salty sweat is!
- **Calcium (Ca2+):** Not just for bones! It's involved in blood clotting, nerve function, and muscle contractions.
- **Magnesium (Mg2+):** Important for everything from muscle contractions and nerve function to regulating bone density.

**Common Imbalances**
- **Hyponatremia (low sodium):** Can be caused by overhydration, vomiting, diarrhea, or certain medications. Symptoms can include confusion, headache, and seizures in severe cases.
- **Hypernatremia (high sodium):** Usually due to not drinking enough fluids or excessive fluid loss. You see this in dehydrated patients who may be confused and lethargic.
- **Hyperkalemia (high potassium):** Critically important to identify! Renal failure, certain medications, and even cell damage can cause it. EKG changes and potentially life-threatening arrhythmias are key concerns.

**Exam Tip:** Know the normal ranges for common electrolytes and be able to identify the causes and clinical manifestations of imbalances.

An elderly patient presents to the clinic feeling weak and confused after enduring several days of vomiting and diarrhea. You suspect hyponatremia as a contributing factor and order lab work to confirm.

**Treatment Strategies**
- **Fluid Management:** IV fluids (often with precise electrolyte concentrations) are a mainstay of treatment. Oral rehydration solutions (for milder cases) contain a tailored mix of fluids and electrolytes.
- **Medication Adjustments:** Diuretics? ACE inhibitors? Medications sometimes need tweaking to help restore electrolyte balance.
- **Dietary Changes:** In some chronic cases (like certain types of kidney disease), dietary adjustments in sodium or potassium intake may be needed.

Fluid and electrolyte management is both an art and a science. Understanding the delicate balance, identifying signs of trouble, and knowing your treatment options will empower you to provide informed care and help your patients quickly get back on their feet!

Let's now talk about dialysis modalities – a lifeline for patients with kidney failure. Think of dialysis as stepping in to do the heavy lifting when the kidneys can no longer filter waste products and excess fluid from the blood. There are two main flavors you should know about:

**Hemodialysis (HD): The Cleaning Machine**
- **The Gist:** The patient's blood is routed through a dialyzer (also known as an "artificial kidney"), where a special solution (dialysate) helps remove waste products and balance electrolytes.
- **Vascular Access:** This requires a special point of entry into the bloodstream, usually a fistula (a surgically created connection between an artery and vein), a graft, or a central line catheter.
- **Frequency:** Typically done several times a week for a few hours each session. It's most often performed in a dialysis center, though home hemodialysis options exist.

**Peritoneal Dialysis (PD): Using Your Own Peritoneum**
- **The Setup:** A catheter is surgically placed in the abdomen. Dialysate is instilled into the peritoneal cavity (the space around your abdominal organs), where it dwells for a set time.
- **The Magic:** Your peritoneum (the lining of your abdominal cavity) acts as a filter. Waste products and excess fluid move from your blood into the dialysate, which is then drained out.
- **Types:** There's continuous ambulatory peritoneal dialysis (CAPD), where exchanges are done manually throughout the day, and automated peritoneal dialysis (APD), using a machine to perform exchanges overnight while you sleep.

Know the basic principles of each dialysis modality, potential complications, and important nursing considerations like vascular access monitoring and fluid balance assessments.

**Choosing a Modality: It's Not One-Size-Fits-All**

Factors like the patient's overall health, lifestyle preferences, and available support systems play a big role in deciding which modality is the best fit.

Imagine a patient with end-stage renal disease who values flexibility and wants to manage their treatments at home. Peritoneal dialysis might be a suitable option for them, while hemodialysis in a center would likely be preferred for a patient who is less medically stable or requires close monitoring. Dialysis modalities offer patients with kidney failure a chance to continue living despite their diagnosis. Understanding how they work, their advantages, and their limitations empowers you to educate and advocate for your patients as they navigate this life-changing journey.

## Chapter 8: Neurological System

Let's now shift our focus to the intricate workings of the neurological system – your body's command center! Think of it as the complex network of nerves and specialized cells that control movement, sensations, thoughts, emotions... essentially everything that makes you YOU. Let's dive in and explore its marvels!

**The Central Nervous System (CNS): HQ of Operations**
- **The Brain:** This master control room houses billions of neurons. Key regions include:
  - **Cerebrum:** Responsible for higher-level functions like thought, consciousness, and voluntary movement.
  - **Brainstem:** Relays messages between the brain and spinal cord, controls vital functions like breathing and heart rate.
  - **Cerebellum:** Crucial for coordination, balance, and fine motor skills.
- **Spinal Cord:** This bundle of nerves within your spinal column acts as an information superhighway, transmitting signals between the brain and the rest of your body.

**The Peripheral Nervous System (PNS): Connecting the Dots**
- **Somatic Nervous System:** Controls voluntary movements through skeletal muscle control.
- **Autonomic Nervous System:** The master regulator of those automatic functions we never think about! Further divides into:
  - **Sympathetic ("Fight-or-flight"):** Primes your body for action in response to stress.
  - **Parasympathetic ("Rest-and-digest"):** Promotes relaxation and those "housekeeping" bodily functions.

**Neurons: The Messengers**
These specialized cells are the cornerstone of communication within the nervous system. They transmit signals via electrical impulses and chemical messengers called neurotransmitters. Think of neurotransmitters like keys fitting into specific locks (receptors) on neighboring cells, triggering various actions.

Know the major brain regions and their functions, and don't forget those cranial nerves. Plus, having a grasp of key neurotransmitters (like acetylcholine and dopamine) comes in handy!

**The Blood-Brain Barrier: A Highly Selective Gatekeeper**
This protective layer shields the brain from harmful substances in the bloodstream, while regulating the passage of essential nutrients. However, it also poses a challenge in delivering medications to treat brain disorders.

The nervous system is a testament to both complexity and elegant organization. Understanding its structure and function is like deciphering the wiring diagram of your body – it's the first step to understanding neurological conditions and the interventions we use to treat them.

Let's now talk about those dreaded neurological conditions that can disrupt even the most robust nervous system. These emergencies require swift recognition and intervention to preserve brain function and minimize long-term consequences.

**Stroke: When Blood Flow Gets Blocked**
- **Ischemic Stroke:** The most common type! A clot obstructs a blood vessel in the brain, depriving cells of oxygen and nutrients. Think of it like a clogged drain in your brain's plumbing.

- **Hemorrhagic Stroke:** A less common, but often more severe form. Here, a weakened blood vessel in the brain ruptures, causing bleeding into brain tissue.
- **"Time is Brain":** Rapid intervention is CRUCIAL! Clot-busting drugs (tPA for ischemic strokes) have a narrow window of efficacy, so door-to-needle time is key.

**TBI (Traumatic Brain Injury): Impact and Aftermath**

From concussion to severe head trauma, TBI can have devastating consequences. The damage occurs not just from primary impact but also from a cascade of secondary injuries within the brain:

- **Swelling and increased intracranial pressure (ICP):** A dangerous complication threatening brain function.
- **Diffuse axonal injury:** Microscopic shearing of nerve fibers that can result in widespread dysfunction.
- **Long-Term Effects:** Depending on severity, TBI can lead to cognitive deficits, personality changes, and persistent neurological impairments.

**Seizures: Electrical Storm in the Brain**

Think of seizures as bursts of abnormal electrical activity in the brain causing a range of effects:

- **Focal Seizures:** Limited to a specific area of the brain, may involve specific symptoms like twitching of a limb or sensory changes.
- **Generalized Seizures:** Involve widespread brain activity. Tonic-clonic seizures ("grand mal") are characterized by muscle stiffening, followed by rhythmic jerking and loss of consciousness.
- **Status Epilepticus:** A medical emergency! A prolonged seizure or repeated seizures without recovery in between.

**Increased Intracranial Pressure (ICP): When the Brain is Under Pressure**

Elevated ICP, whether due to trauma, stroke, tumor, or infection, is a critical complication. Signs include:

- **Decreased level of consciousness:** Lethargy may progress to coma.
- **Headache and vomiting:** Common symptoms as pressure increases.
- **Cushing's Triad:** A late warning sign! Includes elevated blood pressure, slow heart rate, and abnormal breathing pattern.

Know the classic stroke signs (facial droop, weakness, slurred speech), the different seizure types, and the worrisome signs associated with increasing ICP.

A patient arrives in the emergency department with sudden onset of left-sided paralysis and slurred speech. Stroke is the top concern, and a rapid workup including CT scan and neurological assessment will guide immediate treatment decisions.

Neurological emergencies put time sensitivity to the test! Your mastery of these conditions, their rapid assessment, and recognizing signs of deterioration are essential for saving lives and preserving patient function.

### Cracking the Code: Mastering the Neurological Assessment

Imagine yourself as a detective, meticulously gathering clues to solve the mystery of a patient's neurological state. This skillset is paramount for effective patient care, and absolutely essential for acing the CMSRN exam. So, grab your metaphorical magnifying glass, and let's unravel the secrets of a top-notch neurological assessment, step-by-step.

**Level of Consciousness: The Foundation**

First things first, we need to assess the patient's level of consciousness – their awareness and responsiveness to the environment. Think of it as the cornerstone of your neurological assessment. Is your patient wide awake and chatty (alert and oriented – A&Ox4)? Perhaps a bit drowsy but easily arousable (lethargic)? Here's where the legendary **AVPU** scale comes in handy:

- **Alert:** Fully awake and engaged
- **Verbal:** Responds to verbal stimuli (like your voice)
- **Pain:** Responds only to painful stimuli (a pinch on the arm)
- **Unresponsive:** No response to any stimuli

Remember, the AVPU scale is a quick and dirty tool. A more detailed assessment, like the Glasgow Coma Scale (GCS), provides a more nuanced picture of consciousness.

### Mental Status: A Peek into the Mind

Now, let's delve deeper into the patient's mental state. This involves assessing their orientation (to person, place, time), memory (recent and remote), language skills (aphasia?), and emotional state. Imagine you're having a conversation with the patient – are they following along, making sense, and expressing themselves clearly? A helpful mnemonic for orientation is "What, Where, When, Who" – test their knowledge of these basic details.

**Fun Fact:** Did you know that some neurological conditions can cause a person to speak gibberish (aphasia) or fabricate stories (confabulation)? Being familiar with these signs can be a real asset during your assessment.

### Cranial Nerves: The Information Highway

Think of the cranial nerves as twelve special highways carrying sensory and motor information between the brain and various parts of the head and neck. Your assessment here involves checking things like visual fields, pupillary response, facial symmetry, hearing, and gag reflex. A fun trick to remember the cranial nerves in order is: "Oh, Such Good Blood Vessels To Run In My Dear Young Neck!" (Though, some prefer a less colorful version!).

### Motor Function: Moving and Grooving

Onward to motor function! Here, we assess muscle strength, coordination, and the presence of abnormal movements (like tremors or rigidity). Imagine asking the patient to squeeze your hand or walk heel-toe – their ability to follow these instructions tells you a lot about their motor capabilities.

### Sensory Function: Feeling the World

Now, let's see how the patient perceives the world through their senses. Test their ability to feel light touch, pain, temperature, and vibration in different parts of the body. Imagine yourself being a magician, gently touching the patient's arm and asking them to identify whether it feels warm or cold.

### Reflexes: Testing the Basics

Reflexes are involuntary muscle responses to stimuli. We use tools like a reflex hammer to tap tendons and elicit reflexes (like the knee jerk). Think of reflexes as your body's built-in safety features – an abnormal reflex response can indicate underlying neurological issues.

### Putting It All Together: The Art of Storytelling

Remember, a neurological assessment isn't just a collection of isolated findings. It's a cohesive story that paints a picture of the patient's overall neurological health. By weaving together all the pieces – level of consciousness, mental status, cranial nerves, motor and sensory function, and reflexes – you can form a preliminary diagnosis and guide further evaluation and treatment plans.

### Conquering the Exam: Test-Taking Strategies

The key to success on the CMSRN exam lies in mastering the art of applying your knowledge. Here are some power tips to remember:

- **Focus on abnormal findings:** Pay close attention to any deviations from normal during your assessment. These are the red flags that can point towards a neurological problem.
- **Practice, Practice, Practice:** Role-play different neurological scenarios with classmates to hone your assessment skills and build confidence.

- **Visualize Success:** Imagine yourself calmly and efficiently performing a neurological assessment on a patient. Positive visualization is a powerful tool for exam success!

By following these steps and embracing a curious, detective-like approach, you'll be well on your way to mastering the art of neurological assessment and excelling in your CMSRN exams.

Think about those little pills and potent IV drips that can profoundly alter the delicate landscape of the nervous system. Neurological medications are fascinating, wielding the power to quiet a seizure, soothe a migraine, or even slow the relentless progression of degenerative diseases. Let's dive into their diverse mechanisms and unravel the complexities of how we select these pharmacological marvels for our patients.

Taming Seizures: Restoring Calm

Anti-epileptic drugs (AEDs) work like bouncers in the brain, trying to keep those wild electrical parties from getting out of control. There are many different AEDs, and they work in various ways:

Sodium Channel Blockers: Like shutting down the gateways to the dancefloor, these drugs decrease excitable neurons from firing like crazy (examples: phenytoin, carbamazepine).

GABA Enhancers: Remember GABA? Your brain's natural chill-out neurotransmitter? Some AEDs boost its effects to dampen overactive neurons (think: benzodiazepines, phenobarbital).

Exam Tip: Know your AEDs! Be familiar with common side effects (dizziness, drowsiness, etc.) and drug interactions, as these are frequently tested.

Combating Chronic Pain: Turning Down the Volume

When it comes to pain, the nervous system is the DJ spinning the tunes. From throbbing migraines to nerve pain, medications target the pain signals themselves:

Old-School, Multi-Purpose: Tricyclic antidepressants (like amitriptyline) and anticonvulsants (like gabapentin) have some surprising side benefits by modulating how the brain perceives pain.

NSAIDs and Beyond: Familiar friends like ibuprofen and acetaminophen offer mild to moderate pain relief. Stronger opioids (tramadol, codeine, etc.) should be used judiciously due to their high abuse potential.

Neurodegenerative Diseases: Slowing the Progression

Sadly, for some illnesses like Alzheimer's or Parkinson's, medications aren't a cure-all. But they can still improve quality of life:

Boosting Neurotransmitters: Donepezil and similar drugs help preserve memory function in Alzheimer's by increasing acetylcholine levels. In Parkinson's, levodopa helps replenish depleted dopamine stores.

Thinking Outside the Box: While primarily used for depression, some SSRIs can help manage behavioral changes often accompanying neurodegenerative diseases.

Real-World Scenario

Imagine a patient with Parkinson's disease and increasing difficulty managing their motor symptoms. Adding carbidopa-levodopa to their regimen may offer significant tremor control and improve their ability to perform their daily activities.

Managing Neurological Medications: It's All About Balance

It's not just about the drug itself. As a CMSRN, you'll be a master juggler, carefully balancing:
Monitoring Effectiveness: Does the medication actually achieve the desired outcome? Are there any troublesome side effects?
Drug Interactions: Polypharmacy is common in patients with complex neurological conditions. Being vigilant about potential interactions is essential to prevent unwanted complications.
Patient Education: Empowering patients to understand their medications, side effects to watch for, and what to report to their provider is crucial for safe and effective treatment.

Neurological medications offer powerful tools to manage a diverse range of conditions. But they're not a one-size-fits-all answer! Understanding their mechanisms, indications, contraindications, and side effects will help you provide tailored care and confidently navigate the complexities of treatment.

Imagine what happens after a stroke, a traumatic injury, or a major surgery. The body often needs a helping hand to regain strength, function, and independence. That's where the field of rehabilitation comes in, offering a bridge from illness or injury back to a patient's fullest possible life. Let's dive into the core principles driving the world of rehab.

**The Multifaceted Team**
Rehabilitation isn't a solo act. Think of it like a symphony orchestra, with each team member playing an essential role:
- **Physiatrists:** The conductors of the rehab world, specializing in physical medicine and rehabilitation. They direct the overall treatment plan.
- **Physical Therapists:** Masters of movement! They help patients regain strength, mobility, and balance through exercise, hands-on techniques, and assistive devices.
- **Occupational Therapists:** Focus on those essential daily activities, helping patients relearn skills like dressing, eating, and navigating their environment.
- **Speech-Language Pathologists:** Tackle issues with speech, swallowing, and cognition, crucial for safe eating and effective communication.
- **Nurses:** The backbone of the team, providing hands-on care, medication management, patient education, and advocating for the patient's overall well-being.

**Rehab Settings: Tailor-Made Care**
Where a patient receives rehab matters! Let's break it down:
- **Acute Rehab Units:** Think high-intensity! Patients typically require frequent therapy sessions within a hospital setting.
- **Skilled Nursing Facilities:** Provide continued rehab on a less intensive level, with a focus on helping patients transition back home or to long-term care.
- **Outpatient Rehab:** Ideal for patients who live independently but need continued therapy to progress towards their goals.
- **Home Health:** Sometimes, rehab comes to you! Therapists provide targeted care within the patient's own environment.

Know the different rehab settings and the types of patients typically served in each.

**The Rehabilitation Process: Steps Towards Recovery**
While each patient's journey is unique, there are key principles that guide successful rehabilitation:
- **SMART Goals:** Specific, Measurable, Achievable, Relevant, and Time-Based goals provide a roadmap for progress.
- **Early Intervention:** The sooner rehab starts, the better the potential outcomes. Let's not let those muscles get lazy!

- **Individualized Approach:** Rehab isn't cookie-cutter. It's tailored to the patient's specific impairments, goals, and living environment.
- **Assistive Devices:** Walkers, canes, adapted utensils...the right tools can be game-changers in maximizing independence.

**Challenges and Triumphs**

Rehab can be tough – physically and emotionally demanding. Patients may experience setbacks, frustration, and grief over their changed abilities. However, a skilled rehab team knows how to navigate these challenges, celebrating incremental progress and empowering patients every step of the way.

Imagine a young adult who suffered a spinal cord injury in a car accident. Rehab begins with teaching even the basics like transferring from bed to wheelchair and regaining bladder and bowel control. Months later, with hard work and the support of their rehab team, they may walk again with assistance.

Rehab professionals don't just treat impairments; they help patients reclaim their lives! By understanding the principles of rehabilitation, the multifaceted team approach, and the importance of a patient-centered focus, you'll be equipped to support your patients on their journeys towards renewed function and independence.

## Chapter 9: Musculoskeletal System

Think of this chapter as your backstage pass to understanding the bones, joints, muscles, and connective tissues that give us the power to move, support our bodies, and literally make our mark on the world.

We'll start with the foundations – those sturdy bones that form the framework of our bodies. They're not just dusty skeletons in a science lab; they're living tissues constantly remodeling themselves and serving as storage vaults for important minerals.

Then we'll get into the fascinating world of joints – where flexibility meets stability! Get ready to learn about the different types of joints (hinge, ball-and-socket, you name it) and the cartilage and ligaments that allow them to move smoothly. But just like with old hinges, things can go awry, leading to conditions like arthritis, strains, and sprains.

And finally, let's not forget the powerhouses that set things in motion – our muscles! Get ready to discover how muscle contraction works on a microscopic level, why exercise is so important for muscle health, and what happens when muscles are injured or strained.

Understanding the musculoskeletal system empowers you as a nurse. It's the knowledge you need to accurately assess patients with orthopedic injuries, interpret diagnostic tests, and help patients with their rehabilitation journey. So let's dive in and get those mental muscles working as we explore the intricate workings of the musculoskeletal system!

Think of your body as an intricate architectural masterpiece. Much like a skyscraper needs a robust framework, the musculoskeletal system provides structural support and enables movement. Let's embark on a journey through this system, starting with the skeletal foundation, exploring the intricate joints, and concluding with muscle power!

**The Bony Framework**

Your skeleton serves many vital functions beyond Halloween costume inspiration:

- **Support and Shape:** Bones give your body structure, like beams in a building.
- **Protection:** Think of your skull safeguarding the brain or the ribcage shielding your heart and lungs.
- **Movement:** Bones act as levers, providing attachment points for muscles.
- **Mineral Storage:** Your bones are a calcium vault, essential for healthy nerve and muscle function.
- **Blood Cell Production:** The spongy center of many bones (bone marrow) is a factory for new blood cells.

Know the major bone classifications (long, short, flat, irregular) and have a basic understanding of skeletal anatomy—skull, spine, pelvis, major limb bones—it will come in handy across various exam topics!

**Where Bones Connect: The Joints**

Imagine joints as the hinges and pivots that make movement possible. Here's a quick classification breakdown:

- **Synovial Joints:** These champs of movement contain synovial fluid for lubrication (your knees, hips, shoulders).
- **Cartilaginous Joints:** Slightly movable, with cartilage connecting the bones (think your spine).

- **Fibrous Joints:** Mostly immovable (like the sutures in your skull).

**Let's Talk Muscles**

Muscles, your body's powerhouses, come in three flavors:
- **Skeletal Muscle:** Attaches to bones via tendons, responsible for voluntary movement. Big players like your biceps and quads fall into this category.
- **Smooth Muscle:** Found in organs like your intestines and blood vessels, responsible for involuntary contractions.
- **Cardiac Muscle:** The tireless workhorse of your heart! Its unique properties enable the steady beat-by-beat contractions.

**The Muscle Contraction Dance**

Imagine tiny muscle fibers sliding across each other with the release of energy, shortening the entire muscle. This microscopic action powers everything from lifting weights to the subtle movement of your facial expressions.

The musculoskeletal system is an intricate network of bones, joints, and muscles working in harmony. Understanding the structures and functions of these components forms the basis for understanding orthopedic conditions, assessing injuries, and appreciating the incredible ability of the human body to move and adapt.

Speaking of intricate systems, let's now turn our attention to some common musculoskeletal conditions that can disrupt the smooth functioning of your patients' bones, joints, and muscles. Being able to recognize and understand these conditions is key to providing your patients with timely diagnosis, appropriate treatment, and strategies for managing symptoms.

Fractures: When Bones Break

A fracture describes a break or crack in a bone. Imagine your sturdy bones snapping or shattering under excessive force, such as in a fall or car accident. Here's what you should know:

Types of Fractures: Open (the bone pokes through the skin...ouch!), closed (skin remains intact), comminuted (the bone shatters into several fragments)... the classification tells part of the story.
Signs and Symptoms: Pain, swelling, deformity, bruising, and limited mobility around the affected area are common signs.
Treatment: Varies depending on fracture severity. Think: immobilization (cast, splint), pain management, and sometimes surgery to align and stabilize the broken bone.
Exam Tip: Know the different phases of bone healing – understanding this process will help you explain to patients why specific interventions and limitations are needed throughout recovery.

Arthritis: Inflammation Strikes the Joints

Arthritis isn't a single disease but a term covering many conditions that cause joint inflammation, pain, and stiffness. Let's focus on two common culprits:

Osteoarthritis (OA): The "wear-and-tear" type. Cartilage cushioning the joints gradually breaks down over time.
Rheumatoid Arthritis (RA): An autoimmune disease where the body's immune system mistakenly attacks the joints, causing chronic inflammation.

Clinical Picture: Joint pain, stiffness (especially after rest), swelling, limited range of motion, and even deformity might develop, depending on the type of arthritis.

Osteoporosis: When Bones Weaken
Think of osteoporosis as a "silent thief," gradually stealing away bone density. This weakening makes bones more susceptible to fractures, especially in areas like the hips, spine, and wrists. Risk factors include:

Age: Bones naturally lose density as we get older, especially for women post-menopause.
Low Calcium and Vitamin D: Essential building blocks for strong bones!
Certain Medications: Like long-term steroid use.
Real-World Scenario

An older female patient presents to the clinic with a hunched posture and back pain. You consider osteoporosis as a potential cause and might recommend further workup, like a bone density scan (DEXA).

Disruptions within the musculoskeletal system can be painful, debilitating, and impact a patient's quality of life. Understanding the mechanics behind common conditions like fractures, arthritis, and osteoporosis will empower you to effectively assess, educate, and advocate for your patients as they navigate their treatment journey.

Think about pain as your body's alarm system – something's wrong, demanding your attention! It's a complex experience involving physical sensations, emotions, and past experiences. As a CMSRN, mastering the multifaceted approach to pain management is an essential tool in your clinical arsenal and a frequently tested area on the exam.

**The Puzzle of Pain Classification**
Let's break down the different ways we classify pain:
- **Duration:**
  - **Acute Pain:** Usually short-term, a direct response to tissue injury (think broken bone, surgical incision).
  - **Chronic Pain:** Persisting beyond the normal healing time, often for months or years. It can be a disease in itself.
- **Origin:**
  - **Nociceptive:** Triggered by actual or potential damage to non-neural tissues. Think about a sprained ankle or a paper cut.
  - **Neuropathic:** Nerve damage itself is the culprit. It might feel like burning, tingling, or shooting pains – think diabetic neuropathy.

**Exam Tip:** Understanding the different pain types not only guides assessment but also helps you select the most appropriate treatment approach.

**Pain Assessment: Beyond the "1-10 Scale"**
While the numeric pain rating scale is a useful tool, a truly comprehensive pain assessment digs deeper. Consider these key aspects:
- **PQRST:** A handy mnemonic to explore:
  - **P:** Provocative/Palliative (what triggers the pain or makes it better?)
  - **Q:** Quality (describe the feeling – is it sharp, dull, throbbing?)
  - **R:** Region/Radiation (where does it hurt, does it spread?)
  - **S:** Severity (the classic 1-10 scale)

- - **T:** Timing (when did it start, is it constant or intermittent?)
- **Impact on Daily Life:** How does pain affect function, mood, and sleep?

**Treatment: A Toolbox of Strategies**

Pain management is rarely a one-size-fits-all solution. Let's explore some tools at your disposal:

- **Pharmacological:**
  - **Non-Opioids:** Acetaminophen, NSAIDs for milder pain management and inflammation control.
  - **Opioids:** Potent painkillers, but with significant risks (abuse, addiction, respiratory depression). Judicious use is key!
  - **Adjuvant Medications:** Antidepressants, anticonvulsants may offer benefit for certain types of pain, especially neuropathic pain.
- **Non-Pharmacological:** A diverse and essential toolkit!
  - **Physical Therapy:** Exercise and modalities can improve function and reduce pain.
  - **Mind-Body Therapies:** Relaxation techniques, meditation, cognitive behavioral therapy (CBT) for chronic pain management.
  - **Interventional Techniques:** Injections, nerve blocks, implanted devices... sometimes a more specialized approach is needed.

Imagine a patient with chronic low back pain. A holistic approach might involve a combination of acetaminophen, physical therapy exercises, CBT for coping techniques, and potentially a referral for consideration of interventional procedures if initial treatment is unsuccessful.

Pain management is an intricate and individualized journey. Your command of pain assessment techniques, understanding of different treatment modalities, and commitment to a patient-centered approach will empower you to provide comprehensive care and help patients reclaim a better quality of life.

Think for a moment about the effortless joy of movement – whether it's hiking a scenic trail or simply reaching into a cabinet for a cup. Now consider how debilitating it would be if that freedom were taken away. This is why, as a CMSRN, understanding how to promote safe mobility and facilitate wound healing is vital. After all, restoring a patient's ability to function and maintaining skin integrity are critical to their overall well-being.

Mobility: It's All About Balance

Safe mobility requires a symphony of body systems working together:

Musculoskeletal: Strong bones and muscles provide the foundation for movement.
Neurological: The brain coordinates motor signals and our senses give feedback.
Other players: Cardiopulmonary health (supplying oxygen to working muscles) and even vision contribute to safe movement.
Threats to Mobility

The roadblocks to mobility are many:

Acute Illness/Injury: Surgery, a debilitating illness, or trauma can temporarily sideline your patient.
Chronic Conditions: Like arthritis, Parkinson's disease, or heart failure gradually erode mobility.
Aging: Decline in muscle mass, balance, and cognition all increase the risk of falls and loss of independence.

Prevention Is Key

Fall Risk Assessment: Tools like the Morse Fall Scale identify patients at risk. Interventions range from gait training to room modifications to medication adjustments.
Encouraging Exercise: Regular, safe, strength and balance-focused movement, tailored to the patient's abilities, helps maintain function.
Assistive Devices: Walkers, canes...when used correctly, they can be game-changers. Ensure proper sizing and teaching for safe use.
Exam Tip: Know the complications of immobility – from pressure ulcers to pneumonia, these problems become your responsibility to prevent!

Wound Care: The Art of Healing

Think of wound healing as a complex, but well-orchestrated process. Here's the basic breakdown:

Inflammation: Brings immune cells to clean up debris and ward off infection.
Proliferation: New tissue and blood vessels form.
Maturation: Scar tissue forms, the wound closes over time.
Factors That Hinder Healing

Infection: Keep a keen eye for signs of trouble (redness, pus, foul odor).
Poor Nutrition: Protein and other nutrients are the building blocks for tissue repair.
Medical Conditions: Diabetes? Peripheral arterial disease? These compromise healing.
Wound Care Principles

Assessment: Type of wound, signs of infection, healing progress – this guides your management.
Cleansing & Debridement: Removing dead tissue is sometimes needed to jumpstart healing.
Dressings: The variety is mind-boggling! Choosing the right one involves considering wound characteristics.

Imagine a diabetic patient with a slow-healing foot ulcer. Your multi-pronged approach might involve meticulous wound care, off-loading pressure, tight blood sugar control, and perhaps consultation with a wound care specialist.

Optimizing mobility and promoting wound healing are about more than just bandages and physical therapy. It requires a holistic approach, addressing various factors that impact a patient's ability to move and heal. Your knowledge in these areas empowers you to prevent complications and promote a better quality of life for your patients.

Now let's dive into the fascinating world of post-operative orthopedic care. Imagine yourself in the shoes of a nurse overseeing a patient who's just undergone a major orthopedic surgery – hip replacement, spinal fusion, you name it! Your vigilance and comprehensive care are crucial to getting them safely back on their feet. Here's what you need to keep in your arsenal...

Pain Management: Striking the Right Balance

Finding that sweet spot between adequate pain relief and minimizing side effects (like respiratory depression or excessive sedation) is a delicate dance. Consider strategies like:

Multimodal Approach: Combining medications with different mechanisms, such as opioids with acetaminophen or NSAIDs, can be effective.
Regional Anesthesia: Nerve blocks can offer targeted pain control for certain procedures.
Non-pharmacological Techniques: Don't underestimate the power of ice, proper positioning, and distraction to supplement medication.
Monitoring for Complications: Stay One Step Ahead

Neurovascular Checks: Especially important in the immediate post-op period. Assessing distal pulses, movement, and sensation can catch early signs of trouble like compartment syndrome.
Deep Vein Thrombosis (DVT) Prevention: Proactive measures like compression stockings, early mobilization, and sometimes blood thinners are essential.
Surgical Site Infection (SSI): Diligent wound assessment and dressing changes help prevent this potentially serious complication.
Promoting Rehabilitation: Slow and Steady Wins the Race

Close collaboration with physical therapy is key! This includes:

Early Mobilization: The sooner a patient safely starts moving within their limitations, the better their outcomes tend to be.
Progressive Exercises: Tailored to the specific surgery, rebuilding strength, range of motion, and balance takes time and careful guidance.
Assistive Devices: Walkers, crutches, canes...teaching proper use promotes safety and independence.
Patient Education: Knowledge is Power

Activity Restrictions: How much weight can they bear on that leg? When can they drive again? Giving clear instructions is key to preventing setbacks.
Medication Management: Understanding pain medication regimens, potential side effects, and when to seek medical attention is crucial for safe care at home.
Red flags: Teach patients how to recognize signs of complications like increasing swelling, fevers, or wound drainage.
Exam Tip: Know the common complications specifically associated with different types of orthopedic surgeries. For example, hip replacement patients are at higher risk for dislocation.

Imagine a patient who's had a total knee replacement. Your post-op care will involve frequent pain assessments, neurovascular checks, wound monitoring, medication management, collaboration with PT, and educating the patient on their weight-bearing restrictions and home exercise program.

Caring for post-operative orthopedic patients is a dynamic and multi-faceted role. Your mastery of pain management, vigilance for complications, collaboration with the rehab team, and dedication to patient education will empower your patients to reclaim mobility and return to a fulfilling life.

## Chapter 10: Hematology/Oncology

Now, let's get into the fascinating realm of hematology and oncology, a field encompassing the complexities of blood disorders and the battle against cancer. Understanding these conditions is not only crucial for your CMSRN exam but also vital in providing care to the many patients whose lives are affected by these diseases.

Anemias: When Oxygen Delivery Falters

Think of anemia as an oxygen supply shortage for your body! Causes are diverse:

Decreased RBC Production: Iron deficiency? B12 or folate deficiency? Bone marrow suppression (think chemotherapy)?
Blood Loss: Acute (think trauma) or chronic (like insidious GI bleeding).
RBC Destruction (Hemolysis): Certain autoimmune diseases, sickle cell disease, some medications... a case of mistaken identity can wreak havoc.
Clinical Clues

Fatigue, weakness, pale skin...these are common but nonspecific signs of anemia. The type of anemia will have further clues:

Iron Deficiency: Think about potential sources: dietary insufficiency, menstrual losses, GI bleeding
Vitamin Deficiencies: Dietary history and neurological symptoms (in B12 deficiency) provide context.
Hemolytic Anemias: Jaundice (yellowing) may occur from broken-down red blood cells.
Exam Tip: Know the key lab findings that differentiate various anemias: CBC, iron studies, B12/folate levels, and sometimes those specialized tests like haptoglobin or reticulocyte count for hemolytic culprits.

Bleeding Disorders: When Clotting Goes Awry

Maintaining the delicate balance between bleeding and clotting is a complex dance. When things malfunction:

Thrombocytopenia (low platelets): Increased bruising, petechiae (tiny purplish spots), bleeding gums...think about production problems (bone marrow failure) or increased destruction (immune-mediated).
Coagulation Disorders: Hemophilia (missing clotting factors), liver disease (affects production of clotting factors), medications like warfarin.... bleeding can be internal or external.
Hypercoagulability: The other side of the coin, where clots form too easily (deep vein thrombosis, pulmonary embolism). Risk factors include prolonged immobility, certain cancers, genetic predisposition.

Imagine a patient presenting with excessive bruising and a prolonged nosebleed. Your careful assessment will involve a bleeding history, medication review, and labs like a CBC, platelet count, and clotting studies (PT/INR/aPTT).

Alright, let's shift gears and dive headfirst into the complex but fascinating world of cancer. This might seem like a daunting topic, but fear not! We'll break it down into bite-sized pieces to conquer the CMSRN exam and, more importantly, prepare you to care for patients facing this life-altering diagnosis.

Imagine your body as a well-oiled machine. Every cell has a specific job, and they multiply in an orderly fashion to keep things running smoothly. Now, picture a malfunction. Cells start reproducing uncontrollably, forming masses called tumors. These tumors can be benign (don't spread) or malignant (cancerous), wreaking havoc on nearby tissues and potentially traveling to distant organs.

The CMSRN exam will delve into three major categories of cancer: leukemias, lymphomas, and solid tumors. Let's unpack each one:

### 1. Leukemias: Blood Buddies Gone Rogue

Think of your blood as a bustling city. Leukemia is like a civil war within this city. Normally, white blood cells (WBCs) are the good guys, fighting infections. In leukemia, abnormal WBCs become the bad guys, crowding out the good ones and disrupting the immune system. Just like different city districts, leukemias are classified based on the type of WBC involved:

- **Myelogenous:** These cancers originate in the bone marrow, the "city outskirts" where WBCs are produced.
- **Lymphoblastic:** These involve abnormal lymphocytes, a specific type of WBC, kind of like rogue special forces wreaking havoc.

**Exam Tip:** The exam loves acronyms! Know your ALL (Acute Lymphoblastic Leukemia) from your AML (Acute Myeloid Leukemia).

### 2. Lymphomas: When the Lymphatic System Goes Haywire

The lymphatic system is your body's sewage disposal network. Lymph nodes, scattered throughout the body, act like filters, trapping debris and pathogens. In lymphomas, lymphocytes themselves turn cancerous, causing enlarged lymph nodes and disrupting the body's defense system. Just like a clogged drain system, this can lead to infections and other complications.

**Think of It Like This:** Imagine a city with a failing sewage system. Trash backs up, causing problems throughout the city. Similarly, lymphomas disrupt the body's waste disposal, leading to various issues.

### 3. Solid Tumors: Lumps That Can Cause Big Problems

Solid tumors can arise from almost any organ or tissue in the body. They're essentially abnormal clumps of cells that keep growing and can invade surrounding tissues. Common examples include breast cancer, lung cancer, and colon cancer.

**Analogy Alert!** Think of a city with an uncontrolled building boom. Solid tumors are like these out-of-place buildings, disrupting the normal structure and function of the "city."

**Remember:** The exam will likely focus on specific types of solid tumors, so be sure to brush up on high-yield cancers like those mentioned above.

### Mastering the Maze: Tips and Tricks for Exam Success

- **Focus on Classification:** Understanding the different types of leukemias, lymphomas, and solid tumors (and their subtypes) is key.
- **Think Symptoms:** The exam might present cases with vague symptoms like fatigue or weight loss. Recognize these as potential red flags for cancer and think through the possible diagnoses based on the patient's age and other risk factors.
- **The Art of Elimination:** Sometimes, you'll be presented with a list of possible diagnoses. Use your knowledge of symptoms, common cancers, and age groups to rule out unlikely options and arrive at the most fitting answer.

Remember, the CMSRN exam is all about applying your knowledge to real-world scenarios. So, the more you can connect these concepts to actual cases, the better prepared you'll be to ace the exam and care for your future patients.

**Bonus Round: Beyond the Textbook**

Did you know Nobel laureate, Rita Levi-Montalcini, made groundbreaking discoveries about nerve growth factors while studying cancer? This research has implications not just for oncology but also for understanding nervous system disorders! This is just one example of how cancer research has far-reaching benefits across the medical field.

Stay curious, future nurses! The world of cancer is constantly evolving, and your knowledge can make a real difference in the lives of those battling this disease.

so you've grasped the basics of cancer – those rebellious cells wreaking havoc throughout the body. Now let's talk about some of the powerful tools we employ to fight back! Chemotherapy and radiation, while potent, can also take a toll on patients. Let's unravel the complexities so that you can provide the best possible care, both physically and emotionally, to patients undergoing these treatments.

Chemotherapy: Unleashing the Chemical Warriors

Think of chemo drugs as a special forces team infiltrating the body, specifically targeting those rapidly dividing cancer cells. However, it can be like a bomb, harming healthy cells too, hence the well-known side effects. Here's the breakdown:

Different Drugs, Different Missions: There are many chemo drugs, each with their own mechanisms and targets. Some prevent cells from dividing, others damage DNA, disrupting their abnormal growth.
Routes of Administration: Some chemo is given intravenously (IV drip), others as pills or even injected directly into specific areas.
Cycles: Chemo is usually given in cycles... a treatment period followed by a break to allow healthy cells to recover.
Exam Tip: Knowing the broad categories of chemo drugs helps (alkylating agents, antimetabolites...). Focus more on understanding major side effects and how you'll manage them. Think: nausea/vomiting, hair loss, fatigue, increased risk of infection.

Radiation Therapy: Focused Firepower

Imagine radiation as tiny, high-energy beams strategically aimed to blast the DNA of cancer cells. Think laser-guided sniper fire rather than a firestorm like chemo. Here's what you need to know:

External Beam Radiation: The most common type. Imagine a machine precisely aiming the beam at the tumor from the outside.
Internal Radiation: Sometimes, radioactive substances are placed directly inside or near the tumor.
The Goal: It may be given to cure (think smaller, localized tumors) or to control cancer growth and manage symptoms at more advanced stages.
Side Effects: Mostly Localized

Unlike chemo which goes system-wide, radiation side effects are generally confined to the treatment area:

Skin irritation (like a sunburn)
Fatigue
Specific effects depend on what's being treated – think about someone with head and neck cancer getting radiation... they may develop hoarseness, swallowing difficulty, etc.
Your Role as a CMSRN: Expertise Beyond the Treatment

Caring for patients receiving chemo or radiation involves far more than just knowing drug names and radiation doses. Think holistically:

Side Effect Management: You'll become an expert in managing nausea, meticulous wound care for irritated skin, and educating patients on infection prevention.
Emotional Support: These treatments are grueling. Fear, anxiety, and even body image struggles are incredibly common. Your empathetic support is equally vital.
Long-term Considerations: Some patients may experience delayed effects years later. Knowing these risks helps you monitor and guide your patients long-term.
Real World Scenario

Imagine a patient undergoing chemotherapy for breast cancer. They develop a fever and low white blood cell count. You know this places them at high risk for serious infection. Your meticulous assessment, swift communication with the oncologist, and vigilant monitoring for signs of sepsis could be lifesaving.

Chemotherapy and radiation are key weapons in the fight against cancer. Your deep understanding of how they work, their potential side effects, and the nursing complexities of managing them will not only help you ace the CMSRN exam but, more importantly, will translate into the compassionate and expert care your patients deserve.

Let's shift our focus to a life-saving resource – blood and blood products! Transfusions have the power to turn critical situations around. Being transfusion-savvy is essential for your CMSRN exam and in providing skilled and vigilant care.

**The Basics of Blood Types**
Think of blood types as individual ID tags on red blood cells (RBCs). Here's the crash course:
- **ABO System:** The main categories are A, B, AB, and O. If you receive the wrong type, your immune system goes haywire and attacks the transfused RBCs...not good!
- **Rh Factor:** That 'positive' or 'negative' in your blood type. Rh-negative individuals receiving Rh-positive blood can develop antibodies that can cause trouble in future transfusions or pregnancies.
- **Universal Donors and Recipients:** Type O negative blood is the 'universal RBC donor,' as it lacks those trouble-making ID tags. AB positive folks are 'universal recipients.'

Know the ABO compatibility basics! The CMSRN will likely test you on choosing the right blood products in transfusion scenarios.

**Beyond Whole Blood: Components and Their Functions**
Sometimes, patients only need specific blood components. Here's a quick hit-list:
- **Packed RBCs:** Concentrated RBCs, for severe anemia.
- **Platelets:** The clotting heroes! Used when platelet counts are dangerously low.
- **Plasma:** The fluid portion with clotting factors, used for bleeding disorders and sometimes volume replacement in emergencies.

**The Transfusion Process: It's Not Just Hanging a Bag!**
A transfusion is a meticulous process:
1. **Ordering and Crossmatching:** The physician orders the product, lab does meticulous compatibility testing to prevent reactions.
2. **Informed Consent:** You educate the patient about the procedure, risks, and benefits.
3. **Baseline Vitals:** Your starting point for monitoring for any reaction.
4. **Careful Administration:** Start slow, watch closely! Febrile reactions, itching, even life-threatening anaphylaxis can occur.
5. **Staying Vigilant:** Monitoring vitals continues throughout and after the transfusion. Sometimes reactions are delayed.

**The "TAR" of Transfusion Reactions**
Think of the acronym "TAR" to remember those dreaded complications:
- **Transfusion-associated circulatory overload (TACO):** Fluid overload, especially a concern in patients with heart or kidney problems.
- **Allergic Reaction:** Ranges from mild hives (treated with antihistamines) to full-blown anaphylaxis (emergency!).
- **Febrile Reaction:** Fever, chills...can usually be managed, but always rules out a more dangerous reaction.

Imagine a patient who's actively bleeding. You rush to get IV access, anticipate blood product orders, and are ready to monitor closely during the transfusion and afterwards for signs of a reaction.

Blood transfusions can be truly lifesaving. Understanding blood types, the components and their uses, and the potential for complications is essential knowledge for both your CMSRN exam and when caring for critically ill patients. Your attention to detail and vigilance during transfusions could be the difference between an uneventful recovery and a life-threatening reaction.

Now let's dive into the realm of oncology emergencies, a critical area where swift recognition and intervention can make all the difference in patient outcomes. Remember, cancer itself, along with its treatments, can create a complex web of vulnerabilities that increase a patient's risk for life-threatening complications.

Tumor Lysis Syndrome (TLS): When Cancer Cells Die TOO Fast

Picture this: chemotherapy works beautifully, blasting away cancer cells. Sounds great, right? But when large numbers of tumor cells die rapidly, it can overwhelm the body's ability to clear the debris. Imagine a city's plumbing system getting clogged causing chaos! Here's what you need to know:

Electrolyte Mayhem: Potassium, phosphorus, and uric acid rise dangerously within the bloodstream. This can cause life-threatening heart arrhythmias, kidney failure, and seizures.
High-Risk Patients: Think cancers with rapid turnover (leukemias, lymphomas) and patients with poor kidney function to begin with.
Prevention Is Key: Before chemo, it's all about hydration, special meds like allopurinol to lower uric acid levels, and close monitoring of electrolytes and kidney function.
Septic Shock: Infection Hits Hard

Patients with cancer, especially those on chemotherapy, have weakened immune systems. Sepsis, a body-wide, life-threatening response to infection, becomes a major threat. Keep your "sepsis radar" on high alert:

Subtle Signs: Fever, chills, mental status changes, low blood pressure... these might be the only clues in an immunocompromised patient! Don't wait for textbook sepsis presentations in this population.
Rapid Response: Early antibiotics, aggressive IV fluids, and close monitoring are vital. Sepsis protocols are your best friend in this situation.
Spinal Cord Compression: A Neurological Nightmare

When tumors invade or press on the spinal cord, it's a neurological emergency! Here's the red flag roundup:

Back Pain: Often the first, and easily ignored, symptom.
Weakness, Numbness, Bowel/Bladder Trouble: As compression progresses, these alarming signs appear.
Timing is Everything: Timely recognition and treatment (often with high-dose steroids, and sometimes radiation or surgery) can prevent irreversible paralysis!
Hypercalcemia of Malignancy: When Bones Leak Calcium

Some cancers cause bones to release too much calcium into the blood, like a faucet left wide open. Think about it like this: your bones are a bank vault for calcium, and some cancers are master thieves. This calcium overload triggers a cascade of problems:

"Stones, Bones, Groans, and Psychiatric Overtones": A helpful mnemonic to remember the classic symptoms: kidney stones, bone pain, constipation, confusion...and let's not forget, those vague aches and pains that could point to underlying bone involvement.
Treatment: Hydration to dilute the calcium, along with medications that block bone breakdown.
Superior Vena Cava (SVC) Syndrome: Traffic Jam in the Chest

Imagine a major highway being blocked – that's SVC Syndrome! Cancers in the chest (lung cancer, lymphoma) can compress the superior vena cava, a large vein returning blood to the heart. Picture a major traffic jam in your chest! Here's what to watch for:

Swelling: Face, neck, arms may appear puffy and have a bluish discoloration.
Respiratory Distress: Difficulty breathing, cough...as the backup worsens.
Think Treatment, Not Just Diagnosis: Radiation may help shrink the tumor, stents can open up the vein... the exam will likely focus on management interventions.

Imagine a lymphoma patient presenting to the ER with leg weakness and difficulty urinating. Your "oncology emergency radar" goes off, and you immediately suspect spinal cord compression. A quick neurological assessment along with urgent imaging may confirm your suspicion.

Oncology emergencies create a dangerous storm where prompt recognition and intervention are crucial. Your oncology "spidey sense," along with an understanding of these common complications, empowers you to be a lifesaver for your patients with cancer.

## *Chapter 11: Integumentary System*

Think of your skin as a multifunctional marvel! It's your body's first line of defense, a sensory organ, a key player in temperature regulation, and even provides clues about your overall health. Understanding the integumentary system isn't just about diagnosing rashes – it's vital for providing holistic care.

**Layers of Protection**

Let's peel back the layers, starting from the outside in:
- **Epidermis:** The outermost layer, itself divided into thin layers where skin cells (keratinocytes) mature and eventually form that tough, protective top layer.
- **Dermis:** The thick middle layer, packed with blood vessels, nerves, sweat and oil glands, hair follicles...this is where the action happens!
- **Subcutaneous Layer:** Fatty layer providing insulation and cushioning.

Know the basic functions of each layer. This will help you understand why different skin disorders present the way they do.

**More than Meets the Eye: Skin, Hair, and Nails**

These specialized structures are all part of the integumentary family:
- **Hair:** Think beyond looks. Hair offers protection and helps with temperature regulation. Changes in hair texture or distribution can be clues to underlying medical conditions.
- **Nails:** Hardened plates of keratin. Did you know that nail abnormalities can hint at nutritional deficiencies, lung disease, and more?
- **Glands:** Oil (sebaceous) glands keep skin and hair lubricated. Sweat glands are key players in temperature regulation.

**The Skin's Defense System**
- **Physical Barrier:** The tightly packed outer layer helps keep pathogens out.
- **Immune Sentinels:** Specialized immune cells within the skin stand guard against invaders.
- **Good Bugs:** That diverse skin microbiome (bacteria and more) actually helps maintain a balanced, healthy skin environment.

**Skin Assessment: Your Detective Skills Matter**

A thorough skin assessment includes:
- **Inspection:** Color, lesions, distribution of any abnormalities...a systematic head-to-toe assessment is key.
- **Palpation:** Texture, temperature, moisture – your fingertips provide valuable information.
- **Don't Forget the "Hidden Areas":** Scalp, between toes, body folds...sometimes sneaky problems like to hide!

Imagine a patient presenting with a scaling, itchy rash on their elbows and knees. Your knowledge of psoriasis (a buildup of skin cells creating those silvery plaques) helps you recognize the pattern.

The integumentary system offers a window into a patient's overall health and well-being. Your skillful assessment, along with a solid understanding of skin structure and function, empowers you to recognize common skin conditions, identify red flags, and tailor treatment plans. Don't underestimate the importance of skin! It's a complex organ system with a story to tell.

Let's now talk about wounds. Think about them as disruptions in your body's protective armor, leaving it vulnerable to infection and further damage. Proper wound assessment and care aren't just about bandaging, it's crucial for preventing complications, promoting healing, and maintaining a patient's overall well-being.

Pressure Injuries: It's Not Just Lying Around

Also known as pressure ulcers or bedsores, these injuries develop when continuous pressure compromises blood flow to the skin and underlying tissue. Think bony areas like hips, heels, even the back of the head! Here's the breakdown:

Staging: Goes from 1 (intact skin with redness) to 4 (deep tissue loss, muscle and bone might be showing). Never underestimate the early stages!
Who's at Risk: Impaired mobility, poor nutrition, incontinence...these factors make a patient highly susceptible. Prevention is KEY!
Surgical Wounds: Healing After the Cut

Surgical wounds might seem straightforward, but complications can arise:

Types of Healing:
Primary Intention: Clean surgical incision, edges neatly closed...this heals the fastest.
Secondary Intention: Larger wounds left open to heal from the inside out (slower, more scar tissue formation).
Watch Out for Infection: Fever, unusual redness, swelling, drainage – know the red flags!
Principles of Wound Assessment

A systematic approach is key:
Location, Size, Depth
Wound Bed: What does the tissue itself look like? Red, granulating tissue is good. Yellow slough or black eschar needs debridement.
Drainage: Color, amount, odor...purulent drainage means trouble!
Surrounding Skin: Intact, or is there redness, breakdown?
Wound Care: The Toolbox

It's not a one-size-fits-all situation. Wound care is dynamic and individualized:

Cleansing: Gentle is the name of the game! Normal saline often wins.
Dressings: A dizzying variety! Hydrocolloids, alginates, hydrogels...the choice depends on wound characteristics.
Offloading Pressure: Essential for those pressure injuries! Pillow bridges, specialized mattresses...get creative to alleviate the pressure hot spots.
Nutrition Optimization: Wounds need building blocks to heal. Protein intake matters!
Exam Tip: Know the basic dressing categories and their uses. The CMSRN exam will likely test your knowledge of appropriate wound care interventions, NOT specifics of brand names.

Imagine a hospitalized patient with limited mobility who develops a Stage II pressure injury on their sacrum. Your plan will involve frequent repositioning, specialized dressings, and potentially consultation with a wound care specialist.

Wound care is both an art and a science. Your mastery of assessment, knowledge of healing principles, and the diverse tools in your wound care arsenal will empower you to provide that comprehensive care your patients need. Plus, the CMSRN exam expects you to be an expert in all things wound care!

Lets shift gears a little and get into the fascinating world of skin infections and conditions. We touched on the integumentary system's role as a defense system earlier, but infections and dermatological conditions can breach these defenses, causing significant discomfort and sometimes posing serious health risks. Recognizing these conditions and understanding their treatment is crucial for the CMSRN exam and for providing top-notch patient care.

**Bacterial Infections: Common Culprits**
- **Impetigo:** This contagious bacterial infection, particularly prevalent in young children, presents with honey-colored crusted lesions. Keep an eye out for those perioral lesions – a telltale sign!
- **Cellulitis:** This deeper bacterial infection often stems from a break in the skin. Think redness, swelling, warmth, and tenderness – classic signs of inflammation. Early recognition and antibiotic treatment are key to prevent complications like sepsis.
- **Folliculitis:** When bacteria invade hair follicles, you get folliculitis. This can manifest as itchy pustules or papules, sometimes clustered together in a folliculitis "forest."
- **MRSA:** Methicillin-resistant Staphylococcus aureus is a big player here. Remember, MRSA is a particular concern in healthcare settings, so maintaining proper hand hygiene is paramount!

**Fungal Infections: Itchy and Unsightly**

Fungi love warm, moist environments, making the skin between toes and the groin prime targets for these infections. Here are some common fungal foes:
- **Tinea infections:** Ringworm, athlete's foot, jock itch...all caused by various Tinea species. These pesky fungi cause itching, scaling, and sometimes even blistering. Antifungal creams or powders are your weapons of choice.
- **Candida albicans:** This fungus can cause diaper rash in infants and vulvovaginal candidiasis in women. Itching, burning, and irritation are common symptoms. Antifungal creams or suppositories are the mainstay of treatment.

**Viral Infections: A Varied Bunch**

Viruses can wreak havoc on the skin too. Let's look at a couple of common ones:
- **Herpes Zoster (Shingles):** This reactivation of the varicella-zoster virus (chickenpox) causes a painful, blistering rash along a dermatome. Early antiviral treatment can help lessen the severity and duration of the outbreak.
- **Human Papillomavirus (HPV):** Certain strains of HPV cause warts, those rough, bumpy growths on the skin. Genital warts, transmitted through sexual contact, are a particular concern.

**Inflammatory Skin Conditions: When the Immune System Overreacts**

Eczema and Psoriasis are two common inflammatory dermatological conditions. Understanding them is vital for the CMSRN exam:
- **Eczema:** This chronic condition presents with dry, itchy, inflamed skin. It can be exacerbated by stress, allergens, or irritants. Emollients and topical steroids are mainstays of treatment, but identifying and managing triggers is also key.
- **Psoriasis:** This autoimmune condition causes red, scaly patches on the skin. While not contagious, it can be quite visible and affect a person's quality of life. Topical medications, phototherapy, and even systemic medications may be used to manage psoriasis.

**Skin Cancer: Early Detection Saves Lives**

Skin cancer is the most common cancer in the United States. Being familiar with the different types and recognizing the warning signs (think: ABCDE – Asymmetry, Border irregularity, Color variation, Diameter greater than 6mm, Evolving in size or shape) is paramount. As a CMSRN, you'll play a vital role in educating patients about sun protection and performing skin assessments.

This isn't an exhaustive list, but it covers many of the high-yield dermatological conditions you'll likely encounter on the CMSRN exam and in clinical practice. Being a whiz at skin infections and conditions demonstrates your knowledge and ensures you can provide exceptional care to your patients.

## Chapter 12: Perioperative Care

let's explore the fascinating and fast-paced world of perioperative care, where every detail matters. Imagine yourself as part of the surgical team, helping to shepherd a patient safely through every stage of their surgical journey. Your role in the pre-operative phase sets the stage for the best possible outcomes!

**The Pre-Op Detective Work**

Think of the pre-operative assessment as gathering puzzle pieces to create the bigger picture of individual patient risk. Here's what goes into the mix:

- **Medical History: It's Not Just the Headlines:** It's about understanding how chronic conditions (diabetes, heart issues, etc.) could complicate surgery and anesthesia. Know your red flags – poorly controlled hypertension, recent MI, severe COPD...these demand further optimization to decrease risks.
- **Medication List: Beyond the Bottle:** It's not just what they take, but how it might interact with anesthetic medications, impact bleeding risk (blood thinners!), or mask issues during recovery.
- **Physical Exam: Targeted Investigation:** The focus is on cardiac, respiratory systems...any clues suggesting trouble during anesthesia? Don't forget airway assessment – a "difficult airway" can be a major anesthesia concern.
- **Labs & Diagnostics: Filling in the Blanks:** Baseline lab work (CBC, electrolytes), ECG, perhaps chest x-ray based on the patient's history.
- **Nutrition and Hydration: Are They Fueled Up?** Good nutritional status is essential for wound healing and recovery. Dehydration messes with electrolyte balance and kidney function, especially important in older patients.

**Preparing the Patient: It's a Team Effort!**

- **Informed Consent: Beyond a Signature:** This is an open dialogue. It's your job to ensure the patient understands the procedure's risks, benefits, alternatives, and what recovery will entail.
- **Teaching: What to Expect:** NPO instructions, pre-op skin prep, pain management...alleviate anxiety by giving clear instructions and setting realistic expectations.
- **Addressing Fears: It Gets Personal:** Surgery is stressful! Be that reassuring presence who acknowledges their fears and answers their questions with empathy.

**Anesthesia Considerations: A Pre-Op Priority**

Anesthesia deserves its own spotlight. Collaborate closely with the anesthesia team, sharing insights from your assessment:

- **Airway Concerns:** Difficult intubation history? Limited neck range of motion? These are alarm bells!
- **Cardiac Risks:** Recent heart attack, unstable angina? Might change the anesthetic plan (regional vs. general).
- **Malignant Hyperthermia (MH):** Rare but serious! A family history demands a careful pre-op workup.

Know the basic anesthetic categories (general, regional, MAC) and typical medications used. The CMSRN exam might present scenarios where you need to collaborate with anesthesia based on a patient's specific risk factors.

Imagine a patient with poorly controlled diabetes scheduled for elective knee surgery. You anticipate delayed wound healing and higher infection risks. Your pre-op plan will include tight glucose monitoring, potential timing adjustments for their diabetes medications, and meticulous wound care education.

A thorough pre-operative assessment and targeted patient preparation are like laying down a sturdy foundation before construction starts. You're minimizing risks, optimizing outcomes, and empowering the patient to be an active participant in their care. This sets the stage for a smooth surgical journey and a faster path to recovery!

So you've meticulously prepped your patient. Now imagine the curtain rises, and you step into the bright lights of the operating room (OR) itself. This is an intense, dynamic environment where teamwork and safety protocols rule the day!

**The Circulating Nurse: Mission Control of the OR**

Think of the circulating nurse as the OR maestro, ensuring everything runs smoothly. Here's what's in their arsenal:

- **Safety Checklists:** The "surgical time-out"...that final pre-incision moment to confirm the right patient, right procedure, right site. It might sound redundant, but it's a crucial fail-safe against wrong-site surgeries!
- **Sterility Guardian:** Maintaining the sterile field is paramount. The circulating nurse monitors for breaks in technique, and if something unsterile touches the field...it's their call to speak up!
- **Advocate & Resource:** Anticipating needs – an extra pair of hands? Missing equipment? The circulating nurse is the problem-solver who makes the surgical team function.

**The Scrub Role: In the Heart of the Action**

Scrub nurses or surgical techs stand directly across the table from the surgeon. They're masters of instrumentation, and their responsibilities include:

- **Scrubbed and Ready:** Performing the surgical scrub, setting up the sterile instrument table...all with meticulous technique to prevent contamination.
- **Pass the Scalpel, Please:** Knowing surgical instruments and anticipating the surgeon's needs is an art form in itself.
- **Specimen Management:** Any tissues or specimens removed go into the right containers, are labeled correctly...this ensures pathology has everything they need for accurate diagnosis.

**Intraoperative Safety: It's Everyone's Business**

The OR is a potential minefield of hazards. Beyond surgical errors, think broader:

- **Patient Positioning:** Nerve damage from improper positioning is a significant risk! Careful padding of pressure points is key.
- **Fire Prevention:** Electrosurgical units, flammable prep solutions, even oxygen-enriched environments are part of the OR fire risk equation.
- **Falls:** Sounds basic, but a sedated patient + a narrow OR table...safety straps and careful transfer are essential.

**A "Culture of Safety": Beyond Checklists**

While checklists and protocols are important, true safety hinges on a team-focused, "See something, say something" culture. This includes:

- **Speaking Up:** Empowering ANY team member, regardless of title, to voice safety concerns without fear of retribution. Remember, a caught error is far better than a surgical complication!
- **Debriefing:** Taking time after a case to analyze what went well and areas for improvement fosters a culture of continuous learning and safety.

Know the key roles in the OR and their responsibilities. The CMSRN exam loves to test on teamwork and safety principles.

Imagine a surgical tech noticing a small stain on the sterile drape. They bring it to the surgeon's attention. While it might seem minor, this could indicate a break in sterility. Replacing the drape avoids a potential surgical site infection.

The OR can be intimidating, but your meticulous pre-op preparation has already set your patient up for success. Inside the OR, your role as a vigilant patient advocate, team player, and champion of safety protocols makes you an indispensable asset. This is where your knowledge translates directly into the best possible patient outcomes!

Think of the post-operative phase as the patient's journey home after a major storm. They've weathered the surgery itself, but now the focus shifts to careful monitoring, promoting recovery, and catching any early signs of complications. Your role is like a skilled navigator, guiding them safely back to their baseline health.

Immediate Post-Op: The PACU Zone

The Post Anesthesia Care Unit (PACU) is the first stop. Here's where your focus lies:

The ABCs: Airway, Breathing, Circulation. Ensuring the patient is emerging from anesthesia safely is priority one. Vital signs are monitored like a hawk!

Pain Management: It's not just about comfort. Adequate pain control promotes movement, deep breathing...key to preventing post-op complications.

Nausea & Vomiting (PONV): Notorious post-anesthesia culprits. Administering antiemetics and being prepared for this common issue makes all the difference.

Watch for Emergence Delirium: Especially in older patients, agitation and confusion can happen as anesthesia wears off. This generally resolves on its own, but requires close monitoring!

Transition to the Med-Surg Floor: Maintaining Vigilance

Now, your patient's journey continues. Here's what you need to keep on your radar:

Surgical Site Assessment: Redness, warmth, drainage – early signs of infection need prompt intervention.

Wound Care & Dressing Changes: Meticulous technique matters! Educating your patient is key for continued care at home.

Pain Management Shifts Gears: Moving from IV to oral meds – finding the right balance of control with minimal side effects is an ongoing process.

Promoting Mobility: The sooner they're up and moving (within safe limits), the lower the risk of complications like pneumonia and DVT.

Fluid & Electrolyte Balance: Surgery is a major stressor on the body! You'll be keeping an eye on intake, output, and those lab values.

Complications to Anticipate

Even with the best care, complications can happen. Knowing the red flags is key:

Surgical Site Infection (SSI): Fever, wound drainage, or worsening pain beyond the expected post-op course should set off alarm bells.

DVT/Pulmonary Embolism (PE): Leg swelling, pain, new-onset shortness of breath...this deadly duo requires swift action.

Pneumonia: Especially after major surgeries where it may be hard to take deep breaths, crackles in the lungs and productive cough can signal trouble.

Ileus: After abdominal surgery, bowel function can temporarily slow down. Distended abdomen, no bowel sounds... these are worrisome signs.

Exam Tip: Know the most common complications after different types of surgeries. The CMSRN exam will likely test your ability to recognize early signs and interventions.

Discharge Planning: Empowering the Patient

Your post-op care isn't just about the here-and-now. Thorough discharge planning sets patients up for success:

Medication Teaching: What to take, when, potential side effects – making sure they understand is crucial!

Wound Care Instructions: How to do dressing changes, what signs of infection to watch for... empower them to take charge of their healing.

Follow-Up Appointments: Ensure they have clear instructions and understand the importance of follow-up with their surgeon.

Imagine a post-op patient after a bowel resection. Your plan will involve NG tube management, gradual advancement of diet, close monitoring for signs of ileus, and transitioning pain meds to oral forms before their anticipated discharge.

Post-operative care involves a delicate balance of close monitoring for complications, promoting recovery, and preparing patients for the transition home. Your attention to detail, knowledge of potential complications, and commitment to patient education are essential for a smooth recovery and to prevent potential readmissions.

# Chapter 13: Domains of Nursing Practice

Now were going to get into the intricate world of administering and monitoring therapeutic interventions. As a CMSRN, you'll be the medication maestro, ensuring safe and effective delivery and keeping a watchful eye for both desired outcomes and potential side effects.

**The "Five Rights" – Your Guiding Star**
Remember those five rights of medication administration? They seem simple...but in the hustle of a busy unit, these fundamentals can prevent life-altering errors.

- **Right Patient:** Two forms of ID, every single time.
- **Right Drug:** Never assume! Triple-check the label against the order.
- **Right Dose:** Calculations matter! Have a colleague double-check high-risk meds like insulin or heparin.
- **Right Route:** Can this be oral or only IV? The route changes how the drug acts in the body.
- **Right Time:** Is it scheduled, or dependent on parameters (like blood pressure)?

**Beyond the Basics: Your Critical Thinking Cap**

- **Allergies:** That innocuous-looking antibiotic could be a disaster waiting to happen. Always check allergy history meticulously!
- **Patient-Specific Factors:** Age, kidney, or liver function all impact how the body handles drugs. Dosage adjustments might be needed.
- **Drug-Drug Interactions:** Know the common culprits – think warfarin, antibiotics...sometimes adding one med throws another one off balance.

**Monitoring: It's Not "One and Done"**
Giving the med is only the beginning. Here's what you need to be vigilant about:

- **Effectiveness:** Does the blood pressure drop as expected? Is pain relief achieved?
- **Lab Values:** Many drugs need therapeutic monitoring (think digoxin levels, INR for warfarin).
- **Side Effects:** From mild nausea to life-threatening allergic reactions...be ready to recognize and intervene!
- **Watch Out for High-Risk Medications**

Some medications carry extra risks:

- **Heparin:** Bleeding is a major concern. Know the antidote (protamine sulfate) and monitor for bleeding signs.
- **Opioids:** Respiratory depression is always a risk, especially in opioid-naïve patients.
- **Chemotherapy:** Myelosuppression, nausea, complex side effect profiles demand specialized knowledge.

The CMSRN loves to test your knowledge of high-risk meds and their potential complications. Brush up on those!

Imagine a patient receiving IV vancomycin for a MRSA infection. You'll monitor for infusion reactions, watch their kidney function, and be alert for signs of "Red Man Syndrome".

Safe and effective medication administration goes way beyond the mechanics of drawing up meds and hanging IV bags. Your deep understanding of pharmacology, close monitoring for side effects, and astute assessment skills are essential in providing top-notch care and preventing medication-related harm.

Think of your patient as a complex machine with countless blinking lights and dials. Diagnostic tests and monitoring are your tools to read those signals, decipher the body's inner workings, and make informed decisions. Let's delve into how you'll use these tools skillfully!

**Lab Tests: Decoding the Body's Messages**

Labs provide windows into body chemistry and function:
- **Basic Metabolic Panel (BMP):** Electrolytes, kidney markers, glucose – this paints a broad picture of overall health.
- **Complete Blood Count (CBC):** Think infection (white cells!), anemia (low red cells), and clotting ability (platelets).
- **Liver Function Tests (LFTs):** When liver health is in question, these tell the tale.
- **Beyond the Basics:** Think thyroid function, specific markers like troponin for heart damage, or those specialized coagulation studies

**It's Not Just the Number:**

Knowing normal lab ranges is important, but there's more to the story:
- **Context Matters:** That slightly elevated potassium is more worrisome in a patient with kidney failure.
- **Trends Over Time:** Is that creatinine slowly creeping up? Single values only tell part of the story.
- **Patient Factors:** Age, pregnancy, even recent meals can influence certain results.

**Imaging Studies: Seeing Inside the Body**

From plain old x-rays to the high-tech world of MRIs, imaging unveils hidden clues:
- **Chest X-ray:** The go-to for looking at lungs (think pneumonia), heart size, and even rib fractures.
- **CT Scans:** Detailed cross-sectional images – great for finding bleeds, tumors, or internal organ damage.
- **Ultrasound:** From gallbladder stones to peeking at a baby in the womb, this utilizes sound waves for real-time images.

**Continuous Monitoring: The Body's Live Feed**

In critical care settings, patients are wired up, giving you moment-by-moment data:
- **Cardiac Monitoring (EKG):** Rhythm disturbances? Signs of ischemia? The EKG is your early warning system.
- **Pulse Oximetry:** That little finger probe provides continuous oxygen saturation readings.
- **Invasive Lines:** Arterial lines for beat-to-beat blood pressure monitoring, central lines for medication administration...sometimes you need the 'heavy artillery.'

Know the 'why' behind common diagnostic tests, not just what they measure. The CMSRN exam loves scenarios where you must interpret results in context.

Imagine a patient presenting with chest pain. You'll likely order an EKG, troponin levels, and a chest x-ray, each providing a piece of the diagnostic puzzle.

Diagnostic tests and monitoring are the detective tools you'll use to diagnose illnesses, guide treatment, and track a patient's progress. Your ability to order the right tests, interpret results accurately, and integrate these findings into your overall assessment is a hallmark of a skilled CMSRN.

Now let's step away from the medical-surgical world for a moment and delve into the heart of nursing itself – the helping role. Think of it as the invisible thread woven throughout everything you do – from administering medications to providing emotional support. It's easy to forget how powerful this role can be when we're immersed in technical aspects of care.

Therapeutic Communication: More Than Just Words

Effective communication is the foundation of a strong nurse-patient relationship:

Active Listening: It's not just about hearing, but truly absorbing what your patient is saying, both verbally and non-verbally.

Empathy: Stepping into your patient's shoes for a moment, understanding their fears and anxieties, makes a world of difference.

Open-Ended Questions: "Tell me more about..." These invite your patient to share their story and concerns.

Respectful Curiosity

Remember, your patient is the expert on their own lived experience! A sense of genuine curiosity, free from judgment, builds trust and helps you uncover deeper insights into their world.

Patient Education: Empowering Choices

Think of yourself as a translator, breaking down complex medical information into digestible bits your patient understands. This empowers them to be active participants in their own care:

Tailored Approach: Meet your patient where they are. Literacy level, cultural background, all of these impact how you teach.
Visual Aids: Pictures, diagrams, even showing them models of organs can enhance understanding.
"Teach-Back" Method: Having your patient explain things back to you in their own words reveals any gaps in understanding.
Supporting During Difficult Times

There will be times when diagnoses are grim or treatments fail. Your presence and support are invaluable:

The Power of Silence: Sometimes just sitting quietly with your patient, offering a hand to hold, conveys more than words ever could.
Validating Emotions: "It sounds like you're feeling angry and scared..." Letting them know their feelings are heard makes them feel less alone.
Knowing Your Limits: Offering spiritual support (if in your scope) is one thing, but know when to refer to a chaplain or social worker for specialized support.
Interdisciplinary Collaboration: Strength in Teamwork

Your expertise is one piece of the puzzle. Remember those other amazing professionals! Effective collaboration is key to providing holistic care:

Communicating Clearly: Sharing key assessments and changes in your patient's status with physicians, therapists, etc., ensures everyone's on the same page.
Mutual Respect: Each team member brings different skills. Valuing their contributions leads to better care.

Advocating for Your Patient: You have that 'big picture' view. Speak up when you see something missing in the care plan!

The CMSRN exam loves those 'soft skills' scenarios. Focus on therapeutic communication techniques, patient education strategies, and ways to offer support during challenging moments.

Imagine a newly diagnosed diabetic patient. You'll teach them about blood glucose monitoring, medications, and diet modification. You might even connect them with a support group for that sense of community.

Your helping role is not some fluffy extra – it's the bedrock of providing truly person-centered care. Your empathy, skilled communication, and unwavering support can make a profound difference in the lives of your patients, especially when they're facing their most vulnerable moments. This, perhaps more than anything else, defines what you stand for as a CMSRN.

Let's shift our focus from the "what" of patient care to the "how" – the art of teaching and coaching. As a CMSRN, you have life-changing knowledge and skills to share, but knowing how to do so effectively is just as important! Think of yourself as a guide, empowering your patients to become active participants in managing their health, leading to better outcomes and lasting changes.

**Principles of Effective Patient Education**
- **Start With Assessment:** What's their baseline knowledge? Literacy level? Learning style? Tailoring your approach is key!
- **Focus on Priorities:** Don't try and teach them EVERYTHING in one go. Identify the most crucial information first.
- **Break it Down:** Use plain language, avoid medical jargon. Analogies can be incredibly helpful! Think, "Your kidneys are like filters..."
- **"Teach-Back" Technique:** Have your patient explain the instructions back to you. This is where you catch any misunderstandings.
- **Reinforcement is Key:** Written materials, videos, reputable websites...multiple formats support learning and retention.

**Coaching for Behavior Change**

Teaching information is one thing, but supporting your patients to make lasting lifestyle changes is another beast altogether! Here's your toolkit:
- **Motivational Interviewing:** Open-ended questions, exploring ambivalence...get them to voice their own reasons for change.
- **Small, Achievable Goals:** "Lose 50 lbs" is overwhelming. "Walk for 10 minutes daily" feels do-able and builds confidence.
- **Celebrate Successes:** Acknowledging small wins keeps patients motivated and emphasizes those positive changes.
- **Dealing with Setbacks:** Normalize that lapses happen. Help them identify triggers and troubleshoot solutions.

**Written Materials: Making it Stick**

Let's face it, your patients will forget half of what you tell them the minute they walk out the door! Well-designed handouts are your secret weapon:
- **Clear and Concise:** Short sentences, bullet points. Focus on the absolute must-know information.
- **Visually Appealing:** Diagrams, charts...break up text and enhance understanding, especially for visual learners.

- **Reliable Sources:** Reputable websites like the American Heart Association or the CDC provide additional support.

**Beyond the Patient: Teaching Families**

Families, especially for chronically ill or elderly patients, become part of the care team at home. Include them in your teaching whenever possible:
- **Skill Demonstration:** When teaching wound care or injections, having a family member watch and even practice with you strengthens their confidence.
- **Caregiver Support:** Caregiving is TOUGH. Connecting them to support groups or respite resources is vital to prevent burnout.

The CMSRN exam loves scenarios about patient education and behavior change. Think about those communication techniques and how you'd tailor your approach to the individual patient.

Imagine a newly diagnosed heart failure patient. You'll teach them about a low-sodium diet, daily weights, medication management, and when to seek urgent care – that's a lot! Prioritizing the essentials and using multiple teaching strategies will be essential for their long-term success.

Let's now talk about those chaotic, high-pressure moments where a patient's status can take a turn for the worse. Rapid response situations demand not only solid medical knowledge but also the ability to stay calm, think critically, and act decisively. Remember, strong leadership and effective teamwork can make all the difference in those critical moments!

**The ABCs...Always!**

In the midst of chaos, always come back to your foundation:
- **Airway:** Is it patent? Do they need supplemental oxygen or even advanced airway support?
- **Breathing:** Assess rate, effort, oxygen saturation. Are they struggling? Interventions range from repositioning to possible intubation.
- **Circulation:** Blood pressure, heart rate, pulses, mental status...what's their perfusion status like? Fluid boluses or even vasopressors might be needed.

**Rapid Assessment: What's the Problem?**
- **Think Systems:** Is this primarily respiratory distress? Cardiac? Neurologic decline? Each demands a different set of interventions.
- **Focused Exam:** Guided by your initial ABCs, zero in on the problem area. Lung sounds? Heart rhythm? Pupil response?
- **Act on Clues:** Dropping blood pressure in a post-surgical patient? Think bleeding! Low oxygen with wheezing? Exacerbation of asthma or COPD!

**Know Your Role**
- **Team Leader:** As the CMSRN, you'll likely orchestrate the response. Delegate tasks, communicate clearly, and maintain a "big picture" view.
- **Team Member:** Even if not the leader, everyone has a vital role. Performing tasks efficiently, anticipating needs, and communicating findings are essential.
- **Rapid Response Teams:** Know your hospital's protocols for activating a rapid response. This brings additional expertise and resources to the bedside.

**Common Rapid Response Scenarios**
- **Respiratory Distress:** From asthma attacks to pulmonary edema, quick interventions like oxygen, bronchodilators, or even intubation can be lifesavers.
- **Cardiac Arrest:** ACLS protocols kick in. High-quality CPR, early defibrillation, and managing reversible causes are key.

- **Sepsis:** Early recognition is paramount! Fluids, antibiotics, and vasopressors as needed, following the sepsis bundle protocol can improve outcomes.

Be familiar with ACLS algorithms and common medications used in emergency situations. The CMSRN exam might present scenarios where you need to prioritize interventions or demonstrate leadership during a code.

Imagine a patient experiencing worsening shortness of breath, tachycardia, and low oxygen saturation. Your rapid assessment points to a PE (pulmonary embolism). You'll initiate oxygen, alert the physician, and potentially prepare for thrombolytics or anticoagulation.

Rapidly changing situations test both your clinical skills and your ability to stay calm under pressure. Regular participation in simulations, ACLS review, and a solid understanding of common emergency scenarios will empower you to lead your team effectively and potentially save lives.

**Conquering the Organizational and Work-Role Competency Domain: Your Guide to CMSRN Success**

We're about to delve into the fascinating world of **Organizational and Work-Role Competencies**. Don't let the fancy term intimidate you. Here, we'll unpack what it means to be a rockstar nurse who thrives not just in patient care, but also within the bigger picture of the healthcare system.

Think of it like this: you're an exceptional chef, whipping up culinary masterpieces. But even the most skilled chef needs a well-stocked kitchen, a reliable team, and a clear understanding of food safety protocols to truly shine. That's where these competencies come in – they equip you to navigate the organizational aspects of nursing, ensuring you can deliver top-notch care seamlessly.

Now, let's break it down into bite-sized pieces, using the official CMSRN exam topics and subtopics as our guide:

**1. Priority Setting and Time Management:**

Ever feel like you're constantly juggling tasks? You're not alone! This section focuses on mastering the art of prioritization. Here's a handy trick: imagine your patients' needs as color-coded balls. Red balls are critical (think unstable vital signs!), yellow for urgent (like pain management), and green for less pressing matters (like updating paperwork). Learn to identify those red balls first and delegate or reschedule the rest efficiently.

**Exam Tip:** Remember the **ABCDE** method: Airway, Breathing, Circulation, Disability, and Exposure. This framework helps prioritize interventions during critical situations.

**2. Delegation and Supervision:**

As a CMSRN, you'll be a leader, not a lone wolf. Delegation empowers you to utilize your team's strengths effectively. Think of it like conducting an orchestra. You set the tone, assign parts (tasks) based on each musician's (team member's) skillset, and ensure everyone plays in harmony to achieve a beautiful outcome (quality patient care).

**3. Quality Improvement:**

Healthcare is constantly evolving, and so should your approach! This competency focuses on your ability to identify areas for improvement in patient care processes. Imagine you notice a rise in hospital-acquired infections. You'd research best practices, propose implementing new handwashing protocols, and monitor their effectiveness.

**Exam Tip:** The acronym **PDSA** (Plan-Do-Study-Act) is your friend here. It's a framework for implementing and evaluating quality improvement initiatives.

**4. Professional Communication:**

Clear communication is the cornerstone of excellent teamwork and patient safety. This goes beyond just exchanging information. It's about active listening, using respectful language, and adapting your communication style to different audiences (patients, doctors, colleagues). Imagine you're explaining a complex medical procedure to an elderly patient. You'd break down the jargon, use clear visuals, and encourage them to ask questions.

Interdisciplinary rounds are a great example of effective communication. The doctor, nurse, social worker, and therapist all come together to discuss the patient's care plan, ensuring a holistic approach.

**Mnemonics to the Rescue!** Here's a handy acronym to remember the SBAR method for effective communication: **S**ituation, **B**ackground, **A**ssessment, **R**ecommendation.

### 5. Collaboration:

You are a vital part of a healthcare team, and collaboration is key! This means working effectively with doctors, therapists, social workers, and other healthcare professionals. Think of yourselves as superheroes with different superpowers, but united by a common goal – patient well-being.

### 6. Legal and Ethical Considerations:

As a nurse, you have a legal and ethical duty to protect patient confidentiality, practice within your scope, and advocate for your patients' rights. Imagine a patient refusing a specific treatment. You'd explain the risks and benefits, but ultimately respect their decision while exploring alternative options.

These are just some of the key areas covered in the Organizational and Work-Role Competencies domain. By understanding these concepts and practicing them in your clinical rotations, you'll be well on your way to CMSRN success and becoming a well-rounded, adaptable nurse who thrives in any healthcare setting.

Alright, so you've built a strong foundation providing direct patient care, but now let's zoom out a bit. Think of quality healthcare as a symphony. Even the most skilled musicians won't produce great music if they're out of tune, the sheet music has errors, or the conductor is off the beat. This section is all about ensuring all the components of healthcare are working harmoniously to deliver the best possible outcomes.

The Nitty Gritty of Quality Improvement

It's Not Just Lip Service: Every hospital loves to talk about "quality", but what does it mean in practice? It's about constantly evaluating processes, identifying areas for improvement, and implementing evidence-based changes.

Data is Your Friend: Think of quality metrics as your vital signs for healthcare delivery. Things like infection rates, patient falls, readmission rates – these tell you where your system is healthy and where it needs some TLC.

Root Cause Analysis (RCA): When something goes wrong (a sentinel event), a deep dive is needed to figure out why it happened, so you prevent a repeat performance. Was it a medication error? A gap in communication?

Tools of the Trade

Let's peek into your quality improvement toolkit:

PDSA (Plan-Do-Study-Act): This cyclical approach allows for testing changes on a small scale before widespread implementation.

Benchmarking: How do you stack up? Compare your metrics to other hospitals or national standards to measure your performance.

Patient Satisfaction Surveys: Sure, sometimes these get eye-rolls, but they offer valuable insights into the patient experience, an increasingly important part of quality.

The Ethical Angle

Quality healthcare isn't just about numbers; it's about doing things right, even when nobody's looking. Here's where ethics intertwines with quality improvement:

Resource Allocation: What if there's only one ICU bed for two critically ill patients? Having clear, ethically sound triage protocols in place helps navigate these tough decisions.
Disparities in Care: Sadly, factors like race, socioeconomic status, etc. can impact quality of care. Tracking these disparities is the first step in addressing them.
End-of-Life Care: Advance directives, DNRs...these sensitive topics are best addressed proactively, ensuring patients' wishes are respected and families are supported.
Know the major quality initiatives in healthcare...things like National Patient Safety Goals or pay-for-performance models. The CMSRN exam wants you to see the big picture!

Imagine your unit notices a spike in pressure injuries. You launch a quality improvement project focused on skin care protocols, staff education, and even specialized beds. Monitoring those metrics over time shows if your interventions made a difference.

Monitoring and ensuring quality healthcare is an ongoing endeavor. Think of yourself as a detective, constantly searching for clues that point to potential problems and areas for improvement. Your dedication to quality, your comfort with data, and your unwavering commitment to ethical principles make you an invaluable force in ensuring that the healthcare system provides the very best for those it serves.

# **Practice Questions**

Well....Now it's time to put it all to the test – virtually, of course. Consider this your practice orchestra performance, a chance to fine-tune your skills before the real exam.

These practice questions cover a wide range of topics you'll encounter on the CMSRN exam, mimicking the format and difficulty level you can expect. But here's the beauty of this practice test: we won't just leave you hanging after each question. Following each question, you'll find the answer key, along with a detailed explanation for why that answer is the correct choice. Think of it as instant feedback, a chance to learn from both your triumphs and...well, maybe a not-so-perfect answer choice here or there.

The key to mastering any exam is focused practice, and that's exactly what this section is designed for. So, take a deep breath, channel your inner Florence Nightingale, and let's dive into these practice questions. Remember, there's no penalty for getting one wrong here – consider it a valuable learning opportunity that will solidify your knowledge and boost your confidence on exam day!


1. A patient presenting with chest pain, diaphoresis, and nausea is suspected of having an Acute Coronary Syndrome (ACS). Which of the following serum markers is most indicative of myocardial injury?
a. C-reactive protein
b. Myoglobin
c. Troponin
d. Creatine kinase-MB


Answer: c. Troponin. Explanation: Troponin is the most specific and sensitive marker for myocardial injury, as it remains elevated for a longer period following myocardial infarction, making it crucial for diagnosing ACS. While CK-MB was historically used, troponin has largely supplanted it due to its higher specificity for cardiac muscle.


2. In managing a patient with unstable angina, which of the following pharmacological treatments is primarily aimed at preventing platelet aggregation?
a. Beta-blockers
b. ACE inhibitors
c. Thrombolytics
d. Aspirin


Answer: d. Aspirin. Explanation: Aspirin inhibits cyclooxygenase, a key enzyme in the synthesis of thromboxane A2, a potent platelet aggregator and vasoconstrictor, thus playing a critical role in preventing platelet aggregation in the context of ACS management.

3. A 55-year-old patient with a history of stable angina now presents with increased frequency and intensity of chest pain episodes, even at rest. This change in clinical presentation is most consistent with:
a. Stable angina
b. Prinzmetal's angina
c. Unstable angina
d. Myocarditis

Answer: c. Unstable angina. Explanation: Unstable angina is characterized by a change in the usual pattern of angina, such as increased frequency, duration, or intensity of pain, or pain that occurs at rest, indicating a higher risk of myocardial infarction.

4. For a patient diagnosed with NSTEMI, which of the following strategies is typically preferred for immediate management?
a. Emergency coronary artery bypass graft (CABG) surgery
b. Percutaneous coronary intervention (PCI)
c. Immediate discharge with lifestyle modification advice
d. High-dose statin therapy initiation

Answer: b. Percutaneous coronary intervention (PCI). Explanation: PCI is often the preferred immediate management strategy for NSTEMI to restore coronary blood flow, as it can significantly reduce the risk of further cardiac events compared to medical therapy alone.

5. A patient with suspected ACS has a 12-lead ECG performed. The presence of ST-segment elevation in leads II, III, and aVF most likely indicates ischemia in which area of the heart?
a. Anterior wall
b. Lateral wall
c. Inferior wall
d. Posterior wall

Answer: c. Inferior wall. Explanation: ST-segment elevations in leads II, III, and aVF are indicative of inferior wall myocardial infarction, as these leads correspond to the inferior portion of the heart, typically supplied by the right coronary artery.

6. In the context of ACS, which of the following is a key difference between unstable angina and myocardial infarction (MI)?
a. Unstable angina results in permanent myocardial damage
b. MI is always associated with chest pain
c. Unstable angina does not typically show significant enzyme elevation
d. MI can be treated with sublingual nitroglycerin

Answer: c. Unstable angina does not typically show significant enzyme elevation. Explanation: Unlike MI, unstable angina does not usually result in significant myocardial necrosis and, therefore, does not typically show elevations in cardiac enzymes such as troponin.

7. A 63-year-old man with ACS is being evaluated for reperfusion therapy. Which of the following factors is most important in choosing between thrombolytic therapy and PCI?
a. The patient's preference for invasive procedures
b. Presence of contraindications to thrombolytic therapy
c. The cost of PCI compared to thrombolytics
d. Availability of a golf course nearby for post-recovery recreation

Answer: b. Presence of contraindications to thrombolytic therapy. Explanation: The choice between thrombolytic therapy and PCI often hinges on the presence of contraindications to thrombolytics (e.g., risk of bleeding, recent surgery) and the availability and timing of PCI.

8. Regarding secondary prevention in patients post-ACS, which of the following interventions has been shown to reduce the risk of recurrent events?
a. Long-term anticoagulation with warfarin
b. Use of prophylactic antibiotics to prevent infective endocarditis
c. Implementation of a strict low-fat diet alone
d. Initiation of statin therapy

Answer: d. Initiation of statin therapy. Explanation: Statins are a cornerstone of secondary prevention in patients post-ACS due to their ability to lower cholesterol levels and exert pleiotropic effects, such as improving endothelial function and reducing inflammation, which collectively reduce the risk of recurrent cardiovascular events.

9. In a patient with ACS, which imaging modality is most useful for assessing left ventricular function and detecting potential complications like ventricular septal rupture or papillary muscle rupture?
a. Chest X-ray
b. Transthoracic echocardiography (TTE)
c. Coronary angiography
d. Multislice CT angiography

Answer: b. Transthoracic echocardiography (TTE). Explanation: TTE is invaluable for evaluating left ventricular function, wall motion abnormalities, and complications of MI, such as ventricular septal rupture or papillary muscle rupture, providing essential information for guiding management.

10. A patient with a history of ACS is being considered for beta-blocker therapy. Which of the following patient characteristics would necessitate caution or an alternative treatment approach?
a. History of hypertension
b. Asthma with recurrent bronchospasms
c. Previous PCI

d. Elevated LDL cholesterol levels

Answer: b. Asthma with recurrent bronchospasms. Explanation: Beta-blockers can exacerbate bronchospasm and should be used with caution or avoided in patients with asthma or reactive airway disease, necessitating the consideration of alternative therapies.

11. A 58-year-old woman with a history of hypertension and hyperlipidemia presents to the emergency department with crushing chest pain radiating to her left jaw and arm. The pain began at rest 30 minutes prior to arrival and has remained unremitting. On initial EKG, there is sinus tachycardia at 110 bpm and ST-segment depression in leads V1-V4. Troponin levels are elevated at 0.4 ng/mL (reference range <0.1 ng/mL). Based on this presentation, which of the following is the MOST likely initial diagnosis?
a. Stable angina pectoris
b. Pericarditis
c. Non-ST-segment elevation myocardial infarction (NSTEMI)
d. Pulmonary embolism

Answer: c. Non-ST-segment elevation myocardial infarction (NSTEMI). Explanation: While the patient's presentation is consistent with angina, the unremitting nature of the chest pain for over 30 minutes at rest, coupled with EKG findings of ST-segment depression and elevated troponin levels, suggests a higher likelihood of NSTEMI. Stable angina typically presents with chest pain that is provoked by exertion and relieved with rest. Pericarditis can cause chest pain, but it's often pleuritic (sharp, stabbing) and may improve with leaning forward. Pulmonary embolism can cause chest pain, but it's often accompanied by dyspnea (shortness of breath) and less likely to be associated with ST-segment depression.

12. A 72-year-old man with a history of diabetes and chronic kidney disease (CKD) is admitted to the hospital for acute heart failure exacerbation. His EKG shows sinus rhythm with T-wave inversions in leads V1-V4 and a QRS duration of 0.12 seconds. He denies any history of chest pain. Troponin levels are mildly elevated at 0.2 ng/mL. The EKG findings of T-wave inversions in leads V1-V4 are concerning for ischemia in this patient. However, there is no ST-segment depression. How should these findings be interpreted in the context of his presentation?
a. These findings are likely due to old ischemia and do not necessarily indicate an acute coronary event.
b. The T-wave inversions combined with the elevated troponin definitively diagnose NSTEMI.
c. The EKG findings are non-specific and require further investigation with cardiac imaging.
d. The QRS duration prolongation suggests a left bundle branch block, making interpretation of ischemia by EKG unreliable.

Answer: a. These findings are likely due to old ischemia and do not necessarily indicate an acute coronary event. Explanation: In patients with underlying conditions like diabetes and CKD, EKG findings like T-wave inversions can be due to chronic ischemia or cardiomyopathy rather than necessarily reflecting an acute event. The absence of ST-segment depression and a relatively low troponin level argue against an NSTEMI diagnosis in this case. However, the EKG findings do suggest a need for further investigation to assess for underlying coronary artery disease.

13. A 42-year-old woman presents to the emergency department complaining of sharp epigastric pain radiating to her back. She also reports nausea and vomiting. Her EKG shows sinus tachycardia with ST-segment elevation in leads I and aVL. Troponin levels are initially negative. While the EKG findings suggest possible acute coronary syndrome (ACS), this patient's presentation is more typical of another condition. What is the MOST likely alternative diagnosis?
a. Aortic dissection
b. NSTEMI
c. Esophageal rupture
d. Pulmonary embolism

Answer: a. Aortic dissection. Explanation: ST-segment elevation in leads I and aVL can be a sign of ACS, but the patient's young age and atypical presentation with sharp epigastric pain radiating to the back are more suggestive of aortic dissection. Aortic dissection is a life-threatening emergency that requires immediate diagnosis and intervention. While further workup is needed to confirm the diagnosis (chest x-ray, aortography), the clinical suspicion should be high based on the presentation and EKG.

14. In evaluating a patient with suspected STEMI, which EKG change is considered pathognomonic for myocardial infarction?
a. Peaked T waves
b. ST-segment depression
c. Pathological Q waves
d. Biphasic T waves

Answer: c. Pathological Q waves. Explanation: Pathological Q waves indicate necrosis and are a key diagnostic criterion for myocardial infarction, particularly in the context of STEMI. Peaked T waves are more indicative of hyperkalemia, ST-segment depression suggests ischemia but not necessarily infarction, and biphasic T waves can be seen in various cardiac and non-cardiac conditions.

15. During a STEMI, reciprocal changes on an EKG are most often observed in leads:
a. I and aVL.
b. II, III, and aVF.
c. V1 to V4.
d. Opposite to the leads showing ST elevation.

Answer: d. Opposite to the leads showing ST elevation. Explanation: Reciprocal changes, or mirror image changes, occur opposite to the area of injury. For example, if ST elevation is seen in the anterior leads (V1-V4), reciprocal changes might be observed in the inferior or posterior leads.

16. A patient with STEMI has ST-segment elevation in leads II, III, and aVF. Which coronary artery is most likely involved?
a. Left anterior descending (LAD) artery
b. Right coronary artery (RCA)
c. Left circumflex (LCx) artery
d. Left main coronary artery

Answer: b. Right coronary artery (RCA). Explanation: ST-segment elevation in leads II, III, and aVF is indicative of an inferior wall MI, which is most commonly due to occlusion of the RCA.

17. After administering thrombolytic therapy to a STEMI patient, the most critical immediate complication to monitor for is:
a. Reperfusion arrhythmia
b. Hypertension
c. Hemorrhagic stroke
d. Allergic reaction to the medication

Answer: c. Hemorrhagic stroke. Explanation: While reperfusion arrhythmias are common and generally transient, the most severe and life-threatening immediate complication post-thrombolysis is hemorrhagic stroke, especially given the systemic fibrinolytic state induced by the therapy.

18. In the context of a STEMI, the "door-to-balloon time" benchmark set by the American Heart Association is:
a. 30 minutes
b. 60 minutes
c. 90 minutes
d. 120 minutes

Answer: c. 90 minutes. Explanation: The American Heart Association recommends a door-to-balloon time of 90 minutes or less for patients undergoing primary percutaneous coronary intervention (PCI) after presenting with a STEMI, as faster revascularization is associated with better outcomes.

19. The presence of ST-segment elevation in V1-V3 with an accompanying right bundle branch block suggests involvement of the:
a. Inferior wall
b. Anterior wall
c. Lateral wall
d. Posterior wall

Answer: b. Anterior wall. Explanation: ST-segment elevation in leads V1-V3 indicates anterior wall involvement, and when associated with a right bundle branch block, it suggests a significant blockage in the left anterior descending (LAD) artery, affecting the septal and anterior wall of the left ventricle.

20. A patient presenting with STEMI and hypotension should be evaluated for all the following complications except:
a. Acute mitral regurgitation
b. Ventricular septal rupture
c. Pericarditis

d. Right ventricular infarction


Answer: c. Pericarditis. Explanation: While pericarditis can occur post-MI, it is not typically associated with acute hypotension in the setting of STEMI. Hypotension is more indicative of mechanical complications such as acute mitral regurgitation, ventricular septal rupture, or right ventricular infarction.


21. For a patient experiencing a STEMI, early administration of which medication is not typically recommended due to potential for increased bleeding risk with subsequent PCI?
a. Aspirin
b. Clopidogrel
c. Intravenous nitroglycerin
d. Morphine


Answer: b. Clopidogrel. Explanation: While clopidogrel is an important antiplatelet agent in the management of STEMI, its early administration before confirming the need for PCI may increase the bleeding risk, especially if surgery is required. Aspirin, nitroglycerin, and morphine are generally safe and recommended in the acute management of STEMI.


22. A "hyperacute T wave" in the context of STEMI is characterized by:
a. T wave inversion
b. Peaked T waves
c. Flattened T waves
d. Biphasic T waves


Answer: b. Peaked T waves. Explanation: In the very early stages of STEMI, hyperacute T waves are observed, which are characterized by their tall, peaked appearance. This is one of the earliest ECG changes in acute MI and precedes ST-segment elevation.


23. When considering reperfusion therapy for STEMI, contraindications include all of the following except:
a. Recent major surgery
b. A history of ischemic stroke within the past 3 months
c. Uncontrolled hypertension on presentation
d. Well-controlled diabetes


Answer: d. Well-controlled diabetes. Explanation: Well-controlled diabetes is not a contraindication to reperfusion therapy in the setting of STEMI. Contraindications typically include factors that increase the risk of bleeding or hemorrhagic transformation, such as recent major surgery, a history of stroke within 3 months, or uncontrolled hypertension at presentation. A 70-year-old man with a history of hypertension and coronary artery disease (CAD) presents to the clinic for a follow-up appointment. He complains of worsening fatigue and shortness of breath on exertion. Physical exam reveals bibasilar crackles on lung auscultation. Transthoracic echocardiogram (TTE) demonstrates an LVEF (Left Ventricular Ejection Fraction) of 45%, with normal wall thickness but impaired relaxation of the left ventricle. This patient's presentation and TTE findings are most consistent with which type of heart failure?

a. Systolic heart failure with reduced LVEF
b. Diastolic heart failure with preserved LVEF
c. Bi-ventricular heart failure
d. Right-sided heart failure


Answer: b. Diastolic heart failure with preserved LVEF. Explanation: This scenario highlights a key concept: Heart failure can occur even with a preserved LVEF. The patient's symptoms (fatigue, shortness of breath) and impaired LV relaxation on TTE suggest diastolic dysfunction. In diastolic heart failure, the ventricle has difficulty filling with blood during diastole (relaxation phase) despite a seemingly normal LVEF, which reflects systolic contractility.


24. A 45-year-old woman with a history of type 1 diabetes mellitus presents with acute pulmonary edema following a myocardial infarction (MI). Her EKG shows ST-segment elevation in leads V1-V3. TTE demonstrates an LVEF of 20% and diffuse akinesis (lack of movement) of the anterior left ventricular wall. This patient's presentation and TTE findings indicate heart failure. Which principle is MOST important when interpreting LVEF in the context of acute MI?
a. LVEF is a direct measure of myocardial blood flow.
b. LVEF can be transiently depressed following an MI due to stunned myocardium.
c. A low LVEF definitively indicates irreversible heart muscle damage.
d. Medications to improve LVEF should be initiated immediately.


Answer: b. LVEF can be transiently depressed following an MI due to stunned myocardium. Explanation: Myocardial stunning refers to temporary dysfunction of viable heart muscle after an ischemic event (like an MI). While a low LVEF on TTE suggests heart failure, it's crucial to consider the context. In this case, the recent MI explains the LVEF depression. Over time, with reperfusion and recovery, the LVEF might improve. Early intervention focuses on managing the acute MI and preventing further complications.


25. A 65-year-old man with a long history of uncontrolled hypertension is admitted for heart failure exacerbation. He has a jugular venous distention (JVD) and peripheral edema. TTE shows an LVEF of 50%, but with a markedly increased E/A ratio (early diastolic filling velocity to late diastolic filling velocity). The E/A ratio is an important Doppler echocardiography measurement used to assess diastolic function. How does an increased E/A ratio relate to diastolic dysfunction?
a. An E/A ratio > 2 suggests normal diastolic function.
b. In early diastolic dysfunction, the E/A ratio might be normal or mildly elevated.
c. A restrictive filling pattern is characterized by a very high E/A ratio (>2) and impaired A wave.
d. Doppler cannot differentiate between systolic and diastolic dysfunction.


Answer: c. A restrictive filling pattern is characterized by a very high E/A ratio (>2) and impaired A wave. Explanation: The E/A ratio reflects diastolic filling dynamics. In normal filling, the E wave (early filling) is slightly lower than or equal to the A wave (late filling). With diastolic dysfunction, the E/A ratio increases. A very high E/A ratio (>2) along with a decreased or absent A wave suggests a restrictive filling pattern, which is a specific type of diastolic dysfunction often caused by conditions like amyloidosis or pericardial constriction.

26. A 68-year-old male presents with shortness of breath and fatigue. His vital signs are: BP 110/70, HR 120, RR 24, SpO2 92% on room air. ECG shows atrial fibrillation with a rapid ventricular response. Which of the following is the most appropriate initial intervention?
a. administer intravenous digoxin
b. perform synchronized cardioversion
c. initiate amiodarone infusion
d. start diltiazem drip

Answer: b. perform synchronized cardioversion. Explanation: The patient is exhibiting signs of hemodynamic instability (tachycardia, hypoxia) in the setting of atrial fibrillation with rapid ventricular response. In this case, the most appropriate initial intervention is synchronized cardioversion to quickly restore sinus rhythm. Intravenous rate control agents like diltiazem or digoxin may be considered if the patient was stable, but cardioversion takes priority in unstable patients. Amiodarone is an option for pharmacologic cardioversion but is typically reserved for stable patients or after initial electrical cardioversion.

27. A 55-year-old female is admitted with acute onset chest pain. ECG shows ST-segment elevation in leads II, III, and aVF, consistent with an inferior wall STEMI. Which of the following arteries is most likely occluded?
a. left anterior descending (LAD)
b. left circumflex (LCX)
c. right coronary artery (RCA)
d. posterior descending artery (PDA)

Answer: c. right coronary artery (RCA). Explanation: In an inferior wall STEMI, the culprit lesion is typically found in the right coronary artery (RCA) or its branches. The RCA supplies the inferior wall of the left ventricle, so occlusion of this vessel results in ST-segment elevation in the inferior leads (II, III, aVF). The left anterior descending (LAD) artery supplies the anterior wall and septum, while the left circumflex (LCX) supplies the lateral wall. The posterior descending artery (PDA) is a branch of the RCA or LCX, depending on coronary dominance.

28. A hemodynamically stable patient is being treated for acute decompensated heart failure. Despite optimal medical therapy, the patient remains volume overloaded with persistent dyspnea. Pulmonary artery catheterization reveals the following: PA 60/30 mmHg, PCWP 28 mmHg, CO 3.5 L/min. What is the most appropriate next step in management?
a. start inotropic support with milrinone
b. initiate ultrafiltration
c. administer intravenous nitroglycerin
d. perform endotracheal intubation

Answer: b. initiate ultrafiltration. Explanation: The patient's clinical presentation and hemodynamic data suggest volume overload refractory to medical management. The pulmonary capillary wedge pressure (PCWP) of 28 mmHg indicates elevated left ventricular filling pressures, while the low cardiac output (CO) of 3.5 L/min suggests poor forward flow. In this setting, ultrafiltration can be used to remove excess fluid and improve hemodynamics. Inotropic support with milrinone may be considered if the patient remains hypotensive or shows signs of end-organ dysfunction. Intravenous nitroglycerin is a vasodilator that can reduce preload and afterload but may not be as effective for significant volume overload. Endotracheal intubation is not indicated based on the information provided, as the patient is hemodynamically stable and there is no mention of respiratory failure.

29. A 72-year-old male with a history of hypertension and diabetes presents with chest pain and shortness of breath. ECG shows sinus tachycardia with diffuse ST-segment depressions and deep T-wave inversions in the precordial leads. Troponin is elevated at 2.5 ng/mL. What is the most likely diagnosis?
a. unstable angina
b. takotsubo cardiomyopathy
c. non-ST-elevation myocardial infarction (NSTEMI)
d. pulmonary embolism

Answer: c. non-ST-elevation myocardial infarction (NSTEMI). Explanation: The patient's presentation is consistent with an acute coronary syndrome (ACS). The ECG findings of diffuse ST-segment depressions and deep T-wave inversions, along with the elevated troponin, suggest a non-ST-elevation myocardial infarction (NSTEMI). Unstable angina is a type of ACS characterized by chest pain at rest or with minimal exertion, but without significant troponin elevation. Takotsubo cardiomyopathy (also known as stress-induced cardiomyopathy) can mimic ACS but is typically associated with a stressful trigger and shows characteristic apical ballooning on echocardiography. Pulmonary embolism can cause chest pain and dyspnea but would not typically produce the described ECG changes or troponin elevation.

30. A 60-year-old female with a history of atrial fibrillation and chronic heart failure presents with worsening dyspnea and fatigue. ECG shows atrial fibrillation with a ventricular rate of 110 bpm. Echocardiogram reveals an ejection fraction of 30% with moderate mitral regurgitation. Which of the following medications is most likely to improve this patient's symptoms and outcomes?
a. digoxin
b. verapamil
c. sacubitril/valsartan
d. spironolactone

Answer: c. sacubitril/valsartan. Explanation: The patient has chronic heart failure with reduced ejection fraction (HFrEF) and concomitant atrial fibrillation. Sacubitril/valsartan, an angiotensin receptor-neprilysin inhibitor (ARNI), has been shown to reduce morbidity and mortality in patients with HFrEF when compared to traditional ACE inhibitors or ARBs. It works by inhibiting neprilysin, which breaks down natriuretic peptides, and blocking the angiotensin II receptor, leading to vasodilation and reduced neurohormonal activation. While digoxin and verapamil can help control ventricular rate in atrial fibrillation, they do not provide the same mortality benefit as sacubitril/valsartan in HFrEF. Spironolactone, a mineralocorticoid receptor antagonist (MRA), is indicated for HFrEF but is typically used as an adjunct to other guideline-directed medical therapies (GDMTs) like ARNIs, ACE inhibitors, or ARBs.

31. A 58-year-old male with a history of coronary artery disease and a previous myocardial infarction presents with palpitations and lightheadedness. ECG shows sustained ventricular tachycardia at a rate of 180 bpm. The patient is alert and oriented but hypotensive with a blood pressure of 80/50 mmHg. What is the most appropriate initial management?
a. administer intravenous amiodarone
b. perform synchronized cardioversion

c. give intravenous adenosine
d. initiate transcutaneous pacing

Answer: b. perform synchronized cardioversion. Explanation: The patient is presenting with hemodynamically unstable ventricular tachycardia (VT) as evidenced by the hypotension. In this setting, the most appropriate initial management is synchronized cardioversion to quickly restore sinus rhythm and improve hemodynamics. Intravenous amiodarone can be considered for stable VT or as an adjunct after cardioversion, but electrical therapy takes priority in unstable patients. Adenosine is used for supraventricular tachycardias (SVTs) like atrioventricular nodal reentrant tachycardia (AVNRT) or atrioventricular reentrant tachycardia (AVRT) but is not effective for VT. Transcutaneous pacing may be indicated for symptomatic bradycardia or complete heart block but is not the initial treatment for VT.

32. A 65-year-old female with a history of hypertension and hyperlipidemia presents with sudden-onset chest pain radiating to the back. She appears pale and diaphoretic. Vital signs are: BP 180/100, HR 110, RR 24, SpO2 94% on room air. ECG shows sinus tachycardia with nonspecific ST-T wave changes. What is the most likely diagnosis?
a. acute pericarditis
b. aortic dissection
c. pulmonary embolism
d. pneumothorax

Answer: b. aortic dissection. Explanation: The patient's presentation is concerning for an acute aortic dissection. The sudden-onset, tearing chest pain radiating to the back, along with hypertension and signs of hemodynamic instability (tachycardia, pallor, diaphoresis), is highly suggestive of this diagnosis. ECG changes in aortic dissection are often nonspecific and may include sinus tachycardia or ST-T wave changes. Acute pericarditis typically presents with positional chest pain that improves with leaning forward and is associated with diffuse ST-segment elevation on ECG. Pulmonary embolism can cause chest pain, dyspnea, and tachycardia but would not usually produce severe hypertension or pain radiating to the back. Pneumothorax may present with sudden chest pain and dyspnea but would typically show decreased breath sounds and hypotension rather than hypertension.

33. A 70-year-old male with a history of congestive heart failure presents with worsening dyspnea and orthopnea. Physical examination reveals jugular venous distention, bilateral crackles, and pitting edema. Chest X-ray shows pulmonary vascular congestion and pleural effusions. Which of the following diuretics is most appropriate for initial management?
a. acetazolamide
b. furosemide
c. hydrochlorothiazide
d. spironolactone

Answer: b. furosemide. Explanation: The patient is presenting with acute decompensated heart failure and volume overload, as evidenced by the jugular venous distention, pulmonary crackles, peripheral edema, and radiographic findings of pulmonary congestion and pleural effusions. In this setting, a loop diuretic like furosemide is the most appropriate initial choice for diuresis and symptomatic relief. Furosemide works by inhibiting the Na+/K+/2Cl- cotransporter in the thick ascending limb of the loop of Henle, leading to increased sodium and water excretion. Acetazolamide is a carbonic anhydrase inhibitor that is sometimes used for diuresis in heart failure but is not as effective as loop diuretics. Hydrochlorothiazide is a thiazide diuretic that is often used for hypertension but has limited efficacy in acute heart failure. Spironolactone is a potassium-sparing diuretic that is indicated for chronic heart failure with reduced ejection fraction but is typically used in combination with a loop diuretic rather than as monotherapy for acute decompensation.

34. A 62-year-old male with a history of atrial fibrillation on warfarin presents with sudden-onset right-sided weakness and aphasia. INR on admission is 2.5. Head CT shows a large left middle cerebral artery (MCA) infarct with midline shift. What is the most appropriate initial management?
a. administer intravenous alteplase (tPA)
b. give prothrombin complex concentrate (PCC) to reverse anticoagulation
c. start heparin infusion
d. perform emergent decompressive craniectomy

Answer: b. give prothrombin complex concentrate (PCC) to reverse anticoagulation. Explanation: The patient is presenting with an acute ischemic stroke while on therapeutic anticoagulation with warfarin. The large MCA infarct with midline shift suggests a significant neurologic deficit and increased risk of hemorrhagic transformation. In this setting, the most appropriate initial management is to reverse the anticoagulant effect of warfarin using prothrombin complex concentrate (PCC) to minimize the risk of hemorrhagic complications. Intravenous alteplase (tPA) is contraindicated in patients on therapeutic anticoagulation due to the increased risk of bleeding. Starting a heparin infusion would exacerbate the bleeding risk and is not indicated in the acute setting. Decompressive craniectomy may be considered for large hemispheric infarcts with significant edema and mass effect, but only after addressing the anticoagulation status and stabilizing the patient.

35. A 75-year-old female with a history of hypertension and diabetes presents with chest pain and shortness of breath. ECG shows ST-segment elevations in leads V1-V4, consistent with an acute anterior wall myocardial infarction. The patient develops cardiogenic shock with a blood pressure of 70/40 mmHg and signs of end-organ hypoperfusion. Echocardiogram reveals an ejection fraction of 25% with severe anterior and apical hypokinesis. What is the most appropriate next step in management?
a. administer intravenous dopamine
b. insert an intra-aortic balloon pump (IABP)
c. initiate venoarterial extracorporeal membrane oxygenation (VA-ECMO)
d. place an Impella device for left ventricular unloading

Answer: d. place an Impella device for left ventricular unloading. Explanation: The patient is presenting with cardiogenic shock complicating an acute anterior wall myocardial infarction. The ECG findings and echocardiogram suggest a large area of myocardial dysfunction leading to pump failure and hemodynamic instability. In this setting, the most appropriate next step is to provide mechanical circulatory support to unload the left ventricle and maintain end-organ perfusion. The Impella device is a percutaneous left ventricular assist device that can be rapidly inserted and provides up to 5 L/min of forward flow, making it an ideal choice for acute cardiogenic shock. Intravenous dopamine is a vasoactive medication that can increase cardiac output and blood pressure but does not directly unload the left ventricle and may increase myocardial oxygen demand. Intra-aortic balloon pump (IABP) counterpulsation can provide some left ventricular unloading and augment coronary perfusion but typically only adds 0.5-1 L/min of cardiac output, which may not be sufficient in severe cardiogenic shock. Venoarterial extracorporeal membrane oxygenation (VA-ECMO) can provide full cardiopulmonary support but is more invasive and associated with higher complications rates compared to the Impella device in this setting.

36. A 68-year-old man with a history of hypertension and atrial fibrillation presents to the clinic for a follow-up appointment. He complains of mild shortness of breath on exertion (climbing stairs) but denies any chest pain, leg swelling, or difficulty lying flat. On physical exam, his vital signs are stable, and lung auscultation is clear. This patient's symptoms are most consistent with which NYHA (New York Heart Association) functional class?
a. NYHA Class I: No limitation of physical activity
b. NYHA Class II: Slight limitation of physical activity
c. NYHA Class III: Marked limitation of physical activity
d. NYHA Class IV: Inability to perform any physical activity

Answer: b. NYHA Class II: Slight limitation of physical activity. Explanation: The NYHA classification system is a widely used tool for staging heart failure based on functional limitations. This patient's ability to perform daily activities with some limitation upon exertion aligns with NYHA Class II. Class I describes no limitations, Class III denotes significant limitation, and Class IV refers to inability to perform any physical activity without symptoms.

37. A 55-year-old woman with a history of obesity and poorly controlled diabetes is admitted to the hospital for acute heart failure decompensation. She presents with shortness of breath at rest, jugular venous distention, and bibasilar crackles on lung auscultation. An echocardiogram reveals an LVEF (Left Ventricular Ejection Fraction) of 30% and moderate mitral regurgitation. In addition to NYHA classification, the ACC/AHA (American College of Cardiology/American Heart Association) staging system offers a more prognostic evaluation of heart failure. Which stage is most likely for this patient?
a. Stage A: High risk for developing heart failure
b. Stage B: Structural heart disease present but without symptoms
c. Stage C: Symptomatic heart failure with preserved LVEF
d. Stage D: Advanced heart failure with repeated hospitalizations

Answer: d. Stage D: Advanced heart failure with repeated hospitalizations. Explanation: The ACC/AHA staging system classifies heart failure based on structural abnormalities, symptoms, and response to treatment. This patient's presentation with severe symptoms, LVEF dysfunction, and likely requirement for hospitalization aligns with Stage D, indicating advanced heart failure. Stage A refers to high risk but no symptoms, Stage B describes structural abnormalities without symptoms, and Stage C encompasses symptomatic heart failure but with preserved LVEF.

38. A 42-year-old woman with a history of mitral valve prolapse presents to the clinic for a follow-up appointment. She complains of increasing fatigue and occasional palpitations, but denies chest pain or shortness of breath. On physical exam, a low-pitched, rumbling holosystolic murmur is best heard at the apex and radiates to the axilla. EKG reveals sinus rhythm with occasional premature atrial contractions (PACs). This patient's presentation is consistent with mitral regurgitation. However, she does not report shortness of breath, a common symptom. What principle is important to consider in interpreting symptoms of mitral regurgitation?
a. Mitral regurgitation severity always correlates with the degree of symptoms.
b. Fatigue can be an early symptom of mitral regurgitation, even before dyspnea develops.
c. Atrial fibrillation is a more specific symptom of mitral regurgitation than fatigue.
d. The presence of PACs on EKG suggests a low likelihood of mitral regurgitation being the cause of her symptoms.

Answer: b. Fatigue can be an early symptom of mitral regurgitation, even before dyspnea develops. Explanation: While dyspnea (shortness of breath) is a hallmark symptom of advanced mitral regurgitation, fatigue can be an early indicator, especially with exertion. This can be due to various mechanisms, including subtle volume overload or neurohormonal activation. Other symptoms like palpitations (due to PACs) can also occur. The absence of dyspnea doesn't rule out mitral regurgitation, especially in early stages.

39. A 78-year-old man with a history of hypertension and chronic kidney disease (CKD) is admitted to the hospital for acute heart failure decompensation. He presents with dyspnea at rest, jugular venous distention, and bilateral lower extremity edema. Echocardiogram reveals severe mitral regurgitation with an LVEF (Left Ventricular Ejection Fraction) of 40%. This patient's presentation suggests severe mitral regurgitation with secondary pulmonary edema. Mitral regurgitation can worsen with certain maneuvers. Which physical exam finding would further support the diagnosis of mitral regurgitation?
a. A palpable carotid pulse with a slow upstroke
b. A widened pulse pressure (difference between systolic and diastolic BP)
c. Increased intensity of the holosystolic murmur with squatting or handgrip
d. A palpable fluid wave in the jugular veins

Answer: c. Increased intensity of the holosystolic murmur with squatting or handgrip. Explanation: Squatting or handgrip maneuvers (Valsalva maneuver) can transiently increase intrathoracic pressure. In mitral regurgitation, this can worsen the flow of blood back into the left atrium, leading to an augmentable holosystolic murmur (intensity increases with the maneuver). The other listed findings are less specific for mitral regurgitation.

40. A 35-year-old woman with a history of infective endocarditis (IE) is monitored for potential complications. Six months after successful treatment, she develops a new, low-grade fever and progressive dyspnea on exertion. Echocardiogram demonstrates moderate mitral regurgitation with a vegetation on the posterior mitral leaflet. This scenario highlights a potential complication of infective endocarditis. How does infective endocarditis cause mitral regurgitation?
a. Direct infection of the myocardium weakens the ventricle, leading to functional mitral regurgitation.
b. Inflammation and scarring of the mitral valve leaflets impair their ability to close properly.
c. Infection damages the chordae tendineae (fibrous cords supporting the valve leaflets), leading to flail leaflet syndrome.
d. All of the above mechanisms can contribute to mitral regurgitation following infective endocarditis.

Answer: d. All of the above mechanisms can contribute to mitral regurgitation following infective endocarditis. Explanation: Infective endocarditis can damage various mitral valve structures, leading to regurgitation. The inflammatory process can directly affect the leaflets, preventing proper closure (option b). Damage to the chordae tendineae (option c) can cause a flail leaflet that doesn't close effectively. In some cases, myocardial involvement (option a) can also contribute to functional mitral regurgitation.

41. In a patient with chronic heart failure experiencing acute decompensation, which laboratory finding is most indicative of worsening renal function secondary to reduced cardiac output?
a. Decreased serum sodium
b. Elevated blood urea nitrogen (BUN) and creatinine
c. Decreased liver enzymes
d. Elevated white blood cell count

Answer: b. Elevated blood urea nitrogen (BUN) and creatinine. Explanation: In the setting of heart failure, worsening renal function often manifests as an increase in BUN and creatinine levels, a condition known as cardiorenal syndrome. This occurs due to reduced renal perfusion secondary to low cardiac output.

42. A 55-year-old patient with heart failure presents with nocturnal dyspnea and orthopnea. Which of the following interventions is most appropriate to alleviate these symptoms?
a. Increase diuretic dosage before bedtime
b. Administer a short-acting beta-agonist at night
c. Encourage a high-sodium diet to increase intravascular volume
d. Recommend sleeping without a pillow

Answer: a. Increase diuretic dosage before bedtime. Explanation: Nocturnal dyspnea and orthopnea in heart failure patients are often due to fluid redistribution when lying down. Increasing the diuretic dose can help reduce fluid volume and alleviate these symptoms.

43. For a patient with heart failure and preserved ejection fraction (HFpEF), which therapeutic approach is primarily recommended?
a. High-dose beta-blockers
b. Aggressive fluid replacement
c. Management of comorbid conditions and diuretics for fluid overload
d. Immediate referral for heart transplantation

Answer: c. Management of comorbid conditions and diuretics for fluid overload. Explanation: HFpEF management focuses on controlling comorbid conditions such as hypertension and diabetes, and using diuretics to manage symptoms of fluid overload, as there is no definitive treatment to improve ejection fraction in these patients.

44. In assessing a patient with advanced heart failure, which physical exam finding best supports a diagnosis of right-sided heart failure?
a. Pulmonary crackles
b. Jugular venous distension (JVD)
c. Displaced apical impulse
d. Third heart sound (S3 gallop)

Answer: b. Jugular venous distension (JVD). Explanation: JVD is a hallmark sign of right-sided heart failure, indicating increased central venous pressure due to the heart's inability to efficiently pump blood forward through the pulmonary circulation.

45. A heart failure patient is undergoing evaluation for cardiac resynchronization therapy (CRT). Which criterion is not considered when selecting patients for this therapy?
a. Left ventricular ejection fraction (LVEF) ≤ 35%
b. QRS complex duration ≥ 120 ms

c. Presence of a left bundle branch block (LBBB)
d. Acute myocardial infarction within the last month

Answer: d. Acute myocardial infarction within the last month. Explanation: The presence of a recent acute myocardial infarction is not a criterion for CRT. Candidates typically have LVEF ≤ 35%, a widened QRS complex (≥ 120 ms), and often, but not always, LBBB.

46. In heart failure patients, which echocardiographic parameter is most closely associated with diastolic dysfunction?
a. Left ventricular end-diastolic diameter (LVEDD)
b. Ejection fraction (EF)
c. E/A ratio
d. Right ventricular systolic pressure (RVSP)

Answer: c. E/A ratio. Explanation: The E/A ratio, derived from transmitral flow velocities, is an important echocardiographic parameter for assessing diastolic function. An abnormal ratio suggests impaired ventricular filling, which is indicative of diastolic dysfunction.

47. A patient with heart failure is on standard therapy including ACE inhibitors and beta-blockers but continues to have NYHA Class III symptoms. Which medication addition has been shown to reduce hospitalizations in this patient population?
a. Digoxin
b. Ivabradine
c. Amiodarone
d. Atenolol

Answer: b. Ivabradine. Explanation: Ivabradine, a heart rate-reducing agent, has been shown to reduce hospitalizations for patients with symptomatic heart failure (NYHA Class II-III) who are on standard therapy, including ACE inhibitors and beta-blockers, especially when the heart rate remains elevated despite optimal treatment.

48. In the treatment of acute heart failure, which intravenous medication can rapidly reduce preload and afterload, improving symptoms of pulmonary congestion?
a. Dobutamine
b. Nesiritide
c. Sodium nitroprusside
d. Milrinone

Answer: c. Sodium nitroprusside. Explanation: Sodium nitroprusside is a potent vasodilator that effectively reduces both preload and afterload, leading to rapid symptomatic improvement in patients with acute heart failure and pulmonary congestion.

49. Which sign is an early indicator of fluid overload in a patient with heart failure?
a. Weight loss of 2 kg in 24 hours
b. A decrease in jugular venous pressure
c. An increase in daily weight by more than 2-3 pounds
d. Improved exercise tolerance

Answer: c. An increase in daily weight by more than 2-3 pounds. Explanation: A rapid increase in weight over a short period, such as 2-3 pounds in a day, is an early and sensitive indicator of fluid overload in patients with heart failure, reflecting worsening fluid retention.

50. When considering advanced therapies for heart failure, which factor is least likely to influence the decision to proceed with a left ventricular assist device (LVAD) as destination therapy?
a. Age over 75 years
b. Presence of a reversible contraindication to heart transplantation
c. Chronic kidney disease stage 3
d. Refractory NYHA Class IV symptoms

Answer: b. Presence of a reversible contraindication to heart transplantation. Explanation: A reversible contraindication to heart transplantation would not typically influence the decision to use an LVAD as destination therapy, as the contraindication might be resolved, making transplantation a viable option. Age, kidney disease, and refractory symptoms are more critical factors in this decision-making process.

51. In managing a patient with unstable angina, which component of the MONA protocol should be administered with caution due to its potential to mask ischemic pain, thus complicating further assessment?
a. Morphine
b. Oxygen
c. Nitroglycerin
d. Aspirin

Answer: a. Morphine. Explanation: While morphine is used for pain relief in acute coronary syndrome (ACS), it should be administered with caution because it can mask symptoms of ongoing ischemia, making further assessment challenging. Morphine also has vasodilatory effects which can lead to hypotension, necessitating careful monitoring.

52. A 55-year-old presents with chest pain. Initial ECG shows ST-segment elevation. After administering aspirin, what is the next most appropriate step in management according to current guidelines for revascularization?
a. Schedule for elective angiography within the next few weeks
b. Immediate pharmacological thrombolysis, if PCI is not available within 90 minutes
c. Administer a second dose of aspirin and observe
d. Immediate initiation of high-dose statin therapy

Answer: b. Immediate pharmacological thrombolysis, if PCI is not available within 90 minutes. Explanation: For ST-elevation myocardial infarction (STEMI), immediate revascularization is crucial. If percutaneous coronary intervention (PCI) cannot be performed within 90 minutes of diagnosis, pharmacological thrombolysis is recommended as an alternative to quickly restore blood flow.

53. When considering oxygen therapy in the MONA protocol for ACS, current evidence suggests administering supplemental oxygen if SpO2 levels fall below what threshold?
a. 90%
b. 92%
c. 94%
d. 96%

Answer: c. 94%. Explanation: Current guidelines recommend administering supplemental oxygen in ACS only if SpO2 levels fall below 94%, as unnecessary oxygen can lead to increased oxidative stress and potentially adverse outcomes in patients without hypoxemia.

54. In the context of anticoagulation therapy for ACS, which of the following is primarily used to prevent the extension of a coronary thrombus and new thrombus formation?
a. Direct thrombin inhibitors
b. Vitamin K antagonists
c. Antiplatelet agents
d. Low-molecular-weight heparins

Answer: d. Low-molecular-weight heparins. Explanation: Low-molecular-weight heparins (LMWHs) are preferred in the acute management of ACS for their ability to prevent the extension of an existing coronary thrombus and the formation of new thrombi, due to their more predictable anticoagulant effect and better bioavailability compared to unfractionated heparin.

55. Regarding nitroglycerin administration in ACS, what is a significant contraindication that must be evaluated before administration?
a. Recent sildenafil use
b. Hypothyroidism
c. Diabetes mellitus
d. Asthma

Answer: a. Recent sildenafil use. Explanation: Nitroglycerin and phosphodiesterase inhibitors like sildenafil can cause significant vasodilation and severe hypotension if used together. Therefore, patients who have recently used sildenafil (within 24-48 hours) should not be administered nitroglycerin.

56. In the administration of aspirin as part of the MONA protocol, what is the mechanism by which it provides benefit in the setting of ACS?
a. Vasodilation of coronary arteries

b. Reversal of endothelial dysfunction
c. Inhibition of platelet aggregation
d. Stabilization of atherosclerotic plaques

Answer: c. Inhibition of platelet aggregation. Explanation: Aspirin inhibits cyclooxygenase-1 (COX-1) in platelets, leading to a decrease in thromboxane A2 production, a potent promoter of platelet aggregation. This antithrombotic effect is crucial in the management of ACS to prevent further thrombus formation.

57. For a patient with ACS, what is the primary goal of revascularization therapy, such as PCI or CABG?
a. Complete normalization of lipid profiles
b. Immediate cessation of chest pain
c. Restoration of perfusion to ischemic myocardial tissue
d. Long-term modification of cardiac remodeling

Answer: c. Restoration of perfusion to ischemic myocardial tissue. Explanation: The primary goal of revascularization in ACS is to quickly restore blood flow to ischemic myocardial tissue, minimizing infarct size and preserving cardiac function.

58. When considering the use of morphine in ACS management, which of the following is a potential adverse effect that must be monitored?
a. Hyperglycemia
b. Diuresis
c. Respiratory depression
d. Hypertension

Answer: c. Respiratory depression. Explanation: Morphine can cause respiratory depression, which necessitates careful monitoring, especially in patients with compromised respiratory function. Its use should be balanced against its analgesic and anxiolytic benefits in ACS.

59. In the context of ACS, how does nitroglycerin primarily exert its therapeutic effect?
a. By reducing myocardial oxygen demand through preload reduction
b. By increasing heart rate and contractility
c. By direct inotropic effect on the myocardium
d. By irreversible inhibition of platelet aggregation

Answer: a. By reducing myocardial oxygen demand through preload reduction. Explanation: Nitroglycerin dilates venous capacitance vessels, which decreases venous return to the heart (preload) and reduces myocardial wall tension, thereby decreasing myocardial oxygen demand.

60. For a patient presenting with NSTEMI, which anticoagulant strategy is preferred to prevent further thrombus formation while awaiting invasive evaluation?
a. Immediate initiation of vitamin K antagonist therapy
b. Administration of unfractionated heparin or LMWH, guided by risk stratification
c. Sole reliance on dual antiplatelet therapy without anticoagulants
d. Use of direct thrombin inhibitors in all patients regardless of risk

Answer: b. Administration of unfractionated heparin or LMWH, guided by risk stratification. Explanation: In NSTEMI, the use of unfractionated heparin or LMWH is preferred, with the choice and duration guided by the patient's risk stratification and the planned approach for invasive evaluation, ensuring a balance between reducing thrombotic risk and minimizing bleeding risk.

61. A 62-year-old male with a history of hypertension and hyperlipidemia presents to the emergency department with chest pain that has been increasing in frequency and severity over the past week. He reports that the pain now occurs with minimal exertion and sometimes at rest. The pain is described as a heavy, squeezing sensation in the center of his chest that radiates to his left arm. Which of the following is the most appropriate next step in management?
a. administer sublingual nitroglycerin and observe for resolution of symptoms
b. obtain a chest X-ray to evaluate for pulmonary pathology
c. perform a cardiac stress test to assess for inducible ischemia
d. start the patient on high-intensity statin therapy and discharge home

Answer: a. administer sublingual nitroglycerin and observe for resolution of symptoms. Explanation: The patient's presentation is consistent with unstable angina, which is characterized by crescendo angina, new-onset angina, or angina at rest. In this setting, the most appropriate initial management is to administer sublingual nitroglycerin and observe for resolution of symptoms. If the chest pain resolves with nitroglycerin, the patient should be admitted for further evaluation and treatment, which may include antiplatelet therapy, anticoagulation, and coronary angiography. A chest X-ray is not typically indicated in the absence of other symptoms suggestive of pulmonary pathology. While a cardiac stress test can be useful for assessing inducible ischemia in stable patients, it is not the initial test of choice in the acute setting of unstable angina. Starting high-intensity statin therapy is an important component of long-term management for patients with coronary artery disease but does not address the acute symptomatology of unstable angina.

62. A 58-year-old female with a history of diabetes and previous myocardial infarction presents with intermittent chest pain at rest. The pain lasts 10-15 minutes per episode and is not relieved by rest or sublingual nitroglycerin. She denies any recent changes in her medications or activity level. ECG shows T-wave inversions in the inferior leads. Which of the following is the most likely diagnosis?
a. acute pericarditis
b. Prinzmetal's angina
c. unstable angina
d. musculoskeletal chest pain

Answer: c. unstable angina. Explanation: The patient's presentation is consistent with unstable angina, which is defined as chest pain that occurs at rest, lasts more than 10 minutes, and is not relieved by sublingual nitroglycerin. The presence of T-wave inversions on ECG further supports the diagnosis of myocardial ischemia. Acute pericarditis typically presents with positional chest pain that improves with leaning forward and is associated with diffuse ST-segment elevation on ECG. Prinzmetal's angina, also known as vasospastic angina, is caused by coronary artery spasm and often occurs at rest but is usually accompanied by transient ST-segment elevation. Musculoskeletal chest pain is typically described as sharp or pleuritic and is often reproducible with palpation or movement, which is not consistent with the patient's presentation.

63. A 70-year-old male with a history of coronary artery disease and previous coronary artery bypass grafting (CABG) presents with chest pain that has been occurring more frequently over the past month. He reports that the pain now occurs with walking short distances and occasionally at rest. ECG shows ST-segment depressions in the lateral leads. Which of the following medications is most appropriate to add to this patient's regimen?
a. aspirin
b. clopidogrel
c. ticagrelor
d. prasugrel

Answer: c. ticagrelor. Explanation: The patient's presentation is consistent with unstable angina, and the ECG findings of ST-segment depressions suggest active myocardial ischemia. In this setting, the most appropriate medication to add to the patient's regimen is a P2Y12 inhibitor, such as ticagrelor, to provide more potent antiplatelet therapy and reduce the risk of thrombotic events. Ticagrelor has been shown to be superior to clopidogrel in reducing cardiovascular death, myocardial infarction, and stroke in patients with acute coronary syndromes. Aspirin is a cornerstone of antiplatelet therapy for patients with coronary artery disease but is likely already part of this patient's regimen given his history of CABG. Prasugrel is another P2Y12 inhibitor that can be used in patients with acute coronary syndromes, but it is contraindicated in patients with a history of stroke or transient ischemic attack (TIA), which is not mentioned in the case scenario.

64. A 65-year-old female with a history of hypertension and type 2 diabetes presents with new-onset chest pain that occurs with minimal exertion and resolves with rest. The pain is described as a pressure-like sensation in the substernal area. She denies any associated symptoms such as dyspnea, nausea, or diaphoresis. Which of the following risk factors is most strongly associated with the development of unstable angina in this patient?
a. age
b. female gender
c. hypertension
d. diabetes

Answer: d. diabetes. Explanation: While all of the listed risk factors can contribute to the development of unstable angina, diabetes is the most strongly associated with an increased risk of cardiovascular events, including unstable angina. Patients with diabetes have a 2-4 fold increased risk of cardiovascular disease compared to those without diabetes, and this risk is particularly high in women. Diabetes promotes the development of atherosclerosis through multiple mechanisms, including endothelial dysfunction, inflammation, and platelet hyperactivity. Age, female gender, and hypertension are also important risk factors for unstable angina but are not as strongly predictive as diabetes in this patient population.

65. A 72-year-old male with a history of stable angina presents with chest pain that now occurs at rest and lasts for 20-30 minutes per episode. He reports that the pain is similar in character to his usual angina but is more severe and

prolonged. ECG shows ST-segment depressions in the precordial leads. Which of the following is the most appropriate pharmacologic intervention for this patient?
a. sublingual nitroglycerin
b. intravenous morphine
c. oral metoprolol
d. intravenous heparin

Answer: d. intravenous heparin. Explanation: The patient's presentation is consistent with unstable angina, and the prolonged duration of chest pain at rest suggests a high-risk situation that warrants aggressive anticoagulation to prevent thrombotic complications. Intravenous heparin is the most appropriate pharmacologic intervention in this setting, as it provides rapid and effective anticoagulation by enhancing the activity of antithrombin III and inhibiting the formation of fibrin clots. Sublingual nitroglycerin can be used for symptomatic relief of chest pain but does not address the underlying thrombotic process. Intravenous morphine can be used as an adjunctive therapy for pain control and to reduce sympathetic activation but is not the primary intervention for unstable angina. Oral metoprolol is a beta-blocker that can be used for long-term management of stable angina but is not the first-line treatment for acute episodes of unstable angina.

66. A 68-year-old male with a history of coronary artery disease and previous percutaneous coronary intervention (PCI) presents with chest pain that occurs at rest and is not relieved by sublingual nitroglycerin. He reports that the pain has been occurring more frequently over the past few days and is now associated with shortness of breath. ECG shows ST-segment depressions in the anterolateral leads. Which of the following is the most appropriate next step in management?
a. administer intravenous nitroglycerin
b. start a heparin drip and admit to the hospital
c. perform urgent coronary angiography
d. refer for outpatient stress testing

Answer: c. perform urgent coronary angiography. Explanation: The patient's presentation is consistent with unstable angina, and the presence of associated shortness of breath suggests a high-risk situation that warrants urgent evaluation and intervention. In this setting, the most appropriate next step is to perform urgent coronary angiography to assess for significant coronary artery stenosis and guide further management. If a culprit lesion is identified, percutaneous coronary intervention (PCI) can be performed to restore blood flow and relieve symptoms. Intravenous nitroglycerin can be used for symptomatic relief but does not address the underlying pathology. Starting a heparin drip and admitting the patient to the hospital is an important step in management but should be done in conjunction with urgent angiography rather than as a standalone intervention. Outpatient stress testing is not appropriate in the setting of acute, high-risk unstable angina and should be deferred until the patient is stabilized.

67. A 75-year-old female with a history of hypertension and hyperlipidemia presents with new-onset chest pain that occurs at rest and lasts for several minutes per episode. She reports that the pain is pressure-like in quality and radiates to her left shoulder and jaw. ECG shows T-wave inversions in the inferior leads. Which of the following biomarkers is most useful for diagnosing unstable angina in this patient?
a. troponin I
b. creatine kinase (CK)
c. brain natriuretic peptide (BNP)
d. D-dimer

Answer: a. troponin I. Explanation: Troponin I is the most sensitive and specific biomarker for detecting myocardial injury and is the preferred test for diagnosing unstable angina and other acute coronary syndromes. Troponin is a protein complex that regulates muscle contraction, and the cardiac-specific isoforms (troponin I and troponin T) are released into the bloodstream when myocardial cells are damaged. In unstable angina, troponin levels may be normal or only mildly elevated, but they can help to risk-stratify patients and guide further management. Creatine kinase (CK) is an older biomarker that is less specific for myocardial injury and can be elevated in other conditions such as muscle trauma or inflammation. Brain natriuretic peptide (BNP) is a biomarker of heart failure and is not typically used for diagnosing unstable angina. D-dimer is a fibrin degradation product that is elevated in thromboembolic disorders such as pulmonary embolism or deep vein thrombosis but is not specific for unstable angina.

68. A 60-year-old male with a history of hypertension and hyperlipidemia presents with chest pain that occurs at rest and is relieved by sublingual nitroglycerin. He reports that the pain has been occurring more frequently over the past few weeks and is now associated with shortness of breath and diaphoresis. ECG shows ST-segment depressions in the lateral leads. Which of the following is the most appropriate initial antiplatelet therapy for this patient?
a. aspirin alone
b. clopidogrel alone
c. aspirin plus clopidogrel
d. aspirin plus ticagrelor

Answer: d. aspirin plus ticagrelor. Explanation: The patient's presentation is consistent with unstable angina, and the presence of associated symptoms such as shortness of breath and diaphoresis suggests a high-risk situation that warrants aggressive antiplatelet therapy to prevent thrombotic complications. In this setting, the most appropriate initial antiplatelet regimen is a combination of aspirin and ticagrelor. Aspirin irreversibly inhibits cyclooxygenase-1 (COX-1) and prevents the formation of thromboxane A2, which is a potent platelet activator. Ticagrelor is a reversible P2Y12 receptor antagonist that provides more rapid and effective platelet inhibition compared to clopidogrel. The combination of aspirin and ticagrelor has been shown to reduce the risk of cardiovascular death, myocardial infarction, and stroke in patients with acute coronary syndromes, including unstable angina. Aspirin alone or clopidogrel alone may not provide sufficient platelet inhibition in high-risk patients with unstable angina. The combination of aspirin and clopidogrel is an acceptable alternative if ticagrelor is not available or contraindicated.

69. A 55-year-old female with a history of obesity and family history of premature coronary artery disease presents with chest pain that occurs with minimal exertion and is relieved by rest. She reports that the pain has been occurring more frequently over the past month and is now associated with dyspnea on exertion. ECG shows T-wave flattening in the precordial leads. Which of the following is the most appropriate next step in the diagnostic evaluation of this patient?
a. exercise treadmill test
b. coronary computed tomography angiography (CCTA)
c. stress echocardiography
d. cardiac magnetic resonance imaging (MRI)

Answer: c. stress echocardiography. Explanation: The patient's presentation is consistent with new-onset angina, and the presence of multiple risk factors (obesity, family history of premature coronary artery disease) increases the likelihood of underlying obstructive coronary artery disease. In this setting, the most appropriate next step in the diagnostic evaluation is stress echocardiography. Stress echocardiography combines exercise or pharmacologic stress with echocardiographic imaging to assess for inducible myocardial ischemia and wall motion abnormalities. It has a high sensitivity and specificity for detecting obstructive coronary artery disease and can provide important prognostic information. Exercise treadmill testing alone may not be sufficient in this patient, as the ECG changes are nonspecific and the test has a lower sensitivity in women. Coronary computed tomography angiography (CCTA) is a noninvasive imaging modality that can visualize the coronary arteries and detect obstructive lesions, but it may not be necessary as a first-line test in this patient with a high pretest probability of disease. Cardiac magnetic resonance imaging (MRI) can provide detailed information about myocardial structure and function but is not typically used as an initial diagnostic test for suspected coronary artery disease.

70. A 62-year-old male with a history of type 2 diabetes and previous myocardial infarction presents with chest pain that occurs at rest and is not relieved by sublingual nitroglycerin. He reports that the pain has been occurring more frequently over the past week and is now associated with nausea and diaphoresis. ECG shows ST-segment depressions in the inferior and lateral leads. Which of the following is the most appropriate pharmacologic intervention for this patient?
a. intravenous nitroglycerin
b. intravenous heparin
c. intravenous eptifibatide
d. intravenous alteplase

Answer: b. intravenous heparin. Explanation: The patient's presentation is consistent with unstable angina, and the presence of associated symptoms such as nausea and diaphoresis suggests a high-risk situation that warrants aggressive anticoagulation to prevent thrombotic complications. In this setting, the most appropriate pharmacologic intervention is intravenous heparin. Heparin is an indirect thrombin inhibitor that enhances the activity of antithrombin III and prevents the formation of fibrin clots. It has been shown to reduce the risk of myocardial infarction and death in patients with unstable angina, particularly when used in combination with antiplatelet therapy. Intravenous nitroglycerin can be used for symptomatic relief of chest pain but does not address the underlying thrombotic process. Intravenous eptifibatide is a glycoprotein IIb/IIIa inhibitor that can be used as an adjunctive therapy in high-risk patients with unstable angina, but it is not typically used as a standalone intervention. Intravenous alteplase is a thrombolytic agent that is used for the treatment of acute myocardial infarction with ST-segment elevation but is not indicated for unstable angina.

71. A patient with severe aortic stenosis is most likely to present with which classic triad of symptoms?
a. Fever, Roth spots, Osler nodes
b. Cough, dyspnea, wheezing
c. Angina, syncope, heart failure
d. Palpitations, fatigue, dizziness

Answer: c. Angina, syncope, heart failure. Explanation: The classic triad of symptoms associated with severe aortic stenosis includes angina, syncope, and heart failure. These symptoms reflect the increased cardiac workload and reduced cardiac output resulting from the obstruction of blood flow through the stenotic aortic valve.

72. During auscultation of a patient suspected to have aortic stenosis, where is the best location to hear the crescendo-decrescendo murmur characteristic of this condition?
a. Apex of the heart
b. Right sternal border of the 4th intercostal space

c. Right sternal border of the 2nd intercostal space
d. Left sternal border of the 5th intercostal space

Answer: c. Right sternal border of the 2nd intercostal space. Explanation: The crescendo-decrescendo murmur of aortic stenosis is best heard at the right sternal border of the 2nd intercostal space, as this is closest to the aortic valve where the turbulent flow caused by the stenosis occurs.

73. A 70-year-old male with a history of aortic stenosis complains of sudden onset of dyspnea and orthopnea. Echocardiogram shows a decrease in aortic valve area and increased left ventricular pressure. These findings are indicative of:
a. Progression to critical aortic stenosis
b. Mitral valve prolapse
c. Aortic regurgitation
d. Tricuspid stenosis

Answer: a. Progression to critical aortic stenosis. Explanation: A decrease in aortic valve area and increased left ventricular pressure in a patient with known aortic stenosis suggest progression to critical aortic stenosis, which is causing left ventricular overload and resulting in heart failure symptoms like dyspnea and orthopnea.

74. In aortic stenosis, the ejection click heard during auscultation is caused by:
a. Rapid filling of the ventricles
b. Abrupt halting of mitral valve leaflets
c. Opening of a stenotic aortic valve
d. Closure of the aortic valve

Answer: c. Opening of a stenotic aortic valve. Explanation: The ejection click heard in aortic stenosis is caused by the opening of the calcified, stenotic aortic valve. This sound is typically heard just after the first heart sound (S1) and precedes the crescendo-decrescendo murmur.

75. A patient diagnosed with aortic stenosis has an aortic valve area calculated at 0.8 cm². This measurement classifies the stenosis as:
a. Mild
b. Moderate
c. Severe
d. Critical

Answer: c. Severe. Explanation: An aortic valve area of less than 1.0 cm² is typically considered severe aortic stenosis. This level of stenosis significantly impairs cardiac output and correlates with the onset of symptoms.

76. In patients with aortic stenosis, syncope can occur due to:

a. Excessive preload reduction
b. Vasovagal response
c. Fixed cardiac output during exertion
d. Rapid ventricular filling

Answer: c. Fixed cardiac output during exertion. Explanation: In aortic stenosis, syncope often occurs because the stenotic valve prevents an increase in cardiac output during exertion. The inability to adequately increase blood flow to meet the demands of the body can lead to a drop in cerebral perfusion and syncope.

77. For asymptomatic patients with severe aortic stenosis and preserved left ventricular function, the current guideline for intervention is:
a. Immediate surgical valve replacement
b. Watchful waiting with regular echocardiographic monitoring
c. Initiation of beta-blocker therapy
d. Percutaneous balloon valvotomy

Answer: b. Watchful waiting with regular echocardiographic monitoring. Explanation: Current guidelines recommend watchful waiting with regular monitoring for asymptomatic patients with severe aortic stenosis and preserved left ventricular function, with intervention considered upon the onset of symptoms or changes in cardiac function.

78. The phenomenon of "pulsus parvus et tardus" observed in patients with aortic stenosis is characterized by:
a. High-amplitude, bounding pulses
b. Slow-rising, weak arterial pulse
c. Rapid, double-peaked pulse
d. Irregularly irregular pulse

Answer: b. Slow-rising, weak arterial pulse. Explanation: "Pulsus parvus et tardus" describes the slow-rising and weak arterial pulse characteristic of severe aortic stenosis, due to the obstruction of blood flow out of the heart and the prolonged time it takes to reach peak systole.

79. In evaluating a patient for possible aortic stenosis, which imaging modality provides the most direct assessment of valve anatomy and function?
a. Chest X-ray
b. Transthoracic echocardiography (TTE)
c. Magnetic resonance imaging (MRI)
d. Computed tomography (CT) angiography

Answer: b. Transthoracic echocardiography (TTE). Explanation: TTE is the primary imaging modality for the assessment of valvular heart disease, including aortic stenosis, providing detailed information on valve anatomy, function, and hemodynamic measurements such as gradient and valve area.

80. Calcification of the aortic valve, leading to aortic stenosis, is most commonly associated with:
a. Rheumatic fever
b. Infective endocarditis
c. Age-related degenerative changes
d. Congenital bicuspid aortic valve

Answer: c. Age-related degenerative changes. Explanation: While a congenital bicuspid aortic valve is a well-known cause of aortic stenosis in younger individuals, the most common cause in the elderly is age-related calcific degenerative changes of the valve.

81. A patient with acute decompensated heart failure presents with severe dyspnea and evidence of pulmonary edema on chest X-ray. Which initial management step is most appropriate?
a. High-dose beta-blocker therapy
b. Intravenous diuretics
c. Immediate cardioversion
d. Oral ACE inhibitors initiation

Answer: b. Intravenous diuretics. Explanation: In acute decompensated heart failure with pulmonary edema, rapid administration of intravenous diuretics is essential for reducing preload and relieving pulmonary congestion. High-dose beta-blockers are generally avoided initially due to potential for worsening heart failure, cardioversion is not indicated for heart failure without arrhythmia, and oral ACE inhibitors are part of long-term management rather than immediate relief.

82. In cardiogenic shock, characterized by hypotension and signs of poor perfusion following a myocardial infarction, which inotropic agent is preferred for initial hemodynamic support?
a. Dobutamine
b. Digoxin
c. Amiodarone
d. Diltiazem

Answer: a. Dobutamine. Explanation: Dobutamine is preferred in cardiogenic shock for its positive inotropic effect, enhancing myocardial contractility and improving cardiac output without significantly increasing myocardial oxygen demand. Digoxin is not typically used for acute inotropic support in cardiogenic shock, and amiodarone and diltiazem are primarily antiarrhythmics without significant inotropic effects.

83. For a patient exhibiting signs of acute pulmonary edema, which non-pharmacological intervention is most critical while awaiting further treatment?
a. Supine positioning
b. High-flow oxygen therapy via nasal cannula
c. Application of continuous positive airway pressure (CPAP)
d. Cold extremity compresses

Answer: c. Application of continuous positive airway pressure (CPAP). Explanation: CPAP is highly effective in acute pulmonary edema by reducing preload and afterload, improving oxygenation, and reducing the work of breathing. Supine positioning is contraindicated as it can worsen pulmonary congestion, and while high-flow oxygen therapy is important, it is less critical than CPAP in this context.

84. When selecting an inotropic agent for a patient with cardiogenic shock and a history of atrial fibrillation with rapid ventricular response, which consideration is most important to avoid exacerbating arrhythmias?
a. The agent's chronotropic properties
b. The agent's effect on systemic vascular resistance
c. The agent's renal clearance
d. The agent's bioavailability when administered orally

Answer: a. The agent's chronotropic properties. Explanation: In patients with cardiogenic shock and pre-existing arrhythmias like atrial fibrillation, it's crucial to choose an inotropic agent with minimal chronotropic effects to avoid exacerbating arrhythmias. Agents that significantly increase heart rate can worsen atrial fibrillation and lead to hemodynamic instability.

85. In the context of acute heart failure leading to pulmonary edema, which pathophysiological mechanism primarily contributes to fluid accumulation in the alveolar spaces?
a. Decreased colloid osmotic pressure in the pulmonary capillaries
b. Increased hydrostatic pressure in the pulmonary capillaries
c. Decreased permeability of the alveolar-capillary membrane
d. Increased lymphatic drainage from the pulmonary interstitium

Answer: b. Increased hydrostatic pressure in the pulmonary capillaries. Explanation: The primary mechanism for fluid accumulation in acute pulmonary edema due to heart failure is increased hydrostatic pressure in the pulmonary capillaries, leading to fluid transudation into the alveolar spaces.

86. In managing cardiogenic shock, what is the primary goal of inotropic support?
a. To reduce preload and afterload
b. To enhance myocardial contractility and improve cardiac output
c. To induce peripheral vasodilation and decrease blood pressure
d. To increase renal perfusion and diuresis

Answer: b. To enhance myocardial contractility and improve cardiac output. Explanation: The primary goal of inotropic support in cardiogenic shock is to enhance myocardial contractility, thereby improving cardiac output and ensuring adequate tissue perfusion, which is critical in reversing the shock state.

87. For a patient with acute left ventricular failure presenting with pulmonary edema, which vasodilator is most appropriate for reducing afterload and preload?

a. Sodium nitroprusside
b. Hydralazine
c. Amlodipine
d. Metoprolol

Answer: a. Sodium nitroprusside. Explanation: Sodium nitroprusside is a potent vasodilator that effectively reduces both preload and afterload, making it particularly useful in managing acute pulmonary edema secondary to left ventricular failure. Its rapid onset and ease of titration allow for close hemodynamic control.

88. In the treatment of acute cardiogenic pulmonary edema, why is morphine used cautiously, if at all, in contemporary practice?
a. It can lead to acute respiratory depression
b. It increases the risk of thromboembolism
c. It has a pro-arrhythmic effect
d. It exacerbates left ventricular dysfunction

Answer: a. It can lead to acute respiratory depression. Explanation: Morphine has historically been used in acute pulmonary edema for its venodilatory and anxiolytic effects, but it is used cautiously or avoided in contemporary practice due to the risk of acute respiratory depression and worsening of gas exchange, especially in patients with compromised respiratory function.

89. In the setting of acute pulmonary edema, what is the rationale for using diuretics as a first-line treatment?
a. To increase heart rate and improve cardiac efficiency
b. To decrease blood viscosity and improve microcirculation
c. To reduce intravascular volume and pulmonary capillary hydrostatic pressure
d. To enhance renal perfusion and prevent acute kidney injury

Answer: c. To reduce intravascular volume and pulmonary capillary hydrostatic pressure. Explanation: Diuretics are used as a first-line treatment in acute pulmonary edema to rapidly reduce intravascular volume, thereby decreasing pulmonary capillary hydrostatic pressure and mitigating fluid transudation into the alveoli.

90. Considering a patient in cardiogenic shock with a significant left ventricular outflow tract obstruction, why might certain inotropic agents be contraindicated?
a. They may reduce systemic vascular resistance too significantly
b. They can exacerbate obstruction by increasing contractility
c. They often lead to uncontrolled hypertension
d. They decrease heart rate, worsening shock

Answer: b. They can exacerbate obstruction by increasing contractility. Explanation: In patients with cardiogenic shock and left ventricular outflow tract obstruction, such as seen in hypertrophic obstructive cardiomyopathy, inotropic agents that increase myocardial contractility can exacerbate the outflow tract obstruction, leading to a decrease in cardiac output and worsening of shock.

91. For a patient with suspected infective endocarditis, which of the following is considered a major criterion according to the Modified Duke Criteria?
a. Presence of predisposing heart condition
b. Fever of 38.0°C (100.4°F) or higher
c. Positive blood culture for typical IE organisms from two separate blood cultures
d. Vascular phenomena such as Janeway lesions

Answer: c. Positive blood culture for typical IE organisms from two separate blood cultures. Explanation: According to the Modified Duke Criteria, major criteria for the diagnosis of infective endocarditis include positive blood cultures for organisms typical of infective endocarditis from two separate blood cultures or evidence of endocardial involvement from echocardiography. Predisposing heart conditions, fever, and vascular phenomena like Janeway lesions are considered minor criteria.

92. In the management of infective endocarditis caused by methicillin-sensitive Staphylococcus aureus (MSSA), which antibiotic regimen is preferred?
a. Vancomycin
b. Nafcillin or oxacillin plus gentamicin
c. Ciprofloxacin plus rifampin
d. Metronidazole plus ceftriaxone

Answer: b. Nafcillin or oxacillin plus gentamicin. Explanation: For infective endocarditis caused by MSSA, treatment with a beta-lactam antibiotic such as nafcillin or oxacillin is preferred, often in combination with an aminoglycoside like gentamicin for synergistic effects, especially in the initial phase of treatment.

93. A patient with infective endocarditis presents with sudden onset of dyspnea and a new systolic murmur. Transthoracic echocardiogram reveals vegetations on the mitral valve with severe regurgitation. What is the most likely complication?
a. Acute heart failure due to valvular destruction
b. Pulmonary embolism from septic pulmonary infarcts
c. Myocardial infarction due to coronary embolism
d. Aortic dissection secondary to infective lesions

Answer: a. Acute heart failure due to valvular destruction. Explanation: In patients with infective endocarditis, vegetations on the mitral valve causing severe regurgitation can lead to acute heart failure due to the valvular destruction and resultant volume overload on the left ventricle.

94. During the treatment of infective endocarditis, the primary rationale for obtaining serial blood cultures is to:
a. Monitor for the development of antibiotic resistance
b. Confirm the eradication of the causative organism

c. Identify secondary infections
d. Assess the patient's immune response to infection

Answer: b. Confirm the eradication of the causative organism. Explanation: Serial blood cultures are important in the management of infective endocarditis to confirm that the bloodstream has been cleared of the infective organism, indicating effective antibiotic therapy.

95. In infective endocarditis, which echocardiographic finding is considered diagnostic of vegetation?
a. Mitral valve prolapse
b. Oscillating intracardiac mass on valve or supporting structures
c. Dilated left atrium
d. Pericardial effusion

Answer: b. Oscillating intracardiac mass on valve or supporting structures. Explanation: An oscillating intracardiac mass observed on a valve or its supporting structures on echocardiography is considered diagnostic of vegetation in the context of infective endocarditis.

96. A 45-year-old male with a history of intravenous drug use presents with signs of infective endocarditis. Which organism is most commonly associated with infective endocarditis in intravenous drug users?
a. Streptococcus viridans
b. Staphylococcus aureus
c. Enterococci
d. Coxiella burnetii

Answer: b. Staphylococcus aureus. Explanation: Staphylococcus aureus is the most common causative organism of infective endocarditis in intravenous drug users, often affecting the tricuspid valve.

97. When considering surgical intervention in a patient with infective endocarditis, which of the following indications is generally accepted?
a. Presence of a single small vegetation
b. Stable renal function with no evidence of embolization
c. Heart failure resulting from valvular dysfunction
d. Mild valve regurgitation with no symptoms

Answer: c. Heart failure resulting from valvular dysfunction. Explanation: Surgical intervention in infective endocarditis is typically indicated in cases of heart failure due to valvular dysfunction, uncontrolled infection despite appropriate antibiotic therapy, or prevention of embolic events in the presence of large vegetations.

98. In the context of infective endocarditis, Osler's nodes are indicative of:
a. Microembolic phenomena

b. Immune complex deposition
c. Direct bacterial invasion of the skin
d. Hemorrhagic manifestations

Answer: b. Immune complex deposition. Explanation: Osler's nodes, seen in infective endocarditis, are painful, tender nodules usually found on the fingers or toes and are indicative of immune complex deposition in the small vessels.

99. For a patient with prosthetic valve endocarditis, the recommended antibiotic therapy differs from native valve endocarditis primarily due to:
a. The higher risk of fungal infection
b. The need for longer duration of therapy
c. The increased likelihood of infection with more resistant organisms
d. The requirement for combination anticoagulant therapy

Answer: c. The increased likelihood of infection with more resistant organisms. Explanation: Prosthetic valve endocarditis often involves more resistant organisms, including healthcare-associated and more virulent strains, necessitating a different or more aggressive antibiotic regimen compared to native valve endocarditis.

100. The presence of Janeway lesions in a patient with suspected infective endocarditis suggests:
a. A benign cutaneous manifestation requiring no treatment
b. Evidence of acute kidney injury secondary to embolization
c. Septic embolization and microabscess formation in the skin
d. A hypercoagulable state requiring immediate anticoagulation

Answer: c. Septic embolization and microabscess formation in the skin. Explanation: Janeway lesions are non-tender, erythematous macules typically found on the palms or soles in patients with infective endocarditis and are indicative of septic embolization leading to microabscess formation in the skin.

101. A 45-year-old patient presents with sharp, pleuritic chest pain that improves when sitting up and leaning forward. Which of the following findings is most suggestive of acute pericarditis?
a. Bilateral wheezing on auscultation
b. Jugular venous distension
c. Pericardial friction rub
d. Pulsus paradoxus

Answer: c. Pericardial friction rub. Explanation: A pericardial friction rub, caused by the inflamed layers of the pericardium rubbing against each other, is a hallmark sign of acute pericarditis. It is best heard when the patient is sitting up and leaning forward, aligning with the symptomatic relief described.

102. In a patient diagnosed with pericarditis, which ECG change is typically observed?

a. Peaked T waves
b. ST-segment elevation in all leads
c. Prolonged QT interval
d. Deep Q waves in leads II, III, and aVF

Answer: b. ST-segment elevation in all leads. Explanation: Diffuse ST-segment elevation in all ECG leads is characteristic of acute pericarditis, reflecting widespread inflammation of the pericardium. This finding distinguishes pericarditis from myocardial infarction, where ST elevation is usually localized.

103. A patient with acute pericarditis develops dyspnea and hypotension. Echocardiography shows an echogenic swirling mass in the pericardial space. What is the most likely diagnosis?
a. Constrictive pericarditis
b. Myocardial infarction
c. Pericardial effusion with tamponade
d. Aortic dissection

Answer: c. Pericardial effusion with tamponade. Explanation: The presence of an echogenic swirling mass in the pericardial space on echocardiography, accompanied by symptoms of dyspnea and hypotension, strongly suggests a pericardial effusion with cardiac tamponade, where accumulated fluid compresses the heart, impeding its function.

104. In managing a patient with constrictive pericarditis, which surgical intervention is most effective?
a. Pericardiectomy
b. Coronary artery bypass grafting (CABG)
c. Heart transplantation
d. Mitral valve repair

Answer: a. Pericardiectomy. Explanation: Pericardiectomy, the surgical removal of the constricted pericardium, is the most effective treatment for constrictive pericarditis. This procedure relieves the heart from the constrictive layer, allowing for improved cardiac filling and function.

105. When considering the etiologies of pericarditis, which condition is the most common cause in the developed world?
a. Tuberculosis
b. Viral infection
c. Post-myocardial infarction syndrome
d. Rheumatic heart disease

Answer: b. Viral infection. Explanation: Viral infections are the most common cause of acute pericarditis in the developed world, with Coxsackie virus being one of the frequent viral etiologies.

106. A patient with a history of renal failure undergoing hemodialysis presents with pericarditis. What is the likely pathophysiological mechanism in this case?
a. Viral infection
b. Uremic pericarditis
c. Bacterial infection
d. Post-cardiac injury syndrome

Answer: b. Uremic pericarditis. Explanation: In patients with renal failure, particularly those on hemodialysis, uremic pericarditis is a common complication. It is thought to be due to the accumulation of uremic toxins, leading to pericardial inflammation.

107. In the evaluation of a patient with suspected pericarditis, which laboratory finding is commonly elevated and indicative of inflammation?
a. Hemoglobin
b. Serum potassium
c. C-reactive protein (CRP)
d. Serum sodium

Answer: c. C-reactive protein (CRP). Explanation: C-reactive protein (CRP) is an acute phase reactant that is commonly elevated in inflammatory conditions, including pericarditis, making it a useful marker for the presence and severity of inflammation.

108. Which clinical sign is considered pathognomonic for cardiac tamponade, a severe complication of pericarditis?
a. Kussmaul's sign
b. Beck's triad
c. Cannon A waves
d. Pulsus paradoxus

Answer: d. Pulsus paradoxus. Explanation: Pulsus paradoxus, an exaggerated decrease in systolic blood pressure during inspiration, is considered pathognomonic for cardiac tamponade. It reflects the impaired filling of the right ventricle due to increased intrapericardial pressure.

109. A patient with pericarditis is noted to have a low-voltage ECG and electrical alternans. What is the most likely underlying condition?
a. Atrial fibrillation
b. Large pericardial effusion
c. Left ventricular hypertrophy
d. Pulmonary embolism

Answer: b. Large pericardial effusion. Explanation: Low-voltage ECG and electrical alternans (beat-to-beat variations in QRS complex amplitude) are suggestive of a large pericardial effusion, which can dampen the electrical signals reaching the ECG leads.

110. Following a viral illness, a patient presents with chest pain, fever, and a pericardial friction rub. Which therapeutic approach is most appropriate for viral pericarditis?
a. High-dose corticosteroids
b. NSAIDs and colchicine
c. Immediate pericardiocentesis
d. Broad-spectrum antibiotics

Answer: b. NSAIDs and colchicine. Explanation: The mainstay of treatment for viral pericarditis is anti-inflammatory therapy, typically NSAIDs combined with colchicine, to reduce inflammation and prevent recurrence. Corticosteroids are reserved for severe cases or those refractory to standard treatment, and pericardiocentesis is indicated for significant effusions or tamponade. Antibiotics are not indicated unless there is a specific bacterial cause.

111. A patient presents with a BP of 220/120 mmHg and complains of severe headache and blurred vision. There is no evidence of neurological deficit. This presentation is indicative of:
a. Hypertensive urgency
b. Hypertensive emergency with encephalopathy
c. Stable chronic hypertension
d. White coat hypertension

Answer: a. Hypertensive urgency. Explanation: Hypertensive urgency is characterized by severely elevated blood pressure (usually >180/120 mmHg) without acute end-organ damage. Symptoms like severe headache and blurred vision, in the absence of neurological deficits or other end-organ damage signs, suggest urgency rather than emergency.

112. In the management of hypertensive emergency, the initial goal is to reduce the mean arterial pressure (MAP) by no more than:
a. 10% in the first hour
b. 25% in the first hour
c. 50% in the first 2 hours
d. 75% in the first 24 hours

Answer: b. 25% in the first hour. Explanation: In hypertensive emergencies, the initial goal is usually to reduce MAP by no more than 25% within the first hour to decrease the risk of precipitating ischemic events due to too rapid a decrease in blood pressure.

113. A 55-year-old male with a history of hypertension presents with chest pain, dyspnea, and a BP of 210/115 mmHg. ECG shows signs of left ventricular strain. This scenario is most suggestive of:
a. Acute pulmonary edema secondary to hypertensive emergency

b. Myocardial infarction
c. Aortic dissection
d. Stable angina

Answer: a. Acute pulmonary edema secondary to hypertensive emergency. Explanation: The presentation of chest pain, dyspnea, severe hypertension, and ECG changes indicative of left ventricular strain suggests acute pulmonary edema as a complication of hypertensive emergency, rather than stable cardiac conditions.

114. In distinguishing between hypertensive urgency and emergency, which of the following findings is most indicative of emergency?
a. Severe hypertension (>180/120 mmHg)
b. Presence of severe headache
c. Evidence of acute end-organ damage
d. Refractory hypertension despite oral medication

Answer: c. Evidence of acute end-organ damage. Explanation: The critical distinguishing feature of a hypertensive emergency is the presence of acute end-organ damage, which requires immediate intervention to prevent further deterioration, unlike in hypertensive urgency where there is no immediate organ damage.

115. When considering IV antihypertensive agents for hypertensive emergency, which medication is preferred for acute heart failure with pulmonary edema?
a. Nitroglycerin
b. Sodium nitroprusside
c. Labetalol
d. Hydralazine

Answer: a. Nitroglycerin. Explanation: Nitroglycerin, a potent vasodilator, is particularly useful in managing hypertensive emergencies with acute heart failure and pulmonary edema due to its venodilating properties, which reduce preload and cardiac work.

116. A hypertensive patient with a history of renal insufficiency presents with visual disturbances and a BP of 200/130 mmHg. Fundoscopy reveals papilledema. This presentation is consistent with:
a. Hypertensive retinopathy
b. Diabetic retinopathy
c. Hypertensive urgency
d. Malignant hypertension

Answer: d. Malignant hypertension. Explanation: Malignant hypertension is a severe form of hypertensive emergency characterized by very high blood pressure and signs of acute end-organ damage, such as papilledema in hypertensive retinopathy, indicating increased intracranial pressure.

117. For a patient in hypertensive emergency with aortic dissection, which IV antihypertensive agent is first-line to rapidly control blood pressure?
a. Esmolol
b. Enalaprilat
c. Clonidine
d. Furosemide

Answer: a. Esmolol. Explanation: Esmolol, a short-acting beta-blocker, is preferred in the management of hypertensive emergencies with aortic dissection due to its rapid onset of action and ability to decrease shear forces against the vessel wall by reducing heart rate and contractility.

118. A patient with hypertensive emergency is treated with an appropriate IV antihypertensive. After initial stabilization, what is the next step in management?
a. Immediate discharge with oral antihypertensives
b. Gradual reduction to normal BP over 24-48 hours
c. Maintain IV antihypertensives for at least 72 hours
d. Rapid reduction to normal BP within 2 hours

Answer: b. Gradual reduction to normal BP over 24-48 hours. Explanation: After initial stabilization in a hypertensive emergency, the goal is to gradually reduce blood pressure to a safer level over 24-48 hours to avoid the risk of ischemic complications that can result from too rapid a decrease.

119. In a patient with hypertensive urgency, which of the following is the preferred initial management strategy?
a. Oral administration of fast-acting antihypertensives
b. Immediate initiation of IV antihypertensives
c. Observation and non-pharmacological interventions
d. Urgent referral for surgical intervention

Answer: a. Oral administration of fast-acting antihypertensives. Explanation: In hypertensive urgency, where there is no evidence of acute end-organ damage, the preferred initial management is the oral administration of fast-acting antihypertensives to gradually lower blood pressure over 24-48 hours.

120. In a hypertensive emergency with acute aortic dissection, which intravenous antihypertensive is preferred due to its rapid onset and titratability?
a. Metoprolol
b. Nicardipine
c. Hydrochlorothiazide
d. Atenolol

Answer: b. Nicardipine. Explanation: Nicardipine, a calcium channel blocker, is preferred in hypertensive emergencies like acute aortic dissection due to its rapid onset of action, ease of titration, and effective blood pressure control without significant reflex tachycardia.

121. For a patient with severe pre-eclampsia and hypertension, which IV medication is most appropriate to avoid lowering blood pressure too rapidly?
a. Labetalol
b. Furosemide
c. Enalaprilat
d. Nitroglycerin

Answer: a. Labetalol. Explanation: Labetalol, a combined alpha and beta-blocker, is preferred in severe pre-eclampsia for its effective blood pressure control while minimizing the risk of precipitous blood pressure drops, which can compromise placental perfusion.

122. When managing hypertensive urgency in a patient with chronic kidney disease, why is captopril, an oral agent, a preferred choice?
a. It provides diuretic effects
b. It has a vasodilatory effect that reduces afterload
c. It improves glomerular filtration rate
d. It reduces sympathetic outflow

Answer: b. It has a vasodilatory effect that reduces afterload. Explanation: Captopril, an ACE inhibitor, is preferred in hypertensive urgencies, particularly in patients with chronic kidney disease, due to its vasodilatory effects that reduce afterload and its renal protective properties by reducing intraglomerular pressure.

123. In the setting of acute pulmonary edema with hypertension, why is IV nitroglycerin considered beneficial alongside other antihypertensive agents?
a. It selectively dilates renal arteries
b. It provides positive inotropic effects
c. It reduces preload and afterload
d. It increases peripheral resistance

Answer: c. It reduces preload and afterload. Explanation: IV nitroglycerin is beneficial in acute pulmonary edema with hypertension because it effectively reduces preload (venous return) and afterload (vascular resistance), alleviating cardiac workload and pulmonary congestion.

124. For a patient experiencing hypertensive crisis with bradycardia, which antihypertensive agent should be avoided?
a. Clonidine
b. Nicardipine
c. Hydralazine

d. Labetalol

Answer: d. Labetalol. Explanation: Labetalol, with its beta-blocking properties, may exacerbate bradycardia. In hypertensive crises with bradycardia, agents without negative chronotropic effects, such as nicardipine or hydralazine, are more suitable.

125. In the management of acute ischemic stroke with elevated blood pressure, what is the primary goal when using IV antihypertensives like labetalol?
a. Immediate normalization of blood pressure
b. Gradual reduction to prevent cerebral hypoperfusion
c. Rapid increase in cerebral blood flow
d. Immediate reduction to diastolic blood pressure below 60 mmHg

Answer: b. Gradual reduction to prevent cerebral hypoperfusion. Explanation: In acute ischemic stroke, the goal with IV antihypertensives is a gradual reduction of blood pressure to avoid sudden drops that could lead to cerebral hypoperfusion, potentially exacerbating the ischemic injury.

126. Considering a patient with pheochromocytoma presenting with a hypertensive crisis, why is phentolamine an appropriate choice?
a. It acts as a selective beta-blocker
b. It provides rapid renal clearance
c. It is a direct alpha-adrenergic antagonist
d. It enhances catecholamine uptake

Answer: c. It is a direct alpha-adrenergic antagonist. Explanation: Phentolamine, a direct alpha-adrenergic antagonist, is appropriate for hypertensive crises in pheochromocytoma by counteracting the excessive catecholamine-mediated vasoconstriction typical of this condition.

127. When utilizing clonidine for hypertensive urgency, what is a common side effect that requires patient education?
a. Hyperkalemia
b. Rebound hypertension upon abrupt cessation
c. Tachycardia
d. Diuresis

Answer: b. Rebound hypertension upon abrupt cessation. Explanation: Clonidine, a central alpha-2 agonist, can lead to rebound hypertension if abruptly discontinued. Patients should be educated about the importance of gradual tapering under medical supervision.

128. In treating hypertensive emergencies, why is it critical to avoid excessive reduction of blood pressure within the first 24 hours?

a. To prevent reflex tachycardia
b. To minimize the risk of renal artery stenosis
c. To avoid cerebral, coronary, and renal hypoperfusion
d. To reduce the likelihood of hypernatremia

Answer: c. To avoid cerebral, coronary, and renal hypoperfusion. Explanation: In hypertensive emergencies, excessive reduction of blood pressure can lead to cerebral, coronary, and renal hypoperfusion, potentially resulting in ischemia and organ damage. The goal is a controlled, gradual reduction to safe levels.

129. A 68-year-old patient with chronic obstructive pulmonary disease (COPD) presents with an acute exacerbation. Which clinical finding is most indicative of the need for noninvasive positive pressure ventilation (NIPPV)?
a. Respiratory rate of 22 breaths per minute
b. PaCO2 of 55 mmHg with pH 7.32
c. Oxygen saturation of 94% on room air
d. Mild wheezing on auscultation

Answer: b. PaCO2 of 55 mmHg with pH 7.32. Explanation: The presence of respiratory acidosis (elevated PaCO2 with decreased pH) in a COPD patient during an acute exacerbation is an indication for NIPPV to improve ventilation, decrease the work of breathing, and correct gas exchange abnormalities.

130. In assessing a patient with suspected pulmonary embolism (PE), which diagnostic test is considered the gold standard?
a. Chest X-ray
b. D-dimer assay
c. Computed tomography pulmonary angiography (CTPA)
d. Ventilation-perfusion (V/Q) scan

Answer: c. Computed tomography pulmonary angiography (CTPA). Explanation: CTPA is considered the gold standard for diagnosing pulmonary embolism, as it allows direct visualization of the pulmonary arteries and can identify or exclude the presence of emboli with high sensitivity and specificity.

131. A patient presents with sudden onset of dyspnea, pleuritic chest pain, and hemoptysis. Which of the following is the most likely diagnosis?
a. Acute asthma attack
b. Pneumothorax
c. Pulmonary embolism
d. Bronchitis

Answer: c. Pulmonary embolism. Explanation: The classic triad of symptoms for pulmonary embolism includes sudden onset dyspnea, pleuritic chest pain, and hemoptysis. These symptoms, in combination, are highly suggestive of PE and warrant immediate diagnostic evaluation.

132. In a patient with asthma, which spirometry finding is most characteristic during an exacerbation?
a. Increased forced vital capacity (FVC)
b. Decreased FEV1/FVC ratio
c. Increased peak expiratory flow rate (PEFR)
d. Decreased residual volume

Answer: b. Decreased FEV1/FVC ratio. Explanation: Asthma exacerbation typically leads to airway narrowing, which is reflected by a decrease in the FEV1/FVC ratio on spirometry, indicating obstructive lung disease. This is due to a greater reduction in FEV1 compared to FVC.

133. A patient with a history of smoking presents with a new cough and weight loss. A chest CT shows a 3 cm mass in the upper lobe of the right lung. What is the next best step in management?
a. Immediate lobectomy
b. Bronchoscopy with biopsy
c. Start empirical antibiotics for pneumonia
d. Recommend smoking cessation and repeat imaging in 6 months

Answer: b. Bronchoscopy with biopsy. Explanation: In a patient with a lung mass and risk factors for lung cancer, such as a history of smoking, the next best step is diagnostic evaluation with bronchoscopy and biopsy to obtain tissue for histopathological examination.

134. A patient in the ICU with acute respiratory distress syndrome (ARDS) is on mechanical ventilation. What ventilator strategy is most appropriate to minimize lung injury?
a. High tidal volumes (12 mL/kg) with low PEEP
b. Low tidal volumes (6 mL/kg) with higher PEEP
c. High tidal volumes (10 mL/kg) with high PEEP
d. Low tidal volumes (8 mL/kg) with low PEEP

Answer: b. Low tidal volumes (6 mL/kg) with higher PEEP. Explanation: The lung-protective ventilator strategy for ARDS involves using low tidal volumes (approximately 6 mL/kg of ideal body weight) and higher levels of PEEP to prevent alveolar collapse at end expiration, thereby reducing the risk of ventilator-induced lung injury.

135. In a patient with idiopathic pulmonary fibrosis, which clinical feature on high-resolution CT (HRCT) is most characteristic?
a. Centrilobular nodules
b. Pleural plaques
c. Honeycombing
d. Mediastinal lymphadenopathy

Answer: c. Honeycombing. Explanation: Honeycombing, which consists of clustered cystic air spaces typically at the lung peripheries, is a characteristic HRCT finding in idiopathic pulmonary fibrosis and is indicative of advanced fibrotic changes.

136. A 72-year-old patient with heart failure develops acute respiratory distress. Chest X-ray reveals Kerley B lines and perihilar batwing opacities. These findings are most indicative of:
a. Pulmonary edema due to left heart failure
b. Community-acquired pneumonia
c. Chronic obstructive pulmonary disease (COPD)
d. Pulmonary fibrosis

Answer: a. Pulmonary edema due to left heart failure. Explanation: Kerley B lines and perihilar batwing opacities are radiographic signs of pulmonary edema, commonly seen in acute decompensated heart failure, indicating fluid accumulation in the pulmonary interstitium and alveolar spaces.

137. For a patient with a tension pneumothorax, immediate management should include:
a. High-flow oxygen and observation
b. Needle decompression followed by chest tube placement
c. Broad-spectrum antibiotics
d. Therapeutic thoracentesis

Answer: b. Needle decompression followed by chest tube placement. Explanation: Tension pneumothorax is a life-threatening condition requiring immediate decompression to relieve intrathoracic pressure. Needle decompression in the second intercostal space, midclavicular line, followed by definitive management with chest tube placement, is the standard treatment.

138. A patient diagnosed with sarcoidosis presents with bilateral hilar lymphadenopathy and pulmonary infiltrates. Which systemic manifestation is commonly associated with this condition?
a. Erythema nodosum
b. Keratoconjunctivitis
c. Achalasia
d. Peptic ulcer disease

Answer: a. Erythema nodosum. Explanation: Sarcoidosis is a multisystem granulomatous disorder commonly presenting with pulmonary involvement and lymphadenopathy. Erythema nodosum, a painful inflammatory condition of the subcutaneous fat, is a common extrapulmonary manifestation associated with sarcoidosis.

139. A 58-year-old patient with COPD presents with an acute exacerbation and is found to have a PaO2 of 55 mmHg with a normal PaCO2. Which treatment option is most appropriate to address the primary issue?
a. High-dose corticosteroids
b. Non-rebreather mask at 15 L/min
c. Bi-level Positive Airway Pressure (BiPAP)

d. Nebulized short-acting bronchodilators


Answer: c. Bi-level Positive Airway Pressure (BiPAP). Explanation: In patients with COPD experiencing an acute exacerbation leading to hypoxemic (Type I) respiratory failure, BiPAP can be beneficial by improving oxygenation and reducing the work of breathing without the need for intubation, especially when PaCO2 is normal or low.


140. In the setting of acute respiratory failure, which of the following arterial blood gas findings confirms the presence of Type I (hypoxemic) respiratory failure?
a. PaO2 < 60 mmHg, PaCO2 > 45 mmHg
b. PaO2 < 60 mmHg, PaCO2 within normal limits
c. PaO2 > 80 mmHg, PaCO2 < 35 mmHg
d. PaO2 > 80 mmHg, PaCO2 > 45 mmHg


Answer: b. PaO2 < 60 mmHg, PaCO2 within normal limits. Explanation: Type I (hypoxemic) respiratory failure is characterized by a PaO2 of less than 60 mmHg with a normal or low PaCO2. This distinguishes it from Type II (hypercapnic) respiratory failure, where PaCO2 would be elevated.


141. A patient admitted with pneumonia develops sudden worsening of respiratory status with an increase in oxygen requirements. Chest X-ray reveals new bilateral infiltrates. Which of the following is the most likely cause of the hypoxemia?
a. Pulmonary embolism
b. Acute Respiratory Distress Syndrome (ARDS)
c. Cardiac tamponade
d. Pleural effusion


Answer: b. Acute Respiratory Distress Syndrome (ARDS). Explanation: ARDS is characterized by acute onset, severe hypoxemia, and bilateral pulmonary infiltrates on imaging, not fully explained by cardiac failure or fluid overload, fitting the patient's presentation.


142. In managing a patient with acute respiratory failure and a PaO2 of 55 mmHg on room air, which oxygen delivery system ensures the highest fraction of inspired oxygen (FiO2)?
a. Nasal cannula at 6 L/min
b. Simple face mask at 10 L/min
c. Venturi mask set to deliver 40% oxygen
d. Non-rebreather mask with reservoir bag at 10-15 L/min


Answer: d. Non-rebreather mask with reservoir bag at 10-15 L/min. Explanation: A non-rebreather mask with a reservoir bag can deliver the highest FiO2 (up to 90-100%) among the options listed, making it suitable for severe hypoxemia.

143. A patient with acute respiratory failure exhibits signs of increased work of breathing, cyanosis, and a PaO2 of 58 mmHg despite oxygen therapy. Which immediate intervention is most critical?
a. Intravenous diuretics
b. Endotracheal intubation and mechanical ventilation
c. High-dose inhaled corticosteroids
d. Thoracentesis

Answer: b. Endotracheal intubation and mechanical ventilation. Explanation: In cases of severe acute respiratory failure where conservative measures fail and the patient shows signs of significant distress, endotracheal intubation and mechanical ventilation are critical to ensure adequate oxygenation and ventilation.

144. A patient with Type I respiratory failure is on high-flow nasal cannula therapy but not improving. ABG shows a persistent PaO2 of 55 mmHg. What is the next best step in management?
a. Increase the flow rate of the high-flow nasal cannula
b. Switch to a simple face mask
c. Initiate invasive mechanical ventilation
d. Administer subcutaneous epinephrine

Answer: c. Initiate invasive mechanical ventilation. Explanation: When non-invasive measures such as high-flow nasal cannula fail to improve oxygenation in acute hypoxemic respiratory failure, the next step is often invasive mechanical ventilation to ensure adequate oxygen delivery and reduce the work of breathing.

145. In the treatment of hypoxemic respiratory failure, which mechanism explains the benefit of prone positioning in patients with ARDS?
a. It increases lung compliance by reducing pleural pressure
b. It improves ventilation-perfusion (V/Q) mismatch
c. It enhances cardiac output by reducing intrathoracic pressure
d. It decreases airway resistance by relieving bronchospasm

Answer: b. It improves ventilation-perfusion (V/Q) mismatch. Explanation: Prone positioning in patients with ARDS can improve oxygenation by alleviating ventilation-perfusion mismatch. It redistributes pulmonary perfusion toward better-ventilated lung regions, thereby improving gas exchange.

146. Considering a patient with acute hypoxemic respiratory failure due to pulmonary fibrosis, why might high-dose corticosteroids be considered in management?
a. To reduce airway resistance
b. To increase surfactant production
c. To decrease pulmonary inflammation and fibrosis
d. To stimulate central respiratory drive

Answer: c. To decrease pulmonary inflammation and fibrosis. Explanation: In the context of pulmonary fibrosis leading to acute respiratory failure, corticosteroids may be used to decrease inflammation and slow the progression of fibrosis, although their use remains controversial and should be considered in the context of the individual patient's condition.

147. For a patient presenting with hypoxemic respiratory failure and diffuse alveolar hemorrhage, which therapeutic intervention is most directly aimed at addressing the underlying pathology?
a. Administration of broad-spectrum antibiotics
b. Therapeutic bronchoscopy with lavage
c. Cyclophosphamide or other immunosuppressive therapy
d. Continuous positive airway pressure (CPAP) ventilation

Answer: c. Cyclophosphamide or other immunosuppressive therapy. Explanation: In the case of diffuse alveolar hemorrhage, which can cause hypoxemic respiratory failure, the underlying pathology often involves an autoimmune mechanism or vasculitis. Immunosuppressive therapy, such as cyclophosphamide, is used to control the autoimmune response and prevent further hemorrhage.

148. A 68-year-old male with a history of heart failure with reduced ejection fraction (HFrEF) presents with worsening dyspnea on exertion and bilateral lower extremity edema. His current medications include lisinopril, carvedilol, and furosemide. Which of the following medication changes is most appropriate based on the current guidelines for HFrEF management?
a. discontinue lisinopril and start losartan
b. discontinue carvedilol and start metoprolol succinate
c. discontinue furosemide and start spironolactone
d. add sacubitril/valsartan to the current regimen

Answer: d. add sacubitril/valsartan to the current regimen. Explanation: According to the current guidelines for the management of heart failure with reduced ejection fraction (HFrEF), patients who remain symptomatic despite treatment with an ACE inhibitor, beta-blocker, and diuretic should be considered for the addition of sacubitril/valsartan. Sacubitril/valsartan is an angiotensin receptor-neprilysin inhibitor (ARNI) that has been shown to reduce morbidity and mortality in patients with HFrEF compared to ACE inhibitors alone. Switching from lisinopril to losartan (an angiotensin receptor blocker) or from carvedilol to metoprolol succinate (another beta-blocker) is not likely to provide additional benefit in this patient who is already on optimal doses of these medications. Switching from furosemide to spironolactone (a mineralocorticoid receptor antagonist) may be considered in select patients with HFrEF, but this should be done in addition to, rather than instead of, a loop diuretic like furosemide.

149. A 72-year-old female with a history of hypertension and type 2 diabetes presents with shortness of breath and fatigue. Echocardiography reveals a left ventricular ejection fraction of 35%. Which of the following medications should be initiated first in the management of this patient's heart failure?
a. enalapril
b. metoprolol tartrate
c. spironolactone
d. furosemide

Answer: a. enalapril. Explanation: According to the current guidelines for the management of heart failure with reduced ejection fraction (HFrEF), an ACE inhibitor should be initiated as first-line therapy in all patients with HFrEF, unless contraindicated. ACE inhibitors have been shown to reduce morbidity and mortality in patients with HFrEF by inhibiting the renin-angiotensin-aldosterone system (RAAS) and preventing adverse cardiac remodeling. Enalapril is a commonly used ACE inhibitor that has been extensively studied in patients with HFrEF. Beta-blockers like metoprolol tartrate should be initiated after an ACE inhibitor, as they provide additional mortality benefit by reducing heart rate and myocardial oxygen demand. Spironolactone is a mineralocorticoid receptor antagonist that can be added to an ACE inhibitor and beta-blocker in select patients with HFrEF, but it is not typically used as first-line therapy. Furosemide is a loop diuretic that can be used to manage fluid retention and symptoms of congestion in patients with HFrEF, but it does not address the underlying pathophysiology of the disease and should not be used as monotherapy.

150. A 65-year-old male with a history of heart failure with preserved ejection fraction (HFpEF) presents with increasing dyspnea on exertion and orthopnea. His current medications include amlodipine and furosemide. Which of the following medications is most likely to improve this patient's symptoms and functional capacity?
a. lisinopril
b. carvedilol
c. spironolactone
d. digoxin

Answer: c. spironolactone. Explanation: Heart failure with preserved ejection fraction (HFpEF) is a distinct clinical entity that is characterized by symptoms of heart failure in the setting of a normal or near-normal left ventricular ejection fraction. Unlike heart failure with reduced ejection fraction (HFrEF), there are no specific guideline-directed medical therapies that have been shown to improve outcomes in patients with HFpEF. However, recent studies have suggested that spironolactone, a mineralocorticoid receptor antagonist, may be beneficial in reducing symptoms and improving functional capacity in patients with HFpEF. The TOPCAT trial showed that spironolactone reduced the risk of hospitalization for heart failure in patients with HFpEF, although it did not significantly reduce the risk of cardiovascular death. ACE inhibitors like lisinopril and beta-blockers like carvedilol have not been consistently shown to improve outcomes in patients with HFpEF, although they may be used to manage comorbidities like hypertension and coronary artery disease. Digoxin is not typically used in patients with HFpEF, as it has not been shown to improve symptoms or outcomes in this population.

151. A 58-year-old female with a history of dilated cardiomyopathy and atrial fibrillation presents with palpitations and fatigue. Her current medications include metoprolol succinate, lisinopril, and furosemide. Echocardiography reveals a left ventricular ejection fraction of 30%. Which of the following medications is most appropriate to add to this patient's regimen for rate control of atrial fibrillation?
a. digoxin
b. verapamil
c. amiodarone
d. flecainide

Answer: a. digoxin. Explanation: In patients with heart failure with reduced ejection fraction (HFrEF) and atrial fibrillation, the primary goal of treatment is to control the ventricular rate and prevent tachycardia-induced cardiomyopathy. Beta-blockers like metoprolol succinate are the first-line agents for rate control in these patients, as they have been shown to improve symptoms and reduce mortality in HFrEF. However, in patients who remain symptomatic or have inadequate rate control on beta-blocker therapy, digoxin can be added as a second-line agent. Digoxin works by inhibiting the sodium-potassium ATPase pump in cardiac myocytes, which leads to an increase in intracellular calcium and enhanced contractility. It also has vagotonic effects that can slow conduction through the AV node and reduce the ventricular rate in atrial fibrillation. Verapamil is a non-dihydropyridine calcium channel blocker that can be used for rate control in atrial fibrillation, but it is contraindicated in patients with HFrEF due to its negative inotropic effects. Amiodarone and flecainide are antiarrhythmic agents that can be used for rhythm control in atrial fibrillation, but they are not typically used for rate control and may be proarrhythmic in patients with structural heart disease.

152. A 62-year-old male with a history of heart failure with reduced ejection fraction (HFrEF) presents with increasing dyspnea and orthopnea. His current medications include lisinopril, carvedilol, and furosemide. Physical examination reveals jugular venous distention and bilateral pulmonary crackles. Which of the following is the most appropriate next step in managing this patient's acute decompensation?
a. double the dose of lisinopril
b. switch carvedilol to metoprolol tartrate
c. add spironolactone to the current regimen
d. administer intravenous furosemide

Answer: d. administer intravenous furosemide. Explanation: This patient is presenting with signs and symptoms of acute decompensated heart failure, likely due to volume overload. In this setting, the most appropriate next step is to administer intravenous diuretics, specifically furosemide, to promote natriuresis and diuresis and relieve congestion. Intravenous furosemide has a rapid onset of action and can be titrated to achieve the desired level of diuresis. Doubling the dose of lisinopril or switching carvedilol to metoprolol tartrate is not likely to provide immediate relief of symptoms and may actually worsen hypotension in the setting of acute decompensation. Adding spironolactone to the current regimen may be considered in select patients with HFrEF who remain symptomatic despite optimal doses of an ACE inhibitor, beta-blocker, and diuretic, but it is not the most appropriate choice for managing acute decompensation. In addition to intravenous diuretics, other supportive measures for acute decompensated heart failure may include oxygen therapy, nitrates for preload reduction, and inotropic support if there is evidence of cardiogenic shock.

153. A 55-year-old female with a history of heart failure with reduced ejection fraction (HFrEF) secondary to ischemic cardiomyopathy presents with worsening dyspnea at rest. Her current medications include lisinopril, carvedilol, spironolactone, and furosemide. Vital signs reveal a blood pressure of 80/50 mmHg and a heart rate of 110 beats per minute. Physical examination reveals cool extremities and diminished peripheral pulses. Which of the following is the most appropriate next step in managing this patient's cardiogenic shock?
a. start dobutamine infusion
b. administer intravenous nitroglycerin
c. increase the dose of carvedilol
d. initiate vasopressin infusion

Answer: a. start dobutamine infusion. Explanation: This patient is presenting with signs and symptoms of cardiogenic shock, which is a medical emergency characterized by hypotension, hypoperfusion, and end-organ dysfunction due to a primary cardiac disorder. In this setting, the most appropriate next step is to initiate inotropic support with dobutamine, a synthetic catecholamine that stimulates beta-1 receptors in the heart and increases contractility and cardiac output. Dobutamine is the preferred inotrope for cardiogenic shock due to its relatively selective effects on the heart and its ability to improve systemic perfusion without causing significant vasodilation. Intravenous nitroglycerin is a vasodilator that can be used to reduce preload and afterload in patients with acute decompensated heart failure, but it is contraindicated in patients with cardiogenic shock due to its hypotensive effects. Increasing the dose of carvedilol or initiating vasopressin infusion is not appropriate in this setting, as these interventions may worsen hypotension and further compromise end-organ perfusion. In addition to inotropic support, other management strategies for cardiogenic shock may include mechanical circulatory support (e.g., intra-aortic balloon pump, extracorporeal membrane oxygenation), coronary revascularization if there is evidence of acute myocardial ischemia, and treatment of any precipitating factors (e.g., sepsis, arrhythmias).

154. A 70-year-old male with a history of heart failure with reduced ejection fraction (HFrEF) presents with worsening dyspnea and fatigue. His current medications include lisinopril, carvedilol, and furosemide. Echocardiography reveals a left ventricular ejection fraction of 25% and moderate mitral regurgitation. Which of the following medications should be added to this patient's regimen based on the current guidelines for HFrEF management?
a. hydralazine and isosorbide dinitrate
b. sacubitril/valsartan
c. ivabradine
d. digoxin

Answer: b. sacubitril/valsartan. Explanation: According to the current guidelines for the management of heart failure with reduced ejection fraction (HFrEF), patients who remain symptomatic despite treatment with an ACE inhibitor, beta-blocker, and diuretic should be considered for the addition of sacubitril/valsartan, an angiotensin receptor-neprilysin inhibitor (ARNI). The PARADIGM-HF trial showed that sacubitril/valsartan reduced the risk of cardiovascular death and hospitalization for heart failure compared to enalapril in patients with HFrEF. The combination of hydralazine and isosorbide dinitrate can be considered in African American patients with HFrEF who remain symptomatic despite optimal medical therapy, based on the results of the A-HeFT trial. However, this combination is not typically used as a first-line therapy in all patients with HFrEF. Ivabradine is a selective inhibitor of the hyperpolarization-activated cyclic nucleotide-gated (HCN) channel that can be used to reduce heart rate in patients with HFrEF who remain symptomatic despite optimal medical therapy, but it is not indicated in all patients with HFrEF. Digoxin is an oral inotrope that can be used to improve symptoms and reduce hospitalizations in patients with HFrEF, but it is not considered a first-line therapy and should be used with caution due to its narrow therapeutic window and potential for toxicity.

155. A 65-year-old female with a history of hypertension and type 2 diabetes presents with dyspnea and fatigue. Echocardiography reveals a left ventricular ejection fraction of 40% and mild diastolic dysfunction. Her current medications include amlodipine and metformin. Which of the following is the most appropriate initial therapy for this patient's heart failure with mid-range ejection fraction (HFmrEF)?
a. lisinopril
b. carvedilol
c. spironolactone
d. furosemide

Answer: a. lisinopril. Explanation: Heart failure with mid-range ejection fraction (HFmrEF) is a relatively new clinical entity that is defined by a left ventricular ejection fraction between 40-49% and evidence of diastolic dysfunction. The optimal management of HFmrEF is not well established, but current guidelines recommend treating these patients similarly to those with heart failure with reduced ejection fraction (HFrEF). ACE inhibitors like lisinopril have been shown to reduce morbidity and mortality in patients with HFrEF and are considered first-line therapy for both HFrEF and HFmrEF. Beta-blockers like carvedilol have also been shown to improve outcomes in patients with HFrEF and can be added to ACE inhibitor therapy in patients with HFmrEF. Spironolactone is a mineralocorticoid receptor antagonist that can be considered in select patients with HFrEF who remain symptomatic despite optimal medical therapy, but it is not typically used as initial therapy in patients with HFmrEF. Furosemide is a loop diuretic that can be used to manage fluid retention and symptoms of congestion in patients with heart failure, but it does not address the underlying pathophysiology of the disease and should not be used as monotherapy in patients with HFmrEF.

156. A 60-year-old male with a history of heart failure with reduced ejection fraction (HFrEF) secondary to dilated cardiomyopathy presents with worsening dyspnea and peripheral edema. His current medications include lisinopril, carvedilol, spironolactone, and furosemide. Physical examination reveals jugular venous distention and bilateral lower extremity edema. Serum creatinine is 1.8 mg/dL, up from a baseline of 1.2 mg/dL. Which of the following is the most appropriate adjustment to this patient's diuretic regimen?
a. increase the dose of furosemide
b. switch furosemide to bumetanide
c. add metolazone to the current regimen
d. discontinue spironolactone

Answer: c. add metolazone to the current regimen. Explanation: This patient is presenting with signs and symptoms of volume overload despite being on optimal doses of an ACE inhibitor, beta-blocker, mineralocorticoid receptor antagonist, and loop diuretic. In this setting, the most appropriate adjustment to the diuretic regimen is to add a thiazide diuretic like metolazone to promote sequential nephron blockade and enhance diuresis. The combination of a loop diuretic and a thiazide diuretic has been shown to be more effective than loop diuretics alone in patients with resistant edema. Increasing the dose of furosemide or switching to a more potent loop diuretic like bumetanide may be considered, but these interventions may not be as effective in overcoming diuretic resistance. Discontinuing spironolactone is not appropriate in this setting, as mineralocorticoid receptor antagonists have been shown to reduce morbidity and mortality in patients with HFrEF and should be continued unless there are contraindications (e.g., hyperkalemia, acute kidney injury). However, it is important to monitor renal function and electrolytes closely when adding a thiazide diuretic to a regimen that includes an ACE inhibitor, beta-blocker, and mineralocorticoid receptor antagonist, as there is an increased risk of hypokalemia, hyponatremia, and worsening renal function.

157. In a patient with chronic obstructive pulmonary disease (COPD) experiencing an exacerbation, which ABG finding is most indicative of acute hypercapnic respiratory failure?
a. PaCO2 of 55 mmHg and pH of 7.45
b. PaCO2 of 70 mmHg and pH of 7.25
c. PaO2 of 60 mmHg and PaCO2 of 40 mmHg
d. PaO2 of 80 mmHg and pH of 7.35

Answer: b. PaCO2 of 70 mmHg and pH of 7.25. Explanation: Acute hypercapnic respiratory failure is characterized by an increased PaCO2 (>50 mmHg) with accompanying acidemia (pH <7.35). A PaCO2 of 70 mmHg with a pH of 7.25 clearly indicates respiratory acidosis due to CO2 retention, common in acute COPD exacerbations.

158. In managing acute hypercapnic respiratory failure, which intervention is most effective in reducing PaCO2 levels?
a. High-flow nasal cannula oxygen therapy
b. Noninvasive ventilation (NIV)
c. Intravenous bicarbonate infusion
d. High-dose corticosteroid therapy

Answer: b. Noninvasive ventilation (NIV). Explanation: NIV, especially bilevel positive airway pressure (BiPAP), is effective in reducing PaCO2 levels in patients with hypercapnic respiratory failure by improving alveolar ventilation and reducing the work of breathing.

159. A patient with hypercapnic respiratory failure has a PaCO2 of 65 mmHg. Which clinical sign would most likely accompany this gas exchange abnormality?
a. Digital clubbing
b. Peripheral cyanosis
c. Asterixis
d. Tachypnea

Answer: c. Asterixis. Explanation: Asterixis, a flapping tremor of the hands, can occur in patients with significant hypercapnia and is a sign of CO2 narcosis, which can affect the central nervous system.

160. In the context of hypercapnic respiratory failure, the term "ventilatory failure" refers to:
a. Failure to maintain normal oxygen levels
b. Failure to adequately remove CO2 from the blood
c. Structural failure of the lungs leading to pneumothorax
d. Cardiovascular failure secondary to pulmonary hypertension

Answer: b. Failure to adequately remove CO2 from the blood. Explanation: Ventilatory failure, in the context of hypercapnia, specifically refers to the respiratory system's inability to remove CO2 efficiently, leading to increased PaCO2 levels and respiratory acidosis.

161. Which underlying condition is most commonly associated with chronic hypercapnic respiratory failure?
a. Pulmonary fibrosis
b. Asthma
c. Chronic obstructive pulmonary disease (COPD)
d. Pulmonary arterial hypertension

Answer: c. Chronic obstructive pulmonary disease (COPD). Explanation: COPD is the most common cause of chronic hypercapnic respiratory failure due to the progressive airflow limitation and impaired gas exchange inherent to the disease.

162. When assessing a patient with suspected hypercapnic respiratory failure, which symptom is most indicative of increased CO2 levels?
a. Sharp chest pain on deep inhalation
b. Morning headaches
c. Wheezing during exhalation

d. Sudden onset of leg swelling

Answer: b. Morning headaches. Explanation: Morning headaches are a classic symptom of hypercapnic respiratory failure, likely due to vasodilation from retained CO2 during sleep, leading to cerebral edema and headache.

163. In hypercapnic respiratory failure, which compensatory mechanism is observed in arterial blood gas (ABG) analysis over time?
a. Decreased bicarbonate levels
b. Increased oxygen saturation
c. Increased bicarbonate levels
d. Decreased hemoglobin concentration

Answer: c. Increased bicarbonate levels. Explanation: The kidneys compensate for chronic hypercapnia by retaining bicarbonate, which helps to buffer the excess CO2, leading to an increased bicarbonate level in ABG analysis over time.

164. A patient with severe kyphoscoliosis presents with hypercapnic respiratory failure. The primary mechanism for hypercapnia in this patient is:
a. Alveolar hypoventilation due to chest wall deformity
b. Increased airway resistance
c. Diffusion impairment across the alveolar-capillary membrane
d. Pulmonary vascular remodeling

Answer: a. Alveolar hypoventilation due to chest wall deformity. Explanation: In patients with severe kyphoscoliosis, chest wall deformities can lead to alveolar hypoventilation by restricting lung expansion, thereby reducing ventilation and leading to CO2 retention.

165. For a patient with obesity hypoventilation syndrome (OHS) and hypercapnic respiratory failure, which therapeutic approach is most beneficial?
a. Weight loss and lifestyle modification
b. Continuous oxygen therapy alone
c. Diuretic therapy to reduce fluid overload
d. Immediate lung transplantation

Answer: a. Weight loss and lifestyle modification. Explanation: In OHS, weight loss and lifestyle modifications are foundational treatments that can improve lung function by reducing chest wall and abdominal pressure, thereby improving alveolar ventilation and reducing hypercapnia.

166. In evaluating a patient for potential home mechanical ventilation due to chronic hypercapnic respiratory failure, which factor is least important in the decision-making process?

a. Patient's ability to protect the airway
b. Socioeconomic status
c. Nutritional status
d. Level of daytime hypercapnia

Answer: b. Socioeconomic status. Explanation: While socioeconomic factors may influence the feasibility and support for home mechanical ventilation, clinical criteria such as the patient's ability to protect the airway, nutritional status, and level of daytime hypercapnia are more critical in determining the appropriateness and type of home ventilation support.

167. In a patient with acute exacerbation of COPD, which non-invasive ventilatory support method is preferred to decrease the work of breathing and improve gas exchange?
a. Continuous Positive Airway Pressure (CPAP)
b. Bilevel Positive Airway Pressure (BiPAP)
c. High-flow nasal cannula oxygen therapy
d. Incentive spirometry

Answer: b. Bilevel Positive Airway Pressure (BiPAP). Explanation: BiPAP is preferred in acute exacerbations of COPD as it provides both inspiratory and expiratory positive airway pressure, reducing the work of breathing, improving alveolar ventilation, and facilitating gas exchange by stenting open the airways and preventing alveolar collapse.

168. For a patient with acute pulmonary edema secondary to congestive heart failure, which non-invasive ventilation strategy is most effective in rapidly improving oxygenation and reducing preload and afterload?
a. CPAP
b. BiPAP with low inspiratory positive airway pressure
c. Oxygen therapy via Venturi mask
d. Nebulized beta-agonist therapy

Answer: a. CPAP. Explanation: CPAP is most effective for acute pulmonary edema secondary to congestive heart failure as it increases intrathoracic pressure, reduces preload and afterload, and improves oxygenation by preventing alveolar collapse, thereby improving functional residual capacity.

169. In selecting invasive mechanical ventilation settings for a patient with ARDS, which strategy is recommended to minimize ventilator-induced lung injury?
a. High tidal volume (10-12 ml/kg) and low PEEP
b. Low tidal volume (4-6 ml/kg) and high PEEP
c. High tidal volume (10-12 ml/kg) and high PEEP
d. Low tidal volume (4-6 ml/kg) and low PEEP

Answer: b. Low tidal volume (4-6 ml/kg) and high PEEP. Explanation: For ARDS, a low tidal volume strategy (4-6 ml/kg of predicted body weight) with higher levels of PEEP is recommended to minimize ventilator-induced lung injury by avoiding overdistension (volutrauma) and maintaining alveolar recruitment, thereby preventing atelectasis.

170. When transitioning a patient from invasive mechanical ventilation to spontaneous breathing, which of the following is a common method to assess readiness for extubation?
a. Rapid shallow breathing index (RSBI)
b. Peak inspiratory pressure (PIP) measurement
c. Total static lung compliance calculation
d. Maximum inspiratory force (MIF) test

Answer: a. Rapid shallow breathing index (RSBI). Explanation: The RSBI, calculated as the ratio of respiratory rate to tidal volume (f/VT) during a spontaneous breathing trial, is a common and reliable method to assess readiness for extubation. An RSBI lower than 105 breaths/min/L is generally considered predictive of successful extubation.

171. For a patient with obstructive sleep apnea and nocturnal hypoventilation, which ventilatory support modality is most appropriate to ensure airway patency and adequate ventilation during sleep?
a. CPAP
b. BiPAP with a backup respiratory rate
c. Invasive mechanical ventilation via tracheostomy
d. Supplemental oxygen via a nasal cannula

Answer: b. BiPAP with a backup respiratory rate. Explanation: BiPAP with a backup respiratory rate is suitable for patients with obstructive sleep apnea and nocturnal hypoventilation as it provides variable inspiratory and expiratory pressures to maintain airway patency and supports ventilation, with the backup rate ensuring adequate minute ventilation during apneic episodes.

172. In the context of weaning a patient from mechanical ventilation, which parameter is most indicative of potential weaning success?
a. Arterial blood gas (ABG) analysis showing respiratory alkalosis
b. Positive fluid balance over the past 24 hours
c. A decrease in oxygen saturation below 88% during a spontaneous breathing trial
d. A stable mental status with the ability to follow commands

Answer: d. A stable mental status with the ability to follow commands. Explanation: A stable mental status and the ability to follow commands indicate adequate neurological function, which is crucial for successful weaning from mechanical ventilation. Patients must be able to protect their airway and participate in spontaneous breathing efforts to be considered for weaning.

173. In managing a patient with hypercapnic respiratory failure, which of the following ventilatory support options directly targets the reduction of carbon dioxide levels?
a. CPAP with supplemental oxygen

b. BiPAP with an emphasis on increased expiratory positive airway pressure (EPAP)
c. High-frequency oscillatory ventilation
d. BiPAP with an emphasis on increased inspiratory positive airway pressure (IPAP)

Answer: d. BiPAP with an emphasis on increased inspiratory positive airway pressure (IPAP). Explanation: In hypercapnic respiratory failure, increasing the IPAP on BiPAP enhances alveolar ventilation by increasing the tidal volume, which directly facilitates the reduction of carbon dioxide levels.

174. For a patient with asthma exacerbation not responding to standard medical therapy, which non-invasive ventilation modality can be considered to avoid intubation?
a. CPAP with supplemental oxygen
b. BiPAP with high EPAP settings
c. BiPAP with low IPAP/EPAP settings
d. High-flow nasal cannula at maximal flow rates

Answer: c. BiPAP with low IPAP/EPAP settings. Explanation: In asthma exacerbations, non-invasive ventilation like BiPAP with low IPAP/EPAP settings can be considered to stave off intubation by reducing the work of breathing, improving ventilation, and helping to overcome airway resistance without causing barotrauma.

175. When initiating invasive mechanical ventilation for a patient with severe ARDS, which of the following approaches is most aligned with lung-protective ventilation strategies?
a. Setting PEEP just above the lower inflection point on the pressure-volume curve
b. Utilizing an inspiratory to expiratory ratio of 1:1
c. Implementing a high-frequency percussive ventilation mode
d. Applying tidal volumes of 8-10 ml/kg of ideal body weight

Answer: a. Setting PEEP just above the lower inflection point on the pressure-volume curve. Explanation: In severe ARDS, setting PEEP just above the lower inflection point on the pressure-volume curve is part of a lung-protective strategy. This approach helps maintain alveolar recruitment and prevents repeated opening and closing of alveoli, thereby minimizing ventilator-induced lung injury.

176. In setting the initial tidal volume for a mechanically ventilated patient with ARDS, which strategy is recommended to minimize ventilator-induced lung injury?
a. 12 mL/kg based on ideal body weight
b. 10 mL/kg based on actual body weight
c. 6-8 mL/kg based on ideal body weight
d. 8-10 mL/kg based on actual body weight

Answer: c. 6-8 mL/kg based on ideal body weight. Explanation: The lung-protective ventilation strategy recommends using a lower tidal volume of 6-8 mL/kg based on ideal body weight, rather than actual body weight, to reduce the risk of ventilator-induced lung injury in patients with ARDS.

177. Which mode of mechanical ventilation allows the patient to initiate all breaths but provides a set level of pressure support for each breath?
a. Volume control ventilation (VCV)
b. Pressure control ventilation (PCV)
c. Continuous positive airway pressure (CPAP)
d. Pressure support ventilation (PSV)

Answer: d. Pressure support ventilation (PSV). Explanation: In pressure support ventilation (PSV), the ventilator provides a preset level of pressure support to augment the patient's spontaneous breaths, allowing for greater patient control over breathing frequency and depth.

178. A patient on mechanical ventilation develops a sudden onset of hypoxemia and decreased breath sounds on the left side. The most likely cause is:
a. Pneumothorax
b. Pulmonary embolism
c. Mucus plugging
d. Ventilator-associated pneumonia

Answer: a. Pneumothorax. Explanation: A sudden onset of hypoxemia and unilateral decrease in breath sounds in a mechanically ventilated patient strongly suggests pneumothorax, particularly if it's on the same side as the decreased breath sounds, as a result of air accumulation in the pleural space causing lung collapse.

179. In managing a patient with obstructive lung disease on mechanical ventilation, which ventilator adjustment is most appropriate to prevent air trapping and auto-PEEP?
a. Increase tidal volume
b. Decrease inspiratory flow rate
c. Increase expiratory time
d. Increase respiratory rate

Answer: c. Increase expiratory time. Explanation: Increasing the expiratory time allows more time for complete exhalation, which is particularly important in obstructive lung disease where expiratory flow is impaired, thereby reducing the risk of air trapping and auto-PEEP.

180. For a patient with acute respiratory distress syndrome (ARDS) on mechanical ventilation, which of the following is a key goal to prevent ventilator-induced lung injury?
a. Maintaining high plateau pressures to ensure adequate oxygenation
b. Using higher PEEP levels to keep the lungs inflated
c. Limiting plateau pressures to ≤30 cm H2O
d. Maximizing tidal volumes to facilitate CO2 removal

Answer: c. Limiting plateau pressures to ≤30 cm H2O. Explanation: One of the key strategies in managing patients with ARDS on mechanical ventilation is to limit plateau pressures to ≤30 cm H2O to minimize alveolar overdistention and prevent ventilator-induced lung injury.

181. When considering weaning a patient from mechanical ventilation, which parameter is NOT typically evaluated?
a. Rapid shallow breathing index (RSBI)
b. Maximal inspiratory pressure (MIP)
c. Serum bicarbonate level
d. Tidal volume

Answer: c. Serum bicarbonate level. Explanation: Serum bicarbonate level is not typically a parameter evaluated during weaning from mechanical ventilation. Weaning assessments usually focus on respiratory parameters like RSBI, MIP, and tidal volume to evaluate the patient's ability to breathe independently.

182. In a mechanically ventilated patient, the presence of "inverse ratio ventilation" refers to:
a. Inspiratory time is longer than expiratory time
b. Expiratory time is longer than inspiratory time
c. Equal inspiratory and expiratory times
d. Variable inspiratory and expiratory times based on patient effort

Answer: a. Inspiratory time is longer than expiratory time. Explanation: Inverse ratio ventilation is a strategy used in certain cases of severe respiratory failure where the inspiratory time is set to be longer than the expiratory time, which can improve oxygenation by increasing mean airway pressure and alveolar recruitment.

183. Which ventilator setting adjustment is most appropriate for a patient with acute respiratory alkalosis due to hyperventilation?
a. Increase tidal volume
b. Decrease tidal volume
c. Increase respiratory rate
d. Decrease respiratory rate

Answer: d. Decrease respiratory rate. Explanation: In a patient experiencing acute respiratory alkalosis due to hyperventilation, decreasing the respiratory rate on the ventilator can help reduce alveolar ventilation, allowing for the retention of CO2 and correction of alkalosis.

184. For a patient on mechanical ventilation, which finding is an indication for the application of positive end-expiratory pressure (PEEP)?
a. Reduced risk of barotrauma
b. Prevention of alveolar collapse at end-expiration
c. Decrease in functional residual capacity
d. Increased pulmonary compliance

Answer: b. Prevention of alveolar collapse at end-expiration. Explanation: PEEP is applied to prevent alveolar collapse at end-expiration, helping to maintain functional residual capacity and improve oxygenation, especially in conditions like ARDS or acute lung injury.

185. A mechanically ventilated patient exhibits a sudden increase in peak airway pressures. Which of the following is the least likely cause?
a. Bronchospasm
b. Patient-ventilator dyssynchrony
c. Endotracheal tube cuff leak
d. Secretion accumulation in the airway

Answer: c. Endotracheal tube cuff leak. Explanation: An endotracheal tube cuff leak would more likely lead to a decrease in peak airway pressures due to loss of delivered volume. Bronchospasm, patient-ventilator dyssynchrony, and secretion accumulation are more likely to increase peak airway pressures by increasing airway resistance or affecting lung compliance.

186. In a patient with acute respiratory distress syndrome (ARDS) on mechanical ventilation, which mode provides full ventilatory support with a set tidal volume and respiratory rate, while still allowing spontaneous breathing?
a. Assist-control (AC)
b. Synchronized intermittent mandatory ventilation (SIMV)
c. Pressure support ventilation (PSV)
d. Continuous positive airway pressure (CPAP)

Answer: b. Synchronized intermittent mandatory ventilation (SIMV). Explanation: SIMV mode provides full ventilatory support by delivering a set number of breaths at a predetermined tidal volume and allows the patient to take spontaneous breaths in between. This mode helps in synchronizing the ventilator support with the patient's spontaneous efforts, making it suitable for weaning and reducing the risk of ventilator-associated lung injury.

187. For a patient transitioning from full mechanical support to spontaneous breathing, which mode of ventilation is most beneficial in strengthening respiratory muscles by providing support only during a spontaneous breath?
a. Assist-control (AC)
b. Volume control ventilation (VCV)
c. Pressure support ventilation (PSV)
d. High-frequency oscillatory ventilation (HFOV)

Answer: c. Pressure support ventilation (PSV). Explanation: PSV aids spontaneous breaths by providing a preset level of positive pressure during inspiration, which decreases the work of breathing and helps strengthen respiratory muscles. It is commonly used during the weaning process from mechanical ventilation.

188. In assist-control (AC) mode, how does the ventilator respond if the patient's spontaneous breathing rate falls below the set mandatory rate?
a. It decreases the tidal volume to match the patient's effort
b. It increases the inspiratory pressure to encourage spontaneous breaths
c. It delivers the set number of mandatory breaths to maintain minute ventilation
d. It switches to a completely spontaneous mode to assess patient's capability

Answer: c. It delivers the set number of mandatory breaths to maintain minute ventilation. Explanation: In AC mode, if the patient's spontaneous breathing rate falls below the set mandatory rate, the ventilator compensates by delivering the set number of mandatory breaths at the predetermined tidal volume, ensuring the maintenance of adequate minute ventilation.

189. When using synchronized intermittent mandatory ventilation (SIMV), what is the primary advantage of synchronizing mandatory breaths with the patient's spontaneous breathing effort?
a. It allows for higher tidal volumes with each breath
b. It reduces the risk of auto-PEEP and barotrauma
c. It improves patient comfort and synchrony with the ventilator
d. It completely takes over the work of breathing from the patient

Answer: c. It improves patient comfort and synchrony with the ventilator. Explanation: Synchronizing mandatory breaths with the patient's spontaneous effort in SIMV mode improves patient-ventilator synchrony and comfort by reducing breath stacking and the risk of dyssynchrony, making the ventilation more physiological.

190. In a patient with chronic obstructive pulmonary disease (COPD) experiencing an exacerbation, why might pressure support ventilation (PSV) be preferred over assist-control (AC) mode?
a. PSV provides a more consistent tidal volume
b. PSV allows for better control of respiratory rate
c. PSV reduces the risk of ventilator-induced lung injury
d. PSV offers more support for spontaneous breathing efforts

Answer: d. PSV offers more support for spontaneous breathing efforts. Explanation: PSV is preferred in COPD exacerbations because it supports spontaneous breathing efforts by providing a preset level of inspiratory pressure, reducing the work of breathing while allowing the patient to control the tidal volume and respiratory rate, leading to better patient-ventilator synchrony and reduced risk of hyperinflation.

191. For a patient requiring mechanical ventilation due to acute respiratory failure, which ventilatory mode ensures a guaranteed tidal volume despite variations in lung compliance or airway resistance?
a. Pressure support ventilation (PSV)
b. Continuous positive airway pressure (CPAP)
c. Assist-control (AC)
d. Synchronized intermittent mandatory ventilation (SIMV)

Answer: c. Assist-control (AC). Explanation: AC mode guarantees delivery of a set tidal volume with each breath, regardless of changes in lung compliance or airway resistance. This ensures consistent minute ventilation and is particularly beneficial in conditions where maintaining adequate alveolar ventilation is crucial.

192. What is a significant benefit of using pressure support ventilation (PSV) during the weaning process from mechanical ventilation?
a. It allows for precise control of arterial carbon dioxide levels
b. It maintains a constant minute ventilation
c. It diminishes the work of breathing by providing inspiratory assistance
d. It ensures a fixed respiratory rate and tidal volume

Answer: c. It diminishes the work of breathing by providing inspiratory assistance. Explanation: PSV reduces the work of breathing during the weaning process by providing adjustable levels of inspiratory pressure support, thereby facilitating the transition to spontaneous breathing by augmenting the patient's inspiratory efforts.

193. In patients ventilated in assist-control (AC) mode, what is a common challenge that may lead to patient discomfort and the need for sedation?
a. Inability to adjust inspiratory flow rates
b. Lack of synchronization between patient efforts and ventilator support
c. Insufficient tidal volume delivery
d. Over-assistance leading to hypoventilation

Answer: b. Lack of synchronization between patient efforts and ventilator support. Explanation: In AC mode, a common challenge is the lack of synchronization between the patient's spontaneous breathing efforts and the ventilator-delivered breaths, which can lead to discomfort, increased work of breathing, and potentially the need for sedation to ensure patient-ventilator synchrony.

194. When considering the application of synchronized intermittent mandatory ventilation (SIMV) for a patient with acute respiratory failure, which situation is most conducive for its use?
a. The need for full ventilatory support without patient effort
b. Initiating the weaning process in a patient showing signs of improved respiratory function
c. Managing patients with stable respiratory drive but requiring high oxygen levels
d. Situations requiring high levels of PEEP for alveolar recruitment

Answer: b. Initiating the weaning process in a patient showing signs of improved respiratory function. Explanation: SIMV is particularly useful in the weaning process as it combines mandatory breaths that ensure a minimum level of ventilation with the ability for the patient to take spontaneous breaths, thereby facilitating the gradual transition to spontaneous breathing by allowing assessment and enhancement of the patient's respiratory effort and capacity.

195. During a spontaneous breathing trial (SBT), a patient exhibits increased anxiety, diaphoresis, and a respiratory rate of 35 breaths/min. What is the most appropriate next step?

a. Immediately extubate the patient
b. Continue the SBT for another 30 minutes
c. Reintubate the patient
d. Terminate the SBT and reassess readiness later

Answer: d. Terminate the SBT and reassess readiness later. Explanation: The patient's signs of increased work of breathing, anxiety, and tachypnea indicate intolerance to the SBT. The trial should be terminated to prevent respiratory muscle fatigue and distress, and the patient's readiness for weaning should be reassessed later.

196. A patient's rapid shallow breathing index (RSBI) is measured at 105 breaths/min/L during an SBT. What does this value suggest regarding weaning from mechanical ventilation?
a. The patient is likely ready for extubation
b. The patient is not ready for extubation and requires further ventilatory support
c. The RSBI is inconclusive, and further testing is needed
d. The patient requires immediate non-invasive ventilation

Answer: b. The patient is not ready for extubation and requires further ventilatory support. Explanation: An RSBI greater than 105 breaths/min/L is generally considered predictive of weaning failure, suggesting the patient may not be ready for extubation and may require additional time on mechanical ventilation or other interventions to improve respiratory muscle strength and endurance.

197. In preparing a patient for a spontaneous breathing trial, which of the following interventions is essential?
a. Administering a sedative to reduce anxiety
b. Ensuring the patient is in a semi-recumbent position
c. Increasing the FIO2 to 100% just before the trial
d. Performing a bronchodilator treatment immediately before the trial

Answer: b. Ensuring the patient is in a semi-recumbent position. Explanation: Placing the patient in a semi-recumbent position (30-45 degrees) optimizes respiratory mechanics and gas exchange, reducing the work of breathing and risk of aspiration, which is crucial for the success of an SBT.

198. Which parameter is not a typical criterion for initiating a spontaneous breathing trial?
a. Hemodynamic stability without vasopressors
b. Absence of fever
c. PaO2/FiO2 ratio > 200
d. Requirement for high levels of PEEP (>8 cm H2O)

Answer: d. Requirement for high levels of PEEP (>8 cm H2O). Explanation: Needing high levels of PEEP suggests significant lung injury or instability, which may not be conducive to initiating an SBT. The other options indicate stability and readiness for a trial of spontaneous breathing.

199. A patient undergoing an SBT develops a heart rate of 120 bpm, up from a baseline of 90 bpm. What is the most likely interpretation of this change?
a. Normal response to increased activity
b. Indication of successful weaning
c. Sign of potential weaning failure
d. Irrelevant to the weaning process

Answer: c. Sign of potential weaning failure. Explanation: A significant increase in heart rate during an SBT can indicate stress or inadequate cardiovascular response to the increased workload of spontaneous breathing, potentially signifying weaning failure.

200. What role does assessing cough strength and secretions play in the weaning process?
a. It helps determine the need for bronchodilators
b. It is critical for deciding when to initiate an SBT
c. It is essential for evaluating the patient's ability to protect their airway post-extubation
d. It is used to adjust PEEP levels

Answer: c. It is essential for evaluating the patient's ability to protect their airway post-extubation. Explanation: Assessing cough strength and the ability to manage secretions is crucial for determining if the patient can protect their airway and prevent aspiration post-extubation, which is a key consideration in the weaning process.

201. During a trial of spontaneous breathing, monitoring which of the following parameters is least important?
a. Respiratory rate
b. Blood pressure
c. Serum creatinine
d. Oxygen saturation

Answer: c. Serum creatinine. Explanation: While serum creatinine is an important indicator of renal function, it is not directly relevant to monitoring a patient's immediate response to a spontaneous breathing trial, where respiratory and hemodynamic parameters are more critical.

202. A patient has been on mechanical ventilation for 3 weeks due to ARDS. Which factor might contribute to difficulty in weaning from mechanical ventilation?
a. Increased lung compliance
b. Diaphragmatic muscle strength
c. Low levels of sedation
d. Minimal secretions

Answer: b. Diaphragmatic muscle strength. Explanation: Prolonged mechanical ventilation can lead to diaphragmatic disuse atrophy, reducing muscle strength and contributing to weaning difficulty. Increased lung compliance, low levels of sedation, and minimal secretions generally facilitate the weaning process.

203. For a patient with chronic hypercapnia, what adjustment to ventilator settings might be necessary during weaning to avoid respiratory acidosis?
a. Decrease the inspiratory flow rate
b. Increase the tidal volume
c. Adjust the respiratory rate to maintain the patient's usual PaCO2
d. Increase the FIO2

Answer: c. Adjust the respiratory rate to maintain the patient's usual PaCO2. Explanation: Patients with chronic hypercapnia (elevated PaCO2) may require careful adjustment of the respiratory rate during weaning to maintain their baseline PaCO2 levels and avoid acute respiratory acidosis, which could complicate the weaning process.

204. According to the Berlin Definition, within how many hours of a known clinical insult or new/worsening respiratory symptoms should acute respiratory distress syndrome (ARDS) onset occur?
a. Within 1 hour
b. Within 12 hours
c. Within 24-48 hours
d. Within 72 hours

Answer: d. Within 72 hours. Explanation: The Berlin Definition specifies that ARDS should occur within 1 week of a known clinical insult or new or worsening respiratory symptoms, providing a specific time frame to help differentiate ARDS from other forms of respiratory failure that might have a more insidious onset.

205. In the assessment of a patient suspected of having ARDS, which radiographic finding is considered a hallmark of the syndrome?
a. Unilateral pulmonary infiltrates
b. Bilateral opacities not fully explained by effusions, lobar/lung collapse, or nodules
c. Isolated left lower lobe consolidation
d. Pleural thickening and calcification

Answer: b. Bilateral opacities not fully explained by effusions, lobar/lung collapse, or nodules. Explanation: The Berlin Definition of ARDS includes the presence of bilateral opacities on chest imaging that cannot be fully explained by effusions, lobar/lung collapse, or nodules, highlighting the diffuse pulmonary involvement characteristic of ARDS.

206. In ARDS, what is the primary origin of pulmonary edema?
a. Cardiogenic
b. Renal failure-induced
c. Increased capillary permeability due to lung injury
d. Obstructive pulmonary disease

Answer: c. Increased capillary permeability due to lung injury. Explanation: ARDS is primarily associated with non-cardiogenic pulmonary edema, where increased capillary permeability due to direct or indirect lung injury leads to fluid leakage into the alveolar spaces, distinguishing it from cardiogenic causes of pulmonary edema.

207. Using the Berlin Definition, how is the severity of ARDS determined based on the PaO2/FiO2 ratio?
a. Mild ARDS: PaO2/FiO2 > 300 mmHg
b. Moderate ARDS: PaO2/FiO2 > 200 but ≤ 300 mmHg
c. Severe ARDS: PaO2/FiO2 ≤ 100 mmHg
d. Severe ARDS: PaO2/FiO2 ≤ 200 mmHg

Answer: d. Severe ARDS: PaO2/FiO2 ≤ 200 mmHg. Explanation: The Berlin Definition categorizes ARDS severity based on the PaO2/FiO2 ratio, with severe ARDS defined as a PaO2/FiO2 ratio of ≤ 200 mmHg, indicating a greater impairment in oxygenation.

208. In managing a patient with severe ARDS, what is the primary goal of utilizing a lung-protective ventilation strategy?
a. To achieve a PaO2 > 100 mmHg
b. To maintain a high tidal volume to prevent atelectasis
c. To minimize ventilator-induced lung injury
d. To use the highest possible PEEP to maximize oxygenation

Answer: c. To minimize ventilator-induced lung injury. Explanation: Lung-protective ventilation strategies in ARDS aim to minimize ventilator-induced lung injury by using low tidal volumes and limiting plateau pressures, thus avoiding alveolar overdistention (volutrauma) and barotrauma.

209. In the context of ARDS and the PaO2/FiO2 ratio, which ventilatory adjustment is most appropriate for a patient with a deteriorating ratio despite optimized PEEP and FiO2 settings?
a. Increase tidal volume to 10 ml/kg
b. Initiate prone positioning
c. Transition to high-frequency oscillatory ventilation immediately
d. Reduce inspiratory flow rate to prolong inspiratory time

Answer: b. Initiate prone positioning. Explanation: Prone positioning is an effective strategy in severe ARDS patients not responding to conventional ventilatory adjustments, as it improves oxygenation by enhancing ventilation-perfusion matching and alveolar recruitment, without the risks associated with further increasing tidal volumes or inspiratory pressures.

210. For ARDS patients, why is the maintenance of a conservative fluid management strategy recommended?
a. To enhance renal perfusion

b. To increase preload and improve cardiac output
c. To reduce the risk of pulmonary edema and improve lung compliance
d. To facilitate diuresis and weight loss

Answer: c. To reduce the risk of pulmonary edema and improve lung compliance. Explanation: In ARDS, a conservative fluid management strategy aims to minimize fluid accumulation in the lungs, thereby reducing the risk of exacerbating pulmonary edema, improving lung compliance, and potentially improving oxygenation and outcomes.

211. When considering nutritional support for a patient with ARDS, what factor must be carefully managed to avoid exacerbating respiratory failure?
a. High carbohydrate content leading to increased CO2 production
b. High protein content leading to renal overload
c. Excessive lipid content leading to hyperlipidemia
d. High fiber content leading to gastrointestinal distress

Answer: a. High carbohydrate content leading to increased CO2 production. Explanation: In ARDS patients, particularly those on mechanical ventilation, the high carbohydrate content in nutritional support can lead to increased carbon dioxide production as a byproduct of metabolism, potentially exacerbating respiratory acidosis and making ventilation more challenging.

212. In ARDS, what is the physiological rationale behind applying positive end-expiratory pressure (PEEP)?
a. To decrease functional residual capacity
b. To increase airway resistance and work of breathing
c. To prevent alveolar collapse and maintain alveolar recruitment
d. To enhance oxygen delivery to the myocardium

Answer: c. To prevent alveolar collapse and maintain alveolar recruitment. Explanation: PEEP is used in ARDS to prevent end-expiratory alveolar collapse, maintaining alveolar recruitment, improving gas exchange, and increasing functional residual capacity, thereby enhancing oxygenation while minimizing ventilator-associated lung injury.

213. Considering extracorporeal membrane oxygenation (ECMO) in the management of ARDS, which patient scenario best indicates its potential use?
a. Moderate ARDS with a PaO2/FiO2 ratio of 250 mmHg on 60% FiO2
b. Early ARDS with minimal comorbidities and improving lung compliance
c. Severe ARDS with refractory hypoxemia despite optimal ventilatory and adjunctive therapies
d. ARDS with a primary need for CO2 removal and stable oxygenation

Answer: c. Severe ARDS with refractory hypoxemia despite optimal ventilatory and adjunctive therapies. Explanation: ECMO is considered in severe ARDS cases where conventional therapies, including optimal ventilatory strategies and adjunctive treatments like prone positioning and neuromuscular blockade, fail to improve oxygenation, indicating refractory hypoxemia.

214. In the context of ARDS management, what is the primary rationale for implementing low tidal volume ventilation?
a. To increase oxygenation by maximizing alveolar recruitment
b. To minimize ventilator-associated pneumonia (VAP) risk
c. To reduce ventilator-induced lung injury (VILI) by avoiding overdistension of alveoli
d. To facilitate rapid weaning from mechanical ventilation

Answer: c. To reduce ventilator-induced lung injury (VILI) by avoiding overdistension of alveoli. Explanation: Low tidal volume ventilation is employed in ARDS management to prevent VILI, which can occur from alveolar overdistension. This strategy aims to limit the tidal volume to 6-8 mL/kg of predicted body weight to minimize barotrauma and volutrauma.

215. What is the primary benefit of prone positioning in patients with severe ARDS?
a. It facilitates easier access for bronchial hygiene
b. It reduces the risk of aspiration pneumonia
c. It improves oxygenation by enhancing V/Q matching and alveolar recruitment
d. It allows for higher tidal volumes to be used safely

Answer: c. It improves oxygenation by enhancing V/Q matching and alveolar recruitment. Explanation: Prone positioning in severe ARDS patients improves oxygenation primarily by improving ventilation/perfusion (V/Q) matching and promoting more uniform alveolar recruitment, thereby reducing shunt and improving gas exchange.

216. When considering the use of neuromuscular blocking agents (NMBAs) in ARDS, which statement is true?
a. NMBAs are indicated for all patients as a first-line treatment
b. NMBAs primarily improve oxygenation by allowing higher PEEP levels
c. The use of NMBAs has been shown to improve mortality in all cases of ARDS
d. NMBAs may be used early in severe ARDS to improve oxygenation and reduce oxygen consumption

Answer: d. NMBAs may be used early in severe ARDS to improve oxygenation and reduce oxygen consumption. Explanation: In severe ARDS, NMBAs can be used early in the course to facilitate lung-protective ventilation strategies, improve oxygenation, and reduce metabolic demand by limiting spontaneous breathing efforts and ventilator dyssynchrony.

217. For a patient with ARDS, what is the primary goal of implementing low tidal volume ventilation?
a. To maintain a PaCO2 within normal limits
b. To prevent atelectasis
c. To maintain plateau pressures ≤30 cm H2O
d. To achieve normoxemia

Answer: c. To maintain plateau pressures ≤30 cm H2O. Explanation: The primary goal of low tidal volume ventilation in ARDS is to maintain plateau pressures at or below 30 cm H2O to minimize alveolar overdistension and the risk of barotrauma, which are associated with VILI.

218. In ARDS management, how does prone positioning help in reducing VILI?
a. By decreasing the need for sedation
b. By redistributing lung stress and strain more homogeneously
c. By enabling the use of lower levels of PEEP
d. By increasing thoracic compliance

Answer: b. By redistributing lung stress and strain more homogeneously. Explanation: Prone positioning helps reduce VILI by redistributing lung stress and strain more evenly across the lung parenchyma, thereby minimizing overdistension of less affected alveoli and promoting more uniform lung inflation.

219. When might the use of NMBAs in ARDS management be particularly beneficial?
a. When the patient exhibits severe ventilator asynchrony
b. As a routine measure in all mechanically ventilated patients
c. Only when there is evidence of neuromuscular disease
d. When attempting to reduce FiO2 requirements below 40%

Answer: a. When the patient exhibits severe ventilator asynchrony. Explanation: The use of NMBAs may be particularly beneficial in cases of severe ventilator-patient asynchrony that cannot be managed with sedation alone, as NMBAs can ensure full control of ventilation, reduce oxygen demand, and facilitate lung-protective ventilation strategies.

220. What is a key consideration when weaning a patient from mechanical ventilation who has been on neuromuscular blockade?
a. Rapid reduction in PEEP and FiO2 to baseline levels
b. Assessment of muscle strength and ability to initiate spontaneous breaths
c. Immediate extubation to prevent ventilator-associated lung injury
d. Increasing tidal volumes to assess lung recovery

Answer: b. Assessment of muscle strength and ability to initiate spontaneous breaths. Explanation: After the use of NMBAs, a key consideration in weaning is to assess the recovery of muscle strength and the patient's ability to initiate spontaneous breaths, as prolonged neuromuscular blockade can lead to muscle weakness, impacting the ability to breathe independently.

221. In a patient being ventilated with low tidal volumes for ARDS, what is a common compensatory mechanism to avoid respiratory acidosis?
a. Increasing the respiratory rate
b. Administering bicarbonate infusions
c. Decreasing the inspiratory flow rate

d. Reducing the I:E ratio


Answer: a. Increasing the respiratory rate. Explanation: When using low tidal volumes to minimize VILI in ARDS, increasing the respiratory rate is a common compensatory mechanism to avoid respiratory acidosis by ensuring adequate minute ventilation and CO2 clearance.


222. How does the application of optimal PEEP in ARDS management contribute to lung protection?
a. By maximizing alveolar collapse to rest the lungs
b. By reducing the need for supplemental oxygen
c. By preventing derecruitment and atelectrauma
d. By facilitating diuresis and reducing pulmonary edema


Answer: c. By preventing derecruitment and atelectrauma. Explanation: Optimal PEEP contributes to lung protection in ARDS by preventing the cyclic opening and closing of unstable alveoli (derecruitment), thereby reducing atelectrauma and facilitating more uniform lung inflation during mechanical ventilation.


223. A 28-year-old male presents to the emergency department with sudden-onset chest pain and dyspnea. On physical examination, he appears anxious and diaphoretic. His blood pressure is 80/50 mmHg, heart rate is 120 beats per minute, and jugular veins are distended. Cardiac auscultation reveals distant heart sounds. Which of the following is the most likely diagnosis?
a. acute pericarditis
b. cardiac tamponade
c. pulmonary embolism
d. tension pneumothorax


Answer: b. cardiac tamponade. Explanation: The patient's presentation is consistent with cardiac tamponade, a life-threatening condition caused by the accumulation of fluid in the pericardial space, leading to impaired cardiac filling and decreased cardiac output. The classic findings of cardiac tamponade, known as Beck's triad, include hypotension, muffled heart sounds, and jugular venous distention (JVD). The patient's sudden-onset chest pain, dyspnea, tachycardia, and diaphoresis are also suggestive of a critical cardiac condition. Acute pericarditis can cause chest pain and pericardial effusion but typically presents with a pericardial friction rub and diffuse ST-segment elevation on ECG. Pulmonary embolism and tension pneumothorax can cause chest pain and dyspnea but are less likely to present with the specific findings of Beck's triad.


224. A 45-year-old female with a history of systemic lupus erythematosus presents with progressive dyspnea and fatigue. Her blood pressure is 90/60 mmHg, heart rate is 110 beats per minute, and pulsus paradoxus is present. Echocardiography reveals a large pericardial effusion with right ventricular diastolic collapse. Which of the following is the most appropriate initial management?
a. intravenous fluids and vasopressors
b. urgent pericardiocentesis
c. high-dose corticosteroids
d. broad-spectrum antibiotics

Answer: b. urgent pericardiocentesis. Explanation: The patient's presentation is consistent with cardiac tamponade secondary to a large pericardial effusion, likely related to her underlying systemic lupus erythematosus (SLE). The presence of pulsus paradoxus (an exaggerated decrease in systolic blood pressure during inspiration) and right ventricular diastolic collapse on echocardiography are highly specific findings for cardiac tamponade. In this setting, the most appropriate initial management is urgent pericardiocentesis to drain the pericardial fluid and relieve the hemodynamic compromise. Intravenous fluids and vasopressors may be used as temporizing measures to support blood pressure, but they do not address the underlying cause of the tamponade. High-dose corticosteroids may be indicated for the long-term management of SLE-related pericarditis but are not the initial treatment for acute tamponade. Broad-spectrum antibiotics are not indicated in the absence of signs or symptoms of infection.

225. A 60-year-old male presents with acute-onset chest pain and shortness of breath. His blood pressure is 70/40 mmHg, heart rate is 130 beats per minute, and jugular veins are distended. Pulsus paradoxus is present. ECG shows low-voltage QRS complexes and electrical alternans. Which of the following is the most likely etiology of this patient's condition?
a. acute myocardial infarction
b. aortic dissection
c. malignant pericardial effusion
d. hypovolemic shock

Answer: c. malignant pericardial effusion. Explanation: The patient's presentation is consistent with cardiac tamponade, as evidenced by the presence of hypotension, tachycardia, jugular venous distention, and pulsus paradoxus. The ECG findings of low-voltage QRS complexes and electrical alternans (a beat-to-beat variation in the amplitude of the QRS complexes) are also suggestive of a large pericardial effusion. In an older patient with acute-onset symptoms, malignant pericardial effusion is a likely etiology, as malignancies such as lung cancer, breast cancer, and lymphoma can metastasize to the pericardium and cause effusions. Acute myocardial infarction can cause chest pain and hemodynamic instability but typically presents with ECG changes such as ST-segment elevation or depression. Aortic dissection can cause chest pain and hypotension but is less likely to present with the specific findings of cardiac tamponade. Hypovolemic shock can cause hypotension and tachycardia but would not typically present with jugular venous distention or pulsus paradoxus.

226. A 35-year-old male with a history of end-stage renal disease on hemodialysis presents with chest pain and shortness of breath. His blood pressure is 80/50 mmHg, heart rate is 120 beats per minute, and jugular veins are distended. Pulsus paradoxus is present. Bedside ultrasound reveals a moderate pericardial effusion with right atrial collapse during diastole. Which of the following is the most appropriate next step in management?
a. administer intravenous heparin
b. perform urgent hemodialysis
c. initiate dobutamine infusion
d. perform pericardiocentesis

Answer: d. perform pericardiocentesis. Explanation: The patient's presentation is consistent with cardiac tamponade secondary to a moderate pericardial effusion, likely related to his end-stage renal disease (ESRD). Patients with ESRD are at increased risk of developing uremic pericarditis and pericardial effusions due to the accumulation of uremic toxins and inflammation. The presence of right atrial collapse during diastole on bedside ultrasound is a specific finding for cardiac tamponade and indicates the need for urgent pericardiocentesis to drain the effusion and relieve the hemodynamic compromise. Intravenous heparin is not indicated in the absence of evidence of acute coronary syndrome or other thrombotic disorders. While urgent hemodialysis may be necessary to address the underlying uremia and prevent further accumulation of pericardial fluid, it does not provide immediate relief of the tamponade physiology. Dobutamine infusion may be used to support cardiac output in the setting of cardiogenic shock but is not the definitive treatment for cardiac tamponade.

227. A 42-year-old female presents with pleuritic chest pain and dyspnea. Her blood pressure is 110/70 mmHg, heart rate is 100 beats per minute, and jugular veins are non-distended. ECG shows diffuse ST-segment elevation and PR-segment depression. Bedside ultrasound reveals a small pericardial effusion without evidence of tamponade physiology. Which of the following is the most likely diagnosis?
a. acute pericarditis
b. cardiac tamponade
c. pulmonary embolism
d. myocarditis

Answer: a. acute pericarditis. Explanation: The patient's presentation is consistent with acute pericarditis, an inflammation of the pericardium that typically presents with pleuritic chest pain, dyspnea, and fever. The ECG findings of diffuse ST-segment elevation and PR-segment depression are characteristic of acute pericarditis and help differentiate it from other causes of chest pain such as myocardial infarction or myocarditis. The presence of a small pericardial effusion on bedside ultrasound is also supportive of the diagnosis, as pericardial effusions are common in acute pericarditis. However, the absence of hypotension, jugular venous distention, and other features of tamponade physiology suggests that the effusion is not hemodynamically significant. Cardiac tamponade is less likely in the absence of these findings and with a blood pressure in the normal range. Pulmonary embolism can cause pleuritic chest pain and dyspnea but would not typically present with the ECG changes of pericarditis. Myocarditis can cause chest pain, dyspnea, and ECG changes but is typically associated with elevated cardiac biomarkers and left ventricular dysfunction on imaging.

228. A 55-year-old male with a history of lung cancer presents with dyspnea and hypotension. His blood pressure is 80/60 mmHg, heart rate is 120 beats per minute, and jugular veins are distended. Pulsus paradoxus is present. ECG shows low-voltage QRS complexes and electrical alternans. Bedside ultrasound reveals a large pericardial effusion with right ventricular diastolic collapse. Laboratory studies are significant for a positive D-dimer. Which of the following is the most appropriate next step in management?
a. perform urgent pericardiocentesis
b. administer intravenous thrombolysis
c. initiate broad-spectrum antibiotics
d. perform CT angiography of the chest

Answer: a. perform urgent pericardiocentesis. Explanation: The patient's presentation is most consistent with cardiac tamponade secondary to a malignant pericardial effusion, given his history of lung cancer and the presence of Beck's triad (hypotension, muffled heart sounds, and jugular venous distention) and pulsus paradoxus. The ECG findings of low-voltage QRS complexes and electrical alternans and the bedside ultrasound findings of a large pericardial effusion with right ventricular diastolic collapse further support the diagnosis of tamponade. In this setting, the most appropriate next step is urgent pericardiocentesis to drain the effusion and relieve the hemodynamic compromise. While the positive D-dimer raises the possibility of pulmonary embolism (PE), the patient's presentation is more consistent with tamponade, and delaying pericardiocentesis to perform CT angiography could be life-threatening.

Intravenous thrombolysis is not indicated in the absence of confirmed PE and could potentially worsen bleeding into the pericardial space. Broad-spectrum antibiotics are not indicated in the absence of signs or symptoms of infection.

229. A 68-year-old female presents with chest pain and shortness of breath. Her blood pressure is 90/60 mmHg, heart rate is 110 beats per minute, and jugular veins are distended. Pulsus paradoxus is present. ECG shows low-voltage QRS complexes and electrical alternans. Bedside ultrasound reveals a moderate pericardial effusion with right ventricular diastolic collapse. The patient is on warfarin for atrial fibrillation, and her INR is 3.5. Which of the following is the most appropriate next step in management?
a. administer intravenous vitamin K
b. perform urgent pericardiocentesis
c. initiate heparin infusion
d. perform thoracotomy with pericardial window

Answer: b. perform urgent pericardiocentesis. Explanation: The patient's presentation is consistent with cardiac tamponade, as evidenced by the presence of Beck's triad, pulsus paradoxus, and supportive ECG and ultrasound findings. The fact that she is on warfarin and has a supratherapeutic INR suggests that the pericardial effusion may be hemorrhagic in nature. However, the presence of tamponade physiology necessitates urgent pericardiocentesis to relieve the hemodynamic compromise, regardless of the etiology of the effusion. While administering intravenous vitamin K may help reverse the anticoagulant effects of warfarin, it does not address the acute need for drainage of the pericardial effusion. Initiating heparin infusion is contraindicated in the setting of a hemorrhagic effusion and could potentially worsen the bleeding. Thoracotomy with pericardial window is a surgical procedure that may be indicated for recurrent or loculated effusions but is not the initial treatment of choice for acute tamponade.

230. A 50-year-old male presents with chest pain and dyspnea. His blood pressure is 100/70 mmHg, heart rate is 100 beats per minute, and jugular veins are non-distended. ECG shows diffuse ST-segment elevation and PR-segment depression. Bedside ultrasound reveals a small pericardial effusion without evidence of tamponade physiology. The patient is afebrile and has no history of recent viral illness. Which of the following is the most likely etiology of this patient's condition?
a. viral pericarditis
b. uremic pericarditis
c. idiopathic pericarditis
d. malignant pericardial effusion

Answer: c. idiopathic pericarditis. Explanation: The patient's presentation is consistent with acute pericarditis, as evidenced by the pleuritic chest pain, dyspnea, and characteristic ECG findings of diffuse ST-segment elevation and PR-segment depression. The presence of a small pericardial effusion on bedside ultrasound is also supportive of the diagnosis. However, the absence of fever or recent viral illness makes viral pericarditis less likely, and the lack of a history of end-stage renal disease or other risk factors for uremia makes uremic pericarditis unlikely. In the absence of an identifiable cause, idiopathic pericarditis is the most likely etiology, as it accounts for up to 90% of cases of acute pericarditis in developed countries. Malignant pericardial effusion is also a possibility, particularly in older patients or those with a history of malignancy, but the absence of tamponade physiology and the presence of typical ECG findings of pericarditis make it less likely in this case.

231. A 25-year-old male presents with sudden-onset chest pain and shortness of breath. His blood pressure is 70/40 mmHg, heart rate is 130 beats per minute, and jugular veins are distended. Pulsus paradoxus is present. ECG shows

low-voltage QRS complexes and electrical alternans. Bedside ultrasound reveals a large pericardial effusion with right ventricular diastolic collapse. The patient has no significant past medical history but reports recent use of intravenous drugs. Which of the following is the most likely etiology of this patient's condition?
a. viral pericarditis
b. uremic pericarditis
c. idiopathic pericarditis
d. infectious endocarditis with pericardial extension

Answer: d. infectious endocarditis with pericardial extension. Explanation: The patient's presentation is consistent with cardiac tamponade, as evidenced by the presence of Beck's triad, pulsus paradoxus, and supportive ECG and ultrasound findings. The fact that he is a young, otherwise healthy individual with a history of intravenous drug use raises the possibility of infectious endocarditis as the underlying etiology. Intravenous drug use is a major risk factor for the development of endocarditis, particularly right-sided endocarditis involving the tricuspid valve. In some cases, the infection can extend beyond the valve and involve the pericardium, leading to a purulent pericardial effusion and tamponade. Viral pericarditis is a common cause of pericardial effusions in young adults but typically presents with a more subacute onset and less severe hemodynamic compromise. Uremic pericarditis is unlikely in the absence of a history of end-stage renal disease or other risk factors for uremia. Idiopathic pericarditis is a diagnosis of exclusion and is less likely in the presence of risk factors for alternative etiologies such as intravenous drug use.

232. A 30-year-old female presents with pleuritic chest pain and dyspnea. Her blood pressure is 110/70 mmHg, heart rate is 90 beats per minute, and jugular veins are non-distended. ECG shows diffuse ST-segment elevation and PR-segment depression. Bedside ultrasound reveals a small pericardial effusion without evidence of tamponade physiology. The patient reports a recent upper respiratory infection and has a family history of autoimmune disorders. Which of the following is the most appropriate next step in the diagnostic evaluation?
a. perform pericardiocentesis and send fluid for analysis
b. order antinuclear antibody (ANA) and rheumatoid factor (RF) tests
c. perform cardiac MRI with gadolinium contrast
d. initiate empiric antibiotic therapy

Answer: b. order antinuclear antibody (ANA) and rheumatoid factor (RF) tests. Explanation: The patient's presentation is consistent with acute pericarditis, as evidenced by the pleuritic chest pain, dyspnea, and characteristic ECG findings of diffuse ST-segment elevation and PR-segment depression. The presence of a small pericardial effusion on bedside ultrasound is also supportive of the diagnosis. Given the patient's young age, female sex, and family history of autoimmune disorders, an autoimmune etiology such as systemic lupus erythematosus (SLE) or rheumatoid arthritis (RA) should be considered. Ordering antinuclear antibody (ANA) and rheumatoid factor (RF) tests can help screen for these conditions and guide further diagnostic evaluation and management. Pericardiocentesis is not indicated in the absence of tamponade physiology or other indications for diagnostic or therapeutic drainage.

233. In the management of a COPD exacerbation, which initial pharmacological treatment is recommended to relieve bronchospasm and improve airflow?
a. Oral corticosteroids
b. Short-acting beta-agonists (SABA)
c. Long-acting muscarinic antagonists (LAMA)
d. Theophylline

Answer: b. Short-acting beta-agonists (SABA). Explanation: Short-acting beta-agonists, such as albuterol, are the first-line pharmacological treatment for acute relief of bronchospasm in COPD exacerbations due to their rapid onset of action in dilating the bronchi and improving airflow.

234. For a COPD patient with a chronic productive cough, which class of medication is most effective in reducing mucus hypersecretion?
a. Mucolytics
b. Antitussives
c. Inhaled corticosteroids
d. Antibiotics

Answer: a. Mucolytics. Explanation: Mucolytics, such as N-acetylcysteine, help reduce mucus viscosity and promote its clearance, thereby alleviating symptoms in COPD patients with chronic productive cough by targeting mucus hypersecretion.

235. A patient with COPD is assessed for long-term oxygen therapy. Which criterion must be met for its initiation according to the GOLD guidelines?
a. SpO2 ≥ 92% at rest
b. PaO2 ≤ 55 mmHg or SaO2 ≤ 88% on room air
c. Forced expiratory volume in 1 second (FEV1) < 30% predicted
d. Presence of cor pulmonale

Answer: b. PaO2 ≤ 55 mmHg or SaO2 ≤ 88% on room air. Explanation: The GOLD guidelines recommend long-term oxygen therapy for COPD patients with a resting PaO2 of ≤ 55 mmHg or SaO2 ≤ 88% on room air, as oxygen supplementation has been shown to improve survival in this population.

236. In COPD management, what is the primary purpose of using inhaled corticosteroids (ICS) in combination with long-acting beta-agonists (LABA)?
a. To reduce hypercapnia
b. To decrease the frequency of exacerbations in patients with a history of exacerbations
c. To increase oxygen saturation
d. To cure COPD

Answer: b. To decrease the frequency of exacerbations in patients with a history of exacerbations. Explanation: The combination of inhaled corticosteroids and long-acting beta-agonists is used in COPD management primarily to decrease the frequency of exacerbations in patients with a history of exacerbations, not for the cure, as COPD is a chronic and progressive disease.

237. In evaluating a patient with suspected COPD, which diagnostic test is considered the gold standard for confirming airflow obstruction?
a. Chest X-ray

b. Spirometry with post-bronchodilator FEV1/FVC ratio
c. Complete blood count (CBC)
d. Arterial blood gas (ABG) analysis

Answer: b. Spirometry with post-bronchodilator FEV1/FVC ratio. Explanation: Spirometry is the gold standard diagnostic test for COPD, with a post-bronchodilator FEV1/FVC ratio of less than 0.70 confirming the presence of persistent airflow obstruction characteristic of COPD.

238. For a COPD patient experiencing a moderate exacerbation, why is the addition of oral corticosteroids beneficial?
a. To immediately improve lung function
b. To provide long-term cure of COPD
c. To reduce the duration of the exacerbation and improve outcomes
d. To decrease the need for supplemental oxygen

Answer: c. To reduce the duration of the exacerbation and improve outcomes. Explanation: Oral corticosteroids are beneficial in managing moderate to severe COPD exacerbations as they can reduce the duration of the exacerbation, improve lung function and oxygenation, and potentially decrease the risk of relapse, hospitalization, and treatment failure.

239. What is the role of pulmonary rehabilitation in the management of COPD?
a. To restore lung function to normal
b. To improve exercise tolerance, quality of life, and reduce symptoms
c. To increase the effectiveness of inhaled medications
d. To reduce the size of bullae in advanced COPD

Answer: b. To improve exercise tolerance, quality of life, and reduce symptoms. Explanation: Pulmonary rehabilitation, a comprehensive intervention that includes patient education, exercise training, nutrition advice, and psychosocial support, plays a crucial role in COPD management by improving exercise tolerance, quality of life, and reducing symptoms.

240. When considering non-pharmacological management strategies for COPD, which intervention is crucial for all patients, regardless of disease severity?
a. Lung volume reduction surgery
b. Smoking cessation
c. Long-term antibiotic therapy
d. Continuous positive airway pressure (CPAP)

Answer: b. Smoking cessation. Explanation: Smoking cessation is the single most effective and crucial intervention for all patients with COPD, regardless of disease severity, as it can slow disease progression, improve symptoms, and enhance quality of life.

241. In the management of severe COPD, what is the indication for considering lung volume reduction surgery (LVRS)?
a. Presence of diffuse emphysema without significant hyperinflation
b. FEV1 and DLCO > 20% predicted
c. Presence of large bullae comprising > 30% of lung volume
d. Severe hyperinflation with upper lobe predominant emphysema and low exercise capacity despite optimal medical therapy

Answer: d. Severe hyperinflation with upper lobe predominant emphysema and low exercise capacity despite optimal medical therapy. Explanation: LVRS is considered for select patients with severe COPD characterized by upper lobe predominant emphysema and severe hyperinflation who have a low exercise capacity despite receiving optimal medical management, as it can improve lung function, exercise capacity, and quality of life.

242. A COPD patient on long-term home oxygen therapy is admitted with an exacerbation. What adjustment in their oxygen therapy might be necessary during hospitalization?
a. Discontinuation of oxygen therapy to assess baseline saturation
b. Increase in oxygen flow rate to achieve SaO2 of 100%
c. Titration of oxygen to maintain SaO2 within 88-92%
d. Switching from continuous to intermittent oxygen therapy

Answer: c. Titration of oxygen to maintain SaO2 within 88-92%. Explanation: In hospitalized COPD patients on long-term oxygen therapy, titration of oxygen to maintain SaO2 within 88-92% is often necessary to ensure adequate oxygenation without risking hypercapnia and acidosis, which can occur from oxygen-induced suppression of ventilatory drive in patients with COPD.

243. In distinguishing emphysema from chronic bronchitis, which clinical feature is most characteristic of emphysema?
a. Productive cough for 3 months in two consecutive years
b. Prolonged expiration with a decreased FEV1/FVC ratio
c. Presence of wheezing and dyspnea on exertion
d. Increased anteroposterior diameter of the chest

Answer: d. Increased anteroposterior diameter of the chest. Explanation: An increased anteroposterior diameter of the chest, often referred to as "barrel chest," is more characteristic of emphysema due to hyperinflation of the lungs and destruction of alveolar walls, whereas chronic bronchitis is primarily defined by the presence of a productive cough for 3 months in two consecutive years, as per the classic definition.

244. The primary pathophysiological change in emphysema is:
a. Hypertrophy of bronchial smooth muscles
b. Destruction of alveolar walls and loss of lung elasticity
c. Hypersecretion of mucus in the bronchi
d. Chronic inflammation and fibrosis of the bronchial wall

Answer: b. Destruction of alveolar walls and loss of lung elasticity. Explanation: The hallmark of emphysema is the destruction of alveolar walls and loss of lung elasticity, leading to air trapping and reduced gas exchange. The other options describe changes more typical of chronic bronchitis or asthma.

245. Which symptom is more commonly associated with chronic bronchitis than emphysema?
a. Pink puffer phenotype
b. "Blue bloater" phenotype
c. Digital clubbing
d. Quiet chest on auscultation

Answer: b. "Blue bloater" phenotype. Explanation: The "blue bloater" phenotype, characterized by cyanosis and fluid retention, is more commonly associated with chronic bronchitis due to chronic hypoxia and hypercapnia. The "pink puffer" phenotype is typically associated with emphysema, characterized by dyspnea and prolonged expiration without significant cyanosis.

246. In the assessment of a patient with COPD, the presence of which finding would suggest a predominance of emphysema?
a. Frequent episodes of acute bronchitis
b. A history of significant tobacco smoking
c. Diminished breath sounds and hyperresonance on percussion
d. Daily productive cough

Answer: c. Diminished breath sounds and hyperresonance on percussion. Explanation: Diminished breath sounds and hyperresonance on percussion are indicative of lung hyperinflation and air trapping, which are characteristic findings in emphysema. While smoking is a risk factor for both conditions, the specific physical exam findings suggest emphysema predominance.

247. A patient with COPD presents with worsening dyspnea and a significant increase in sputum production. This presentation is most consistent with an exacerbation of:
a. Emphysema due to increased air trapping
b. Chronic bronchitis due to acute infection superimposed on chronic inflammation
c. Asthma due to reversible airway obstruction
d. Pulmonary embolism due to immobilization

Answer: b. Chronic bronchitis due to acute infection superimposed on chronic inflammation. Explanation: An increase in sputum production and worsening dyspnea, especially if associated with signs of infection, is indicative of an acute exacerbation of chronic bronchitis, where acute infections can superimpose on chronic bronchial inflammation and exacerbate symptoms.

248. In evaluating a patient for COPD, which diagnostic criterion is essential for the diagnosis of chronic bronchitis?
a. Decreased FEV1/FVC ratio on spirometry
b. Chest X-ray showing flattened diaphragms
c. Chronic productive cough for at least three months for two consecutive years
d. CT scan showing emphysematous changes in the lungs

Answer: c. Chronic productive cough for at least three months for two consecutive years. Explanation: The classic definition of chronic bronchitis requires the presence of a chronic productive cough for at least three months in each of two consecutive years, in the absence of any other identifiable cause.

249. The primary mechanism leading to hypoxemia in emphysema is:
a. Mucous plugging and airway obstruction
b. Ventilation-perfusion (V/Q) mismatch
c. Shunting of blood through the pulmonary circulation
d. Reduced diffusing capacity of the alveolar-capillary membrane

Answer: b. Ventilation-perfusion (V/Q) mismatch. Explanation: In emphysema, the destruction of alveolar walls and the consequent loss of capillary beds lead to ventilation-perfusion mismatch, which is the primary mechanism for hypoxemia, as some areas of the lung receive oxygen without adequate blood flow for gas exchange.

250. Which of the following pulmonary function test findings is indicative of chronic bronchitis?
a. Increased total lung capacity (TLC)
b. Normal FEV1/FVC ratio with decreased diffusing capacity
c. Reduced FEV1/FVC ratio with normal TLC
d. Increased residual volume with reduced vital capacity

Answer: c. Reduced FEV1/FVC ratio with normal TLC. Explanation: Chronic bronchitis is characterized by airflow obstruction, evidenced by a reduced FEV1/FVC ratio on spirometry. Total lung capacity may remain normal or slightly increased due to mucus hypersecretion and inflammation, unlike emphysema, where significant hyperinflation increases TLC.

251. The presence of cor pulmonale is more commonly associated with:
a. Emphysema due to primary alveolar destruction
b. Chronic bronchitis due to prolonged hypoxemia and pulmonary hypertension
c. Asthma due to episodic bronchospasm
d. Pulmonary fibrosis due to restrictive lung disease

Answer: b. Chronic bronchitis due to prolonged hypoxemia and pulmonary hypertension. Explanation: Cor pulmonale, or right-sided heart failure, is more commonly associated with chronic bronchitis, where prolonged hypoxemia leads to pulmonary hypertension and subsequent right ventricular hypertrophy and failure.

252. In managing a patient with predominant emphysema, which therapeutic intervention is most beneficial for improving lung function and quality of life?
a. Aggressive antibiotic therapy
b. Long-term oxygen therapy if chronic hypoxemia is present
c. Daily chest physiotherapy to clear secretions
d. High-dose inhaled corticosteroids

Answer: b. Long-term oxygen therapy if chronic hypoxemia is present. Explanation: Long-term oxygen therapy has been shown to improve survival and quality of life in patients with COPD, particularly in those with predominant emphysema and chronic hypoxemia, by correcting hypoxia, reducing pulmonary hypertension, and decreasing the workload on the heart.

253. According to the GOLD criteria, what defines Stage I (Mild) COPD?
a. FEV1/FVC < 0.70 and FEV1 ≥ 80% predicted
b. FEV1/FVC < 0.70 and FEV1 < 30% predicted
c. FEV1/FVC < 0.70 and 30% ≤ FEV1 < 50% predicted
d. FEV1/FVC < 0.70 and 50% ≤ FEV1 < 80% predicted

Answer: a. FEV1/FVC < 0.70 and FEV1 ≥ 80% predicted. Explanation: Stage I (Mild) COPD is defined by a post-bronchodilator FEV1/FVC ratio of less than 0.70, indicating the presence of airflow limitation, and an FEV1 of 80% or more of the predicted value, signifying only mild reduction in lung function.

254. In Stage II (Moderate) COPD as per GOLD criteria, what is the FEV1 range after bronchodilator use?
a. FEV1 ≥ 80% predicted
b. 30% ≤ FEV1 < 50% predicted
c. 50% ≤ FEV1 < 80% predicted
d. FEV1 < 30% predicted

Answer: c. 50% ≤ FEV1 < 80% predicted. Explanation: Stage II (Moderate) COPD is characterized by a post-bronchodilator FEV1/FVC ratio below 0.70, indicating persistent airflow limitation, and an FEV1 between 50% and 80% of the predicted value, indicating a moderate decrease in pulmonary function.

255. For a COPD patient classified in Stage III (Severe) according to GOLD criteria, what is the FEV1 level after bronchodilator administration?
a. FEV1 ≥ 80% predicted
b. 50% ≤ FEV1 < 80% predicted
c. 30% ≤ FEV1 < 50% predicted
d. FEV1 < 30% predicted

Answer: c. 30% ≤ FEV1 < 50% predicted. Explanation: Stage III (Severe) COPD is defined by a post-bronchodilator FEV1/FVC ratio less than 0.70, showing significant airflow obstruction, and an FEV1 between 30% and 50% of the predicted value, indicating severe impairment of lung function.

256. What characterizes Stage IV (Very Severe) COPD in the GOLD staging system?
a. FEV1/FVC < 0.70 and FEV1 ≥ 80% predicted with chronic respiratory failure
b. FEV1/FVC < 0.70 and 50% ≤ FEV1 < 80% predicted
c. FEV1/FVC < 0.70 and 30% ≤ FEV1 < 50% predicted
d. FEV1/FVC < 0.70 and FEV1 < 30% predicted or FEV1 < 50% predicted with chronic respiratory failure

Answer: d. FEV1/FVC < 0.70 and FEV1 < 30% predicted or FEV1 < 50% predicted with chronic respiratory failure. Explanation: Stage IV (Very Severe) COPD is defined by a post-bronchodilator FEV1/FVC ratio below 0.70 and an FEV1 below 30% predicted or FEV1 below 50% predicted in the presence of chronic respiratory failure, indicating very severe airflow limitation and impaired gas exchange.

257. How does the GOLD system incorporate symptoms and exacerbation history into COPD assessment beyond spirometric classification?
a. By solely focusing on the FEV1/FVC ratio
b. Through a combined assessment of symptoms using tools like the mMRC or CAT score and exacerbation risk
c. By assessing only the frequency of exacerbations
d. Using chest X-rays and CT scans to assess lung damage

Answer: b. Through a combined assessment of symptoms using tools like the mMRC or CAT score and exacerbation risk. Explanation: The GOLD system uses a multidimensional approach that includes spirometric classification and assesses symptoms using the mMRC dyspnea scale or the COPD Assessment Test (CAT), along with the patient's exacerbation history, to guide treatment decisions more comprehensively.

258. In the GOLD staging for COPD, what significance does a CAT score greater than 10 have?
a. It indicates a mild level of symptoms
b. It is used to classify COPD into one of the four stages
c. It suggests a higher symptom burden and may influence the choice of therapy
d. It directly correlates with the FEV1/FVC ratio

Answer: c. It suggests a higher symptom burden and may influence the choice of therapy. Explanation: A CAT score greater than 10 indicates a higher symptom burden in COPD patients. This assessment, combined with the history of exacerbations, helps determine the appropriate management and treatment strategies, beyond the spirometric classification alone.

259. In considering the risk of exacerbations in COPD, how does the GOLD system classify patients with two or more moderate exacerbations or one hospitalization in the past year?
a. Low risk
b. Intermediate risk

c. High risk
d. Not specified

Answer: c. High risk. Explanation: The GOLD system classifies patients as high risk if they have had two or more moderate exacerbations or at least one exacerbation leading to hospitalization in the past year, guiding more aggressive management strategies to reduce future exacerbation risk.

260. What is the primary goal of treatment in GOLD Stage II (Moderate) COPD?
a. To completely reverse lung damage
b. To slow disease progression and improve quality of life
c. To prepare for lung transplantation
d. To reduce the need for supplemental oxygen

Answer: b. To slow disease progression and improve quality of life. Explanation: The primary goal of treatment in GOLD Stage II (Moderate) COPD is to slow the progression of the disease, relieve symptoms, improve exercise tolerance, and overall quality of life, and prevent and treat exacerbations.

261. In GOLD Stage III (Severe) COPD, why is pulmonary rehabilitation considered an essential component of management?
a. It has been shown to reverse lung function decline
b. It significantly improves symptoms, exercise capacity, and quality of life
c. It eliminates the need for inhaled medications
d. It is a prerequisite for lung volume reduction surgery

Answer: b. It significantly improves symptoms, exercise capacity, and quality of life. Explanation: Pulmonary rehabilitation is a cornerstone in the management of GOLD Stage III (Severe) COPD, as it significantly improves dyspnea, exercise capacity, and quality of life, even though it does not directly improve lung function. It addresses the systemic effects of COPD and enhances the overall health status of patients.

262. In a patient with COPD, which class of bronchodilators is typically used as first-line therapy for symptom management?
a. Short-acting beta-agonists (SABAs)
b. Long-acting beta-agonists (LABAs)
c. Short-acting muscarinic antagonists (SAMAs)
d. Long-acting muscarinic antagonists (LAMAs)

Answer: d. Long-acting muscarinic antagonists (LAMAs). Explanation: LAMAs are often used as first-line maintenance therapy in COPD management due to their effectiveness in providing prolonged bronchodilation, improving lung function, reducing exacerbations, and improving symptoms and quality of life.

263. For acute asthma exacerbations, which medication is preferred for immediate relief of bronchospasm?
a. Oral corticosteroids
b. Inhaled corticosteroids
c. Short-acting beta-agonists (SABAs)
d. Long-acting beta-agonists (LABAs)

Answer: c. Short-acting beta-agonists (SABAs). Explanation: SABAs, such as albuterol, are the treatment of choice for quick relief of acute bronchospasm in asthma exacerbations due to their rapid onset of action in dilating the bronchi and relieving symptoms.

264. A patient with persistent asthma is not well controlled on a moderate dose of inhaled corticosteroid (ICS). What is the next best step in management according to current guidelines?
a. Increase the dose of ICS to the maximum recommended dose
b. Add a long-acting beta-agonist (LABA) to the current ICS regimen
c. Switch from ICS to an oral corticosteroid
d. Initiate short-acting beta-agonist (SABA) as monotherapy

Answer: b. Add a long-acting beta-agonist (LABA) to the current ICS regimen. Explanation: For patients with asthma not well controlled on a moderate dose of ICS, adding a LABA to the existing ICS regimen is recommended to improve control before increasing the ICS to a higher dose.

265. In the management of chronic asthma, which medication is primarily used to control inflammation and reduce the frequency of exacerbations?
a. Oral corticosteroids
b. Inhaled corticosteroids
c. Long-acting beta-agonists (LABAs)
d. Leukotriene receptor antagonists

Answer: b. Inhaled corticosteroids. Explanation: Inhaled corticosteroids are the cornerstone of chronic asthma management for their anti-inflammatory effects, which reduce airway hyperresponsiveness, control chronic symptoms, and decrease the frequency of exacerbations.

266. For a COPD patient with a PaO2 of 55 mmHg or an oxygen saturation of 88% at rest, which intervention is indicated to improve survival?
a. High-dose inhaled corticosteroids
b. Long-term oxygen therapy for ≥15 hours per day
c. Intermittent use of short-acting beta-agonists
d. Pulmonary rehabilitation program

Answer: b. Long-term oxygen therapy for ≥15 hours per day. Explanation: Long-term oxygen therapy is indicated for COPD patients with chronic respiratory failure, evidenced by a resting PaO2 ≤55 mmHg or SaO2 ≤88%, to improve survival, reduce hospitalizations, and enhance quality of life.

267. In COPD management, which treatment strategy has been shown to improve exercise tolerance, quality of life, and reduce hospital readmissions?
a. Antibiotic prophylaxis
b. Pulmonary rehabilitation
c. Nebulized hypertonic saline
d. Continuous oral corticosteroid therapy

Answer: b. Pulmonary rehabilitation. Explanation: Pulmonary rehabilitation, a comprehensive intervention including exercise training, education, and behavior change, is beneficial in COPD for improving exercise tolerance, quality of life, and reducing the risk of hospital readmissions.

268. When considering the use of systemic corticosteroids for an acute exacerbation of COPD, which potential side effect is of greatest concern?
a. Hypoglycemia
b. Osteoporosis
c. Tachycardia
d. Bronchospasm

Answer: b. Osteoporosis. Explanation: Systemic corticosteroids, while effective for treating acute exacerbations of COPD, are associated with significant side effects including osteoporosis, especially with long-term use, necessitating careful consideration of risks and benefits.

269. For a patient with severe asthma uncontrolled by high-dose inhaled corticosteroids and LABA, which additional therapy could be considered?
a. Short-acting muscarinic antagonist (SAMA)
b. Oral leukotriene receptor antagonist
c. Biologic therapy targeting specific inflammatory pathways
d. Increased frequency of SABA use

Answer: c. Biologic therapy targeting specific inflammatory pathways. Explanation: For patients with severe asthma uncontrolled by standard therapies, biologic therapies targeting specific inflammatory pathways (e.g., anti-IgE, anti-IL5) can be effective in reducing exacerbations and improving asthma control.

270. A COPD patient undergoing mechanical ventilation for acute respiratory failure requires sedation. Which agent is preferred due to its minimal impact on respiratory drive?
a. Midazolam
b. Propofol
c. Ketamine

d. Dexmedetomidine

Answer: d. Dexmedetomidine. Explanation: Dexmedetomidine is often preferred in ventilated COPD patients requiring sedation due to its analgesic and sedative effects with minimal impact on respiratory drive, allowing for better coordination with mechanical ventilation and easier weaning.

271. In an acute asthma exacerbation, which clinical sign is most indicative of severe airway obstruction and impending respiratory failure?
a. Loud wheezing on auscultation
b. Pulsus paradoxus exceeding 25 mmHg
c. Use of accessory muscles of respiration
d. Peak expiratory flow rate (PEFR) of 50% predicted

Answer: b. Pulsus paradoxus exceeding 25 mmHg. Explanation: Pulsus paradoxus, an exaggerated decrease in systolic blood pressure during inspiration, is indicative of severe asthma exacerbation. A value exceeding 25 mmHg suggests significant airway obstruction and is a warning sign of impending respiratory failure, necessitating immediate intervention.

272. In managing a patient with asthma, what is the primary goal of using inhaled corticosteroids (ICS)?
a. Immediate relief of bronchospasm
b. Reduction of airway inflammation
c. Prevention of respiratory infections
d. Increase in bronchial diameter

Answer: b. Reduction of airway inflammation. Explanation: The primary goal of using inhaled corticosteroids in asthma management is to reduce chronic airway inflammation, which is a fundamental pathophysiological feature of asthma. This leads to decreased hyper-responsiveness and improved control of asthma symptoms.

273. For a patient with asthma not controlled by low-dose inhaled corticosteroids, which step-up therapy is recommended according to most asthma guidelines?
a. Oral corticosteroids
b. High-dose inhaled corticosteroids
c. Addition of a long-acting beta-agonist (LABA) to existing ICS therapy
d. Leukotriene receptor antagonist as monotherapy

Answer: c. Addition of a long-acting beta-agonist (LABA) to existing ICS therapy. Explanation: When asthma is not well-controlled with low-dose inhaled corticosteroids, guidelines recommend the addition of a long-acting beta-agonist to the existing ICS therapy. This combination has been shown to improve asthma control more effectively than increasing the dose of ICS alone.

274. Which spirometric measurement is most crucial in the diagnosis and monitoring of asthma?
a. Total lung capacity (TLC)
b. Forced vital capacity (FVC)
c. Forced expiratory volume in 1 second (FEV1)
d. Diffusing capacity of the lungs for carbon monoxide (DLCO)

Answer: c. Forced expiratory volume in 1 second (FEV1). Explanation: FEV1 is the most crucial spirometric measurement in the diagnosis and monitoring of asthma, as it quantifies the maximum volume of air that can be forcefully exhaled in one second and is a key indicator of airflow obstruction, which is reversible in asthma.

275. In a patient with suspected asthma, what is the significance of a positive bronchodilator reversibility test?
a. Confirms the diagnosis of chronic obstructive pulmonary disease (COPD)
b. Indicates irreversible airway obstruction
c. Demonstrates reversible airflow obstruction, supporting the diagnosis of asthma
d. Suggests the presence of a fixed stenosis in the airway

Answer: c. Demonstrates reversible airflow obstruction, supporting the diagnosis of asthma. Explanation: A positive bronchodilator reversibility test, showing significant improvement in FEV1 following the administration of a bronchodilator, indicates reversible airflow obstruction, which is a hallmark characteristic of asthma, thus supporting the diagnosis.

276. For an asthmatic patient with exercise-induced bronchoconstriction, which preventive measure is most effective?
a. Pre-exercise administration of a short-acting beta-agonist (SABA)
b. Long-term oral corticosteroid therapy
c. Daily leukotriene receptor antagonist therapy
d. Use of anticholinergic agents before exercise

Answer: a. Pre-exercise administration of a short-acting beta-agonist (SABA). Explanation: The pre-exercise administration of a short-acting beta-agonist, such as albuterol, is the most effective measure for preventing exercise-induced bronchoconstriction in asthmatic patients, providing rapid bronchodilation and protection during physical activity.

277. In assessing asthma control, which symptom frequency categorizes a patient's asthma as "well-controlled"?
a. Symptoms more than twice a week but not daily
b. Nighttime awakenings once a week
c. Symptoms no more than twice a month and no nighttime awakenings
d. Daily use of a short-acting beta-agonist for symptom control

Answer: c. Symptoms no more than twice a month and no nighttime awakenings. Explanation: Asthma is considered "well-controlled" if symptoms occur no more than twice a month and there are no nighttime awakenings due to asthma. This indicates that the disease is being effectively managed, minimizing the impact on the patient's quality of life.

278. What is the role of tiotropium in asthma management, especially in patients over 6 years old?
a. It serves as a first-line rescue medication for acute symptoms
b. It is used as an add-on therapy when asthma is not controlled by ICS and LABA
c. It replaces the need for inhaled corticosteroids in mild asthma
d. It is the preferred monotherapy in severe asthma

Answer: b. It is used as an add-on therapy when asthma is not controlled by ICS and LABA. Explanation: Tiotropium, a long-acting muscarinic antagonist, has been shown to be effective as an add-on therapy in asthma management for patients aged 6 years and older whose asthma is not adequately controlled with inhaled corticosteroids and long-acting beta-agonists, improving lung function and decreasing exacerbations.

279. When is omalizumab indicated in the management of asthma?
a. As a first-line treatment in all asthma patients
b. In patients with moderate to severe persistent asthma who have a documented allergy and are not controlled with ICS
c. For immediate relief of acute asthma symptoms
d. In all steroid-resistant asthma cases

Answer: b. In patients with moderate to severe persistent asthma who have a documented allergy and are not controlled with ICS. Explanation: Omalizumab, an anti-IgE monoclonal antibody, is indicated for patients with moderate to severe persistent asthma who have evidence of allergen sensitivity and whose symptoms are inadequately controlled with high-dose inhaled corticosteroids, offering a targeted therapy to reduce the frequency of asthma exacerbations.

280. A 68-year-old male with a history of COPD is admitted to the ICU with acute hypercapnic respiratory failure. His initial arterial blood gas shows a pH of 7.28, PaCO2 of 68 mmHg, and PaO2 of 55 mmHg on 50% FiO2. The patient is initiated on mechanical ventilation. Which of the following is the most appropriate initial tidal volume setting?
a. 4 mL/kg of ideal body weight
b. 6 mL/kg of ideal body weight
c. 8 mL/kg of ideal body weight
d. 10 mL/kg of ideal body weight

Answer: b. 6 mL/kg of ideal body weight. Explanation: In patients with COPD and acute respiratory failure, the goal of mechanical ventilation is to provide adequate ventilation and oxygenation while minimizing the risk of ventilator-induced lung injury (VILI). Current guidelines recommend using a low tidal volume strategy, starting with a tidal volume of 6 mL/kg of ideal body weight and adjusting as needed based on the patient's response. This approach has been shown to reduce the risk of VILI and improve outcomes in patients with acute respiratory distress syndrome (ARDS), and similar principles are applied to patients with COPD. A tidal volume of 4 mL/kg may be too low and result in inadequate ventilation, while tidal volumes of 8-10 mL/kg may increase the risk of VILI, particularly in patients with pre-existing lung disease.

281. A 55-year-old female with a history of asthma presents with acute respiratory failure secondary to a severe asthma exacerbation. She is intubated and mechanically ventilated. Her initial ventilator settings include a tidal volume of 400 mL, respiratory rate of 12 breaths/min, FiO2 of 0.5, and PEEP of 5 cmH2O. Despite these settings, her peak airway pressure is 45 cmH2O, and she has persistent wheezing and poor air movement. Which of the following is the most appropriate adjustment to her ventilator settings?
a. Increase the tidal volume to 500 mL
b. Increase the respiratory rate to 16 breaths/min
c. Increase the FiO2 to 0.8
d. Decrease the respiratory rate to 8 breaths/min

Answer: d. Decrease the respiratory rate to 8 breaths/min. Explanation: In patients with severe asthma exacerbations, the primary goal of mechanical ventilation is to provide adequate oxygenation while avoiding dynamic hyperinflation and barotrauma. Dynamic hyperinflation occurs when there is insufficient time for complete exhalation before the next breath is delivered, leading to progressive air trapping and increased intrathoracic pressure. This can result in decreased venous return, hypotension, and increased risk of pneumothorax. To minimize dynamic hyperinflation, the ventilator strategy should aim to prolong the expiratory time by decreasing the respiratory rate and/or tidal volume. In this case, decreasing the respiratory rate to 8 breaths/min would be the most appropriate initial adjustment, as it would allow more time for exhalation and reduce the risk of dynamic hyperinflation. Increasing the tidal volume or respiratory rate could worsen dynamic hyperinflation, while increasing the FiO2 may improve oxygenation but does not address the underlying issue of air trapping.

282. A 72-year-old male with a history of interstitial lung disease is admitted with acute hypoxemic respiratory failure. He is intubated and mechanically ventilated with a tidal volume of 400 mL, respiratory rate of 20 breaths/min, FiO2 of 0.8, and PEEP of 8 cmH2O. His arterial blood gas shows a pH of 7.35, PaCO2 of 40 mmHg, and PaO2 of 60 mmHg. Which of the following is the most appropriate adjustment to his ventilator settings?
a. Increase the tidal volume to 500 mL
b. Increase the PEEP to 12 cmH2O
c. Decrease the FiO2 to 0.6
d. Increase the respiratory rate to 24 breaths/min

Answer: b. Increase the PEEP to 12 cmH2O. Explanation: In patients with interstitial lung disease and acute hypoxemic respiratory failure, the primary goal of mechanical ventilation is to provide adequate oxygenation while minimizing the risk of ventilator-induced lung injury (VILI). These patients often have reduced lung compliance and require higher levels of positive end-expiratory pressure (PEEP) to maintain alveolar recruitment and improve oxygenation. In this case, increasing the PEEP to 12 cmH2O would be the most appropriate adjustment, as it may help to improve oxygenation by increasing the functional residual capacity and reducing ventilation-perfusion mismatch. Increasing the tidal volume or respiratory rate could increase the risk of VILI, particularly in patients with pre-existing lung disease. Decreasing the FiO2 may be appropriate once oxygenation improves, but it should not be the initial adjustment in a patient with significant hypoxemia.

283. A 60-year-old female with a history of obesity and obstructive sleep apnea presents with acute hypercapnic respiratory failure secondary to a drug overdose. She is intubated and mechanically ventilated with a tidal volume of 500 mL, respiratory rate of 16 breaths/min, FiO2 of 0.4, and PEEP of 5 cmH2O. Her arterial blood gas shows a pH of

7.25, PaCO2 of 70 mmHg, and PaO2 of 90 mmHg. Which of the following is the most appropriate adjustment to her ventilator settings?
a. Increase the tidal volume to 600 mL
b. Increase the respiratory rate to 20 breaths/min
c. Decrease the FiO2 to 0.3
d. Decrease the PEEP to 0 cmH2O

Answer: b. Increase the respiratory rate to 20 breaths/min. Explanation: In patients with obesity and obstructive sleep apnea, the primary goal of mechanical ventilation is to provide adequate ventilation and oxygenation while minimizing the risk of hypoventilation and respiratory acidosis. These patients often have reduced chest wall compliance and increased airway resistance, which can lead to hypoventilation and CO2 retention. In this case, increasing the respiratory rate to 20 breaths/min would be the most appropriate adjustment, as it would help to increase minute ventilation and reduce the PaCO2. Increasing the tidal volume could increase the risk of ventilator-induced lung injury and may not be necessary if adequate ventilation can be achieved with a higher respiratory rate. Decreasing the FiO2 or PEEP is not indicated in a patient with significant hypercapnia and respiratory acidosis, as this could worsen ventilation-perfusion mismatch and further impair gas exchange.

284. A 75-year-old male with a history of COPD presents with acute hypercapnic respiratory failure secondary to a pneumonia. He is intubated and mechanically ventilated with volume control ventilation, with an initial tidal volume of 400 mL and respiratory rate of 12 breaths/min. Despite an FiO2 of 0.5 and PEEP of 5 cmH2O, his arterial blood gas shows a pH of 7.28, PaCO2 of 65 mmHg, and PaO2 of 60 mmHg. Which of the following is the most appropriate change to his ventilator mode?
a. Switch to pressure control ventilation
b. Switch to pressure support ventilation
c. Switch to airway pressure release ventilation (APRV)
d. Continue with volume control ventilation

Answer: a. Switch to pressure control ventilation. Explanation: In patients with COPD and acute hypercapnic respiratory failure, the choice of ventilator mode can have a significant impact on patient outcomes. Volume control ventilation, which delivers a fixed tidal volume with each breath, may be less effective in these patients due to the increased airway resistance and reduced lung compliance associated with COPD. Pressure control ventilation, which delivers a fixed inspiratory pressure with each breath, may be more effective in improving ventilation and reducing the risk of dynamic hyperinflation. In this case, switching to pressure control ventilation would be the most appropriate change, as it may help to improve ventilation and reduce the PaCO2 while minimizing the risk of ventilator-induced lung injury. Pressure support ventilation is primarily used for weaning and may not provide adequate support for a patient with significant respiratory failure. Airway pressure release ventilation (APRV) is a specialized mode that may be useful in patients with severe ARDS but is not typically used as a first-line mode in patients with COPD.

285. A 62-year-old female with a history of asthma presents with acute hypercapnic respiratory failure secondary to a severe asthma exacerbation. She is intubated and mechanically ventilated with pressure control ventilation, with an initial inspiratory pressure of 20 cmH2O, respiratory rate of 12 breaths/min, FiO2 of 0.6, and PEEP of 0 cmH2O. Despite these settings, her peak airway pressure is 40 cmH2O, and she has persistent wheezing and poor air movement. Which of the following is the most appropriate adjustment to her ventilator settings?
a. Increase the inspiratory pressure to 25 cmH2O
b. Increase the PEEP to 5 cmH2O

c. Increase the FiO2 to 1.0
d. Decrease the inspiratory time to 0.8 seconds

Answer: d. Decrease the inspiratory time to 0.8 seconds. Explanation: In patients with severe asthma exacerbations, the primary goal of mechanical ventilation is to provide adequate oxygenation while avoiding dynamic hyperinflation and barotrauma. Pressure control ventilation can be useful in these patients, as it allows for a variable inspiratory flow and may reduce the risk of dynamic hyperinflation compared to volume control ventilation. However, the inspiratory time should be kept short to allow for adequate expiratory time and minimize air trapping. In this case, decreasing the inspiratory time to 0.8 seconds would be the most appropriate adjustment, as it would help to reduce dynamic hyperinflation and improve expiratory flow. Increasing the inspiratory pressure or PEEP could worsen dynamic hyperinflation and increase the risk of barotrauma. Increasing the FiO2 may be necessary to maintain adequate oxygenation but does not address the underlying issue of air trapping.

286. A 70-year-old male with a history of COPD presents with acute hypercapnic respiratory failure secondary to a COPD exacerbation. He is intubated and mechanically ventilated with pressure control ventilation, with an initial inspiratory pressure of 15 cmH2O, respiratory rate of 12 breaths/min, FiO2 of 0.4, and PEEP of 5 cmH2O. His arterial blood gas shows a pH of 7.32, PaCO2 of 60 mmHg, and PaO2 of 65 mmHg. Which of the following is the most appropriate adjustment to his ventilator settings?
a. Increase the inspiratory pressure to 20 cmH2O
b. Increase the respiratory rate to 16 breaths/min
c. Decrease the FiO2 to 0.3
d. Increase the PEEP to 8 cmH2O

Answer: b. Increase the respiratory rate to 16 breaths/min. Explanation: In patients with COPD and acute hypercapnic respiratory failure, the primary goal of mechanical ventilation is to provide adequate ventilation and oxygenation while minimizing the risk of dynamic hyperinflation and ventilator-induced lung injury. Pressure control ventilation can be useful in these patients, as it allows for a variable inspiratory flow and may reduce the risk of dynamic hyperinflation compared to volume control ventilation. However, the respiratory rate should be adjusted to achieve adequate minute ventilation and reduce the PaCO2. In this case, increasing the respiratory rate to 16 breaths/min would be the most appropriate adjustment, as it would help to increase minute ventilation and reduce the PaCO2 without significantly increasing the risk of dynamic hyperinflation. Increasing the inspiratory pressure could improve ventilation but may also increase the risk of barotrauma and ventilator-induced lung injury. Decreasing the FiO2 is not indicated in a patient with significant hypoxemia, as this could worsen ventilation-perfusion mismatch and further impair gas exchange. Increasing the PEEP may be necessary in patients with significant atelectasis or hypoxemia but is not typically used as a first-line adjustment in patients with COPD.

287. A 65-year-old female with a history of obesity hypoventilation syndrome presents with acute hypercapnic respiratory failure secondary to a pulmonary embolism. She is intubated and mechanically ventilated with volume control ventilation, with an initial tidal volume of 500 mL, respiratory rate of 16 breaths/min, FiO2 of 0.5, and PEEP of 8 cmH2O. Her arterial blood gas shows a pH of 7.25, PaCO2 of 75 mmHg, and PaO2 of 70 mmHg. Which of the following is the most appropriate adjustment to her ventilator settings?
a. Increase the tidal volume to 600 mL
b. Increase the respiratory rate to 20 breaths/min
c. Decrease the FiO2 to 0.4
d. Decrease the PEEP to 5 cmH2O

Answer: b. Increase the respiratory rate to 20 breaths/min. Explanation: In patients with obesity hypoventilation syndrome and acute hypercapnic respiratory failure, the primary goal of mechanical ventilation is to provide adequate ventilation and oxygenation while minimizing the risk of hypoventilation and respiratory acidosis. These patients often have reduced chest wall compliance and increased airway resistance, which can lead to hypoventilation and CO2 retention. In this case, increasing the respiratory rate to 20 breaths/min would be the most appropriate adjustment, as it would help to increase minute ventilation and reduce the PaCO2. Increasing the tidal volume could improve ventilation but may also increase the risk of ventilator-induced lung injury, particularly in obese patients who may have reduced functional residual capacity. Decreasing the FiO2 or PEEP is not indicated in a patient with significant hypoxemia and respiratory acidosis, as this could worsen ventilation-perfusion mismatch and further impair gas exchange. It is important to note that these patients may also require higher levels of PEEP to maintain alveolar recruitment and improve oxygenation, particularly in the setting of acute pulmonary embolism.

288. A 58-year-old male with a history of interstitial lung disease presents with acute hypoxemic respiratory failure secondary to a pneumocystis pneumonia. He is intubated and mechanically ventilated with pressure control ventilation, with an initial inspiratory pressure of 25 cmH2O, respiratory rate of 20 breaths/min, FiO2 of 0.8, and PEEP of 10 cmH2O. His arterial blood gas shows a pH of 7.30, PaCO2 of 45 mmHg, and PaO2 of 55 mmHg. Which of the following is the most appropriate adjustment to his ventilator settings?
a. Increase the inspiratory pressure to 30 cmH2O
b. Increase the PEEP to 15 cmH2O
c. Decrease the respiratory rate to 16 breaths/min
d. Switch to volume control ventilation

Answer: b. Increase the PEEP to 15 cmH2O. Explanation: In patients with interstitial lung disease and acute hypoxemic respiratory failure, the primary goal of mechanical ventilation is to provide adequate oxygenation while minimizing the risk of ventilator-induced lung injury (VILI). These patients often have reduced lung compliance and may require higher levels of positive end-expiratory pressure (PEEP) to maintain alveolar recruitment and improve oxygenation. In this case, increasing the PEEP to 15 cmH2O would be the most appropriate adjustment, as it may help to improve oxygenation by increasing the functional residual capacity and reducing ventilation-perfusion mismatch. Increasing the inspiratory pressure could improve ventilation but may also increase the risk of VILI, particularly in patients with pre-existing lung disease. Decreasing the respiratory rate is not indicated in a patient with significant hypoxemia and may worsen ventilation-perfusion mismatch. Switching to volume control ventilation is not typically recommended in patients with interstitial lung disease, as it may increase the risk of VILI compared to pressure control ventilation. It is important to note that these patients may also require a conservative fluid management strategy and adjunctive therapies such as prone positioning or inhaled

289. Which of the following is a primary indication for the use of inhaled corticosteroids (ICS) in respiratory management?
a. As a quick-relief medication during an acute asthma attack
b. For long-term control to reduce inflammation in chronic asthma
c. To immediately reverse bronchoconstriction in COPD exacerbations
d. As a monotherapy in mild intermittent asthma

Answer: b. For long-term control to reduce inflammation in chronic asthma. Explanation: Inhaled corticosteroids are the cornerstone of long-term control therapy in asthma, aimed at reducing chronic inflammation, decreasing the frequency and severity of exacerbations, and improving overall lung function.

290. In a patient with asthma, adding a long-acting beta-agonist (LABA) to inhaled corticosteroid therapy is recommended when:
a. The patient's symptoms are well-controlled with ICS alone
b. The patient requires more than occasional use of a short-acting beta-agonist (SABA)
c. Immediately before exercise to prevent exercise-induced bronchospasm
d. As the first-line treatment in newly diagnosed asthma

Answer: b. The patient requires more than occasional use of a short-acting beta-agonist (SABA). Explanation: LABAs are added to ICS therapy when asthma is not adequately controlled with ICS alone, manifested by the need for frequent SABA use. LABAs improve control but are not used as monotherapy due to increased risk of asthma-related death.

291. Leukotriene modifiers are particularly useful in asthma management for patients who:
a. Have contraindications to the use of inhaled corticosteroids
b. Experience aspirin-exacerbated respiratory disease
c. Require rapid relief of acute bronchospasm
d. Show intolerance to LABA therapy

Answer: b. Experience aspirin-exacerbated respiratory disease. Explanation: Leukotriene modifiers, such as montelukast, are beneficial in patients with aspirin-exacerbated respiratory disease (AERD) as they block the leukotriene pathway, which is involved in the pathophysiology of AERD, leading to improved control of asthma symptoms and decreased sensitivity to aspirin.

292. The main mechanism of action of inhaled corticosteroids (ICS) in the management of chronic respiratory diseases is to:
a. Induce bronchodilation by relaxing smooth muscle in the airways
b. Inhibit the inflammatory response in the airways
c. Block the action of leukotrienes
d. Stimulate beta-2 adrenergic receptors to increase airflow

Answer: b. Inhibit the inflammatory response in the airways. Explanation: ICS work primarily by inhibiting the inflammatory response in the airways, reducing airway hyperresponsiveness, and decreasing the frequency of exacerbations in chronic respiratory conditions like asthma and COPD.

293. A major advantage of using long-acting beta-agonists (LABAs) in conjunction with inhaled corticosteroids (ICS) for asthma management is:
a. Immediate reduction of airway inflammation
b. Quick relief of acute asthma symptoms

c. Enhanced control of asthma symptoms and reduction in exacerbation frequency
d. Replacement of the need for short-acting beta-agonists (SABAs)

Answer: c. Enhanced control of asthma symptoms and reduction in exacerbation frequency. Explanation: The combination of LABAs with ICS enhances control of asthma symptoms and reduces the frequency of exacerbations more effectively than either component used alone. LABAs provide sustained bronchodilation, while ICS reduce inflammation.

294. When prescribing leukotriene modifiers for asthma management, it's important to monitor for:
a. Immediate hypersensitivity reactions
b. Potential impact on growth in children
c. Changes in bone mineral density
d. Neuropsychiatric events

Answer: d. Neuropsychiatric events. Explanation: While leukotriene modifiers like montelukast are generally well-tolerated, there have been reports of neuropsychiatric events, including agitation, aggression, hallucinations, and depression, which necessitates monitoring and caution in their use.

295. The use of inhaled corticosteroids (ICS) in COPD management is specifically indicated for patients:
a. With mild COPD and no history of exacerbations
b. Who are symptomatic with a FEV1 > 80% predicted
c. With a history of frequent exacerbations
d. As the first-line treatment regardless of disease severity

Answer: c. With a history of frequent exacerbations. Explanation: ICS are indicated in COPD management for patients with a history of frequent exacerbations, particularly those with a history of hospitalizations due to exacerbations, as they can reduce the frequency of future exacerbations when used in combination with bronchodilators.

296. A potential side effect of long-term use of inhaled corticosteroids (ICS) that requires monitoring is:
a. Tachycardia
b. Oral candidiasis
c. Hypokalemia
d. QT prolongation

Answer: b. Oral candidiasis. Explanation: Oral candidiasis (thrush) is a common side effect of long-term ICS use due to the deposition of steroids in the oral cavity, which can disrupt the normal flora. Patients should be advised to rinse their mouth after ICS use to minimize this risk.

297. In considering the addition of a LABA to an asthma patient's regimen, it is critical to assess:
a. The patient's preference for inhaler device type

b. The patient's current level of asthma control and use of SABA
c. The presence of comorbid allergic rhinitis
d. The patient's ability to perform peak flow monitoring

Answer: b. The patient's current level of asthma control and use of SABA. Explanation: Before adding a LABA to an asthma patient's regimen, it's crucial to assess the current level of asthma control and the frequency of SABA use, as LABAs are indicated when asthma is not well-controlled with ICS alone.

298. In pulmonary rehabilitation for patients with severe COPD, the primary goal of incorporating bronchodilators into the treatment plan is to:
a. Cure the underlying lung disease
b. Improve exercise tolerance and participation in activities
c. Completely reverse airway obstruction
d. Eliminate the need for supplemental oxygen

Answer: b. Improve exercise tolerance and participation in activities. Explanation: The primary goal of incorporating bronchodilators into the pulmonary rehabilitation plan for COPD patients is to improve exercise tolerance and participation in activities by reducing airway obstruction, relieving symptoms, and enhancing overall quality of life.

299. In assessing a patient with suspected acute kidney injury (AKI), which laboratory finding is most indicative of intrinsic renal damage?
a. Elevated serum creatinine with normal urine output
b. Presence of muddy brown casts in urine sediment
c. Hyperkalemia with an ECG showing no changes
d. Isolated proteinuria without hematuria

Answer: b. Presence of muddy brown casts in urine sediment. Explanation: The presence of muddy brown casts in urine sediment is highly indicative of acute tubular necrosis, a type of intrinsic renal damage seen in acute kidney injury. These casts result from the sloughing of renal tubular epithelial cells, which is a hallmark of tubular injury.

300. For a patient with chronic kidney disease (CKD), what is the significance of calculating the estimated glomerular filtration rate (eGFR)?
a. To determine the need for renal replacement therapy
b. To assess the stage of CKD and guide management decisions
c. To decide on the dosage of renally cleared medications
d. To evaluate for renal artery stenosis

Answer: b. To assess the stage of CKD and guide management decisions. Explanation: The eGFR is crucial in assessing the stage of chronic kidney disease, which is important for guiding management decisions and monitoring disease progression. It reflects the level of kidney function and helps in planning treatment strategies, including the timing of referral for renal replacement therapy.

301. In the context of renal system physiology, what role does the juxtaglomerular apparatus play in blood pressure regulation?
a. It secretes aldosterone in response to low blood volume
b. It directly activates the parasympathetic nervous system to decrease heart rate
c. It releases renin in response to decreased renal perfusion pressure
d. It filters plasma to form urine without any adjustments

Answer: c. It releases renin in response to decreased renal perfusion pressure. Explanation: The juxtaglomerular apparatus (JGA) is essential for blood pressure regulation through the renin-angiotensin-aldosterone system (RAAS). It releases renin in response to decreased renal perfusion pressure, initiating a cascade that ultimately leads to vasoconstriction and sodium retention, thereby increasing blood pressure.

302. A patient with end-stage renal disease (ESRD) on hemodialysis develops pericarditis. What is the most likely etiology of this complication?
a. Viral infection
b. Uremic pericarditis
c. Autoimmune response
d. Myocardial infarction

Answer: b. Uremic pericarditis. Explanation: Uremic pericarditis is a serious complication of end-stage renal disease (ESRD) and is associated with the accumulation of uremic toxins due to inadequate dialysis. It presents as an inflammatory condition of the pericardium and is a direct consequence of renal failure.

303. In managing a patient with polycystic kidney disease (PKD), what is the primary goal of treatment?
a. To shrink renal cysts using aggressive diuresis
b. To manage hypertension and slow the progression of renal damage
c. To initiate early renal replacement therapy before the onset of symptoms
d. To perform surgical cyst decompression routinely

Answer: b. To manage hypertension and slow the progression of renal damage. Explanation: The primary goal in managing polycystic kidney disease is to control hypertension, which is both a cause and a consequence of the disease, and to implement strategies that may slow the progression of renal damage, such as lifestyle modifications and pharmacological treatment.

304. What is the most common cause of intrinsic acute kidney injury (AKI) in hospitalized patients?
a. Drug-induced nephrotoxicity
b. Acute glomerulonephritis
c. Acute tubular necrosis (ATN)
d. Renal artery embolism

Answer: c. Acute tubular necrosis (ATN). Explanation: Acute tubular necrosis (ATN) is the most common cause of intrinsic acute kidney injury in hospitalized patients, often resulting from ischemia, nephrotoxins, or sepsis. It involves damage to the renal tubular epithelial cells, leading to acute renal dysfunction.

305. For a patient undergoing contrast-enhanced imaging studies, which preventive measure is most effective in reducing the risk of contrast-induced nephropathy (CIN)?
a. Administration of acetylcysteine prior to and after the procedure
b. High-volume intravenous hydration with isotonic saline
c. Immediate initiation of dialysis post-procedure
d. Use of low molecular weight heparin during the procedure

Answer: b. High-volume intravenous hydration with isotonic saline. Explanation: High-volume intravenous hydration with isotonic saline is the most effective preventive measure against contrast-induced nephropathy (CIN), as it helps dilute the nephrotoxic contrast agent and maintains renal perfusion, reducing the risk of renal injury.

306. In evaluating a patient with nephrotic syndrome, which clinical feature is least likely to be present?
a. Hyperlipidemia
b. Hypoalbuminemia
c. Hematuria
d. Edema

Answer: c. Hematuria. Explanation: While hematuria can occur in nephrotic syndrome, it is more characteristic of nephritic syndromes. Nephrotic syndrome is primarily characterized by proteinuria leading to hypoalbuminemia, edema, and hyperlipidemia due to the loss of protein in the urine and compensatory protein synthesis by the liver.

307. What dietary modification is most recommended for patients with chronic kidney disease to slow disease progression?
a. High protein intake
b. Low sodium intake
c. High carbohydrate intake
d. Low fat intake

Answer: b. Low sodium intake. Explanation: A low sodium intake is recommended for patients with chronic kidney disease to help control blood pressure and reduce the risk of fluid overload, both of which can contribute to the progression of renal damage and exacerbate cardiovascular complications associated with CKD.

308. In a patient with diabetic nephropathy, which finding on urinalysis is most indicative of early renal involvement?
a. Waxy casts
b. Broad casts
c. Microalbuminuria
d. Gross hematuria

Answer: c. Microalbuminuria. Explanation: Microalbuminuria, the excretion of a small amount of albumin in the urine, is an early indicator of diabetic nephropathy. It precedes overt proteinuria and reflects early glomerular damage in patients with diabetes, signaling the need for interventions to prevent further renal progression.

309. In an acute asthma exacerbation, a significant decrease in Peak Expiratory Flow Rate (PEFR) indicates:
a. Mild obstruction and the need for short-acting beta-agonists (SABA) only
b. Moderate obstruction and potential need for systemic corticosteroids
c. Severe obstruction and immediate hospitalization
d. Normal airway function, no intervention needed

Answer: c. Severe obstruction and immediate hospitalization. Explanation: A significant decrease in PEFR in the context of an acute asthma exacerbation indicates severe airway obstruction, necessitating immediate medical intervention, which may include hospitalization for advanced respiratory support and aggressive treatment.

310. When initiating treatment for an acute asthma exacerbation, the first-line medication to relieve bronchospasm is:
a. An oral corticosteroid
b. A short-acting beta-agonist (SABA) via inhalation
c. A long-acting beta-agonist (LABA) via inhalation
d. An inhaled corticosteroid (ICS)

Answer: b. A short-acting beta-agonist (SABA) via inhalation. Explanation: SABAs are the first-line treatment for immediate relief of bronchospasm in acute asthma exacerbations due to their rapid onset of action in dilating the bronchi.

311. For a patient experiencing an acute exacerbation of COPD, the initial management should include:
a. High-dose inhaled corticosteroids
b. Oral corticosteroids and short-acting bronchodilators
c. Long-acting muscarinic antagonists (LAMA)
d. Antibiotic therapy, irrespective of infection signs

Answer: b. Oral corticosteroids and short-acting bronchodilators. Explanation: The initial management of an acute COPD exacerbation typically includes oral corticosteroids to reduce airway inflammation and short-acting bronchodilators (SABAs and/or SAMAs) to relieve bronchospasm.

312. In the management of an acute asthma exacerbation, the effectiveness of treatment is best monitored by:
a. Frequency of cough
b. Improvement in PEFR or FEV1
c. Reduction in wheezing heard on auscultation

d. Patient's subjective feeling of relief

Answer: b. Improvement in PEFR or FEV1. Explanation: Objective measures such as PEFR (Peak Expiratory Flow Rate) or FEV1 (Forced Expiratory Volume in the first second) are reliable indicators to monitor the effectiveness of treatment in an acute asthma exacerbation, reflecting improvement in airway obstruction.

313. When prescribing oral corticosteroids for an acute exacerbation of asthma, the typical course duration is:
a. 24 hours
b. 3-5 days
c. 7-14 days
d. Indefinite, until symptoms resolve

Answer: c. 7-14 days. Explanation: A typical course of oral corticosteroids for an acute asthma exacerbation ranges from 7-14 days to effectively reduce airway inflammation and prevent the recurrence of exacerbations.

314. A patient with a known history of asthma presents with an acute exacerbation and is not responding to repeated SABA treatments. The next step should be:
a. Discontinuation of all asthma medications due to potential adverse effects
b. Administration of a LABA for long-term control
c. Initiation of systemic corticosteroids
d. Performance of a chest X-ray to rule out pneumonia

Answer: c. Initiation of systemic corticosteroids. Explanation: If an asthma exacerbation is not responsive to repeated SABA treatments, systemic corticosteroids should be initiated promptly to control the inflammation and prevent progression of the exacerbation.

315. In the context of acute exacerbations of COPD, the role of systemic corticosteroids is to:
a. Provide immediate bronchodilation
b. Reduce airway inflammation and improve lung function
c. Serve as maintenance therapy to prevent future exacerbations
d. Replace the need for inhaled bronchodilators

Answer: b. Reduce airway inflammation and improve lung function. Explanation: Systemic corticosteroids are used in acute COPD exacerbations to reduce airway inflammation, thereby improving lung function and expediting recovery from the exacerbation.

316. For patients with recurrent exacerbations of COPD, which therapy has been shown to reduce the frequency of exacerbations?
a. Antibiotic prophylaxis
b. Continuous oxygen therapy

c. Regular use of inhaled corticosteroids combined with long-acting beta-agonists (ICS/LABA)
d. Nebulized hypertonic saline

Answer: c. Regular use of inhaled corticosteroids combined with long-acting beta-agonists (ICS/LABA). Explanation: Regular use of combined ICS/LABA therapy has been shown to reduce the frequency of exacerbations in patients with COPD, particularly those with a history of recurrent exacerbations.

317. In an acute exacerbation of asthma unresponsive to initial treatments, which adjunct therapy can be considered for rapid bronchodilation?
a. Intravenous magnesium sulfate
b. Intravenous antibiotics
c. Oral leukotriene receptor antagonists
d. High-dose inhaled anticholinergics

Answer: a. Intravenous magnesium sulfate. Explanation: Intravenous magnesium sulfate can be considered as an adjunct therapy in acute asthma exacerbations unresponsive to initial treatments, due to its bronchodilating properties and ability to induce smooth muscle relaxation.

318. In acute kidney injury (AKI), which parameter is most indicative of renal function and used to classify the severity of AKI?
a. Urine output
b. Serum creatinine
c. Blood urea nitrogen (BUN)
d. Serum potassium

Answer: b. Serum creatinine. Explanation: Serum creatinine is a key parameter for assessing renal function and is used to classify the severity of AKI based on the RIFLE (Risk, Injury, Failure, Loss, End-stage kidney disease) and AKIN (Acute Kidney Injury Network) criteria. Changes in serum creatinine levels reflect alterations in glomerular filtration rate (GFR), a critical indicator of kidney function.

319. In chronic kidney disease (CKD), what is the primary goal of using angiotensin-converting enzyme inhibitors (ACEIs) or angiotensin receptor blockers (ARBs)?
a. To increase urine output
b. To reduce proteinuria and slow the progression of renal damage
c. To elevate serum potassium levels
d. To decrease calcium absorption

Answer: b. To reduce proteinuria and slow the progression of renal damage. Explanation: ACEIs and ARBs are used in CKD primarily to reduce proteinuria, a marker of kidney damage, and to slow the progression of renal disease by lowering intraglomerular pressure and providing renal-protective effects.

320. In managing a patient with end-stage renal disease (ESRD) on hemodialysis, what is a common complication that needs to be monitored?
a. Hypotension during dialysis sessions
b. Hypercalcemia
c. Decreased risk of infection
d. Reduction in serum phosphate levels

Answer: a. Hypotension during dialysis sessions. Explanation: Hypotension is a common complication during hemodialysis sessions due to rapid fluid removal and changes in intravascular volume, requiring careful monitoring and management to prevent adverse outcomes.

321. Which electrolyte imbalance is typically associated with renal tubular acidosis (RTA)?
a. Hyperkalemia
b. Hypokalemia
c. Hypernatremia
d. Hyponatremia

Answer: b. Hypokalemia. Explanation: Renal tubular acidosis, particularly Type 1 (distal RTA) and Type 2 (proximal RTA), is often associated with hypokalemia due to impaired potassium reabsorption or increased renal potassium excretion, contributing to the acid-base and electrolyte disturbances seen in this condition.

322. In the diagnosis of nephrotic syndrome, which clinical feature is essential for diagnosis?
a. Hematuria
b. Proteinuria exceeding 3.5 grams per day
c. Hypertension
d. Increased serum albumin

Answer: b. Proteinuria exceeding 3.5 grams per day. Explanation: Nephrotic syndrome is characterized by significant proteinuria exceeding 3.5 grams per day, leading to hypoalbuminemia, edema, and hyperlipidemia. This hallmark feature distinguishes nephrotic syndrome from other kidney disorders.

323. For a patient with polycystic kidney disease (PKD), what is a major risk associated with the disease?
a. Decreased risk of renal cell carcinoma
b. Development of renal calculi
c. Increased risk of urinary tract infections (UTIs)
d. Intracranial aneurysms

Answer: d. Intracranial aneurysms. Explanation: Patients with polycystic kidney disease have an increased risk of developing intracranial aneurysms, in addition to renal complications. Screening for intracranial aneurysms in selected cases, especially in those with a family history of aneurysms, is recommended due to the potential risk of rupture.

324. What is the primary mechanism of action of loop diuretics like furosemide in the management of fluid overload in CKD?
a. Inhibition of sodium and chloride reabsorption in the distal convoluted tubule
b. Inhibition of sodium and chloride reabsorption in the proximal convoluted tubule
c. Inhibition of sodium and chloride reabsorption in the thick ascending limb of the loop of Henle
d. Potassium-sparing effects in the collecting duct

Answer: c. Inhibition of sodium and chloride reabsorption in the thick ascending limb of the loop of Henle. Explanation: Loop diuretics, such as furosemide, act on the thick ascending limb of the loop of Henle to inhibit sodium and chloride reabsorption, resulting in significant diuresis and reduction of fluid overload, making them effective in managing volume overload in CKD and heart failure.

325. In a patient with diabetic nephropathy, what finding in the urinary albumin-to-creatinine ratio (UACR) indicates the presence of microalbuminuria?
a. UACR < 30 mg/g
b. 30-300 mg/g
c. >300 mg/g
d. >500 mg/g

Answer: b. 30-300 mg/g. Explanation: Microalbuminuria in diabetic nephropathy is indicated by a UACR of 30-300 mg/g. This range signifies increased urinary albumin excretion, which is an early marker of diabetic kidney disease and an important risk factor for cardiovascular disease and progression to overt nephropathy.

326. When considering the pathophysiology of glomerulonephritis, what is a key immunological mechanism involved in most cases?
a. Decreased circulating immune complexes
b. Antibody-mediated damage to the glomerular basement membrane
c. Activation of the parasympathetic nervous system
d. Reduction in complement activation

Answer: b. Antibody-mediated damage to the glomerular basement membrane. Explanation: The key immunological mechanism involved in most cases of glomerulonephritis is antibody-mediated damage to the glomerular basement membrane, often through the formation of immune complexes or antibodies directed against glomerular antigens, leading to inflammation and damage to the glomeruli.

327. Under the RIFLE criteria, a patient whose glomerular filtration rate (GFR) has declined by 25% from baseline is classified as:
a. Risk
b. Injury

c. Failure
d. Loss

Answer: a. Risk. Explanation: The 'Risk' category in the RIFLE criteria is defined by either a decrease in GFR by 25% from baseline, an increase in serum creatinine by 1.5 times the baseline, or a reduction in urine output (oliguria) to less than 0.5 mL/kg/hour for 6 hours.

328. A patient with acute kidney injury (AKI) shows a doubling of serum creatinine from the baseline. According to the RIFLE criteria, this patient falls into which category?
a. Risk
b. Injury
c. Failure
d. End-stage

Answer: b. Injury. Explanation: The 'Injury' stage in the RIFLE criteria is characterized by a doubling (or a 100% increase) of serum creatinine from baseline or a reduction in GFR by 50%, indicating more severe renal dysfunction than the 'Risk' stage.

329. For a patient to be classified under the 'Failure' category of the RIFLE criteria, there must be:
a. A tripling of baseline serum creatinine
b. Urine output of less than 0.3 mL/kg/hour for 24 hours or anuria for 12 hours
c. A 25% decrease in GFR from baseline
d. Persistent AKI symptoms for over 4 weeks

Answer: a. A tripling of baseline serum creatinine. Explanation: The 'Failure' stage in the RIFLE criteria is defined by a tripling of the baseline serum creatinine, an acute rise in serum creatinine to ≥4.0 mg/dL with an acute increase of at least 0.5 mg/dL, or a reduction in GFR by 75% or more.

330. The 'Loss' category in the RIFLE criteria refers to:
a. Complete loss of kidney function for more than 4 weeks
b. A GFR decrease of 90% from baseline
c. The need for temporary renal replacement therapy
d. Permanent renal failure requiring long-term dialysis

Answer: a. Complete loss of kidney function for more than 4 weeks. Explanation: The 'Loss' stage indicates a complete loss of kidney function (i.e., requiring renal replacement therapy) for more than 4 weeks but less than 3 months, suggesting a progression from acute to potentially chronic kidney disease.

331. 'End-stage' in the RIFLE criteria is characterized by:
a. Complete dependence on renal replacement therapy for less than 3 months

b. Complete dependence on renal replacement therapy for more than 3 months
c. Reversible kidney injury with potential for full recovery
d. A GFR reduction of 50% from baseline

Answer: b. Complete dependence on renal replacement therapy for more than 3 months. Explanation: The 'End-stage' category signifies complete dependence on renal replacement therapy (e.g., dialysis) for more than 3 months, indicating the transition from acute kidney injury to end-stage renal disease (ESRD).

332. In a patient with acute kidney injury, urine output less than 0.5 mL/kg/hour for 12 hours is indicative of which RIFLE category?
a. Risk
b. Injury
c. Failure
d. Loss

Answer: a. Risk. Explanation: A urine output of less than 0.5 mL/kg/hour for 12 hours places a patient in the 'Risk' category of the RIFLE criteria, signifying a reduced urine output and potential risk for further renal deterioration.

333. A patient with acute kidney injury requiring renal replacement therapy (dialysis) for a duration of 2 weeks is classified under which RIFLE category?
a. Failure
b. Loss
c. End-stage
d. Injury

Answer: a. Failure. Explanation: The need for renal replacement therapy in the context of acute kidney injury classifies the patient under the 'Failure' category of the RIFLE criteria, reflecting severe impairment of kidney function.

334. In the context of the RIFLE criteria, a patient with a GFR decrease of 60% from baseline would be classified as:
a. Risk
b. Injury
c. Failure
d. Loss

Answer: b. Injury. Explanation: A 60% decrease in GFR from baseline signifies a significant decline in renal function, placing the patient in the 'Injury' category of the RIFLE criteria, which denotes a greater severity than the 'Risk' stage but not as severe as 'Failure'.

335. A patient's serum creatinine has increased to 3.5 mg/dL from a baseline of 1.0 mg/dL. This change falls into which category of the RIFLE criteria?

a. Risk
b. Injury
c. Failure
d. Loss

Answer: c. Failure. Explanation: A more than threefold increase in serum creatinine from baseline (in this case, from 1.0 to 3.5 mg/dL) places the patient in the 'Failure' category of the RIFLE criteria, indicating a severe decline in renal function.

336. Persistent acute kidney injury for more than 6 weeks would be categorized in the RIFLE criteria as:
a. Loss
b. End-stage
c. Failure
d. Injury

Answer: a. Loss. Explanation: Persistent acute kidney injury for more than 4 weeks but less than 3 months is categorized as 'Loss' in the RIFLE criteria, indicating a significant duration of kidney dysfunction without full recovery to baseline function.

337. For a patient to be classified under Stage 1 of the Acute Kidney Injury Network (AKIN) criteria, the serum creatinine must:
a. Increase by ≥0.3 mg/dL within 48 hours
b. Double from the baseline value
c. Increase by 1.5-1.9 times the baseline within 7 days
d. Exceed 4.0 mg/dL with an acute rise of at least 0.5 mg/dL

Answer: a. Increase by ≥0.3 mg/dL within 48 hours. Explanation: Stage 1 of the AKIN criteria is defined by an increase in serum creatinine by ≥0.3 mg/dL within 48 hours or an increase to 1.5-1.9 times baseline, which is known or presumed to have occurred within the prior 7 days, highlighting the importance of acute changes in kidney function for early detection and intervention.

338. In AKIN Stage 2, the urine output criteria specify that the patient must have:
a. <0.5 mL/kg/hr for more than 6 hours
b. <0.5 mL/kg/hr for more than 12 hours
c. <0.5 mL/kg/hr for 2-12 hours
d. Anuria for 12 hours

Answer: b. <0.5 mL/kg/hr for more than 12 hours. Explanation: AKIN Stage 2 is characterized by a urine output of <0.5 mL/kg/hr for more than 12 hours, indicating a more severe reduction in kidney function compared to Stage 1 and necessitating more aggressive interventions to prevent further deterioration.

339. A patient's serum creatinine has increased to 2.5 times the baseline value. According to AKIN criteria, this patient would be classified as:
a. Stage 1
b. Stage 2
c. Stage 3
d. Not classifiable due to lack of urine output data

Answer: c. Stage 3. Explanation: An increase in serum creatinine to 3.0 times baseline or more (or serum creatinine of ≥4.0 mg/dL with an acute increase of at least 0.5 mg/dL) qualifies for AKIN Stage 3, indicating severe acute kidney injury and potentially requiring renal replacement therapy.

340. For a patient with known chronic kidney disease, the AKIN staging requires:
a. A new baseline creatinine to be established at admission
b. Use of the lowest previous creatinine level as the baseline
c. Doubling of the baseline creatinine irrespective of the absolute value
d. A fixed baseline creatinine value of 1.0 mg/dL for all patients

Answer: a. A new baseline creatinine to be established at admission. Explanation: In patients with chronic kidney disease, establishing a new baseline creatinine level at the time of admission is crucial for accurately assessing acute changes in kidney function according to the AKIN criteria, as their baseline creatinine may already be elevated due to underlying chronic kidney disease.

341. In the context of AKIN staging, how is a patient with no prior baseline creatinine data assessed for acute kidney injury?
a. Estimation of baseline using the MDRD equation
b. Assuming a baseline creatinine of 1.0 mg/dL
c. Utilizing the admission creatinine as the baseline
d. AKIN staging cannot be applied without prior baseline creatinine

Answer: a. Estimation of baseline using the MDRD equation. Explanation: When no prior baseline creatinine data is available, the baseline can be estimated using predictive equations such as the Modification of Diet in Renal Disease (MDRD) equation, which considers factors like age, sex, and race, allowing for the application of AKIN staging to assess the presence and severity of acute kidney injury.

342. A patient under AKIN Stage 3 due to acute kidney injury shows no improvement in renal function after 48 hours. The next step in management should include:
a. Immediate initiation of renal replacement therapy
b. Repeat kidney ultrasound to assess for structural abnormalities
c. Conservative management with fluids and diuretics
d. Administration of nephrotoxic agents to stimulate renal response

Answer: a. Immediate initiation of renal replacement therapy. Explanation: In patients classified under AKIN Stage 3, especially those showing no improvement in renal function after 48 hours, the consideration for renal replacement therapy (RRT) is critical to manage severe azotemia, fluid overload, electrolyte imbalances, and acidosis, thereby preventing further complications.

343. In assessing urine output for AKIN staging, the importance of measuring urine output lies in its ability to:
a. Directly measure glomerular filtration rate (GFR)
b. Provide immediate insights into changes in kidney perfusion
c. Reflect tubular function independently of serum creatinine
d. Serve as the sole criterion for diagnosing acute kidney injury

Answer: b. Provide immediate insights into changes in kidney perfusion. Explanation: Measuring urine output is crucial in AKIN staging as it provides immediate and sensitive insights into changes in kidney perfusion and function, often preceding changes in serum creatinine, and helps in the early detection and staging of acute kidney injury.

344. When considering fluid resuscitation in a patient with acute kidney injury as per AKIN criteria, which factor must be carefully monitored to avoid exacerbating the injury?
a. Urine sodium concentration
b. Rate of fluid administration
c. Choice of crystalloid vs. colloid
d. Development of fluid overload

Answer: d. Development of fluid overload. Explanation: In patients with acute kidney injury, careful monitoring for the development of fluid overload is essential during fluid resuscitation, as excessive fluid can exacerbate kidney injury, increase the risk of pulmonary edema, and lead to complications associated with volume overload.

345. In a patient with acute kidney injury classified as AKIN Stage 1, the primary therapeutic goal is to:
a. Immediately start renal replacement therapy
b. Identify and manage the underlying cause of kidney injury
c. Increase urine output to >3 mL/kg/hr
d. Maintain serum creatinine levels below 1.5 mg/dL

Answer: b. Identify and manage the underlying cause of kidney injury. Explanation: For a patient classified under AKIN Stage 1, the primary therapeutic focus should be on identifying and managing the underlying cause of the acute kidney injury, such as resolving hemodynamic instability, discontinuing nephrotoxic agents, or treating sepsis, to prevent further renal damage and promote recovery.

346. A 70-year-old patient presents with acute kidney injury (AKI) following a severe bout of gastroenteritis with significant vomiting and diarrhea. The most likely etiology of this AKI is:
a. Pre-renal due to hypovolemia
b. Intrinsic due to acute tubular necrosis

c. Intrinsic due to interstitial nephritis
d. Post-renal due to urinary tract obstruction

Answer: a. Pre-renal due to hypovolemia. Explanation: Severe vomiting and diarrhea can lead to significant fluid loss and hypovolemia, reducing renal perfusion and leading to pre-renal AKI, characterized by decreased glomerular filtration rate (GFR) without intrinsic damage to the kidney tissue.

347. A patient with a history of benign prostatic hyperplasia (BPH) presents with elevated creatinine and bilateral hydronephrosis on ultrasound. The AKI is most likely:
a. Pre-renal due to reduced cardiac output
b. Intrinsic due to glomerulonephritis
c. Intrinsic due to acute tubular necrosis
d. Post-renal due to urinary tract obstruction

Answer: d. Post-renal due to urinary tract obstruction. Explanation: In patients with BPH, enlarged prostate can cause urinary tract obstruction, leading to post-renal AKI. Bilateral hydronephrosis is indicative of obstruction at the level of the bladder or urethra, causing back pressure and kidney dysfunction.

348. A patient with lupus presents with AKI and urine analysis showing red blood cell casts. This type of AKI is most likely:
a. Pre-renal due to hypoperfusion
b. Intrinsic due to glomerulonephritis
c. Post-renal due to nephrolithiasis
d. Pre-renal due to dehydration

Answer: b. Intrinsic due to glomerulonephritis. Explanation: In patients with lupus, an autoimmune disease, glomerulonephritis is a common cause of intrinsic AKI. The presence of red blood cell casts in urine analysis is indicative of glomerular injury, which is characteristic of glomerulonephritis.

349. Following a major surgery, a patient develops AKI with urine output less than 0.5 mL/kg/hour. The patient had significant blood loss during surgery. The AKI in this scenario is most likely:
a. Pre-renal due to volume depletion
b. Intrinsic due to rhabdomyolysis
c. Intrinsic due to contrast-induced nephropathy
d. Post-renal due to abdominal compartment syndrome

Answer: a. Pre-renal due to volume depletion. Explanation: Significant blood loss during surgery can lead to hypovolemia and volume depletion, resulting in reduced renal perfusion and pre-renal AKI. The low urine output further supports the diagnosis of pre-renal AKI due to volume depletion.

350. A patient on long-term non-steroidal anti-inflammatory drugs (NSAIDs) presents with AKI. The NSAIDs are most likely to cause this type of AKI through:
a. Pre-renal mechanisms by affecting renal perfusion
b. Intrinsic damage due to acute interstitial nephritis
c. Intrinsic damage due to nephrolithiasis
d. Post-renal mechanisms by causing urinary retention

Answer: b. Intrinsic damage due to acute interstitial nephritis. Explanation: NSAIDs can cause AKI through intrinsic mechanisms, most commonly acute interstitial nephritis, which is an immune-mediated injury to the renal interstitium, leading to decreased renal function.

351. A patient with heart failure exacerbation develops AKI. The echocardiogram shows reduced ejection fraction. This type of AKI is typically:
a. Pre-renal due to decreased cardiac output
b. Intrinsic due to myocardial infarction-induced nephropathy
c. Intrinsic due to cardiorenal syndrome
d. Post-renal due to venous congestion

Answer: a. Pre-renal due to decreased cardiac output. Explanation: In patients with heart failure exacerbation and reduced ejection fraction, decreased cardiac output can lead to reduced renal perfusion and pre-renal AKI, as the kidneys receive inadequate blood flow to maintain normal function.

352. A diabetic patient with a recent history of antibiotic use for a urinary tract infection now presents with AKI. Urinalysis shows white blood cell casts. This presentation suggests AKI due to:
a. Pre-renal azotemia from dehydration
b. Intrinsic AKI from acute pyelonephritis
c. Post-renal AKI from ureteral obstruction by stones
d. Intrinsic AKI from diabetic nephropathy

Answer: b. Intrinsic AKI from acute pyelonephritis. Explanation: In the context of recent antibiotic use for a urinary tract infection and the presence of white blood cell casts in urinalysis, the AKI is most likely due to intrinsic renal damage from acute pyelonephritis, an upper urinary tract infection that can involve the kidneys.

353. In patients with CKD, maintaining a blood pressure below which target is recommended to slow the progression of renal disease?
a. 140/90 mmHg
b. 130/80 mmHg
c. 120/70 mmHg
d. 150/100 mmHg

Answer: b. 130/80 mmHg. Explanation: For patients with CKD, particularly those with proteinuria, maintaining a target blood pressure below 130/80 mmHg is recommended to slow the progression of renal disease and reduce the risk of cardiovascular complications.

354. Which dietary modification is most commonly recommended for patients with advanced CKD to delay the progression to end-stage renal disease?
a. High protein intake
b. Low sodium intake
c. Restricted potassium intake
d. Reduced phosphorus intake

Answer: d. Reduced phosphorus intake. Explanation: Patients with advanced CKD are often advised to limit dietary phosphorus intake to help manage hyperphosphatemia, reduce the risk of bone disease, and delay the progression to end-stage renal disease by minimizing mineral and bone disorders associated with CKD.

355. What is the significance of an elevated serum parathyroid hormone (PTH) level in a patient with CKD?
a. It indicates improved calcium absorption from the gut.
b. It is a compensatory response to hypocalcemia and hyperphosphatemia.
c. It suggests an increased risk of acute kidney injury.
d. It is indicative of effective erythropoiesis.

Answer: b. It is a compensatory response to hypocalcemia and hyperphosphatemia. Explanation: In CKD, elevated PTH levels are part of secondary hyperparathyroidism, a compensatory response to hypocalcemia and hyperphosphatemia, aiming to maintain calcium and phosphate balance but potentially contributing to renal osteodystrophy and vascular calcification if uncontrolled.

356. For CKD patients not on dialysis, which erythropoiesis-stimulating agent (ESA) dosing strategy is recommended to manage anemia?
a. High doses to rapidly increase hemoglobin
b. Starting with low doses and titrating to maintain hemoglobin within a target range
c. Use only in cases of severe anemia with hemoglobin below 7 g/dL
d. ESAs are not recommended for CKD patients not on dialysis

Answer: b. Starting with low doses and titrating to maintain hemoglobin within a target range. Explanation: For CKD patients not on dialysis, ESA therapy should be initiated at low doses and carefully titrated to avoid rapid increases in hemoglobin, aiming to maintain hemoglobin levels within a target range that minimizes transfusions and cardiovascular risks.

357. In CKD, what is the primary reason for administering sodium bicarbonate therapy to patients with metabolic acidosis?
a. To increase serum potassium levels
b. To enhance calcium absorption

c. To correct the acid-base balance and ameliorate the effects of acidosis on kidney function
d. To reduce serum phosphorus levels

Answer: c. To correct the acid-base balance and ameliorate the effects of acidosis on kidney function. Explanation: Sodium bicarbonate therapy in CKD patients with metabolic acidosis is primarily aimed at correcting the acid-base balance, as chronic acidosis can exacerbate kidney damage and contribute to the progression of CKD.

358. When considering the use of ACE inhibitors or ARBs in CKD, what is a potential adverse effect that requires close monitoring?
a. Hyperkalemia
b. Hyponatremia
c. Hypokalemia
d. Hypercalcemia

Answer: a. Hyperkalemia. Explanation: ACE inhibitors and ARBs can increase the risk of hyperkalemia in CKD patients by reducing aldosterone levels, which impairs potassium excretion. Close monitoring of serum potassium levels is necessary when using these medications in CKD management.

359. What is the role of kidney ultrasound in the evaluation of CKD?
a. To assess the effectiveness of dialysis treatment
b. To evaluate the size, structure, and potential obstructions in the kidneys
c. To measure the glomerular filtration rate directly
d. To identify the specific type of glomerulonephritis

Answer: b. To evaluate the size, structure, and potential obstructions in the kidneys. Explanation: Kidney ultrasound in CKD evaluation is used to assess the size and structure of the kidneys, detect abnormalities such as cysts or tumors, and identify potential obstructions, providing valuable information for diagnosis and management without direct measurement of glomerular filtration rate or specific kidney diseases.

360. In the management of CKD, why is it important to control proteinuria?
a. Proteinuria is the primary cause of hyperkalemia in CKD.
b. Reducing proteinuria can slow the progression of kidney damage.
c. High protein intake is associated with improved kidney function.
d. Proteinuria indicates an overactive erythropoiesis.

Answer: b. Reducing proteinuria can slow the progression of kidney damage. Explanation: Proteinuria is not only a marker of kidney damage but also a contributor to further renal decline. Controlling proteinuria, through measures such as ACE inhibitors or ARBs, can help slow the progression of CKD by reducing intraglomerular pressure and the subsequent damage to the renal parenchyma.

361. For a patient with CKD and recurrent calcium oxalate kidney stones, which dietary recommendation is most appropriate?
a. Increase oxalate intake to enhance oxalate excretion
b. Increase fluid intake to reduce urine concentration
c. Restrict calcium intake to decrease stone formation
d. Increase sodium intake to facilitate calcium excretion

Answer: b. Increase fluid intake to reduce urine concentration. Explanation: Increasing fluid intake is a key strategy in preventing recurrent calcium oxalate stones in CKD patients, as it dilutes the urine, reduces the concentration of stone-forming substances like calcium and oxalate, and promotes their excretion, thereby reducing the risk of stone formation.

362. A patient has a GFR of 88 mL/min/1.73 m². According to the GFR categories, this patient would be classified as:
a. G1
b. G2
c. G3a
d. G3b

Answer: b. G2. Explanation: GFR categories are defined as follows: G1 is a GFR ≥90 mL/min/1.73 m² (normal or high), G2 is a GFR of 60-89 mL/min/1.73 m² (mildly decreased), G3a is a GFR of 45-59 mL/min/1.73 m² (mildly to moderately decreased), and G3b is a GFR of 30-44 mL/min/1.73 m² (moderately to severely decreased). A GFR of 88 mL/min/1.73 m² falls into the G2 category.

363. In a urine albumin-to-creatinine ratio (UACR) test, a result of 25 mg/g would place the patient in which albuminuria category?
a. A1
b. A2
c. A3
d. The result is inconclusive and needs retesting

Answer: b. A2. Explanation: Albuminuria categories are defined as follows: A1 is a UACR <30 mg/g (normal to mildly increased), A2 is a UACR of 30-300 mg/g (moderately increased), and A3 is a UACR >300 mg/g (severely increased). A UACR result of 25 mg/g falls into the A1 category, indicating normal to mildly increased albuminuria.

364. A patient's recent lab results indicate a GFR of 55 mL/min/1.73 m². This GFR would classify the patient's kidney function in which stage?
a. G1
b. G2
c. G3a
d. G4

Answer: c. G3a. Explanation: Based on the GFR categories, a GFR of 55 mL/min/1.73 m² falls into the G3a category, indicating a mildly to moderately decreased kidney function.

365. For a patient with diabetes, a UACR of 350 mg/g would indicate what level of albuminuria?
a. Normal
b. Moderately increased
c. Severely increased
d. Below detectable limits

Answer: c. Severely increased. Explanation: In the context of albuminuria categories, a UACR of 350 mg/g falls into the A3 category, which indicates severely increased albuminuria, a common complication in patients with diabetes.

366. If a patient's estimated GFR falls below 15 mL/min/1.73 m², they would be classified in which stage of kidney disease?
a. G3b
b. G4
c. G5
d. A1

Answer: c. G5. Explanation: A GFR below 15 mL/min/1.73 m² classifies a patient in the G5 category, which corresponds to kidney failure or end-stage renal disease (ESRD), necessitating renal replacement therapy such as dialysis or transplantation.

367. A patient with hypertension has a UACR of 40 mg/g. This result would suggest what level of albuminuria?
a. A1
b. A2
c. A3
d. The result is within the normal range and does not suggest albuminuria

Answer: b. A2. Explanation: A UACR of 40 mg/g indicates moderately increased albuminuria (A2 category), which is significant for a patient with hypertension as it may indicate early kidney damage.

368. In a patient with chronic kidney disease (CKD), a consistent GFR of 32 mL/min/1.73 m² would be categorized as:
a. G2
b. G3a
c. G3b
d. G4

Answer: c. G3b. Explanation: A GFR of 32 mL/min/1.73 m² falls into the G3b category, indicating a moderately to severely decreased kidney function, which is a characteristic of advancing CKD.

369. A 60-year-old patient with a history of cardiovascular disease presents with a UACR of 280 mg/g. This finding indicates:
a. Normal albuminuria
b. Moderately increased albuminuria
c. Severely increased albuminuria
d. Insufficient data for categorization

Answer: b. Moderately increased albuminuria. Explanation: A UACR of 280 mg/g falls into the A2 category, indicating moderately increased albuminuria. This is significant in a patient with cardiovascular disease, as it may suggest an increased risk of worsening cardiovascular and kidney outcomes.

370. When assessing a patient's CKD stage with a GFR of 20 mL/min/1.73 m², the appropriate classification would be:
a. G2
b. G3a
c. G3b
d. G4

Answer: d. G4. Explanation: A GFR of 20 mL/min/1.73 m² is classified as G4, indicating a severely decreased kidney function, which is one stage before kidney failure (G5).

371. For a patient who has a UACR result of 15 mg/g, the albuminuria would be classified as:
a. A1
b. A2
c. A3
d. This value indicates the need for immediate renal replacement therapy

Answer: a. A1. Explanation: A UACR result of 15 mg/g falls into the A1 category, indicating normal to mildly increased albuminuria, suggesting that the patient's kidney function may be relatively preserved, with no immediate indication for renal replacement therapy based solely on this result.

372. In the management of CKD, what is the target blood pressure for most patients to reduce the risk of progression to end-stage renal disease?
a. <140/90 mmHg
b. <130/80 mmHg
c. <120/70 mmHg
d. <150/100 mmHg

Answer: b. <130/80 mmHg. Explanation: For most patients with chronic kidney disease, especially those with proteinuria, the target blood pressure to reduce the risk of progression to end-stage renal disease is <130/80 mmHg. This target helps in minimizing the progression of renal damage and managing cardiovascular risk factors.

373. In a patient with diabetic nephropathy, what is the primary reason for tight glycemic control as part of the management plan?
a. To increase urinary glucose excretion
b. To reduce systemic blood pressure
c. To decrease the progression of kidney damage
d. To enhance the action of diuretics

Answer: c. To decrease the progression of kidney damage. Explanation: Tight glycemic control in patients with diabetic nephropathy is crucial for slowing the progression of kidney damage. Maintaining blood glucose levels as close to the normal range as possible reduces hyperglycemia-induced damage in the glomeruli, thereby delaying the progression of nephropathy.

374. For CKD patients with proteinuria, why are ACE inhibitors or ARBs recommended as part of the therapeutic regimen?
a. They directly reduce protein synthesis in the liver.
b. They have a diuretic effect that reduces blood volume.
c. They decrease intraglomerular pressure, reducing proteinuria.
d. They increase renal blood flow, enhancing glomerular filtration.

Answer: c. They decrease intraglomerular pressure, reducing proteinuria. Explanation: ACE inhibitors or ARBs are recommended for CKD patients with proteinuria because they decrease intraglomerular pressure by dilating the efferent arterioles of the glomerulus. This reduction in pressure leads to a decrease in proteinuria, which is beneficial in slowing the progression of kidney damage.

375. When using erythropoiesis-stimulating agents (ESAs) in CKD patients with anemia, what is a critical parameter to monitor due to the risk of adverse outcomes?
a. White blood cell count
b. Blood glucose levels
c. Hemoglobin levels
d. Platelet count

Answer: c. Hemoglobin levels. Explanation: When administering ESAs to CKD patients with anemia, it is critical to monitor hemoglobin levels closely. Overcorrection of anemia (hemoglobin levels >13 g/dL) can increase the risk of cardiovascular events, hypertension, and stroke. The goal is to maintain hemoglobin at the lowest level that both reduces the need for red blood cell transfusions and alleviates symptoms of anemia.

376. In CKD management, why is strict blood pressure control more crucial in patients with proteinuria than in those without?

a. Proteinuria is associated with an increased risk of hypotension.
b. Proteinuria indicates a more severe form of kidney damage that is sensitive to blood pressure changes.
c. Proteinuria can be directly reduced by lowering blood pressure.
d. Blood pressure medications have a protein-sparing effect in the kidney.

Answer: b. Proteinuria indicates a more severe form of kidney damage that is sensitive to blood pressure changes. Explanation: Strict blood pressure control is particularly crucial in CKD patients with proteinuria because proteinuria is a marker of more severe kidney damage. These patients are more susceptible to the deleterious effects of high blood pressure on the kidney, and tighter control can significantly slow the progression of renal disease.

377. What is the main goal of using diuretics in the management of fluid overload in CKD patients?
a. To increase potassium excretion
b. To decrease blood pressure by reducing blood volume
c. To enhance renal clearance of urea and creatinine
d. To reduce the risk of hypercalcemia

Answer: b. To decrease blood pressure by reducing blood volume. Explanation: In CKD patients, diuretics are primarily used to manage fluid overload by promoting diuresis, which reduces blood volume and, consequently, blood pressure. This helps in controlling hypertension and mitigating symptoms associated with fluid overload, such as edema and pulmonary congestion.

378. When initiating ACE inhibitors in CKD patients, what biochemical parameter should be closely monitored within the first few weeks of therapy?
a. Serum sodium
b. Serum potassium
c. Blood urea nitrogen (BUN)
d. Serum magnesium

Answer: b. Serum potassium. Explanation: When initiating ACE inhibitors in CKD patients, it is important to closely monitor serum potassium levels, as these medications can reduce aldosterone secretion, leading to hyperkalemia. This is especially critical in CKD, where potassium excretion may already be compromised.

379. In managing CKD, what is the rationale behind recommending a low-protein diet?
a. To decrease the metabolic burden on the kidneys
b. To prevent the absorption of phosphorus from dietary sources
c. To reduce the risk of developing renal osteodystrophy
d. To increase insulin sensitivity and improve glycemic control

Answer: a. To decrease the metabolic burden on the kidneys. Explanation: A low-protein diet is recommended in CKD management to decrease the metabolic burden on the kidneys by reducing the amount of nitrogenous waste products, such as urea, that the kidneys need to filter. This can help slow the progression of kidney damage and manage uremic symptoms.

380. For a CKD patient at risk of cardiovascular disease, why is statin therapy often included in the management plan?
a. Statins have a direct protective effect on the kidney glomeruli.
b. They enhance the excretion of cholesterol in the urine.
c. Statins reduce LDL cholesterol, decreasing the risk of cardiovascular events.
d. They increase the effectiveness of antihypertensive medications.

Answer: c. Statins reduce LDL cholesterol, decreasing the risk of cardiovascular events. Explanation: In CKD patients, particularly those at risk of cardiovascular disease, statin therapy is often included in the management plan to reduce low-density lipoprotein (LDL) cholesterol levels. This helps in decreasing the risk of cardiovascular events, which are a leading cause of morbidity and mortality in this population.

381. How does metabolic acidosis in CKD contribute to the progression of kidney disease, and why is bicarbonate supplementation beneficial?
a. Acidosis increases renal synthesis of ammonia, which is nephrotoxic.
b. Low pH levels directly damage the kidney tubules.
c. Acidosis promotes protein catabolism, leading to increased nitrogenous waste.
d. Acidosis enhances calcium excretion, leading to kidney stone formation.

Answer: c. Acidosis promotes protein catabolism, leading to increased nitrogenous waste. Explanation: Metabolic acidosis in CKD can contribute to the progression of kidney disease by promoting protein catabolism, which increases the production of nitrogenous waste that the kidneys must filter. Bicarbonate supplementation helps correct acidosis, reducing this catabolic effect and potentially slowing the progression

382. In a patient with chronic kidney disease, which condition most urgently indicates the initiation of dialysis?
a. Serum potassium of 5.5 mEq/L
b. Presence of pedal edema
c. Metabolic acidosis with a bicarbonate level of 15 mEq/L
d. Uremic symptoms including pericarditis and encephalopathy

Answer: d. Uremic symptoms including pericarditis and encephalopathy. Explanation: Uremic symptoms, such as pericarditis and encephalopathy, indicate severe uremia and are urgent indications for the initiation of dialysis to remove toxins and prevent life-threatening complications.

383. A patient presents with acute pulmonary edema due to fluid overload. Which treatment is most appropriate to immediately address this condition?
a. Oral loop diuretics
b. Intravenous (IV) loop diuretics
c. Hemodialysis with ultrafiltration
d. Conservative fluid management with restriction

Answer: c. Hemodialysis with ultrafiltration. Explanation: In cases of acute pulmonary edema due to fluid overload where rapid intervention is needed, hemodialysis with ultrafiltration is effective in removing excess fluid quickly, especially if the patient's condition does not respond to medical therapy like IV diuretics.

384. Which laboratory finding is a direct indication for emergency dialysis in a patient with end-stage renal disease (ESRD)?
a. Hyperkalemia with serum potassium >6.5 mEq/L and ECG changes
b. Hyponatremia with serum sodium 130 mEq/L
c. Isolated increase in blood urea nitrogen (BUN)
d. Mild metabolic alkalosis

Answer: a. Hyperkalemia with serum potassium >6.5 mEq/L and ECG changes. Explanation: Severe hyperkalemia (>6.5 mEq/L) with ECG changes such as peaked T waves, prolonged PR interval, or widened QRS complex is a life-threatening condition requiring emergency dialysis to prevent fatal cardiac arrhythmias.

385. For a patient with metabolic acidosis secondary to renal failure, which condition would necessitate the use of dialysis?
a. pH 7.32 with bicarbonate 18 mEq/L
b. pH 7.1 with bicarbonate <10 mEq/L and hemodynamic instability
c. Compensation with respiratory alkalosis
d. Mild acidosis with pH 7.25 and stable condition

Answer: b. pH 7.1 with bicarbonate <10 mEq/L and hemodynamic instability. Explanation: Severe metabolic acidosis (pH <7.1) with significantly low bicarbonate (<10 mEq/L) and associated hemodynamic instability is an indication for dialysis to correct the acid-base balance and improve the patient's condition.

386. In managing a patient with acute kidney injury, which criterion indicates the need for renal replacement therapy?
a. Creatinine clearance of 20 mL/min
b. Anuria for 12 hours
c. Oliguria with volume overload unresponsive to diuretics
d. Proteinuria >3.5 grams per 24 hours

Answer: c. Oliguria with volume overload unresponsive to diuretics. Explanation: Oliguria with associated volume overload that is unresponsive to diuretic therapy indicates the need for renal replacement therapy such as dialysis to remove excess fluid and prevent complications like pulmonary edema.

387. A patient with ESRD on hemodialysis develops severe dyspnea and anasarca. Chest X-ray reveals extensive bilateral pleural effusions. The most likely cause is:

a. Inadequate dialysis with fluid retention
b. Dialysis-related pericarditis
c. Uremic pneumonitis
d. Dialysate leakage

Answer: a. Inadequate dialysis with fluid retention. Explanation: In a patient with ESRD on hemodialysis, extensive bilateral pleural effusions and anasarca are indicative of fluid overload, likely due to inadequate dialysis sessions leading to insufficient fluid removal.

388. Which of the following is a contraindication for the immediate use of peritoneal dialysis in a patient with acute renal failure?
a. Recent abdominal surgery
b. Hyperkalemia with ECG changes
c. Volume overload with pulmonary edema
d. Severe metabolic acidosis

Answer: a. Recent abdominal surgery. Explanation: Recent abdominal surgery is a contraindication for the immediate initiation of peritoneal dialysis due to the risk of peritoneal membrane damage or infection. Other options are indications for dialysis but not specific to the type of dialysis.

389. In a patient with acute kidney injury, the decision to initiate dialysis is least dependent on:
a. Absolute serum creatinine value
b. Volume status and responsiveness to diuretics
c. Degree of metabolic acidosis
d. Severity of hyperkalemia

Answer: a. Absolute serum creatinine value. Explanation: The decision to initiate dialysis in acute kidney injury is more dependent on clinical factors such as volume status, metabolic acidosis, and hyperkalemia rather than the absolute value of serum creatinine, as creatinine can vary based on muscle mass and other factors.

390. When considering renal replacement therapy, which factor is not typically used to determine the modality (hemodialysis vs. peritoneal dialysis)?
a. Patient's lifestyle and preference
b. Presence of abdominal adhesions
c. Blood pressure control
d. Geographic location and access to medical facilities

Answer: c. Blood pressure control. Explanation: The choice between hemodialysis and peritoneal dialysis is usually based on patient preference, lifestyle, medical and surgical history (such as abdominal adhesions), and logistical considerations (such as geographic location and access to medical facilities), rather than blood pressure control, which can be managed in both modalities.

391. In which clinical scenario is intermittent hemodialysis (IHD) most likely contraindicated?
a. Stable chronic kidney disease requiring routine maintenance dialysis
b. Acute kidney injury with hemodynamic instability
c. Volume overload unresponsive to diuretics in a hemodynamically stable patient
d. Electrolyte imbalance in a patient with end-stage renal disease

Answer: b. Acute kidney injury with hemodynamic instability. Explanation: IHD may be contraindicated or used with caution in patients with acute kidney injury who are hemodynamically unstable because the rapid fluid shifts and changes in blood pressure associated with IHD can further compromise their stability. Continuous renal replacement therapy (CRRT) is often preferred in these situations due to its gentler and more continuous fluid removal and solute clearance.

392. Which modality of renal replacement therapy is typically preferred for patients with acute kidney injury in the intensive care unit, especially those with hemodynamic instability?
a. Intermittent hemodialysis (IHD)
b. Continuous renal replacement therapy (CRRT)
c. Peritoneal dialysis (PD)
d. Nocturnal hemodialysis

Answer: b. Continuous renal replacement therapy (CRRT). Explanation: CRRT is generally preferred for patients with acute kidney injury in the ICU, particularly those who are hemodynamically unstable. CRRT offers the advantage of slower, continuous fluid removal and solute clearance, which can be better tolerated by critically ill patients.

393. For a patient with end-stage renal disease who prefers a home-based dialysis treatment with the ability to maintain a flexible schedule, which modality would be most appropriate?
a. Intermittent hemodialysis (IHD)
b. Continuous renal replacement therapy (CRRT)
c. Peritoneal dialysis (PD)
d. In-center nocturnal hemodialysis

Answer: c. Peritoneal dialysis (PD). Explanation: Peritoneal dialysis is often the preferred choice for patients seeking home-based renal replacement therapy that allows for a more flexible treatment schedule. PD can be performed at home, at work, or while traveling, providing a degree of autonomy and flexibility not typically available with in-center hemodialysis.

394. In the context of renal replacement therapy modalities, which factor is a significant advantage of peritoneal dialysis (PD) over hemodialysis (HD)?
a. Faster clearance of small and large molecules
b. Less requirement for vascular access
c. Shorter treatment times per session
d. Lower risk of hemodynamic instability

Answer: b. Less requirement for vascular access. Explanation: A significant advantage of PD over HD is the reduced need for vascular access, as PD utilizes the peritoneal membrane as the dialyzing surface. This can decrease the complications associated with vascular access, such as infections and stenosis.

395. When considering the initiation of CRRT, which patient factor most strongly supports this choice over IHD?
a. The need for rapid correction of hyperkalemia
b. Desire for a modality suitable for home use
c. Presence of significant hemodynamic instability
d. Patient preference for treatment modality

Answer: c. Presence of significant hemodynamic instability. Explanation: The most compelling indication for choosing CRRT over IHD is the presence of significant hemodynamic instability. CRRT's slow and continuous nature makes it better suited for critically ill patients who might not tolerate the rapid fluid and electrolyte shifts associated with IHD.

396. What is a primary consideration in choosing intermittent hemodialysis (IHD) for a patient with chronic kidney disease?
a. The patient's ability to perform self-care at home
b. The need for continuous solute and fluid removal
c. The efficiency of solute removal in shorter time frames
d. The patient's preference for nocturnal treatment

Answer: c. The efficiency of solute removal in shorter time frames. Explanation: A primary consideration in choosing IHD is its efficiency in removing solutes and fluids within shorter treatment times, typically several hours per session, making it suitable for patients who can tolerate the rapid changes and prefer the convenience of less frequent treatments.

397. For patients undergoing peritoneal dialysis (PD), what is a common complication that requires vigilant monitoring and prevention?
a. Air embolism
b. Peritonitis
c. Hemolysis
d. Dialyzer clotting

Answer: b. Peritonitis. Explanation: Peritonitis, an infection of the peritoneal cavity, is a common and serious complication of PD that requires vigilant monitoring and prompt management. Patients are educated on aseptic technique and signs of infection to prevent and detect peritonitis early.

398. In evaluating renal replacement therapy options for a patient with residual renal function, which modality is most likely to preserve this function longer?

a. Intermittent hemodialysis (IHD)
b. Continuous renal replacement therapy (CRRT)
c. Peritoneal dialysis (PD)
d. High-flux hemodialysis

Answer: c. Peritoneal dialysis (PD). Explanation: Peritoneal dialysis is often associated with a slower decline in residual renal function compared to hemodialysis. The continuous, gentle nature of PD and the avoidance of hemodynamic shifts seen in hemodialysis may contribute to the preservation of remaining kidney function.

399. When choosing between CRRT and IHD for a patient with multi-organ failure in the ICU, which factor would favor the use of CRRT?
a. The need for rapid correction of life-threatening hyperkalemia
b. The patient's long-term preference for renal replacement therapy modality
c. The presence of hemodynamic instability and the need for meticulous fluid management
d. The availability of trained personnel to perform bedside IHD

Answer: c. The presence of hemodynamic instability and the need for meticulous fluid management. Explanation: CRRT is favored for patients with multi-organ failure in the ICU, particularly when hemodynamic instability is a concern. CRRT allows for more precise and gradual fluid and solute management, which can be critical in the setting of multi-organ failure where fluid balance and stability are paramount.

400. A 72-year-old male with a history of chronic kidney disease stage 3 presents with a 3-day history of decreased urine output, nausea, and vomiting. His serum creatinine is found to be 4.2 mg/dL, increased from a baseline of 1.8 mg/dL. His fractional excretion of sodium (FENa) is calculated to be 0.8%. Which of the following is the most likely cause of this patient's acute kidney injury?
a. prerenal azotemia
b. acute tubular necrosis
c. obstructive uropathy
d. contrast-induced nephropathy

Answer: a. prerenal azotemia. Explanation: The patient's presentation of decreased urine output, nausea, and vomiting, along with a acute increase in serum creatinine and a low fractional excretion of sodium (FENa < 1%), suggests prerenal azotemia as the most likely cause of his acute kidney injury (AKI). Prerenal azotemia occurs when there is a decrease in renal perfusion, leading to a reduction in glomerular filtration rate (GFR) and an increase in serum creatinine. Common causes of prerenal azotemia include volume depletion, decreased cardiac output, and renal vasoconstriction. The low FENa is a key finding that suggests a prerenal cause of AKI, as the kidneys attempt to conserve sodium in response to decreased perfusion. Acute tubular necrosis typically presents with a higher FENa (> 2%) and may have a more gradual onset. Obstructive uropathy is less likely in the absence of flank pain, hematuria, or imaging findings of hydronephrosis. Contrast-induced nephropathy is a possibility if the patient had recent exposure to contrast dye, but the low FENa and absence of exposure history make it less likely.

401. A 58-year-old female with a history of type 2 diabetes and hypertension is admitted to the hospital with sepsis secondary to pneumonia. She develops oliguria and her serum creatinine rises from 1.0 mg/dL to 3.5 mg/dL over the

course of 48 hours. Her urine output is 20 mL/hour. According to the KDIGO criteria, what stage of acute kidney injury (AKI) is this patient experiencing?
a. stage 1
b. stage 2
c. stage 3
d. renal replacement therapy required

Answer: c. stage 3. Explanation: The patient's acute increase in serum creatinine from 1.0 mg/dL to 3.5 mg/dL (a more than 3-fold increase) and urine output of 20 mL/hour (< 0.3 mL/kg/hour for more than 24 hours) meet the KDIGO (Kidney Disease: Improving Global Outcomes) criteria for stage 3 acute kidney injury (AKI). The KDIGO criteria define AKI stages based on changes in serum creatinine and urine output. Stage 1 AKI is defined as a 1.5-1.9 times increase in serum creatinine from baseline or a urine output < 0.5 mL/kg/hour for 6-12 hours. Stage 2 AKI is defined as a 2.0-2.9 times increase in serum creatinine from baseline or a urine output < 0.5 mL/kg/hour for more than 12 hours. Stage 3 AKI is defined as a more than 3-fold increase in serum creatinine from baseline, a serum creatinine ≥ 4.0 mg/dL with an acute increase of at least 0.5 mg/dL, a urine output < 0.3 mL/kg/hour for more than 24 hours, or anuria for more than 12 hours. Renal replacement therapy may be required in patients with stage 3 AKI, but it is not an automatic indication based on the KDIGO criteria alone.

402. A 65-year-old male with a history of heart failure and chronic kidney disease presents with shortness of breath and decreased urine output. His serum creatinine is found to be 4.5 mg/dL, increased from a baseline of 2.5 mg/dL. His urine sodium is 30 mEq/L, and his fractional excretion of urea (FEUrea) is calculated to be 35%. Which of the following is the most likely cause of this patient's acute kidney injury (AKI)?
a. cardiorenal syndrome type 1
b. hepatorenal syndrome
c. obstructive nephropathy
d. acute interstitial nephritis

Answer: a. cardiorenal syndrome type 1. Explanation: The patient's presentation of shortness of breath and decreased urine output in the setting of heart failure, along with an acute increase in serum creatinine and a high fractional excretion of urea (FEUrea > 35%), suggests cardiorenal syndrome type 1 as the most likely cause of his acute kidney injury (AKI). Cardiorenal syndrome type 1 is characterized by acute worsening of heart failure leading to AKI, and is thought to be mediated by a combination of reduced renal perfusion, venous congestion, and neurohormonal activation. The high FEUrea is a key finding that helps to differentiate cardiorenal syndrome from prerenal azotemia, as it suggests that the kidneys are still able to excrete urea despite a decrease in glomerular filtration rate (GFR). Hepatorenal syndrome is a type of functional renal failure that occurs in patients with advanced liver disease, but the absence of liver disease history and the presence of heart failure make it less likely. Obstructive nephropathy and acute interstitial nephritis are less likely in the absence of supportive clinical or imaging findings.

403. A 50-year-old male with a history of hypertension and gout presents with acute onset flank pain and hematuria. His serum creatinine is found to be 3.0 mg/dL, increased from a baseline of 1.2 mg/dL. Urinalysis shows numerous uric acid crystals and white blood cell casts. Which of the following is the most appropriate initial management of this patient's acute kidney injury (AKI)?
a. intravenous fluids and allopurinol
b. intravenous fluids and rasburicase
c. oral prednisone and colchicine
d. emergent hemodialysis

Answer: b. intravenous fluids and rasburicase. Explanation: The patient's presentation of acute flank pain and hematuria, along with an acute increase in serum creatinine and the presence of uric acid crystals and white blood cell casts on urinalysis, suggests acute uric acid nephropathy as the most likely cause of his acute kidney injury (AKI). Acute uric acid nephropathy occurs when there is a rapid increase in serum uric acid levels, leading to the precipitation of uric acid crystals in the renal tubules and collecting ducts. This can cause obstruction, inflammation, and damage to the renal parenchyma. The most appropriate initial management of acute uric acid nephropathy is aggressive intravenous hydration to increase urine flow and promote the excretion of uric acid crystals, along with the use of rasburicase, a recombinant urate oxidase enzyme that rapidly lowers serum uric acid levels. Allopurinol is a xanthine oxidase inhibitor that can be used to prevent future attacks of gout and uric acid nephropathy, but it does not rapidly lower serum uric acid levels and may actually worsen acute uric acid nephropathy if started during an acute attack. Oral prednisone and colchicine are used for the treatment of acute gout flares but are not effective for the management of acute uric acid nephropathy. Emergent hemodialysis may be necessary in patients with severe AKI or hyperuricemia that is refractory to medical management, but it is not typically the initial treatment of choice.

404. A 60-year-old female with a history of chronic kidney disease presents with a 2-week history of progressively worsening fatigue, nausea, and pruritus. Her serum creatinine is found to be 8.5 mg/dL, increased from a baseline of 3.5 mg/dL. Her serum potassium is 6.2 mEq/L, and her serum bicarbonate is 14 mEq/L. Which of the following is the most appropriate management of this patient's uremic symptoms?
a. intravenous sodium bicarbonate
b. oral sodium polystyrene sulfonate
c. urgent hemodialysis initiation
d. oral calcitriol supplementation

Answer: c. urgent hemodialysis initiation. Explanation: The patient's presentation of fatigue, nausea, and pruritus in the setting of a significantly elevated serum creatinine and electrolyte abnormalities (hyperkalemia and metabolic acidosis) suggests uremia secondary to advanced chronic kidney disease. Uremia is a clinical syndrome that occurs when there is an accumulation of nitrogenous waste products and other uremic toxins in the blood, leading to a variety of systemic symptoms. The most appropriate management of uremic symptoms in this patient is urgent initiation of hemodialysis, which can rapidly remove excess fluid, correct electrolyte abnormalities, and clear uremic toxins from the blood. Intravenous sodium bicarbonate may be used to temporarily correct metabolic acidosis, but it does not address the underlying cause of the patient's symptoms and may worsen fluid overload. Oral sodium polystyrene sulfonate is a potassium-binding resin that can be used to treat hyperkalemia, but it is not effective for the management of other uremic symptoms and may cause gastrointestinal side effects. Oral calcitriol is a vitamin D analog that can be used to treat secondary hyperparathyroidism in patients with chronic kidney disease, but it is not indicated for the acute management of uremic symptoms.

405. A 45-year-old male with a history of type 1 diabetes presents with nausea, vomiting, and abdominal pain. His serum creatinine is found to be 2.5 mg/dL, increased from a baseline of 1.0 mg/dL. His serum lipase is 3,000 U/L, and his serum triglycerides are 1,500 mg/dL. Which of the following is the most likely etiology of this patient's acute kidney injury (AKI)?
a. acute tubular necrosis
b. diabetic ketoacidosis
c. hypertriglyceridemia-induced pancreatitis
d. urinary tract obstruction

Answer: c. hypertriglyceridemia-induced pancreatitis. Explanation: The patient's presentation of nausea, vomiting, and abdominal pain, along with an acute increase in serum creatinine and significantly elevated serum lipase and triglyceride levels, suggests hypertriglyceridemia-induced pancreatitis as the most likely cause of his acute kidney injury (AKI). Hypertriglyceridemia is a well-recognized cause of acute pancreatitis, and it can occur in patients with poorly controlled diabetes or other disorders of lipid metabolism. The release of pancreatic enzymes and inflammatory mediators during acute pancreatitis can lead to systemic inflammation, microvascular damage, and acute tubular necrosis (ATN). While ATN is a common cause of AKI in hospitalized patients, the presence of severe hypertriglyceridemia and pancreatitis makes it a secondary rather than primary diagnosis in this case. Diabetic ketoacidosis (DKA) can cause AKI through a combination of volume depletion, hypoperfusion, and direct tubular injury from ketoacids, but the absence of clinical features of DKA (such as hyperglycemia, metabolic acidosis, and ketonuria) makes it less likely. Urinary tract obstruction is a potentially reversible cause of AKI, but it is not typically associated with the degree of pancreatitis and hypertriglyceridemia seen in this patient.

406. A 70-year-old male with a history of benign prostatic hyperplasia presents with decreased urine output and suprapubic pain. His serum creatinine is found to be 4.0 mg/dL, increased from a baseline of 1.5 mg/dL. Bladder scan shows a post-void residual volume of 800 mL. Which of the following is the most appropriate initial management of this patient's acute kidney injury (AKI)?
a. intravenous furosemide
b. oral doxazosin
c. percutaneous nephrostomy tube placement
d. indwelling urinary catheter placement

Answer: d. indwelling urinary catheter placement. Explanation: The patient's presentation of decreased urine output and suprapubic pain, along with an acute increase in serum creatinine and a significantly elevated post-void residual volume on bladder scan, suggests obstructive uropathy secondary to benign prostatic hyperplasia (BPH) as the most likely cause of his acute kidney injury (AKI). Obstructive uropathy is a potentially reversible cause of AKI that occurs when there is a mechanical obstruction to urine flow, leading to increased intratubular pressure, tubular dilatation, and ultimately, a decrease in glomerular filtration rate (GFR). The most appropriate initial management of obstructive uropathy in this patient is placement of an indwelling urinary catheter to relieve the obstruction and allow for urine drainage. This can help to improve renal function and alleviate symptoms of urinary retention. Intravenous furosemide is a loop diuretic that can be used to promote diuresis in patients with AKI, but it is not effective in the setting of urinary tract obstruction and may actually worsen kidney injury by increasing intratubular pressure. Oral doxazosin is an alpha-1 adrenergic antagonist that can be used to treat the symptoms of BPH, but it does not address the acute obstruction and may cause hypotension in patients with AKI. Percutaneous nephrostomy tube placement is an invasive procedure that involves the direct drainage of urine from the renal pelvis and may be necessary in patients with severe or prolonged obstruction, but it is not typically the initial treatment of choice in patients with BPH-related obstruction.

407. A 55-year-old female with a history of lupus nephritis presents with fever, rash, and acute onset anuria. Her serum creatinine is found to be 6.0 mg/dL, increased from a baseline of 2.0 mg/dL. Urinalysis shows numerous white blood cells and white blood cell casts. Which of the following is the most appropriate management of this patient's acute kidney injury (AKI)?
a. intravenous methylprednisolone
b. intravenous cyclophosphamide
c. oral mycophenolate mofetil
d. urgent hemodialysis initiation

Answer: a. intravenous methylprednisolone. Explanation: The patient's presentation of fever, rash, and acute onset anuria in the setting of lupus nephritis, along with an acute increase in serum creatinine and the presence of white blood cells and white blood cell casts on urinalysis, suggests acute lupus nephritis as the most likely cause of her acute kidney injury (AKI). Lupus nephritis is a common and serious complication of systemic lupus erythematosus (SLE) that occurs when autoantibodies and immune complexes deposit in the kidneys, leading to inflammation, fibrosis, and damage to the renal parenchyma. The most appropriate initial management of acute lupus nephritis in this patient is intravenous pulse methylprednisolone, a high-dose corticosteroid that can rapidly suppress inflammation and prevent further kidney damage. This is typically followed by a gradual taper and maintenance therapy with oral prednisone, along with other immunosuppressive agents such as cyclophosphamide or mycophenolate mofetil. Intravenous cyclophosphamide is a cytotoxic alkylating agent that can be used for induction therapy in severe cases of lupus nephritis, but it is not typically used as initial monotherapy due to its potential for toxicity. Oral mycophenolate mofetil is an immunosuppressive agent that can be used for maintenance therapy in lupus nephritis, but it is not as effective as intravenous corticosteroids for the initial management of acute disease. Urgent hemodialysis may be necessary in patients with severe AKI or life-threatening complications such as hyperkalemia or fluid overload, but it does not address the underlying autoimmune process and is not the primary treatment for lupus nephritis.

408. A patient presents with muscle weakness, arrhythmias, and a serum potassium level of 6.8 mEq/L. This condition is known as:
a. Hyponatremia
b. Hyperkalemia
c. Hypokalemia
d. Hypercalcemia

Answer: b. Hyperkalemia. Explanation: Hyperkalemia is characterized by elevated serum potassium levels, which can lead to muscle weakness and cardiac arrhythmias. A potassium level of 6.8 mEq/L is significantly above the normal range, indicating hyperkalemia.

409. In the setting of severe dehydration, which electrolyte imbalance is most likely to occur?
a. Hyponatremia
b. Hypernatremia
c. Hypokalemia
d. Hypercalcemia

Answer: b. Hypernatremia. Explanation: Severe dehydration can lead to hypernatremia, characterized by elevated serum sodium levels, due to the loss of water exceeding the loss of sodium.

410. A patient with prolonged vomiting is at risk for developing:
a. Hyperkalemia
b. Hypokalemia
c. Hypercalcemia
d. Hyperphosphatemia

Answer: b. Hypokalemia. Explanation: Prolonged vomiting can lead to hypokalemia due to the loss of gastric contents rich in potassium, as well as secondary hyperaldosteronism from volume depletion, which further promotes renal potassium loss.

411. A patient diagnosed with hyperparathyroidism is likely to exhibit which electrolyte imbalance?
a. Hypocalcemia
b. Hypercalcemia
c. Hypokalemia
d. Hyponatremia

Answer: b. Hypercalcemia. Explanation: Hyperparathyroidism leads to increased parathyroid hormone (PTH) secretion, which elevates serum calcium levels through increased bone resorption, renal reabsorption of calcium, and increased intestinal calcium absorption, resulting in hypercalcemia.

412. In a patient with diabetic ketoacidosis (DKA), which electrolyte disturbance is commonly seen due to osmotic diuresis?
a. Hyperkalemia
b. Hypokalemia
c. Hypernatremia
d. Hyponatremia

Answer: b. Hypokalemia. Explanation: Although patients with DKA may initially present with hyperkalemia due to acidosis shifting potassium out of cells, the osmotic diuresis caused by hyperglycemia leads to substantial urinary losses of potassium, often resulting in significant hypokalemia as treatment progresses.

413. A patient on loop diuretics for heart failure management should be monitored for:
a. Hyperkalemia
b. Hypokalemia
c. Hypercalcemia
d. Hypernatremia

Answer: b. Hypokalemia. Explanation: Loop diuretics increase the excretion of sodium, water, and potassium in the urine, leading to a risk of hypokalemia, which necessitates monitoring and potentially supplementation of potassium.

414. The development of Chvostek's sign and Trousseau's sign in a postoperative patient suggests:
a. Hypernatremia
b. Hypokalemia
c. Hypercalcemia
d. Hypocalcemia

Answer: d. Hypocalcemia. Explanation: Chvostek's sign (facial muscle spasm upon tapping the facial nerve) and Trousseau's sign (carpopedal spasm induced by inflating a blood pressure cuff) are clinical manifestations of neuromuscular irritability seen in hypocalcemia.

415. A patient with chronic renal failure is at risk for developing:
a. Hypophosphatemia
b. Hyperphosphatemia
c. Hypomagnesemia
d. Hyponatremia

Answer: b. Hyperphosphatemia. Explanation: Patients with chronic renal failure often develop hyperphosphatemia due to decreased renal phosphate excretion. The kidneys play a crucial role in regulating phosphate levels, and their impaired function in renal failure leads to phosphate accumulation.

416. An elderly patient taking thiazide diuretics for hypertension might exhibit:
a. Hypocalcemia
b. Hypercalcemia
c. Hypokalemia
d. Hypernatremia

Answer: b. Hypercalcemia. Explanation: Thiazide diuretics decrease calcium excretion by the kidneys, which can lead to hypercalcemia, especially in the elderly or in patients with other predisposing factors for elevated calcium levels.

417. The administration of intravenous insulin to a patient with hyperkalemia is intended to:
a. Increase renal excretion of potassium
b. Bind excess potassium in the gut
c. Shift potassium from the extracellular to the intracellular space
d. Increase potassium absorption from the gastrointestinal tract

Answer: c. Shift potassium from the extracellular to the intracellular space. Explanation: Insulin helps to lower serum potassium levels by facilitating the shift of potassium from the extracellular fluid into the cells, a critical immediate management step in patients with hyperkalemia.

418. In distinguishing between SIADH and cerebral salt wasting (CSW), which clinical finding is more indicative of CSW?
a. Decreased serum osmolality
b. Increased urine sodium excretion with hypovolemia
c. Hyponatremia with urine osmolality greater than serum osmolality
d. Euvolemic hyponatremia

Answer: b. Increased urine sodium excretion with hypovolemia. Explanation: CSW is characterized by the renal loss of salt and water, leading to hyponatremia and hypovolemia, distinguished by increased urine sodium excretion. In contrast, SIADH typically presents with euvolemic hyponatremia, without the significant volume depletion seen in CSW.

419. In the management of SIADH, which therapeutic intervention is initially recommended for mild to moderate chronic hyponatremia?
a. Intravenous hypertonic saline
b. Fluid restriction
c. Loop diuretics
d. Vasopressin receptor antagonists

Answer: b. Fluid restriction. Explanation: For mild to moderate chronic hyponatremia associated with SIADH, fluid restriction is often the initial management strategy to decrease water intake and help correct the dilutional hyponatremia, without the risks associated with more aggressive interventions.

420. A patient with SIADH is being treated with fluid restriction, but their serum sodium remains low. What is the next step in management?
a. Increase fluid intake to stimulate diuresis
b. Administer a vasopressin receptor antagonist
c. Start intravenous administration of 0.9% saline
d. Discontinue all medications that might be causing SIADH

Answer: b. Administer a vasopressin receptor antagonist. Explanation: If fluid restriction is ineffective in managing SIADH, the next step can include the use of vasopressin receptor antagonists (vaptans), which block the action of antidiuretic hormone (ADH) at the kidney, promoting free water excretion (aquaresis) and correcting hyponatremia.

421. What is a major risk associated with the rapid correction of hyponatremia in patients with SIADH?
a. Osmotic demyelination syndrome
b. Acute renal failure
c. Hypertensive crisis
d. Pulmonary edema

Answer: a. Osmotic demyelination syndrome. Explanation: Rapid correction of hyponatremia, especially in chronic cases, can lead to osmotic demyelination syndrome, a serious and potentially irreversible condition characterized by demyelination in the central nervous system, due to the sudden shift of water out of brain cells.

422. Which diagnostic criterion is essential for confirming the diagnosis of SIADH?
a. Serum sodium >135 mEq/L
b. Urine osmolality less than serum osmolality

c. Normal adrenal and thyroid function
d. Evidence of hypovolemia

Answer: c. Normal adrenal and thyroid function. Explanation: Confirming the diagnosis of SIADH requires the exclusion of other causes of hyponatremia, including adrenal insufficiency and hypothyroidism, making normal adrenal and thyroid function tests essential for the accurate diagnosis of SIADH.

423. In a patient with suspected cerebral salt wasting post-subarachnoid hemorrhage, what hallmark sign differentiates it from SIADH?
a. Elevated hematocrit due to hemoconcentration
b. Positive water balance with weight gain
c. Increased thirst and polydipsia
d. Negative water balance with signs of dehydration

Answer: d. Negative water balance with signs of dehydration. Explanation: CSW is characterized by renal salt loss leading to hyponatremia and a negative water balance, often manifesting as signs of dehydration, which differentiates it from SIADH where patients are typically euvolemic.

424. For a patient with cerebral salt wasting, what is the primary treatment goal?
a. Fluid restriction to manage hyponatremia
b. Replacement of both sodium and volume losses
c. Administration of vasopressin receptor antagonists
d. High-dose loop diuretics to reduce intracranial pressure

Answer: b. Replacement of both sodium and volume losses. Explanation: The primary treatment goal for cerebral salt wasting is the replacement of both sodium and volume losses to address the underlying hypovolemia and hyponatremia, typically requiring administration of isotonic or hypertonic saline solutions.

425. When considering the treatment for SIADH, which option is particularly useful for severe symptomatic hyponatremia?
a. Oral salt tablets
b. Intravenous hypertonic saline
c. Increased water intake
d. Potassium supplementation

Answer: b. Intravenous hypertonic saline. Explanation: In cases of severe symptomatic hyponatremia due to SIADH, intravenous hypertonic saline (3% NaCl) is used to acutely raise serum sodium levels and prevent or treat serious complications like seizures, while carefully monitoring to avoid overly rapid correction.

426. In distinguishing SIADH from dehydration, which laboratory finding is indicative of SIADH?

a. High serum sodium
b. High serum osmolality
c. Low urine sodium despite normal salt intake
d. Concentrated urine with high urine osmolality

Answer: d. Concentrated urine with high urine osmolality. Explanation: In SIADH, despite the presence of hyponatremia, the urine remains inappropriately concentrated with high urine osmolality, reflecting the continued renal reabsorption of water under the influence of inappropriately secreted antidiuretic hormone.

427. Which ECG change is most commonly associated with severe hyperkalemia?
a. Prolonged PR interval
b. ST-segment elevation
c. Peaked T waves
d. Presence of U waves

Answer: c. Peaked T waves. Explanation: Peaked T waves are an early and common electrocardiographic manifestation of hyperkalemia, particularly when serum potassium levels are significantly elevated, reflecting the effects of increased extracellular potassium on cardiac myocyte action potentials.

428. In the management of hyperkalemia with ECG changes, the immediate administration of which substance is recommended to stabilize the myocardial cell membrane?
a. Insulin
b. Sodium polystyrene sulfonate
c. Calcium gluconate
d. Dextrose

Answer: c. Calcium gluconate. Explanation: Calcium gluconate is administered in the setting of hyperkalemia with ECG changes to stabilize the myocardial cell membrane and counteract the cardiotoxic effects of potassium, even though it does not lower serum potassium levels.

429. The combination of insulin and dextrose in hyperkalemia management serves to:
a. Increase urinary potassium excretion
b. Stabilize the myocardial cell membrane
c. Shift potassium from the extracellular to the intracellular space
d. Bind potassium in the gastrointestinal tract

Answer: c. Shift potassium from the extracellular to the intracellular space. Explanation: The administration of insulin, accompanied by dextrose to prevent hypoglycemia, facilitates the intracellular uptake of potassium, thereby temporarily reducing serum potassium levels in hyperkalemia.

430. Sodium polystyrene sulfonate (Kayexalate) is used in hyperkalemia management to:
a. Enhance renal potassium excretion
b. Bind potassium in the gastrointestinal tract for elimination
c. Stabilize cardiac membranes
d. Shift potassium intracellularly

Answer: b. Bind potassium in the gastrointestinal tract for elimination. Explanation: Sodium polystyrene sulfonate works by exchanging sodium ions for potassium ions in the gastrointestinal tract, leading to the binding and subsequent fecal elimination of potassium, which helps to lower serum potassium levels over hours to days.

431. In a patient with hyperkalemia, which ECG finding indicates an urgent need for intervention?
a. Sinus bradycardia
b. Widened QRS complexes
c. Inverted T waves
d. Isolated premature atrial contractions

Answer: b. Widened QRS complexes. Explanation: Widened QRS complexes in the context of hyperkalemia indicate severe potassium elevation with significant cardiac toxicity, necessitating urgent treatment to prevent progression to life-threatening arrhythmias.

432. Which therapeutic intervention is considered first-line for acute management of hyperkalemia without ECG changes?
a. Hemodialysis
b. Oral calcium supplements
c. Nebulized albuterol
d. Insulin and dextrose infusion

Answer: d. Insulin and dextrose infusion. Explanation: Insulin (with dextrose to prevent hypoglycemia) is a first-line therapy for acute hyperkalemia management to promote the intracellular shift of potassium, even in the absence of ECG changes, due to its rapid onset of action.

433. A patient with renal failure presents with hyperkalemia. Which of the following treatments should be used cautiously due to the patient's renal status?
a. Calcium gluconate
b. Insulin and dextrose
c. Sodium polystyrene sulfonate
d. Oral potassium supplements

Answer: c. Sodium polystyrene sulfonate. Explanation: Sodium polystyrene sulfonate's effectiveness may be limited in patients with renal failure due to decreased bowel movement and potential for sodium overload. Additionally, there's a risk of intestinal necrosis, especially in patients with reduced bowel motility.

434. In treating hyperkalemia, the role of calcium gluconate is primarily to:
a. Reduce serum potassium levels
b. Increase potassium excretion via the kidneys
c. Protect the heart from the effects of elevated potassium
d. Increase gastrointestinal elimination of potassium

Answer: c. Protect the heart from the effects of elevated potassium. Explanation: Calcium gluconate does not lower serum potassium levels but is crucial in protecting the heart from the toxic effects of hyperkalemia by stabilizing cardiac cell membranes.

435. The administration of nebulized albuterol in hyperkalemia management is intended to:
a. Bind serum potassium for renal excretion
b. Induce a diuretic effect to remove potassium
c. Promote the intracellular shift of potassium
d. Counteract the effects of hyperkalemia on the ECG

Answer: c. Promote the intracellular shift of potassium. Explanation: Nebulized albuterol, a beta-agonist, can cause a temporary shift of potassium from the extracellular space into cells, thereby reducing serum potassium levels and mitigating hyperkalemia.

436. When considering the use of sodium polystyrene sulfonate for hyperkalemia, it's important to remember that:
a. Its action is immediate, suitable for emergency use
b. It should be combined with calcium gluconate for membrane stabilization
c. It works by exchanging sodium for potassium in the colon, leading to fecal potassium excretion
d. It is the treatment of choice for hyperkalemia with severe ECG changes

Answer: c. It works by exchanging sodium for potassium in the colon, leading to fecal potassium excretion. Explanation: Sodium polystyrene sulfonate acts in the colon to exchange sodium ions for potassium ions, which are then eliminated in the stool. This action is not immediate and is therefore not suitable for emergency use in the presence of severe ECG changes.

437. What is the primary physiological mechanism responsible for neuromuscular irritability in hypocalcemia?
a. Decreased threshold for nerve and muscle excitation
b. Increased potassium efflux in neuronal cells
c. Enhanced sodium-potassium ATPase activity
d. Inhibition of acetylcholine release at neuromuscular junctions

Answer: a. Decreased threshold for nerve and muscle excitation. Explanation: Hypocalcemia leads to neuromuscular irritability primarily due to a decreased threshold for nerve and muscle excitation. Calcium plays a key role in stabilizing nerve cell membranes, and lower levels make cells more easily excitable, leading to symptoms such as muscle spasms and tingling.

438. Chvostek's sign, indicative of hypocalcemia, is elicited by:
a. Tapping over the facial nerve anterior to the ear
b. Occluding the brachial artery with a blood pressure cuff
c. Stroking the lateral aspect of the thigh
d. Applying pressure over the carpal tunnel

Answer: a. Tapping over the facial nerve anterior to the ear. Explanation: Chvostek's sign is a clinical sign of hypocalcemia where tapping over the facial nerve just anterior to the ear induces a twitch of the facial muscles, reflecting neuromuscular excitability due to low calcium levels.

439. Trousseau's sign, a clinical indicator of latent tetany in hypocalcemia, is demonstrated by:
a. Contraction of facial muscles in response to facial nerve percussion
b. Carpal spasm induced by inflating a blood pressure cuff above systolic pressure for several minutes
c. Extension of the big toe upon plantar stimulation
d. Involuntary contraction of the diaphragm leading to hiccups

Answer: b. Carpal spasm induced by inflating a blood pressure cuff above systolic pressure for several minutes. Explanation: Trousseau's sign is positive when inflation of a blood pressure cuff on the arm to a pressure above systolic level induces carpal spasm, such as flexion of the wrist and metacarpophalangeal joints, reflecting latent tetany due to hypocalcemia.

440. In the management of acute symptomatic hypocalcemia, which intervention is most immediately required?
a. Oral calcium supplementation
b. Intravenous administration of calcium gluconate
c. Magnesium repletion
d. Vitamin D therapy

Answer: b. Intravenous administration of calcium gluconate. Explanation: In acute symptomatic hypocalcemia, immediate treatment involves the intravenous administration of calcium gluconate to rapidly increase serum calcium levels and alleviate symptoms, particularly neuromuscular irritability and cardiac effects.

441. Which electrolyte imbalance is often associated with hypocalcemia and must be corrected to effectively treat hypocalcemia?
a. Hyponatremia
b. Hypomagnesemia
c. Hyperkalemia
d. Hyperphosphatemia

Answer: b. Hypomagnesemia. Explanation: Hypomagnesemia is commonly associated with hypocalcemia and can impair the release of parathyroid hormone (PTH), exacerbating hypocalcemia. Correction of magnesium levels is often necessary to effectively manage and treat hypocalcemia.

442. In a patient with chronic kidney disease, what is a common cause of hypocalcemia?
a. Excessive intake of calcium supplements
b. Decreased production of 1,25-dihydroxyvitamin D
c. Increased calcium excretion due to diuretic therapy
d. Overactivity of the parathyroid gland

Answer: b. Decreased production of 1,25-dihydroxyvitamin D. Explanation: In patients with chronic kidney disease, hypocalcemia commonly results from decreased production of 1,25-dihydroxyvitamin D due to impaired renal function. This form of vitamin D is crucial for calcium absorption from the gut.

443. What is the underlying pathophysiology of hypocalcemia in the setting of acute pancreatitis?
a. Calcium sequestration in areas of fat necrosis
b. Excessive urinary calcium loss
c. Hyperphosphatemia-induced calcium precipitation
d. Parathyroid hormone resistance

Answer: a. Calcium sequestration in areas of fat necrosis. Explanation: In acute pancreatitis, hypocalcemia can occur due to the sequestration of calcium in areas of fat necrosis, where saponification of fat by pancreatic lipases leads to the formation of calcium soaps, reducing the bioavailable serum calcium.

444. When considering the differential diagnosis of hypocalcemia, what role does the measurement of serum albumin play?
a. It helps differentiate between renal and non-renal causes of hypocalcemia.
b. It is used to calculate the corrected serum calcium level in hypoalbuminemic states.
c. It determines the need for vitamin D supplementation.
d. It identifies patients at risk for developing calcium stones.

Answer: b. It is used to calculate the corrected serum calcium level in hypoalbuminemic states. Explanation: The measurement of serum albumin is crucial in the evaluation of hypocalcemia because calcium binds to albumin, and hypoalbuminemia can lead to low total serum calcium levels. Correcting the calcium level for albumin concentration helps determine the true free calcium level.

445. In the treatment of chronic hypocalcemia, what is the main reason for combining calcium supplements with vitamin D analogs?
a. Vitamin D enhances renal calcium reabsorption.
b. Vitamin D increases calcium absorption from the gastrointestinal tract.
c. Calcium alone can lead to hyperphosphatemia.

d. Vitamin D suppresses parathyroid hormone secretion.

Answer: b. Vitamin D increases calcium absorption from the gastrointestinal tract. Explanation: In the treatment of chronic hypocalcemia, combining calcium supplements with vitamin D analogs is essential because vitamin D enhances the intestinal absorption of calcium, ensuring effective treatment of hypocalcemia by increasing the bioavailability of calcium.

446. A patient presents with melena and a history of epigastric pain that improves with eating. Endoscopy reveals a gastric ulcer. Which factor is most commonly associated with this condition?
a. Chronic alcohol consumption
b. Helicobacter pylori infection
c. Excessive intake of spicy foods
d. Use of acetaminophen

Answer: b. Helicobacter pylori infection. Explanation: Helicobacter pylori infection is a common cause of peptic ulcer disease, which can lead to gastric ulcers. The bacteria damage the stomach's protective lining, leading to ulcer formation.

447. A 45-year-old patient with a history of rheumatoid arthritis has been taking ibuprofen regularly for joint pain. They now present with hematemesis. What is the most likely cause of their upper gastrointestinal bleeding?
a. Barrett's esophagus
b. Zollinger-Ellison syndrome
c. NSAID-induced gastropathy
d. Esophageal varices

Answer: c. NSAID-induced gastropathy. Explanation: Chronic use of nonsteroidal anti-inflammatory drugs (NSAIDs) like ibuprofen can cause gastropathy, leading to the development of ulcers in the stomach or duodenum, which can result in upper gastrointestinal bleeding manifested as hematemesis.

448. In a patient diagnosed with Zollinger-Ellison syndrome, which clinical feature is most characteristic of this condition?
a. Decreased gastric acid secretion
b. Multiple peptic ulcers resistant to standard treatments
c. Absence of Helicobacter pylori infection
d. Gastric ulcers located exclusively in the antrum

Answer: b. Multiple peptic ulcers resistant to standard treatments. Explanation: Zollinger-Ellison syndrome is characterized by the presence of one or more gastrin-secreting tumors (gastrinomas) leading to excessive gastric acid secretion, resulting in multiple peptic ulcers that are often resistant to standard ulcer treatments.

449. A patient with peptic ulcer disease is found to have Helicobacter pylori infection. What is the most appropriate first-line treatment?
a. Proton pump inhibitor (PPI) monotherapy
b. Triple therapy with a PPI, clarithromycin, and amoxicillin
c. High-dose antacids
d. Corticosteroids

Answer: b. Triple therapy with a PPI, clarithromycin, and amoxicillin. Explanation: First-line treatment for Helicobacter pylori-associated peptic ulcer disease typically involves triple therapy, including a proton pump inhibitor (PPI) to reduce acid production and two antibiotics (commonly clarithromycin and amoxicillin) to eradicate the H. pylori infection.

450. In assessing a patient with suspected upper gastrointestinal bleeding, which diagnostic procedure is considered the gold standard for identifying the source of bleeding?
a. Abdominal ultrasound
b. Barium swallow study
c. Upper gastrointestinal endoscopy
d. CT scan of the abdomen

Answer: c. Upper gastrointestinal endoscopy. Explanation: Upper gastrointestinal endoscopy is the gold standard for diagnosing and identifying the source of upper gastrointestinal bleeding, allowing for direct visualization of the esophagus, stomach, and duodenum.

451. A patient on long-term NSAID therapy for osteoarthritis reports dark, tarry stools. What is the most likely diagnosis?
a. Esophageal varices
b. NSAID-induced peptic ulcer with upper GI bleeding
c. Gastric cancer
d. Ileal diverticulosis

Answer: b. NSAID-induced peptic ulcer with upper GI bleeding. Explanation: Long-term NSAID use is a risk factor for the development of peptic ulcers, which can lead to upper gastrointestinal bleeding, often presenting as melena (dark, tarry stools).

452. A patient with recurrent epigastric pain undergoes endoscopy, which reveals duodenal ulcers. A rapid urease test is positive. What is the most likely etiology?
a. Stress-induced gastritis
b. Helicobacter pylori infection
c. Crohn's disease
d. Intake of corticosteroids

Answer: b. Helicobacter pylori infection. Explanation: A positive rapid urease test suggests the presence of Helicobacter pylori, a common cause of duodenal ulcers due to its ability to survive in the acidic environment of the stomach and duodenum, leading to inflammation and ulceration.

453. For a patient with Zollinger-Ellison syndrome and recurrent peptic ulcers, which treatment approach is most effective in controlling gastric acid hypersecretion?
a. High-dose H2 receptor antagonists
b. Surgical resection of gastrin-secreting tumors
c. Proton pump inhibitors at standard doses
d. Proton pump inhibitors at high doses

Answer: d. Proton pump inhibitors at high doses.

454. What is the primary pathophysiological mechanism leading to the development of esophageal varices in patients with liver cirrhosis?
a. Decreased hepatic arterial blood flow
b. Portal hypertension due to increased resistance to portal blood flow
c. Direct liver cell damage by hepatotoxins
d. Splanchnic vasoconstriction reducing portal venous inflow

Answer: b. Portal hypertension due to increased resistance to portal blood flow. Explanation: Esophageal varices develop primarily due to portal hypertension, which is an increase in the blood pressure within the portal venous system, often resulting from cirrhosis. The increased resistance to portal blood flow leads to the formation of collateral pathways, including those in the esophagus, to bypass the obstruction.

455. In the management of acute bleeding from esophageal varices, what is the role of octreotide?
a. To mechanically compress the varices and stop the bleeding
b. To reduce portal venous pressure by splanchnic vasoconstriction
c. To sclerose the varices and prevent rebleeding
d. To enhance clot formation by increasing platelet aggregation

Answer: b. To reduce portal venous pressure by splanchnic vasoconstriction. Explanation: Octreotide, a somatostatin analog, is used in the acute management of bleeding esophageal varices to reduce portal venous pressure. It works by causing splanchnic vasoconstriction, which decreases the blood flow to the portal system, thereby helping to control the bleeding.

456. What is the primary advantage of banding over sclerotherapy in the treatment of esophageal varices?
a. Banding can permanently eliminate the risk of variceal bleeding
b. Banding is less invasive and can be performed without endoscopy
c. Banding is associated with fewer complications, such as esophageal stricture
d. Banding provides immediate control of bleeding by direct compression

Answer: c. Banding is associated with fewer complications, such as esophageal stricture. Explanation: Banding, or endoscopic variceal ligation, is preferred over sclerotherapy for the treatment of esophageal varices due to its lower complication rate, particularly a reduced risk of post-procedure esophageal strictures, ulcers, and other mucosal damage.

457. For a patient with known esophageal varices, which preventive measure is most effective in reducing the risk of a first variceal hemorrhage?
a. Prophylactic antibiotics
b. Non-selective beta-blockers to reduce portal pressure
c. Regular endoscopic surveillance without primary prophylaxis
d. Immediate band ligation of all detected varices

Answer: b. Non-selective beta-blockers to reduce portal pressure. Explanation: Non-selective beta-blockers, such as propranolol or nadolol, are effective in primary prophylaxis against the first variceal hemorrhage in patients with known esophageal varices. They work by reducing portal venous pressure, thus decreasing the risk of bleeding from varices.

458. During an acute esophageal variceal bleed, what is the initial step in management before specific treatments like banding or octreotide?
a. Administration of high-dose proton pump inhibitors
b. Endoscopic examination to determine the source of bleeding
c. Volume resuscitation and stabilization of hemodynamics
d. Immediate oral intake restriction and initiation of total parenteral nutrition

Answer: c. Volume resuscitation and stabilization of hemodynamics. Explanation: The initial management of an acute esophageal variceal bleed involves volume resuscitation to stabilize hemodynamics, ensuring the patient is hemodynamically stable before proceeding with specific treatments like endoscopic banding or pharmacotherapy.

459. In patients with cirrhosis, why is screening for esophageal varices recommended upon diagnosis?
a. To initiate dietary changes and reduce alcohol consumption
b. To start prophylactic treatment with non-selective beta-blockers if varices are present
c. To determine the need for liver transplantation
d. To prepare the patient for elective banding of varices

Answer: b. To start prophylactic treatment with non-selective beta-blockers if varices are present. Explanation: Screening for esophageal varices in patients newly diagnosed with cirrhosis is recommended to identify those at risk of variceal bleeding. If varices are present, prophylactic treatment with non-selective beta-blockers can be initiated to reduce the risk of the first hemorrhage.

460. What is the main goal of secondary prophylaxis in patients who have experienced an episode of variceal bleeding?
a. To completely eradicate esophageal varices
b. To prevent rebleeding by managing portal hypertension
c. To perform liver transplantation as a definitive cure
d. To switch from banding to sclerotherapy for long-term management

Answer: b. To prevent rebleeding by managing portal hypertension. Explanation: The main goal of secondary prophylaxis in patients who have had an episode of variceal bleeding is to prevent rebleeding, which is achieved by managing portal hypertension through measures such as non-selective beta-blockers and repeat endoscopic band ligation.

461. When considering the use of transjugular intrahepatic portosystemic shunt (TIPS) in the management of esophageal varices, in which scenario is it most commonly indicated?
a. As first-line treatment for all patients with esophageal varices
b. In patients with refractory ascites who are not candidates for paracentesis
c. For patients in whom both pharmacological and endoscopic therapies have failed to control bleeding
d. As a preventive measure in patients with compensated cirrhosis

Answer: c.

462. A patient presents with hematemesis following a prolonged episode of severe vomiting after a heavy alcohol intake session. The most likely diagnosis is:
a. Esophageal varices
b. Peptic ulcer disease
c. Mallory-Weiss tear
d. Gastric cancer

Answer: c. Mallory-Weiss tear. Explanation: A Mallory-Weiss tear is characterized by a mucosal tear at the gastroesophageal junction, often precipitated by severe vomiting, which can lead to hematemesis. This condition is commonly associated with heavy alcohol intake or any event that significantly increases intra-abdominal pressure.

463. In the diagnosis of a Mallory-Weiss tear, which diagnostic procedure is considered the gold standard?
a. Abdominal ultrasound
b. CT scan
c. Endoscopy
d. Barium swallow

Answer: c. Endoscopy. Explanation: Endoscopy is the gold standard for diagnosing a Mallory-Weiss tear, as it allows direct visualization of the mucosal tear at the gastroesophageal junction and assessment of the severity of bleeding.

464. A patient with a suspected Mallory-Weiss tear has a history of chronic NSAID use. This is relevant because NSAIDs are known to:
a. Reduce the risk of such tears by protecting the gastric lining
b. Increase the risk of tears by inhibiting prostaglandin synthesis
c. Have no effect on the gastrointestinal mucosa
d. Increase gastric pH, thus providing a protective effect

Answer: b. Increase the risk of tears by inhibiting prostaglandin synthesis. Explanation: NSAIDs can increase the risk of gastrointestinal mucosal injury by inhibiting prostaglandin synthesis, which normally protects the gastric lining by promoting mucus and bicarbonate secretion and maintaining mucosal blood flow.

465. Following the endoscopic diagnosis of a Mallory-Weiss tear, the first-line management usually involves:
a. Surgical repair
b. Administration of proton pump inhibitors (PPIs)
c. Immediate cessation of all oral intake
d. Intravenous corticosteroids

Answer: b. Administration of proton pump inhibitors (PPIs). Explanation: The first-line management for a Mallory-Weiss tear typically involves the administration of proton pump inhibitors to reduce gastric acid secretion and promote mucosal healing.

466. A patient with a Mallory-Weiss tear develops signs of shock. The most appropriate next step in management is:
a. Oral administration of antacids
b. Endoscopic hemostasis
c. Scheduling for elective surgery
d. Initiation of H2 receptor antagonists

Answer: b. Endoscopic hemostasis. Explanation: In the case of a Mallory-Weiss tear with significant bleeding leading to shock, endoscopic hemostasis is the most appropriate next step to control bleeding actively. Techniques may include thermal coagulation, clipping, or banding.

467. The differentiation between a Mallory-Weiss tear and Boerhaave syndrome is critical because:
a. Both conditions present with identical symptoms and require the same treatment
b. Boerhaave syndrome involves a full-thickness esophageal rupture and is a surgical emergency
c. Mallory-Weiss tears are typically managed with emergency surgery, while Boerhaave syndrome is not
d. Boerhaave syndrome is self-limiting and does not require medical intervention

Answer: b. Boerhaave syndrome involves a full-thickness esophageal rupture and is a surgical emergency. Explanation: Boerhaave syndrome, characterized by a spontaneous full-thickness esophageal rupture, typically requires immediate surgical intervention due to the risk of mediastinitis and other severe complications, distinguishing it from a Mallory-Weiss tear, which is usually a mucosal tear without full-thickness involvement.

468. A patient with a Mallory-Weiss tear reports relief of symptoms after conservative management. The most appropriate follow-up is:
a. Repeat endoscopy in 24 hours
b. Discharge with oral PPI therapy and outpatient follow-up
c. Immediate surgical consultation
d. Administration of intravenous PPIs for 72 hours

Answer: b. Discharge with oral PPI therapy and outpatient follow-up. Explanation: For a patient with a Mallory-Weiss tear who reports symptom relief following conservative management, discharge with oral PPI therapy and outpatient follow-up is appropriate, as many such tears heal spontaneously with supportive care.

469. In a patient with a known Mallory-Weiss tear, the presence of melena suggests:
a. The tear has spontaneously healed
b. A potential underlying peptic ulcer disease
c. Continued bleeding from the tear
d. Development of esophageal varices

Answer: c. Continued bleeding from the tear. Explanation: The presence of melena (black, tarry stools) in a patient with a known Mallory-Weiss tear suggests continued or delayed bleeding from the tear, as blood has had time to be digested as it passes through the gastrointestinal tract.

470. The role of helicobacter pylori eradication in a patient with a Mallory-Weiss tear and concurrent peptic ulcer disease is to:
a. Promote immediate healing of the tear
b. Prevent future episodes of hematemesis
c. Reduce the risk of recurrent peptic ulcers and associated bleeding
d. Increase gastric pH to facilitate tear healing

Answer: c. Reduce the risk of recurrent peptic ulcers and associated bleeding. Explanation: Eradication of Helicobacter pylori in patients with peptic ulcer disease is aimed at reducing the risk of recurrent ulcers and associated complications, including bleeding, which can indirectly benefit patients with a Mallory-Weiss tear by minimizing additional sources of gastrointestinal bleeding.

471. Which symptom is commonly associated with moderate to severe ulcerative colitis (UC)?
a. Constipation
b. Greasy, foul-smelling stools
c. Bloody diarrhea with abdominal pain
d. Intermittent rectal bleeding without diarrhea

Answer: c. Bloody diarrhea with abdominal pain. Explanation: Patients with moderate to severe ulcerative colitis often present with bloody diarrhea accompanied by abdominal pain. The inflammatory process in UC primarily affects the colon and rectum, leading to the hallmark symptom of bloody diarrhea, which reflects mucosal ulceration and inflammation.

472. Tenesmus, a distressing symptom of ulcerative colitis, is best described as:
a. A constant urge to defecate without significant stool passage
b. Severe abdominal cramping without bowel movement
c. Sudden onset of watery diarrhea
d. The passage of large, hard stools

Answer: a. A constant urge to defecate without significant stool passage. Explanation: Tenesmus in ulcerative colitis is characterized by a distressing and continuous feeling of needing to pass stool, but with little to no stool actually being passed. This symptom reflects rectal inflammation and irritation.

473. In ulcerative colitis, pseudopolyps are formed as a result of:
a. Excessive growth of normal colonic tissue
b. Regeneration of the mucosa between areas of ulceration
c. Malignant transformation of colonic cells
d. Accumulation of submucosal fat

Answer: b. Regeneration of the mucosa between areas of ulceration. Explanation: Pseudopolyps in ulcerative colitis are formed due to the regeneration of the mucosa in areas between ulcerations. They are non-neoplastic lesions that arise in the context of chronic inflammation and mucosal damage.

474. Toxic megacolon, a serious complication of ulcerative colitis, is characterized by:
a. Colon dilation >6cm with signs of systemic toxicity
b. Focal narrowing of the colon with obstruction
c. The formation of multiple transverse colonic ulcers
d. Rapid onset of colonic bleeding without dilation

Answer: a. Colon dilation >6cm with signs of systemic toxicity. Explanation: Toxic megacolon is a life-threatening complication of ulcerative colitis characterized by acute colonic dilation (typically >6cm) and signs of systemic toxicity. It represents a transmural inflammatory process leading to colonic distension, loss of muscle tone, and potential for perforation.

475. In the management of mild ulcerative colitis, which medication class is typically considered first-line therapy?
a. Corticosteroids
b. Aminosalicylates (5-ASA)
c. TNF-alpha inhibitors

d. Immunomodulators

Answer: b. Aminosalicylates (5-ASA). Explanation: Aminosalicylates (5-ASA) are considered first-line therapy for mild to moderate ulcerative colitis due to their anti-inflammatory properties. They can be administered orally or topically (enemas or suppositories) depending on the disease extent and are effective in inducing and maintaining remission.

476. Which diagnostic tool is most definitive for establishing the diagnosis of ulcerative colitis?
a. Abdominal X-ray
b. Colonoscopy with biopsy
c. CT scan of the abdomen
d. Stool culture

Answer: b. Colonoscopy with biopsy. Explanation: Colonoscopy with biopsy is the most definitive tool for diagnosing ulcerative colitis. It allows for direct visualization of the mucosal inflammation, ulceration, and other characteristic changes of UC, and biopsies can provide histological confirmation of the diagnosis.

477. When considering the risk of colorectal cancer in ulcerative colitis, which factor most significantly increases this risk?
a. The presence of pseudopolyps
b. Duration of disease >8-10 years
c. Use of 5-ASA medications
d. Isolated proctitis

Answer: b. Duration of disease >8-10 years. Explanation: The risk of colorectal cancer in patients with ulcerative colitis significantly increases with the duration of the disease, particularly after 8-10 years. Other risk factors include the extent of colonic involvement and a family history of colorectal cancer.

478. In a patient with ulcerative colitis, what is the main goal of nutritional therapy during a flare?
a. To increase dietary fiber intake
b. To maintain nutritional balance and manage symptoms
c. To initiate a high-fat diet
d. To strictly limit fluid intake

Answer: b. To maintain nutritional balance and manage symptoms. Explanation: During a flare of ulcerative colitis, the main goal of nutritional therapy is to maintain nutritional balance and manage symptoms. This may involve modifying the diet to ensure adequate nutrition while minimizing symptoms such as diarrhea and abdominal pain, rather than focusing on restrictive or specific dietary regimens.

479. For severe flares of ulcerative colitis unresponsive to conventional therapy, which treatment may be considered?
a. Oral aminosalicylates (5-ASA) only

b. Increased dietary fiber supplementation
c. Intravenous corticosteroids or biologic therapy
d. Immediate surgical intervention without trying medical therapy

Answer: c. Intravenous corticosteroids or biologic therapy. Explanation: For severe flares of ulcerative colitis unresponsive to conventional therapy, intravenous corticosteroids or the initiation of biologic therapy, such as TNF-alpha inhibitors or integrin receptor antagonists, may be considered to achieve remission.

480. What is the role of colectomy in the management of ulcerative colitis?
a. It is the first-line treatment for mild ulcerative colitis
b. Reserved for cases with dysplasia, refractory disease, or complications like toxic megacolon
c. Routinely performed after 5 years of disease to prevent cancer
d. Only indicated for pseudopolyp management

Answer: b. Reserved for cases with dysplasia, refractory disease, or complications like toxic megacolon. Explanation: Colectomy in ulcerative colitis is reserved for patients with high-grade dysplasia or cancer, refractory disease not responding to medical therapy, or complications such as toxic megacolon. It is considered a definitive cure for the colonic manifestations of the disease but is generally reserved for specific indications.

481. One distinguishing feature of Crohn's disease compared to ulcerative colitis is the presence of:
a. Continuous colonic inflammation
b. Mucosal inflammation only
c. "Skip lesions" with areas of normal tissue between inflamed areas
d. Limited involvement to the rectum

Answer: c. "Skip lesions" with areas of normal tissue between inflamed areas. Explanation: Crohn's disease is characterized by "skip lesions," where areas of inflammation are interspersed with areas of normal tissue, unlike ulcerative colitis, which typically presents with continuous inflammation of the colonic mucosa.

482. A patient with Crohn's disease is most likely to develop which of the following complications due to transmural inflammation?
a. Pseudopolyps
b. Fistulas
c. Toxic megacolon
d. Continuous bleeding

Answer: b. Fistulas. Explanation: The transmural inflammation seen in Crohn's disease, which extends through the entire depth of the intestinal wall, can lead to the formation of fistulas, abnormal connections between the intestine and other structures such as the bladder, vagina, or skin.

483. The development of strictures in Crohn's disease is a result of:
a. Continuous superficial inflammation
b. Healing and scarring from deep transmural inflammation
c. High fiber diet
d. Use of nonsteroidal anti-inflammatory drugs (NSAIDs)

Answer: b. Healing and scarring from deep transmural inflammation. Explanation: In Crohn's disease, strictures often result from the healing and scarring process following deep transmural inflammation, leading to narrowing of the intestinal lumen.

484. A 35-year-old patient with Crohn's disease presents with abdominal pain and a palpable mass in the right lower quadrant. The most likely diagnosis is:
a. Carcinoid tumor
b. Appendicitis
c. Inflammatory fibroid polyp
d. Inflammatory bowel stricture

Answer: d. Inflammatory bowel stricture. Explanation: Patients with Crohn's disease may develop inflammatory bowel strictures due to transmural inflammation and subsequent fibrosis, presenting as abdominal pain and palpable masses, particularly in the right lower quadrant where the terminal ileum is commonly affected.

485. Which of the following best describes the typical distribution of gastrointestinal involvement in Crohn's disease?
a. Limited to the sigmoid colon and rectum
b. Continuous involvement of the entire colon
c. Patchy involvement throughout the gastrointestinal tract, from mouth to anus
d. Confined to the stomach and duodenum

Answer: c. Patchy involvement throughout the gastrointestinal tract, from mouth to anus. Explanation: Crohn's disease can affect any part of the gastrointestinal tract in a discontinuous, patchy manner, known as "skip lesions," with areas of diseased tissue separated by areas of normal tissue, from the mouth to the anus.

486. In the management of Crohn's disease, which medication class is specifically used to close fistulas?
a. Aminosalicylates
b. Antibiotics
c. Corticosteroids
d. Tumor necrosis factor (TNF) inhibitors

Answer: d. Tumor necrosis factor (TNF) inhibitors. Explanation: TNF inhibitors, such as infliximab, are biologic therapies used in the management of Crohn's disease and are particularly effective in closing fistulas and reducing other manifestations of the disease.

487. A patient with Crohn's disease undergoing endoscopy is found to have deep linear ulcers and cobblestone mucosa. This finding is indicative of:
a. Early disease
b. Malignant transformation
c. Advanced transmural inflammation
d. Ischemic colitis

Answer: c. Advanced transmural inflammation. Explanation: Deep linear ulcers and cobblestone appearance of the mucosa are endoscopic findings indicative of advanced Crohn's disease, reflecting transmural inflammation and the characteristic patchy involvement.

488. A Crohn's disease patient complains of pain and swelling in the lower extremities. Upon examination, erythema nodosum is diagnosed. This condition is:
a. Unrelated to Crohn's disease
b. A common gastrointestinal manifestation of Crohn's disease
c. A cutaneous extraintestinal manifestation of Crohn's disease
d. Typically a sign of infectious complications in Crohn's disease

Answer: c. A cutaneous extraintestinal manifestation of Crohn's disease. Explanation: Erythema nodosum is a cutaneous extraintestinal manifestation of Crohn's disease, characterized by painful, red nodules, usually appearing on the lower extremities, and is associated with the inflammatory process of the disease.

489. The use of imaging studies in Crohn's disease is essential for:
a. Diagnosing superficial ulcers only
b. Assessing the extent of mucosal involvement
c. Identifying complications such as fistulas and abscesses
d. Screening for colon cancer exclusively

Answer: c. Identifying complications such as fistulas and abscesses. Explanation: Imaging studies in Crohn's disease, such as MRI or CT enterography, play a crucial role in identifying complications like fistulas and abscesses, which are common due to the transmural nature of the disease.

490. During a flare of Crohn's disease, a patient presents with fever, tachycardia, and a tender abdominal mass. The most immediate concern is:
a. Irritable bowel syndrome overlap
b. Development of a perianal fistula
c. Intra-abdominal abscess formation
d. Lactose intolerance exacerbation

Answer: c. Intra-abdominal abscess formation. Explanation: In the setting of Crohn's disease, the presence of fever, tachycardia, and a tender abdominal mass, especially during a flare, raises immediate concern for an intra-abdominal abscess, a complication of the transmural inflammation and potential fistula formation associated with the disease.

491. A 62-year-old male with a history of end-stage renal disease on hemodialysis presents with shortness of breath and chest pain during his dialysis session. His blood pressure is 80/50 mmHg, and he appears pale and diaphoretic. Which of the following is the most likely cause of this patient's symptoms?
a. dialyzer membrane reaction
b. dialysis disequilibrium syndrome
c. air embolism
d. pericardial tamponade

Answer: c. air embolism. Explanation: The patient's presentation of acute onset shortness of breath, chest pain, hypotension, and altered mental status during hemodialysis is highly suggestive of an air embolism, a rare but potentially fatal complication of hemodialysis. Air embolism occurs when air enters the bloodstream, typically through the venous access site or a break in the dialyzer circuit, and travels to the lungs or brain, causing cardiopulmonary collapse or neurologic symptoms. Dialyzer membrane reactions, such as type A reactions or complement activation-related pseudoallergy (CARPA), can cause similar symptoms but are usually associated with more gradual onset and less severe hypotension. Dialysis disequilibrium syndrome is a neurologic complication of hemodialysis that occurs when the rapid removal of urea causes an osmotic gradient between the brain and the blood, leading to cerebral edema and symptoms such as headache, nausea, and seizures. Pericardial tamponade is a rare complication of end-stage renal disease that can cause hypotension and cardiovascular collapse, but it is not typically associated with the acute onset of symptoms during hemodialysis.

492. A 55-year-old female with a history of congestive heart failure and chronic kidney disease presents with volume overload and acute kidney injury. Her serum creatinine is 4.5 mg/dL, up from a baseline of 2.0 mg/dL. Her blood pressure is 180/100 mmHg, and she has bilateral pulmonary crackles and pitting edema. Which of the following is the most appropriate initial renal replacement therapy for this patient?
a. intermittent hemodialysis
b. continuous venovenous hemofiltration (CVVH)
c. slow low-efficiency dialysis (SLED)
d. peritoneal dialysis

Answer: b. continuous venovenous hemofiltration (CVVH). Explanation: The patient's presentation of acute kidney injury with volume overload and hemodynamic instability (as evidenced by hypertension and pulmonary edema) suggests that continuous renal replacement therapy (CRRT) may be the most appropriate initial modality. CRRT, such as continuous venovenous hemofiltration (CVVH), provides gradual and continuous removal of fluid and solutes, which can be better tolerated by patients with hemodynamic instability or acute illness. Intermittent hemodialysis, while effective at removing fluid and solutes, can cause rapid shifts in fluid and electrolyte balance that may not be well tolerated by critically ill patients. Slow low-efficiency dialysis (SLED) is a hybrid modality that combines the longer treatment time of CRRT with the intermittent nature of hemodialysis, but it may not provide as much hemodynamic stability as CVVH. Peritoneal dialysis is a home-based modality that uses the patient's peritoneal membrane as a filter and is not typically used for the management of acute kidney injury in the hospital setting.

493. A 70-year-old male with a history of diabetes and hypertension is admitted to the ICU with septic shock and acute kidney injury. His serum creatinine is 5.0 mg/dL, and his blood pressure is 80/40 mmHg on norepinephrine infusion. He is anuric and has severe metabolic acidosis with a pH of 7.1. Which of the following is the most appropriate renal replacement therapy prescription for this patient?
a. intermittent hemodialysis with a blood flow rate of 200 mL/min and a dialysate flow rate of 500 mL/min
b. continuous venovenous hemodialysis (CVVHD) with a blood flow rate of 150 mL/min and a dialysate flow rate of 1500 mL/hr
c. continuous venovenous hemodiafiltration (CVVHDF) with a blood flow rate of 200 mL/min, a dialysate flow rate of 1000 mL/hr, and a replacement fluid rate of 1000 mL/hr
d. sustained low-efficiency dialysis (SLED) with a blood flow rate of 200 mL/min and a dialysate flow rate of 300 mL/min

Answer: c. continuous venovenous hemodiafiltration (CVVHDF) with a blood flow rate of 200 mL/min, a dialysate flow rate of 1000 mL/hr, and a replacement fluid rate of 1000 mL/hr. Explanation: The patient's presentation of septic shock, anuric acute kidney injury, and severe metabolic acidosis suggests that a high-intensity continuous renal replacement therapy modality may be necessary to provide adequate solute clearance and acid-base correction. Continuous venovenous hemodiafiltration (CVVHDF) combines the convective clearance of hemofiltration with the diffusive clearance of hemodialysis, allowing for higher total effluent rates and greater control over fluid balance and solute removal. A blood flow rate of 200 mL/min is typically used to ensure adequate circuit flow and prevent clotting, while a dialysate flow rate of 1000 mL/hr and a replacement fluid rate of 1000 mL/hr can provide a total effluent rate of 2000 mL/hr, which is considered a high-intensity prescription. Intermittent hemodialysis and sustained low-efficiency dialysis (SLED) may not provide adequate clearance or hemodynamic stability in this critically ill patient. Continuous venovenous hemodialysis (CVVHD) alone may not provide as much convective clearance as CVVHDF and may require higher dialysate flow rates to achieve similar total effluent rates.

494. A 45-year-old female with a history of lupus nephritis presents with volume overload and acute kidney injury. Her serum creatinine is 6.0 mg/dL, up from a baseline of 1.5 mg/dL. She is started on continuous venovenous hemofiltration (CVVH) with a prescribed fluid removal rate of 100 mL/hr. After 6 hours of therapy, her net fluid balance is positive 500 mL. Which of the following is the most likely explanation for this discrepancy?
a. the prescribed fluid removal rate was too low
b. the replacement fluid rate was higher than the prescribed fluid removal rate
c. the patient received additional intravenous fluids or blood products during the treatment
d. the ultrafiltration coefficient of the hemofilter was lower than expected

Answer: c. the patient received additional intravenous fluids or blood products during the treatment. Explanation: The discrepancy between the prescribed fluid removal rate and the actual net fluid balance suggests that the patient received additional fluids during the continuous renal replacement therapy (CRRT) session that were not accounted for in the original prescription. This is a common occurrence in critically ill patients who may require intravenous medications, blood products, or nutrition that can affect fluid balance. The prescribed fluid removal rate of 100 mL/hr is a reasonable starting point for most patients and can be adjusted based on the patient's response and ongoing fluid balance. The replacement fluid rate is typically set to match the prescribed fluid removal rate plus any additional fluid needed to maintain hemodynamic stability or replace ongoing losses. A lower-than-expected ultrafiltration coefficient of the hemofilter could theoretically lead to less fluid removal than prescribed, but this is a relatively rare occurrence with modern hemofilters and would not typically cause a large discrepancy in fluid balance.

495. A 60-year-old male with a history of chronic kidney disease presents with uremic symptoms and a serum creatinine of 8.0 mg/dL. He is interested in starting home hemodialysis and is evaluated for arteriovenous (AV) access creation. Which of the following is the preferred type of AV access for home hemodialysis?
a. tunneled dialysis catheter
b. arteriovenous fistula (AVF)
c. arteriovenous graft (AVG)
d. peritoneal dialysis catheter

Answer: b. arteriovenous fistula (AVF). Explanation: Arteriovenous fistula (AVF) is the preferred type of vascular access for all forms of hemodialysis, including home hemodialysis, due to its lower rates of infection, thrombosis, and interventions compared to other access types. An AVF is created by surgically connecting an artery to a vein, typically in the forearm or upper arm, allowing the vein to become larger and stronger over time and providing reliable access for repeated needle insertions. Tunneled dialysis catheters are often used as a temporary or bridging access while an AVF is maturing, but they have higher rates of infection and dysfunction and are not recommended for long-term use. Arteriovenous grafts (AVGs) are synthetic tubes that connect an artery to a vein and can be used when a patient's vasculature is not suitable for an AVF, but they also have higher rates of complications compared to AVFs. Peritoneal dialysis catheters are used for a different modality of dialysis that uses the patient's peritoneal membrane as a filter and are not suitable for hemodialysis access.

496. A 50-year-old male with a history of end-stage renal disease presents with fever, chills, and purulent drainage from his tunneled dialysis catheter exit site. Blood cultures are positive for methicillin-resistant Staphylococcus aureus (MRSA). Which of the following is the most appropriate management of this patient's catheter-related bloodstream infection?
a. intravenous vancomycin and catheter exchange over a guidewire
b. intravenous daptomycin and catheter removal with delayed replacement
c. oral linezolid and antibiotic lock therapy
d. intravenous cefazolin and catheter salvage

Answer: b. intravenous daptomycin and catheter removal with delayed replacement. Explanation: Catheter-related bloodstream infections (CRBSIs) are a serious complication of tunneled dialysis catheters and require prompt diagnosis and management to prevent morbidity and mortality. In this case, the patient has a confirmed CRBSI with MRSA, a highly virulent and potentially resistant pathogen. The Infectious Diseases Society of America (IDSA) guidelines recommend catheter removal and delayed replacement for all patients with MRSA CRBSIs, along with systemic antibiotic therapy targeted to the specific pathogen. Daptomycin is a lipopeptide antibiotic with excellent activity against MRSA and is preferred over vancomycin for MRSA bacteremia due to its higher rates of clinical success and lower rates of treatment failure. Catheter exchange over a guidewire is not recommended for MRSA CRBSIs due to the high risk of recurrent infection. Oral linezolid is an alternative agent for MRSA infections but is not typically used as monotherapy for CRBSIs due to its lower blood and catheter penetration compared to intravenous agents. Antibiotic lock therapy, in which a high concentration of antibiotic is instilled into the catheter lumen, can be used as an adjunctive therapy for CRBSIs but is not sufficient as a standalone treatment. Cefazolin is a first-generation cephalosporin that is not active against MRSA and would not be an appropriate choice for this patient.

497. A 65-year-old female with a history of end-stage renal disease on peritoneal dialysis presents with abdominal pain, cloudy effluent, and a peritoneal fluid cell count of 800 cells/μL with 80% neutrophils. Which of the following is the most likely diagnosis?
a. acute pancreatitis

b. peritoneal dialysis-associated peritonitis
c. abdominal wall cellulitis
d. peritoneal dialysis catheter migration

Answer: b. peritoneal dialysis-associated peritonitis. Explanation: The patient's presentation of abdominal pain and cloudy effluent, along with an elevated peritoneal fluid cell count with neutrophil predominance, is highly suggestive of peritoneal dialysis-associated peritonitis, a common and potentially serious complication of peritoneal dialysis. Peritonitis occurs when bacteria or other pathogens enter the peritoneal cavity, typically through contamination of the catheter or extension tubing during exchanges or through transmural migration from the bowel or skin. The diagnosis of peritonitis is based on the presence of at least two of the following criteria: abdominal pain, cloudy effluent, and peritoneal fluid cell count > 100 cells/µL with > 50% neutrophils. Treatment typically involves intraperitoneal antibiotics targeted to the specific pathogen, along with supportive care and monitoring for complications such as sepsis or catheter dysfunction. Acute pancreatitis can cause abdominal pain and elevated peritoneal fluid cell counts but is not typically associated with cloudy effluent and would not be the most likely diagnosis in this patient. Abdominal wall cellulitis can cause localized pain and erythema but would not typically cause cloudy effluent or peritoneal fluid neutrophilia. Peritoneal dialysis catheter migration can cause drainage problems or localized pain but would not typically cause cloudy effluent or peritonitis in the absence of contamination.

498. A 70-year-old male with a history of end-stage renal disease on hemodialysis presents with confusion, myoclonus, and seizures during his dialysis session. His serum sodium is 118 mEq/L, and his osmolality is 250 mOsm/kg. Which of the following is the most likely diagnosis?
a. dialysis disequilibrium syndrome
b. uremic encephalopathy
c. hyponatremia-induced seizures
d. subdural hematoma

Answer: a. dialysis disequilibrium syndrome. Explanation: The patient's presentation of neurologic symptoms (confusion, myoclonus, seizures) during hemodialysis, along with a low serum sodium and osmolality, is consistent with dialysis disequilibrium syndrome, a rare but potentially serious complication of hemodialysis. Dialysis disequilibrium syndrome occurs when the rapid removal of urea and other osmolytes during dialysis leads to a transient osmotic gradient between the brain and the blood, causing water to shift into the brain and resulting in cerebral edema and neurologic symptoms. Risk factors for dialysis disequilibrium syndrome include severe uremia, high interdialytic weight gain, and rapid or aggressive dialysis prescriptions. Treatment typically involves slowing the rate of dialysis, using smaller dialyzers or lower blood flow rates, and gradually increasing the osmolality of the dialysate to prevent rapid shifts in osmolality. Uremic encephalopathy can cause similar neurologic symptoms but is typically associated with high serum osmolality and would be expected to improve, rather than worsen, with dialysis. Hyponatremia-induced seizures can occur with severe hyponatremia (serum sodium < 120 mEq/L) but are not typically associated with dialysis and would not explain the other neurologic symptoms or the low osmolality. Subdural hematoma can cause neurologic symptoms in patients with end-stage renal disease due to platelet dysfunction and anticoagulation but would not typically present during dialysis and would not be associated with low sodium or osmolality.

499. A 55-year-old female with a history of diabetic nephropathy is initiated on continuous venovenous hemofiltration (CVVH) for acute kidney injury and septic shock. Her initial blood flow rate is 200 mL/min, and her replacement fluid rate is 2000 mL/hr. After 24 hours of therapy, her serum creatinine has decreased from 6.0 mg/dL

to 2.5 mg/dL, but her urine output remains < 100 mL/day. Which of the following is the most appropriate next step in her management?
a. discontinue CVVH and transition to intermittent hemodialysis
b. increase the blood flow rate to 250 mL/min and continue CVVH
c. decrease the replacement fluid rate to 1500 mL/hr and continue CVVH
d. continue current CVVH settings and reassess in 24 hours

Answer: d. continue current CVVH settings and reassess in 24 hours. Explanation: The patient's significant improvement in serum creatinine after 24 hours of continuous venovenous hemofiltration (CVVH) suggests that the current prescription is providing adequate solute clearance and is well-tolerated by the patient. The lack of urine output is not uncommon in the early stages of acute kidney injury and does not necessarily indicate inadequate therapy or the need for adjustments in CVVH settings. In fact, the patient's urine output may take several days to recover, even with adequate renal replacement therapy and resolution of the underlying sepsis.

500. Which class of medication is considered first-line therapy for mild to moderate ulcerative colitis due to its anti-inflammatory properties in the colon?
a. Corticosteroids
b. 5-aminosalicylic acid (5-ASA) agents
c. Immunomodulators
d. Biologic therapies

Answer: b. 5-aminosalicylic acid (5-ASA) agents. Explanation: 5-ASA agents are considered first-line therapy for mild to moderate ulcerative colitis due to their topical anti-inflammatory effects on the colonic mucosa. They are effective in inducing and maintaining remission in ulcerative colitis.

501. In the management of acute severe ulcerative colitis, what is the role of intravenous corticosteroids?
a. They are used as maintenance therapy to prevent relapse.
b. They are the first-line treatment for inducing remission in severe cases.
c. They are only used in patients who fail to respond to biologic therapies.
d. They are contraindicated due to the risk of infection.

Answer: b. They are the first-line treatment for inducing remission in severe cases. Explanation: Intravenous corticosteroids are the first-line treatment for inducing remission in acute severe ulcerative colitis due to their potent anti-inflammatory effects, providing rapid improvement in clinical symptoms and inflammatory markers.

502. For a patient with Crohn's disease who has not responded to conventional therapy, which class of drugs represents a targeted approach by inhibiting tumor necrosis factor-alpha (TNF-α)?
a. Corticosteroids
b. 5-ASA agents
c. Immunomodulators
d. Biologic therapies

Answer: d. Biologic therapies. Explanation: Biologic therapies, specifically anti-TNF agents, represent a targeted approach in the management of Crohn's disease for patients who have not responded to conventional therapy. These agents block TNF-α, a cytokine involved in inflammation, and are effective in inducing and maintaining remission.

503. When considering the use of immunomodulators such as azathioprine in IBD management, what is a key consideration due to potential side effects?
a. Immediate onset of action
b. Risk of nephrotoxicity
c. Need for regular monitoring of blood counts and liver enzymes
d. Short-term use only

Answer: c. Need for regular monitoring of blood counts and liver enzymes. Explanation: When using immunomodulators like azathioprine in IBD, it's crucial to regularly monitor blood counts and liver enzymes due to potential side effects such as bone marrow suppression and hepatotoxicity, ensuring patient safety during long-term therapy.

504. In the management of IBD, 5-ASA agents are available in various formulations. Which factor primarily influences the choice of formulation?
a. The patient's age
b. The site and extent of intestinal inflammation
c. Preference for oral versus injectable medication
d. Cost of medication

Answer: b. The site and extent of intestinal inflammation. Explanation: The choice of 5-ASA formulation in IBD management is primarily influenced by the site and extent of intestinal inflammation. Different formulations are designed to release the active drug at specific locations in the gastrointestinal tract, targeting the inflamed areas effectively.

505. For a patient with moderate to severe Crohn's disease who develops antibodies to an anti-TNF agent, what is an appropriate subsequent therapeutic strategy?
a. Discontinue all biologic therapy due to cross-reactivity.
b. Switch to a different class of biologic therapy, such as integrin receptor antagonists.
c. Increase the dose of the current anti-TNF agent.
d. Add an oral corticosteroid to the existing anti-TNF regimen.

Answer: b. Switch to a different class of biologic therapy, such as integrin receptor antagonists. Explanation: For patients who develop antibodies to an anti-TNF agent, an appropriate strategy is to switch to a different class of biologic therapy, such as integrin receptor antagonists, to overcome the loss of response and target different pathways involved in the inflammatory process.

506. What is the primary mechanism of action of methotrexate when used as an immunomodulator in the treatment of Crohn's disease?
a. It stimulates the production of anti-inflammatory cytokines.
b. It inhibits dihydrofolate reductase, leading to anti-proliferative and anti-inflammatory effects.
c. It directly suppresses TNF-α production.
d. It enhances epithelial barrier function in the intestine.

Answer: b. It inhibits dihydrofolate reductase, leading to anti-proliferative and anti-inflammatory effects. Explanation: Methotrexate, when used as an immunomodulator in Crohn's disease, inhibits dihydrofolate reductase, which leads to anti-proliferative and anti-inflammatory effects. This action helps reduce the immune response that contributes to inflammation in Crohn's disease.

507. In the context of IBD management, under what circumstance is surgical intervention typically considered for patients with ulcerative colitis?
a. When there is a failure to respond to maximum medical therapy
b. As a first-line treatment in mild cases
c. After the first episode of acute severe colitis
d. In all patients as a curative approach

Answer: a. When there is a failure to respond to maximum medical therapy. Explanation: Surgical intervention is typically considered for patients with ulcerative colitis when there is a failure to respond to maximum medical therapy, the presence of dysplasia or cancer, or complications such as toxic megacolon. Surgery can be curative for the colonic manifestations of ulcerative colitis but is reserved for specific indications.

508. How do biologic therapies targeting integrin receptors, such as vedolizumab, function in the treatment of IBD?
a. They neutralize circulating TNF-α.
b. They inhibit leukocyte migration into the gut mucosa.
c. They promote mucosal healing by stimulating fibroblast growth.
d. They decrease the production of IL-12 and IL-23.

Answer: b. They inhibit leukocyte migration into the gut mucosa. Explanation: Biologic therapies targeting integrin receptors, such as vedolizumab, function by inhibiting the migration of leukocytes into the gut mucosa. This action helps reduce the inflammation that characterizes IBD by preventing immune cells from reaching the sites of inflammation in the gastrointestinal tract.

509. On admission, a patient with acute pancreatitis has a white blood cell count of 18,000/μL. According to Ranson's criteria, this finding is an indicator of:
a. Mild pancreatitis with a low risk of mortality
b. Moderate pancreatitis requiring IV fluids and monitoring
c. Severe pancreatitis with an increased risk of complications
d. Insufficient information for prognostic determination

Answer: c. Severe pancreatitis with an increased risk of complications. Explanation: In Ranson's criteria, a white blood cell count greater than 16,000/μL at admission is one of the indicators suggesting severe pancreatitis, which is associated with an increased risk of complications and potentially higher mortality.

510. A patient with acute pancreatitis has a BISAP score of 3 on admission, indicating:
a. Minimal risk of morbidity and mortality
b. Moderate risk requiring close observation
c. High risk of severe pancreatitis and organ failure
d. The need for immediate surgical intervention

Answer: c. High risk of severe pancreatitis and organ failure. Explanation: The Bedside Index for Severity in Acute Pancreatitis (BISAP) score ranges from 0 to 5, with higher scores indicating a greater risk of mortality and severe pancreatitis. A score of 3 suggests a high risk of severe disease and potential for organ failure.

511. In assessing the severity of acute pancreatitis via the CT severity index, which finding contributes to a higher score?
a. Peripancreatic fat stranding
b. Pancreatic necrosis involving 30% of the pancreas
c. Single small peripancreatic fluid collection
d. Absence of pancreatic enlargement

Answer: b. Pancreatic necrosis involving 30% of the pancreas. Explanation: The CT severity index for acute pancreatitis takes into account the extent of pancreatic necrosis. Necrosis involving 30% of the pancreas would significantly increase the severity score, indicating a more severe form of the disease.

512. A patient with acute pancreatitis presents with a serum glucose level of 250 mg/dL at admission. According to Ranson's criteria, this finding suggests:
a. Mild acute pancreatitis
b. A moderate need for nutritional support
c. An increased risk for severe pancreatitis
d. No significant impact on pancreatitis outcome

Answer: c. An increased risk for severe pancreatitis. Explanation: In Ranson's criteria, a serum glucose level greater than 200 mg/dL at admission is one of the factors indicating a higher risk for severe pancreatitis and associated complications.

513. For a patient with acute pancreatitis, a BISAP score includes all of the following EXCEPT:
a. Blood urea nitrogen increase
b. Impaired mental status
c. Age over 60 years
d. Serum calcium level

Answer: d. Serum calcium level. Explanation: The BISAP score for predicting the severity of acute pancreatitis includes blood urea nitrogen increase, impaired mental status, evidence of systemic inflammatory response syndrome (SIRS), age over 60 years, and pleural effusion on imaging, but not serum calcium level.

514. During the first 48 hours of hospitalization for acute pancreatitis, the development of hypoxemia (PaO2 <60 mmHg) is considered in Ranson's criteria as an indicator of:
a. Expected complication in mild pancreatitis
b. Moderate severity with a favorable prognosis
c. Severe pancreatitis with a high risk of mortality
d. Unrelated to pancreatitis severity

Answer: c. Severe pancreatitis with a high risk of mortality. Explanation: The development of hypoxemia (PaO2 <60 mmHg) within the first 48 hours of hospitalization is considered in Ranson's criteria as a sign of severe pancreatitis, associated with a high risk of complications and mortality.

515. A CT severity index score of 7 in a patient with acute pancreatitis predicts:
a. Mild disease with minimal intervention required
b. Moderate pancreatitis with potential for recovery
c. Severe disease with a high likelihood of complications
d. Indeterminate severity, requiring further evaluation

Answer: c. Severe disease with a high likelihood of complications. Explanation: The CT severity index scores range from 0 to 10, with higher scores indicating more severe disease. A score of 7 is associated with severe pancreatitis and a high likelihood of developing complications such as necrosis, organ failure, or pseudocysts.

516. In the context of acute pancreatitis, Ranson's criteria assess the presence of anemia (hematocrit drop >10%) to:
a. Confirm the diagnosis of pancreatitis
b. Evaluate the adequacy of fluid resuscitation
c. Predict the severity and potential complications of pancreatitis
d. Determine the need for blood transfusion

Answer: c. Predict the severity and potential complications of pancreatitis. Explanation: In Ranson's criteria, a drop in hematocrit greater than 10% during the initial 48 hours is used to predict the severity of acute pancreatitis and the potential for complications, reflecting significant fluid sequestration and systemic inflammation.

517. For a patient with acute pancreatitis and a BISAP score of 4, the recommended management approach would likely include:
a. Outpatient management with oral medications
b. Standard inpatient care with IV fluids and analgesia

c. Intensive care monitoring and potential for advanced interventions
d. Immediate exploratory surgery

Answer: c. Intensive care monitoring and potential for advanced interventions. Explanation: A BISAP score of 4 indicates a high risk of mortality and severe pancreatitis, necessitating intensive care monitoring and the possibility of advanced interventions such as mechanical ventilation or renal replacement therapy, depending on the development of organ failure.

518. What is the primary cause of steatorrhea in chronic pancreatic insufficiency?
a. Inadequate bile acid production
b. Decreased gastric acid secretion
c. Deficiency of pancreatic lipase
d. Overgrowth of intestinal bacteria

Answer: c. Deficiency of pancreatic lipase. Explanation: Steatorrhea in chronic pancreatic insufficiency is primarily due to a deficiency of pancreatic lipase, an enzyme critical for the digestion and absorption of dietary fats. Without sufficient lipase, fats are not adequately broken down, leading to fatty stools characteristic of steatorrhea.

519. Which nutritional deficiency is most commonly associated with malabsorption due to chronic pancreatic insufficiency?
a. Vitamin C
b. Vitamin B12
c. Iron
d. Fat-soluble vitamins (A, D, E, K)

Answer: d. Fat-soluble vitamins (A, D, E, K). Explanation: Chronic pancreatic insufficiency often leads to malabsorption of fat-soluble vitamins (A, D, E, K) due to inadequate digestion and absorption of dietary fats, which are necessary for the absorption of these vitamins.

520. When prescribing pancreatic enzyme replacement therapy (PERT), what is a crucial consideration to ensure effectiveness?
a. The enzymes should be taken on an empty stomach.
b. Enzyme doses should be adjusted based on the fat content of the meal.
c. Patients should avoid consuming liquids during meals.
d. Enzymes should be taken with antacid to prevent degradation.

Answer: b. Enzyme doses should be adjusted based on the fat content of the meal. Explanation: The effectiveness of pancreatic enzyme replacement therapy is closely linked to the fat content of meals, as enzymes are needed to digest dietary fats. Adjusting enzyme doses according to the fat content ensures adequate enzyme activity where it's needed most.

521. In a patient with chronic pancreatitis, which symptom is indicative of malabsorption and requires further evaluation?
a. Epigastric pain radiating to the back
b. Weight loss despite adequate caloric intake
c. Jaundice with dark urine
d. Intermittent episodes of hypoglycemia

Answer: b. Weight loss despite adequate caloric intake. Explanation: Weight loss in a patient with chronic pancreatitis, despite adequate caloric intake, is indicative of malabsorption. This suggests that nutrients are not being properly absorbed in the gastrointestinal tract, warranting further evaluation and management.

522. For effective pancreatic enzyme replacement therapy (PERT), the timing of enzyme administration is critical. When should enzymes be taken in relation to meals?
a. 30 minutes before meals
b. With the first bites of a meal
c. Immediately after meals
d. 1 hour after meals

Answer: b. With the first bites of a meal. Explanation: Pancreatic enzymes are most effective when taken with the first bites of a meal to ensure they mix properly with food and facilitate the digestion of fats, proteins, and carbohydrates throughout the digestive process.

523. What is a common complication of long-term pancreatic enzyme replacement therapy (PERT) at high doses?
a. Hypoglycemia
b. Fibrosing colonopathy
c. Hypercalcemia
d. Peptic ulcer disease

Answer: b. Fibrosing colonopathy. Explanation: A potential complication of long-term high-dose pancreatic enzyme replacement therapy is fibrosing colonopathy, a condition characterized by thickening and fibrosis of the colon wall, which can lead to intestinal obstruction.

524. In assessing the effectiveness of pancreatic enzyme replacement therapy (PERT) in a patient with chronic pancreatic insufficiency, what improvement should be primarily observed?
a. Resolution of epigastric pain
b. Decrease in serum amylase and lipase levels
c. Improvement in steatorrhea and nutritional status
d. Normalization of fasting blood glucose levels

Answer: c. Improvement in steatorrhea and nutritional status. Explanation: The primary indicator of effective pancreatic enzyme replacement therapy is the improvement in steatorrhea and overall nutritional status, as these enzymes aid in the digestion and absorption of essential nutrients, particularly fats.

525. How does chronic pancreatic insufficiency lead to bone density loss and osteoporosis?
a. Through the malabsorption of calcium and vitamin D
b. By increasing renal calcium excretion
c. Due to the direct toxic effects of unabsorbed fatty acids on bone tissue
d. By stimulating parathyroid hormone secretion

Answer: a. Through the malabsorption of calcium and vitamin D. Explanation: Chronic pancreatic insufficiency can lead to bone density loss and osteoporosis primarily through the malabsorption of calcium and vitamin D, which are crucial for bone health. Fat malabsorption associated with pancreatic insufficiency impairs the absorption of these nutrients, contributing to bone density loss.

526. Which of the following is most likely to precipitate hepatic encephalopathy in a patient with cirrhosis?
a. Administration of a lactulose enema
b. A high-protein meal
c. Intravenous infusion of normal saline
d. Oral intake of a glucose solution

Answer: b. A high-protein meal. Explanation: A high-protein meal can precipitate hepatic encephalopathy in patients with cirrhosis by increasing the production of ammonia and other nitrogenous substances from the gut, which can't be adequately detoxified by the liver due to impaired function.

527. In the management of hepatic encephalopathy, lactulose is used to:
a. Increase serum ammonia levels
b. Decrease the absorption of ammonia from the gut
c. Provide nutritional support to the damaged liver
d. Correct electrolyte imbalances

Answer: b. Decrease the absorption of ammonia from the gut. Explanation: Lactulose is a non-absorbable disaccharide used in the treatment of hepatic encephalopathy. It acidifies the colonic contents, converting ammonia to ammonium, which is less easily absorbed, and promotes its excretion.

528. A patient with liver cirrhosis presents with worsening confusion. Laboratory tests reveal hyponatremia. This electrolyte imbalance can exacerbate:
a. Renal failure
b. Hepatic encephalopathy
c. Ascites
d. Portal hypertension

Answer: b. Hepatic encephalopathy. Explanation: Hyponatremia can exacerbate hepatic encephalopathy by promoting cerebral edema, further impairing neurological function in patients with liver cirrhosis.

529. Infection is a common precipitant of hepatic encephalopathy because it:
a. Leads to increased production and absorption of toxins due to increased intestinal motility
b. Causes direct hepatocellular damage, worsening liver function
c. Increases the catabolic state, elevating ammonia and other nitrogenous waste products
d. Results in overutilization of lactulose, leading to electrolyte imbalances

Answer: c. Increases the catabolic state, elevating ammonia and other nitrogenous waste products. Explanation: Infections increase the catabolic state, leading to elevated production of ammonia and other nitrogenous waste products, which can precipitate or worsen hepatic encephalopathy in patients with compromised liver function.

530. Constipation can precipitate hepatic encephalopathy by:
a. Reducing the efficacy of diuretics used in cirrhosis management
b. Increasing the absorption of ammonia and other toxins from the intestines
c. Decreasing serum albumin levels, leading to reduced toxin binding
d. Inducing electrolyte imbalances, particularly hypokalemia

Answer: b. Increasing the absorption of ammonia and other toxins from the intestines. Explanation: Constipation can lead to an increased absorption of ammonia and other toxins from the intestines due to prolonged transit time, which can precipitate or exacerbate hepatic encephalopathy.

531. A patient with cirrhosis and hepatic encephalopathy develops gastrointestinal bleeding. The bleeding is likely to worsen encephalopathy due to:
a. Increased iron absorption leading to oxidative stress
b. Blood acting as a protein source, increasing ammonia production in the gut
c. Loss of clotting factors exacerbating cerebral hemorrhage
d. Direct toxic effect of blood on hepatic cells

Answer: b. Blood acting as a protein source, increasing ammonia production in the gut. Explanation: Gastrointestinal bleeding provides an additional protein load in the gut, which is broken down into ammonia and other nitrogenous substances, potentially exacerbating hepatic encephalopathy.

532. The use of non-selective beta-blockers in cirrhotic patients with hepatic encephalopathy:
a. Directly reduces ammonia production
b. Can exacerbate encephalopathy by impairing renal function
c. Is the treatment of choice for reducing portal hypertension-associated encephalopathy
d. Has no impact on the course of hepatic encephalopathy

Answer: b. Can exacerbate encephalopathy by impairing renal function. Explanation: Non-selective beta-blockers can indirectly exacerbate hepatic encephalopathy by impairing renal function, leading to the retention of ammonia and other neurotoxins.

533. In a cirrhotic patient, the development of hepatic encephalopathy following a paracentesis procedure may be due to:
a. Rapid shifts in fluid and electrolyte balance
b. Introduction of infectious agents during the procedure
c. Direct removal of ammonia and toxins from the ascitic fluid
d. Increased hepatic blood flow post-procedure

Answer: a. Rapid shifts in fluid and electrolyte balance. Explanation: Rapid shifts in fluid and electrolyte balance following a large-volume paracentesis can precipitate hepatic encephalopathy, particularly if there is significant removal of ascitic fluid without adequate volume replacement.

534. The role of rifaximin in the management of hepatic encephalopathy is to:
a. Increase renal clearance of ammonia
b. Reduce systemic inflammation and oxidative stress
c. Decrease the absorption of ammonia-producing bacteria from the gut
d. Stimulate hepatic regeneration and improve liver function

Answer: c. Decrease the absorption of ammonia-producing bacteria from the gut. Explanation: Rifaximin is a non-absorbable antibiotic used in the management of hepatic encephalopathy. It reduces the load of ammonia-producing bacteria in the gut, thereby decreasing the production and absorption of ammonia.

535. In hepatic encephalopathy, the administration of intravenous albumin is primarily aimed at:
a. Enhancing the excretion of ammonia through the kidneys
b. Binding circulating toxins, including ammonia, in the bloodstream
c. Directly reducing the production of ammonia in the gut
d. Counteracting the effects of hyponatremia on brain edema

Answer: b. Binding circulating toxins, including ammonia, in the bloodstream. Explanation: Albumin has a role in binding various substances, including toxins, in the bloodstream. In hepatic encephalopathy, the administration of albumin can help bind circulating toxins, potentially ameliorating the symptoms, although its primary use is for volume expansion and management of complications such as spontaneous bacterial peritonitis.

536. In assessing a patient with suspected hyperthyroidism, which clinical manifestation is most commonly associated with this condition?
a. Bradycardia
b. Weight gain

c. Cold intolerance
d. Exophthalmos

Answer: d. Exophthalmos. Explanation: Exophthalmos, or protrusion of the eyeballs, is a common and distinctive clinical manifestation of hyperthyroidism, particularly in Graves' disease. It results from the autoimmune process causing inflammation and edema in the orbital tissues.

537. A patient presents with fatigue, weight gain, and constipation. Laboratory tests reveal elevated TSH and low free T4 levels. Which condition do these findings suggest?
a. Hyperthyroidism
b. Hypothyroidism
c. Adrenal insufficiency
d. Pheochromocytoma

Answer: b. Hypothyroidism. Explanation: Elevated TSH and low free T4 levels are indicative of primary hypothyroidism, where the thyroid gland is underactive, leading to symptoms such as fatigue, weight gain, and constipation due to decreased metabolic processes.

538. In the management of Addison's disease, why is it important to increase glucocorticoid doses during periods of stress?
a. To counteract the excessive production of ACTH
b. To prevent adrenal crisis due to increased physiological demands
c. To enhance the metabolic clearance of cortisol
d. To suppress the immune response and prevent autoimmune damage

Answer: b. To prevent adrenal crisis due to increased physiological demands. Explanation: In Addison's disease, the adrenal glands do not produce sufficient cortisol, which is crucial for the body's response to stress. During periods of stress, the physiological demand for cortisol increases, necessitating an increase in glucocorticoid doses to prevent an adrenal crisis, characterized by severe hypotension and shock.

539. Which diagnostic test is most specific for diagnosing Cushing's syndrome?
a. 24-hour urinary free cortisol
b. Overnight dexamethasone suppression test
c. Serum ACTH level
d. Salivary cortisol level at midnight

Answer: b. Overnight dexamethasone suppression test. Explanation: The overnight dexamethasone suppression test is specific for diagnosing Cushing's syndrome. It involves administering a low dose of dexamethasone, a synthetic glucocorticoid, to suppress ACTH production. Failure to suppress serum cortisol levels the next morning suggests Cushing's syndrome.

540. A patient with type 1 diabetes mellitus is scheduled for surgery in the morning. How should insulin management be adjusted on the day of surgery?
a. Omit insulin doses to prevent hypoglycemia during fasting
b. Administer the usual daily dose of insulin
c. Give half the usual dose of long-acting insulin and manage with short-acting insulin as needed
d. Increase insulin doses to counteract the stress response

Answer: c. Give half the usual dose of long-acting insulin and manage with short-acting insulin as needed. Explanation: On the day of surgery, it's common to give half the usual dose of long-acting insulin to prevent hypoglycemia due to fasting while ensuring some basal insulin coverage. Blood glucose levels are then managed with short-acting insulin as needed, based on frequent monitoring.

541. In a patient with acromegaly, which clinical feature would you expect to find on physical examination?
a. Moon face
b. Buffalo hump
c. Enlarged hands and feet
d. Hyperpigmentation

Answer: c. Enlarged hands and feet. Explanation: Acromegaly is characterized by the excessive secretion of growth hormone, usually due to a pituitary adenoma, leading to the enlargement of extremities, including hands and feet, along with other somatic features such as coarse facial features and prognathism.

542. What is the primary treatment goal in the management of a patient with pheochromocytoma?
a. To reduce thyroid hormone production
b. To block the effects of excessive catecholamines
c. To increase cortisol synthesis
d. To enhance insulin sensitivity

Answer: b. To block the effects of excessive catecholamines. Explanation: The primary treatment goal in pheochromocytoma, a tumor of the adrenal medulla that secretes excessive catecholamines, is to block the effects of these hormones, typically using alpha and beta-adrenergic blockers, to manage hypertension and prevent catecholamine-induced complications until the tumor can be surgically removed.

543. A patient with suspected primary hyperparathyroidism has elevated serum calcium and PTH levels. What is the most likely cause of these findings?
a. Vitamin D deficiency
b. Parathyroid adenoma
c. Chronic kidney disease
d. Malabsorption syndrome

Answer: b. Parathyroid adenoma. Explanation: The most common cause of primary hyperparathyroidism is a parathyroid adenoma, which leads to excessive production of PTH, resulting in increased serum calcium levels due to enhanced bone resorption, renal reabsorption of calcium, and intestinal absorption.

544. In evaluating a patient with suspected diabetic ketoacidosis (DKA), which laboratory finding is most indicative of this condition?
a. Elevated serum bicarbonate
b. Low anion gap
c. Positive serum ketones
d. Hyponatremia

Answer: c. Positive serum ketones. Explanation: The presence of positive serum ketones is a hallmark finding in diabetic ketoacidosis (DKA), a serious complication of diabetes characterized by hyperglycemia, ketonemia, and metabolic acidosis. Serum ketones are produced from the breakdown of fatty acids when insulin levels are insufficient.

545. For a patient with chronic hypoparathyroidism, what is a common complication requiring regular monitoring?
a. Hypoglycemia
b. Nephrolithiasis
c. Adrenal insufficiency
d. Thyrotoxicosis

Answer: b. Nephrolithiasis. Explanation: Patients with chronic hypoparathyroidism are at increased risk for nephrolithiasis (kidney stones) due to altered calcium and phosphate metabolism. Regular monitoring of renal function and urinary calcium excretion is essential to prevent the formation of kidney stones and manage this complication.

546. In the pathophysiology of Type 1 Diabetes Mellitus (T1DM), which cells are primarily targeted and destroyed by the autoimmune process?
a. Beta cells in the pancreas
b. Alpha cells in the pancreas
c. Hepatocytes in the liver
d. Adipocytes in adipose tissue

Answer: a. Beta cells in the pancreas. Explanation: T1DM is characterized by an autoimmune-mediated destruction of pancreatic beta cells, which are responsible for insulin production. The loss of these cells leads to insulin deficiency and hyperglycemia.

547. What is the hallmark metabolic emergency associated with Type 1 Diabetes Mellitus?
a. Hyperosmolar Hyperglycemic State (HHS)
b. Diabetic Ketoacidosis (DKA)
c. Hypoglycemic coma

d. Lactic acidosis

Answer: b. Diabetic Ketoacidosis (DKA). Explanation: DKA is a life-threatening complication of T1DM characterized by hyperglycemia, ketosis, and metabolic acidosis, primarily due to insulin deficiency.

548. Which of the following is a common initial presenting symptom of Type 1 Diabetes Mellitus in children?
a. Cushingoid appearance
b. Nocturnal enuresis in a previously toilet-trained child
c. Excessive weight gain
d. Slow wound healing

Answer: b. Nocturnal enuresis in a previously toilet-trained child. Explanation: New onset nocturnal enuresis in a previously toilet-trained child can be an initial presenting symptom of T1DM, likely due to osmotic diuresis induced by hyperglycemia.

549. The presence of which antibodies is most indicative of an autoimmune etiology in Type 1 Diabetes Mellitus?
a. Insulin antibodies
b. Glutamic acid decarboxylase (GAD) antibodies
c. Hepatitis C antibodies
d. Anti-smooth muscle antibodies

Answer: b. Glutamic acid decarboxylase (GAD) antibodies. Explanation: GAD antibodies are often present in T1DM and are indicative of an autoimmune etiology. They target an enzyme involved in the synthesis of the neurotransmitter GABA within pancreatic beta cells.

550. In Type 1 Diabetes Mellitus, insulin therapy is required because:
a. The pancreas produces excessive insulin
b. The liver cannot metabolize glucose properly
c. There is a total or near-total deficiency of endogenous insulin
d. The muscle and fat cells are resistant to insulin's effects

Answer: c. There is a total or near-total deficiency of endogenous insulin. Explanation: T1DM involves an autoimmune destruction of insulin-producing beta cells in the pancreas, leading to a total or near-total deficiency of endogenous insulin, necessitating lifelong insulin therapy.

551. The risk of developing Diabetic Ketoacidosis (DKA) is particularly high when a patient with Type 1 Diabetes Mellitus:
a. Engages in moderate physical activity
b. Misses a single dose of insulin
c. Experiences an intercurrent illness or infection

d. Consumes a carbohydrate-rich meal

Answer: c. Experiences an intercurrent illness or infection. Explanation: Intercurrent illnesses or infections can significantly increase the risk of DKA in patients with T1DM by increasing the body's insulin requirements and exacerbating insulin deficiency.

552. In the management of Type 1 Diabetes Mellitus, continuous subcutaneous insulin infusion (CSII) is used to:
a. Temporarily replace the function of the pancreas during acute illness
b. Provide a basal rate of insulin with bolus doses at mealtimes
c. Deliver oral hypoglycemic agents more effectively
d. Stimulate residual beta-cell function in the pancreas

Answer: b. Provide a basal rate of insulin with bolus doses at mealtimes. Explanation: CSII, or insulin pump therapy, allows for continuous subcutaneous infusion of insulin, providing a basal rate of insulin 24/7 with the ability to administer bolus doses at mealtimes or when correcting high blood glucose levels.

553. The detection of islet cell autoantibodies in a patient with hyperglycemia is indicative of:
a. Type 2 Diabetes Mellitus
b. Type 1 Diabetes Mellitus
c. Gestational Diabetes Mellitus
d. Maturity Onset Diabetes of the Young (MODY)

Answer: b. Type 1 Diabetes Mellitus. Explanation: The presence of islet cell autoantibodies is indicative of an autoimmune process targeting the pancreatic beta cells, which is characteristic of Type 1 Diabetes Mellitus.

554. In the context of Type 1 Diabetes Mellitus, the "honeymoon period" refers to:
a. The time immediately after diagnosis when no insulin is required
b. A temporary phase of partial remission when insulin needs decrease
c. The period before the onset of diabetic complications
d. The initial phase of insulin resistance before complete beta-cell failure

Answer: b. A temporary phase of partial remission when insulin needs decrease. Explanation: The "honeymoon period" in T1DM refers to a temporary phase soon after the diagnosis during which the endogenous insulin production is still present, albeit reduced, leading to lower exogenous insulin requirements. This period typically ends as the autoimmune destruction of beta cells progresses.

555. The development of a fistula in a patient with T1DM and recurrent DKA episodes could indicate:
a. A complication related to insulin injection sites
b. An unrelated gastrointestinal disorder
c. The presence of an underlying chronic inflammatory process, such as Crohn's disease

d. Advanced diabetic nephropathy


Answer: c. The presence of an underlying chronic inflammatory process, such as Crohn's disease. Explanation: The development of a fistula in a patient with T1DM, especially in the context of recurrent DKA, may indicate an underlying chronic inflammatory condition like Crohn's disease, as both D


556. What is the primary mechanism by which insulin resistance contributes to hyperglycemia in type 2 diabetes?
a. Decreased glucose uptake by peripheral tissues
b. Increased insulin degradation by the liver
c. Enhanced glucose absorption in the gastrointestinal tract
d. Reduced renal excretion of glucose


Answer: a. Decreased glucose uptake by peripheral tissues. Explanation: Insulin resistance in type 2 diabetes primarily leads to hyperglycemia through decreased glucose uptake by peripheral tissues, especially muscle and adipose tissue, despite the presence of insulin. This results in elevated blood glucose levels as glucose remains in the bloodstream instead of being utilized by cells for energy.


557. Which clinical feature is commonly associated with a relative insulin deficiency in type 2 diabetes?
a. Sudden weight loss
b. Ketoacidosis
c. Polyphagia
d. Gradual onset of symptoms


Answer: d. Gradual onset of symptoms. Explanation: A relative insulin deficiency in type 2 diabetes typically leads to a gradual onset of symptoms, including polyuria, polydipsia, and fatigue. Unlike type 1 diabetes, where insulin deficiency is absolute and symptoms are more abrupt, the partial deficiency in type 2 allows for some insulin activity, delaying symptom onset.


558. In the context of type 2 diabetes, what distinguishes hyperosmolar hyperglycemic state (HHS) from diabetic ketoacidosis (DKA)?
a. Higher blood glucose levels in HHS
b. More severe acidosis in HHS
c. Presence of significant ketonuria in HHS
d. More rapid onset in HHS


Answer: a. Higher blood glucose levels in HHS. Explanation: Hyperosmolar hyperglycemic state (HHS) in type 2 diabetes is characterized by higher blood glucose levels (often >600 mg/dL) compared to diabetic ketoacidosis (DKA), with minimal or no ketosis. This leads to profound dehydration and increased serum osmolality, distinguishing it from DKA, which involves significant ketonemia and acidosis.

559. What is the role of metformin in managing insulin resistance in type 2 diabetes?
a. Stimulates pancreatic insulin secretion
b. Increases sensitivity of peripheral tissues to insulin
c. Inhibits absorption of glucose in the intestine
d. Enhances renal glucose excretion

Answer: b. Increases sensitivity of peripheral tissues to insulin. Explanation: Metformin is a first-line medication for type 2 diabetes that primarily works by increasing the sensitivity of peripheral tissues, such as liver and muscle, to insulin. This helps improve glucose uptake and utilization, thereby lowering blood glucose levels without stimulating additional insulin secretion.

560. Which factor is a major risk for the development of hyperosmolar hyperglycemic state (HHS) in patients with type 2 diabetes?
a. Vigorous exercise
b. Insulin overdose
c. Infection or other acute illness
d. Dietary carbohydrate restriction

Answer: c. Infection or other acute illness. Explanation: Infection or other acute illnesses are major precipitating factors for the development of HHS in patients with type 2 diabetes. These conditions lead to increased insulin resistance and elevated counter-regulatory hormones, resulting in severe hyperglycemia and dehydration.

561. How does obesity contribute to insulin resistance in type 2 diabetes?
a. By enhancing insulin receptor sensitivity
b. Through the secretion of adipokines that impair glucose uptake
c. By increasing the production of insulin-like growth factors
d. Through the stimulation of pancreatic beta-cell regeneration

Answer: b. Through the secretion of adipokines that impair glucose uptake. Explanation: Obesity contributes to insulin resistance in type 2 diabetes through the secretion of adipokines, such as resistin and TNF-alpha, by adipose tissue. These substances impair the insulin signaling pathway, reducing glucose uptake by cells and leading to insulin resistance.

562. What is the primary goal of lifestyle interventions in the management of insulin resistance in type 2 diabetes?
a. To increase body mass index (BMI)
b. To enhance glycogen storage in the liver
c. To reduce body weight and improve insulin sensitivity
d. To eliminate the need for glucose-lowering medications

Answer: c. To reduce body weight and improve insulin sensitivity. Explanation: The primary goal of lifestyle interventions, including diet and exercise, in managing insulin resistance in type 2 diabetes is to reduce body weight and improve insulin sensitivity. Weight loss, particularly the reduction of visceral fat, is effective in enhancing the responsiveness of peripheral tissues to insulin, thereby improving glycemic control.

563. In assessing a patient with type 2 diabetes for the risk of developing HHS, which symptom is an early warning sign?
a. Hyperventilation
b. Fruity odor on the breath
c. Profound dehydration
d. Rapid weight gain

Answer: c. Profound dehydration. Explanation: Profound dehydration is an early warning sign of HHS in patients with type 2 diabetes, characterized by excessive thirst, dry mouth, and decreased urine output. Recognizing and addressing dehydration early can prevent the progression to HHS, a life-threatening emergency.

564. What therapeutic approach is most effective for targeting postprandial hyperglycemia in type 2 diabetes?
a. Long-acting insulin analogs
b. Alpha-glucosidase inhibitors
c. Insulin sensitizers like metformin
d. Beta-cell stimulators like sulfonylureas

Answer: b. Alpha-glucosidase inhibitors. Explanation: Alpha-glucosidase inhibitors are effective in targeting postprandial hyperglycemia in type 2 diabetes by delaying the absorption of carbohydrates in the intestine, leading to a more gradual increase in blood glucose levels after meals. This class of medications is particularly useful for patients who have significant postprandial glucose excursions.

565. For a patient newly diagnosed with Type 1 Diabetes Mellitus, the initial management strategy typically includes:
a. Oral hypoglycemic agents
b. Lifestyle modifications only
c. Basal-bolus insulin therapy
d. Dietary supplements and herbal medications

Answer: c. Basal-bolus insulin therapy. Explanation: In Type 1 Diabetes Mellitus, where there's an absolute deficiency of insulin, the mainstay of management is insulin therapy. Basal-bolus insulin therapy, which includes long-acting (basal) insulin to cover insulin needs for a full day and short-acting (bolus) insulin to cover insulin needs at meals, closely mimics the body's normal insulin pattern.

566. In the management of Type 2 Diabetes Mellitus, Metformin is often the first-line medication due to its:
a. Ability to increase insulin secretion
b. Direct effect on reducing hepatic glucose production
c. Role in significantly increasing body weight
d. Mechanism of decreasing insulin sensitivity

Answer: b. Direct effect on reducing hepatic glucose production. Explanation: Metformin is a first-line medication in the management of Type 2 Diabetes Mellitus primarily due to its effect on reducing hepatic glucose production and improving insulin sensitivity, without causing significant weight gain or hypoglycemia.

567. A patient with diabetes and a recent history of myocardial infarction might benefit most from which oral hypoglycemic agent?
a. Sulfonylureas
b. Thiazolidinediones
c. SGLT2 inhibitors
d. Alpha-glucosidase inhibitors

Answer: c. SGLT2 inhibitors. Explanation: SGLT2 inhibitors have been shown to provide cardiovascular benefits in patients with Type 2 Diabetes Mellitus, including those with a history of myocardial infarction. These agents work by promoting glucose excretion in urine, and recent studies have indicated their role in reducing hospitalization for heart failure and potentially lowering the risk of death from cardiovascular causes.

568. The primary goal of lifestyle modifications in the management of diabetes includes all the following EXCEPT:
a. Achieving and maintaining optimal blood glucose levels
b. Significant and rapid weight loss regardless of initial weight
c. Reducing the risk of diabetes-related complications
d. Improving overall health through diet and exercise

Answer: b. Significant and rapid weight loss regardless of initial weight. Explanation: While weight management is important in diabetes care, the goal is not necessarily significant and rapid weight loss, especially without considering the patient's initial weight and health status. The focus should be on gradual, sustainable weight loss if overweight or obese, alongside achieving optimal blood glucose control and reducing the risk of complications.

569. For a patient with Type 2 Diabetes Mellitus and renal impairment, which oral hypoglycemic agent requires dose adjustment or avoidance?
a. Metformin
b. DPP-4 inhibitors
c. SGLT2 inhibitors
d. Both a and c

Answer: d. Both a and c. Explanation: Both Metformin and SGLT2 inhibitors require careful consideration in patients with renal impairment. Metformin is contraindicated in severe renal impairment due to the risk of lactic acidosis, and SGLT2 inhibitors may require dose adjustment or may be contraindicated depending on the degree of renal dysfunction.

570. Intensive insulin therapy in patients with Type 1 Diabetes Mellitus is aimed at:

a. Only lowering fasting blood glucose levels
b. Achieving tight glycemic control to mimic normal insulin activity
c. Eliminating the need for dietary management
d. Reducing the frequency of insulin injections

Answer: b. Achieving tight glycemic control to mimic normal insulin activity. Explanation: Intensive insulin therapy in Type 1 Diabetes Mellitus aims to achieve tight glycemic control by closely mimicking the body's normal insulin release. This typically involves multiple daily insulin injections or the use of an insulin pump, alongside frequent blood glucose monitoring.

571. In the context of diabetes management, carbohydrate counting is used to:
a. Restrict the total intake of carbohydrates to a bare minimum
b. Match the insulin dose to the carbohydrate content of meals and snacks
c. Calculate the total calorie intake from proteins only
d. Eliminate the need for insulin in Type 2 Diabetes Mellitus

Answer: b. Match the insulin dose to the carbohydrate content of meals and snacks. Explanation: Carbohydrate counting is a meal planning technique used especially in Type 1 Diabetes Mellitus management, where patients adjust their insulin dose based on the carbohydrate content of their meals and snacks to manage blood glucose levels effectively.

572. A patient with Type 2 Diabetes Mellitus on oral hypoglycemics is scheduled for surgery. The perioperative management plan should include:
a. Continuing oral hypoglycemics on the day of surgery
b. Switching to insulin therapy to manage blood glucose during the perioperative period
c. Complete cessation of all diabetes medications 48 hours before surgery
d. Doubling the dose of oral hypoglycemics on the day before surgery

Answer: b. Switching to insulin therapy to manage blood glucose during the perioperative period. Explanation: In the perioperative period, especially for major surgery or in patients with poorly controlled diabetes, switching from oral hypoglycemic agents to insulin therapy is often necessary to maintain optimal blood glucose control, as it allows for more flexible and precise management of blood glucose levels.

573. In a patient with diabetes and hypertension, lifestyle modifications that can effectively manage both conditions include:
a. High-protein, low-carbohydrate diets exclusively
b. Salt restriction, DASH diet, and increased physical activity
c. Elimination of all fats from the diet
d. Consumption of high-sodium sports drinks during exercise

Answer: b. Salt restriction, DASH diet, and increased physical activity. Explanation: Lifestyle modifications such as salt restriction, adherence to the Dietary Approaches to Stop Hypertension (DASH) diet, and increased physical activity are effective in managing both diabetes and hypertension by promoting weight management, improving insulin sensitivity, and controlling blood pressure.

574. A 68-year-old male with a history of GERD presents with dysphagia to both solids and liquids. He reports a sensation of food getting stuck in his chest, and has lost 15 pounds over the past 2 months. Upper endoscopy reveals concentric rings and furrows in the esophageal mucosa. Which of the following is the most likely diagnosis?
a. achalasia
b. eosinophilic esophagitis
c. peptic stricture
d. esophageal carcinoma

Answer: b. eosinophilic esophagitis. Explanation: The patient's presentation of dysphagia to both solids and liquids, along with weight loss and endoscopic findings of concentric rings and furrows in the esophageal mucosa, is highly suggestive of eosinophilic esophagitis (EoE). EoE is a chronic immune-mediated disorder characterized by eosinophilic infiltration of the esophageal mucosa, leading to inflammation, fibrosis, and esophageal dysfunction. The typical endoscopic appearance of EoE includes linear furrows, concentric rings (also known as trachealization), and white exudates or plaques. Achalasia is characterized by impaired relaxation of the lower esophageal sphincter and can cause dysphagia, but it typically does not cause weight loss or mucosal changes on endoscopy. Peptic strictures are a complication of GERD and can cause dysphagia, but they typically affect the distal esophagus and do not cause concentric rings or furrows. Esophageal carcinoma can cause dysphagia and weight loss, but it typically appears as a mass or ulceration on endoscopy and is less likely to cause diffuse mucosal changes.

575. A 55-year-old female presents with abdominal pain, nausea, and vomiting. She reports that the pain began suddenly in the epigastric region and then migrated to the right lower quadrant. Physical examination reveals rebound tenderness at McBurney's point. Which of the following is the most appropriate initial imaging study?
a. abdominal ultrasound
b. computed tomography (CT) of the abdomen and pelvis with contrast
c. magnetic resonance imaging (MRI) of the abdomen
d. plain radiographs of the abdomen

Answer: b. computed tomography (CT) of the abdomen and pelvis with contrast. Explanation: The patient's presentation of abdominal pain that began in the epigastric region and migrated to the right lower quadrant, along with nausea, vomiting, and rebound tenderness at McBurney's point, is highly suggestive of acute appendicitis. In patients with suspected appendicitis, computed tomography (CT) of the abdomen and pelvis with intravenous contrast is the most accurate and widely used imaging modality for diagnosis. CT has a high sensitivity and specificity for detecting appendicitis and can also identify alternative diagnoses or complications such as perforation or abscess. Abdominal ultrasound is sometimes used as an initial imaging study in children or pregnant women to avoid radiation exposure, but it is less sensitive and specific than CT in adults. Magnetic resonance imaging (MRI) can also be used to diagnose appendicitis, but it is more time-consuming and less widely available than CT. Plain radiographs of the abdomen are not typically useful for diagnosing appendicitis and may delay definitive diagnosis and treatment.

576. A 60-year-old male with a history of alcohol use disorder presents with jaundice, abdominal distension, and confusion. Laboratory studies reveal a serum bilirubin of 8.0 mg/dL, INR of 2.5, and ammonia level of 100 μmol/L. Which of the following is the most likely cause of this patient's presentation?
a. acute viral hepatitis
b. alcoholic hepatitis
c. primary biliary cholangitis
d. hepatocellular carcinoma

Answer: b. alcoholic hepatitis. Explanation: The patient's presentation of jaundice, abdominal distension (likely due to ascites), and confusion (likely due to hepatic encephalopathy), along with a history of alcohol use disorder and laboratory findings of hyperbilirubinemia, coagulopathy, and hyperammonemia, is highly suggestive of alcoholic hepatitis. Alcoholic hepatitis is a syndrome of jaundice and liver inflammation that occurs in patients with heavy alcohol use, typically after decades of drinking. It is characterized by a rapid onset of jaundice, fever, abdominal pain, and tender hepatomegaly, along with laboratory evidence of hepatocellular injury and cholestasis. Severe cases can lead to hepatic encephalopathy, coagulopathy, and ascites. Acute viral hepatitis can cause jaundice and liver inflammation but is less likely to cause such severe hyperbilirubinemia or coagulopathy in the absence of fulminant liver failure. Primary biliary cholangitis is a chronic autoimmune disorder that causes progressive destruction of the bile ducts, leading to cholestasis and cirrhosis, but it typically has a more insidious onset and does not cause acute hepatic encephalopathy. Hepatocellular carcinoma can cause jaundice and abdominal distension but is less likely to cause such severe coagulopathy or hyperammonemia.

577. A 45-year-old female with a history of chronic pancreatitis presents with severe epigastric pain radiating to the back, nausea, and vomiting. Serum lipase is 1500 U/L. CT of the abdomen reveals a large fluid collection in the pancreatic tail with adjacent necrosis. Which of the following is the most appropriate initial management?
a. intravenous fluids and pain control
b. urgent endoscopic retrograde cholangiopancreatography (ERCP)
c. percutaneous drainage of the fluid collection
d. surgical necrosectomy

Answer: a. intravenous fluids and pain control. Explanation: The patient's presentation of severe epigastric pain radiating to the back, nausea, and vomiting, along with a significantly elevated serum lipase and CT findings of a pancreatic fluid collection with necrosis, is consistent with acute pancreatitis. The most appropriate initial management of acute pancreatitis is supportive care with intravenous fluids to maintain euvolemia, pain control with opioids or other analgesics, and close monitoring for complications such as organ failure or infection. In patients with necrotizing pancreatitis, as in this case, urgent intervention is not typically necessary unless there is evidence of infected necrosis or clinical deterioration despite supportive care. Endoscopic retrograde cholangiopancreatography (ERCP) is sometimes used to treat biliary pancreatitis by removing obstructing gallstones, but it is not indicated in patients with non-biliary pancreatitis and can potentially worsen pancreatic inflammation. Percutaneous drainage of pancreatic fluid collections is typically reserved for patients with symptomatic or infected pseudocysts that do not resolve with conservative management. Surgical necrosectomy is a highly invasive procedure that involves removing infected or necrotic pancreatic tissue and is typically only performed in patients with severe necrotizing pancreatitis who fail to respond to less invasive interventions.

578. A 75-year-old male presents with bright red blood per rectum and lightheadedness. He reports a history of intermittent constipation and straining with bowel movements. His hemoglobin is 7.5 g/dL, and he is

hemodynamically unstable with a blood pressure of 90/50 mmHg. Which of the following is the most likely source of this patient's lower gastrointestinal bleeding?
a. diverticular bleed
b. angiodysplasia
c. ischemic colitis
d. colorectal cancer

Answer: a. diverticular bleed. Explanation: The patient's presentation of bright red blood per rectum, lightheadedness, and hemodynamic instability, along with a history of constipation and straining, is highly suggestive of a lower gastrointestinal bleed, likely from a diverticular source. Diverticular bleeding is the most common cause of acute lower gastrointestinal bleeding in older adults and is typically caused by rupture of a vasa recta artery in the neck of a diverticulum. Risk factors for diverticular bleeding include advanced age, chronic constipation, and use of non-steroidal anti-inflammatory drugs (NSAIDs). Angiodysplasia is another common cause of lower gastrointestinal bleeding in older adults, but it typically presents with more chronic or recurrent bleeding and is less likely to cause such severe anemia or hemodynamic instability. Ischemic colitis can cause acute lower gastrointestinal bleeding, but it typically presents with abdominal pain and bloody diarrhea rather than bright red blood per rectum. Colorectal cancer is a less common cause of acute lower gastrointestinal bleeding and is more likely to present with chronic iron deficiency anemia or change in bowel habits.

579. A 50-year-old male with a history of Crohn's disease presents with abdominal pain, diarrhea, and fever. CT of the abdomen reveals a complex perianal fistula with adjacent abscess formation. Which of the following is the most appropriate initial management?
a. oral corticosteroids
b. intravenous antibiotics and surgical drainage
c. anti-tumor necrosis factor (TNF) therapy
d. hyperbaric oxygen therapy

Answer: b. intravenous antibiotics and surgical drainage. Explanation: The patient's presentation of abdominal pain, diarrhea, and fever, along with CT findings of a complex perianal fistula with abscess formation, is consistent with a Crohn's disease flare complicated by perianal sepsis. The most appropriate initial management of this condition is intravenous antibiotics to treat the underlying infection and surgical drainage of the abscess to prevent further spread and promote healing. Antibiotics should be broad-spectrum and cover gram-negative and anaerobic organisms, such as a combination of ciprofloxacin and metronidazole. Oral corticosteroids are sometimes used to treat Crohn's disease flares, but they are contraindicated in the setting of perianal sepsis due to the risk of worsening the infection. Anti-tumor necrosis factor (TNF) therapy, such as infliximab or adalimumab, can be highly effective for inducing and maintaining remission in Crohn's disease, but it should be avoided in the acute setting of perianal sepsis due to the risk of exacerbating the infection. Hyperbaric oxygen therapy has been used as an adjunctive treatment for perianal Crohn's disease, but it is not a standard initial therapy and should not delay the use of antibiotics and surgical drainage.

580. A 30-year-old female with a history of ulcerative colitis presents with severe abdominal pain, bloody diarrhea, and fever. She has been on oral mesalamine but reports worsening symptoms over the past week. Flexible sigmoidoscopy reveals diffuse ulceration and friability of the colonic mucosa. Which of the following is the most appropriate next step in management?
a. switch to oral sulfasalazine
b. initiate oral budesonide

c. start intravenous corticosteroids
d. perform total colectomy

Answer: c. start intravenous corticosteroids. Explanation: The patient's presentation of severe abdominal pain, bloody diarrhea, and fever, along with endoscopic findings of diffuse ulceration and friability, is consistent with a severe flare of ulcerative colitis. The most appropriate next step in management is to initiate intravenous corticosteroids, such as methylprednisolone or hydrocortisone, to rapidly reduce inflammation and prevent further complications. Intravenous corticosteroids are typically given at high doses (e.g., methylprednisolone 60 mg daily) and tapered over several weeks as symptoms improve. Oral mesalamine is a first-line maintenance therapy for mild-to-moderate ulcerative colitis, but it is not effective for inducing remission in severe flares. Switching to oral sulfasalazine, another aminosalicylate, is unlikely to provide additional benefit in this setting. Oral budesonide is a topical corticosteroid that can be effective for inducing remission in mild-to-moderate ulcerative colitis, but it is not typically used for severe flares due to limited systemic absorption. Total colectomy is a surgical option for patients with severe, refractory ulcerative colitis, but it is not the initial treatment of choice and should be reserved for patients who fail to respond to medical therapy or develop life-threatening complications such as toxic megacolon.

581. A 65-year-old male with a history of GERD presents with dysphagia, odynophagia, and weight loss. Upper endoscopy reveals a partially obstructing mass in the distal esophagus. Biopsy confirms the diagnosis of esophageal adenocarcinoma. Which of the following is the most appropriate initial treatment?
a. endoscopic mucosal resection
b. chemoradiation therapy
c. esophagectomy
d. palliative stenting

Answer: b. chemoradiation therapy. Explanation: The patient's presentation of dysphagia, odynophagia, and weight loss, along with endoscopic and histologic findings of esophageal adenocarcinoma, is consistent with locally advanced disease. The most appropriate initial treatment for locally advanced esophageal adenocarcinoma is chemoradiation therapy, which combines systemic chemotherapy (typically with a fluoropyrimidine and a platinum agent) with external beam radiation therapy to the esophagus and regional lymph nodes. Chemoradiation therapy can be given as definitive treatment for patients who are not candidates for surgery or as neoadjuvant treatment to shrink the tumor and improve the chances of complete resection. Endoscopic mucosal resection is a minimally invasive procedure that can be used to remove early-stage esophageal cancers that are confined to the mucosa, but it is not appropriate for larger or more invasive tumors. Esophagectomy, or surgical removal of the esophagus, is a potentially curative option for patients with locally advanced esophageal cancer, but it is typically performed after neoadjuvant chemoradiation therapy to reduce the risk of local recurrence. Palliative stenting is a treatment option for patients with unresectable or metastatic esophageal cancer who have severe dysphagia or obstruction, but it does not address the underlying malignancy and is not a curative therapy.

582. A 40-year-old female presents with abdominal pain, bloody diarrhea, and joint pain. She reports a family history of inflammatory bowel disease. Colonoscopy reveals skip lesions and cobblestone appearance of the colonic mucosa. Which of the following extraintestinal manifestations is most commonly associated with this condition?
a. primary sclerosing cholangitis
b. uveitis
c. erythema nodosum
d. ankylosing spondylitis

Answer: c. erythema nodosum. Explanation: The patient's presentation of abdominal pain, bloody diarrhea, and joint pain, along with endoscopic findings of skip lesions and cobblestone appearance, is consistent with Crohn's disease, a type of inflammatory bowel disease (IBD) that can affect any part of the gastrointestinal tract. Crohn's disease is associated with a variety of extraintestinal manifestations that can involve the skin, eyes, joints, and hepatobiliary system. The most common cutaneous manifestation of Crohn's disease is erythema nodosum, a type of panniculitis that presents with tender, red nodules on the shins and other extensor surfaces. Erythema nodosum occurs in up to 15% of patients with Crohn's disease and typically correlates with disease activity. Other cutaneous manifestations of Crohn's disease include pyoderma gangrenosum and oral aphthous ulcers. Uveitis, or inflammation of the uveal tract of the eye, is a less common extraintestinal manifestation of Crohn's disease that can cause eye pain, redness, and vision changes. Primary sclerosing cholangitis, a chronic cholestatic liver disease characterized by inflammation and fibrosis of the bile ducts, is more commonly associated with ulcerative colitis than with Crohn's disease. Ankylosing spondylitis, a type of inflammatory arthritis that affects the spine and sacroiliac joints, is also more common in patients with ulcerative colitis than in those with Crohn's disease.

583. A 55-year-old male with a history of cirrhosis presents with hematemesis and melena. He reports a history of heavy alcohol use and has not been taking his prescribed prophylactic beta-blocker. Physical examination reveals scleral icterus, spider angiomata, and ascites. Which of the following is the most appropriate initial management?
a. intravenous octreotide and proton pump inhibitor
b. emergent endoscopic variceal ligation
c. transjugular intrahepatic portosystemic shunt (TIPS)
d. oral lactulose and rifaximin

Answer: a. intravenous octreotide and proton pump inhibitor.

584. What is the most sensitive initial test for diagnosing primary hypothyroidism?
a. Total T4 levels
b. Thyroid ultrasound
c. Thyroid-stimulating hormone (TSH) levels
d. Thyroid peroxidase (TPO) antibodies

Answer: c. Thyroid-stimulating hormone (TSH) levels. Explanation: TSH levels are the most sensitive initial test for diagnosing primary hypothyroidism because they rise in response to decreased thyroid hormone production, even before T4 levels fall below the normal range.

585. A patient with hypothyroidism presents with profound lethargy, hypothermia, and bradycardia. What is the most immediate concern?
a. Thyroid storm
b. Myxedema coma
c. Graves' disease
d. Toxic multinodular goiter

Answer: b. Myxedema coma. Explanation: Myxedema coma is a life-threatening complication of severe, untreated hypothyroidism characterized by profound lethargy, hypothermia, and bradycardia, among other symptoms. Immediate intervention is critical.

586. Which medication is the treatment of choice for hypothyroidism?
a. Levothyroxine (LT4)
b. Liothyronine (LT3)
c. Methimazole
d. Propylthiouracil (PTU)

Answer: a. Levothyroxine (LT4). Explanation: Levothyroxine (LT4) is the treatment of choice for hypothyroidism, as it is a synthetic form of thyroxine (T4), the primary hormone produced by the thyroid gland, and can effectively normalize thyroid hormone levels.

587. In hypothyroid patients, why is it important to start levothyroxine at a lower dose and titrate slowly, especially in the elderly and those with cardiovascular disease?
a. To minimize the risk of inducing hyperthyroidism
b. To prevent adverse effects on bone density
c. To reduce the risk of precipitating myocardial infarction or arrhythmias
d. To avoid rapid correction of hyponatremia

Answer: c. To reduce the risk of precipitating myocardial infarction or arrhythmias. Explanation: Starting levothyroxine at a lower dose and titrating slowly is crucial in the elderly and those with cardiovascular disease to reduce the risk of precipitating myocardial infarction or arrhythmias due to increased metabolic demands.

588. What is the characteristic feature of myxedema seen in severe hypothyroidism?
a. Exophthalmos
b. Pretibial myxedema
c. Non-pitting edema in the face, hands, and feet
d. Pitting edema in lower extremities

Answer: c. Non-pitting edema in the face, hands, and feet. Explanation: Myxedema in severe hypothyroidism is characterized by non-pitting edema, particularly in the face, hands, and feet, due to the accumulation of mucopolysaccharides in the skin and other tissues.

589. For a hypothyroid patient undergoing surgery, what is a critical preoperative consideration?
a. Temporary discontinuation of levothyroxine
b. Ensuring euthyroid status to reduce surgical risks
c. Switching from levothyroxine to liothyronine for rapid onset
d. Administration of iodine to suppress TSH

Answer: b. Ensuring euthyroid status to reduce surgical risks. Explanation: Ensuring euthyroid status before surgery is critical in hypothyroid patients to reduce surgical risks such as poor wound healing, cardiovascular instability, and increased susceptibility to infection.

590. How does untreated hypothyroidism affect pregnancy outcomes?
a. It decreases the risk of gestational diabetes.
b. It increases the risk of preeclampsia and miscarriage.
c. It leads to shorter gestation periods.
d. It ensures faster postpartum recovery.

Answer: b. It increases the risk of preeclampsia and miscarriage. Explanation: Untreated hypothyroidism during pregnancy is associated with increased risks, including preeclampsia, miscarriage, preterm birth, and adverse neurodevelopmental outcomes in the offspring.

591. In the context of subclinical hypothyroidism, which patient population is most likely to benefit from levothyroxine therapy?
a. Patients with TSH levels <5 mIU/L without symptoms
b. Patients with TSH levels >10 mIU/L, especially if symptomatic or with positive TPO antibodies
c. Young patients with TSH levels <7 mIU/L and negative TPO antibodies
d. Elderly patients with TSH levels <10 mIU/L without cardiovascular risk

Answer: b. Patients with TSH levels >10 mIU/L, especially if symptomatic or with positive TPO antibodies. Explanation: Patients with subclinical hypothyroidism who are most likely to benefit from levothyroxine therapy are those with TSH levels >10 mIU/L, especially if they are symptomatic or have positive thyroid peroxidase (TPO) antibodies, as they are at higher risk for progression to overt hypothyroidism.

592. Which finding on physical examination is suggestive of long-standing untreated hypothyroidism?
a. Warm, moist skin
b. Fine tremors of the hands
c. Delayed relaxation phase of deep tendon reflexes
d. Pretibial myxedema

Answer: c. Delayed relaxation phase of deep tendon reflexes. Explanation: The delayed relaxation phase of deep tendon reflexes, particularly the Achilles reflex, is suggestive of long-standing untreated hypothyroidism. This is due to the accumulation of mucopolysaccharides within muscles and tendons, affecting their function.

593. What is the recommended approach to monitoring levothyroxine therapy in hypothyroidism?
a. Serial T3 measurements every 3 months
b. TSH and free T4 levels 6-8 weeks after initiating or changing the dose
c. Annual thyroid ultrasound
d. Continuous TSH monitoring every month

Answer: b. TSH and free T4 levels 6-8 weeks after initiating or changing the dose. Explanation: The recommended approach to monitoring levothyroxine therapy in hypothyroidism is to check TSH and free T4 levels 6-8 weeks after initiating therapy or after any change in dose to ensure that thyroid hormone levels are within the target range and to adjust the dose accordingly.

594. The primary mechanism of action of thionamides in the treatment of Graves' disease is to:
a. Inhibit the synthesis of thyroid hormones
b. Block the peripheral conversion of T4 to T3
c. Increase the renal excretion of thyroid hormones
d. Neutralize thyroid-stimulating antibodies

Answer: a. Inhibit the synthesis of thyroid hormones. Explanation: Thionamides, such as methimazole and propylthiouracil, work by inhibiting the thyroid peroxidase enzyme, which is involved in the synthesis of thyroid hormones, thereby reducing the levels of circulating thyroid hormones.

595. Which clinical feature is most suggestive of Graves' disease as a cause of hyperthyroidism?
a. Hoarseness and difficulty swallowing
b. Exophthalmos and pretibial myxedema
c. Cold intolerance and weight gain
d. Constipation and bradycardia

Answer: b. Exophthalmos and pretibial myxedema. Explanation: Graves' disease is characterized by unique clinical features such as exophthalmos (protrusion of the eyeballs) and pretibial myxedema (swelling and thickening of the skin on the shins), which are not typically seen in other causes of hyperthyroidism.

596. In managing a thyroid storm, the immediate use of beta-blockers is primarily aimed at:
a. Reducing thyroid hormone levels
b. Controlling heart rate and reducing tremors
c. Inhibiting the peripheral conversion of T4 to T3
d. Suppressing the immune response against the thyroid

Answer: b. Controlling heart rate and reducing tremors. Explanation: In a thyroid storm, a life-threatening exacerbation of hyperthyroidism, beta-blockers are used to provide symptomatic relief by controlling the rapid heart rate, reducing tremors, and helping with anxiety, but they do not directly reduce thyroid hormone levels.

597. The definitive diagnosis of Graves' disease often includes the detection of:
a. Elevated thyroid-stimulating hormone (TSH) levels
b. Thyroid-stimulating immunoglobulins (TSIs)
c. Decreased radioactive iodine uptake

d. Hypoechoic nodules on thyroid ultrasonography

Answer: b. Thyroid-stimulating immunoglobulins (TSIs). Explanation: Graves' disease is an autoimmune disorder characterized by the presence of thyroid-stimulating immunoglobulins (TSIs) that stimulate the thyroid gland to produce excessive amounts of thyroid hormones, leading to hyperthyroidism.

598. Which of the following is a potential side effect of thionamide therapy in the treatment of hyperthyroidism?
a. Hypertension
b. Agraulocytosis
c. Hypercalcemia
d. Myopathy

Answer: b. Agraulocytosis. Explanation: A serious potential side effect of thionamide therapy (e.g., methimazole, propylthiouracil) is agranulocytosis, a condition characterized by a dangerously low level of neutrophils, which increases the risk of infections.

599. A patient with hyperthyroidism is started on beta-blockers. This intervention is contraindicated in patients with:
a. Migraines
b. Asthma
c. Hypercholesterolemia
d. Iron deficiency anemia

Answer: b. Asthma. Explanation: Beta-blockers can exacerbate bronchospasm and are generally contraindicated in patients with asthma or other chronic obstructive pulmonary diseases due to their potential to cause airway constriction.

600. In the context of hyperthyroidism, the use of radioactive iodine therapy is intended to:
a. Stimulate the production of thyroid hormones
b. Destroy overactive thyroid tissue
c. Block the release of thyroid hormones from the gland
d. Suppress the immune system's attack on the thyroid

Answer: b. Destroy overactive thyroid tissue. Explanation: Radioactive iodine therapy is used to treat hyperthyroidism by selectively destroying overactive thyroid tissue, thereby reducing the production of thyroid hormones.

601. The occurrence of thyroid storm is often precipitated by:
a. Starting treatment with levothyroxine
b. Inadequate treatment of hyperthyroidism and stressors such as infection or surgery
c. Long-term use of beta-blockers
d. Dietary iodine deficiency

Answer: b. Inadequate treatment of hyperthyroidism and stressors such as infection or surgery. Explanation: Thyroid storm is a severe and life-threatening exacerbation of hyperthyroidism, often precipitated by inadequate treatment of hyperthyroidism and additional stressors like infection, surgery, or trauma.

602. A patient with newly diagnosed Graves' disease is concerned about the risk of osteoporosis with antithyroid drugs. The best approach to address this concern is to:
a. Discontinue all antithyroid medications
b. Reassure that this is a side effect of hyperthyroidism, not the treatment
c. Switch to high-dose iodine therapy only
d. Start calcium and vitamin D supplementation along with antithyroid drugs

Answer: b. Reassure that this is a side effect of hyperthyroidism, not the treatment. Explanation: Hyperthyroidism, not its treatment with antithyroid drugs, is associated with an increased risk of osteoporosis due to the increased bone turnover. Effective treatment of hyperthyroidism can help reduce this risk.

603. For a patient with Graves' disease and severe liver dysfunction, the preferred treatment option would be:
a. Thionamides
b. Radioactive iodine therapy
c. Beta-blockers only
d. Surgical thyroidectomy

Answer: d. Surgical thyroidectomy. Explanation: In patients with Graves' disease who have severe liver dysfunction, thionamides may be contraindicated due to their potential hepatotoxicity. Radioactive iodine therapy may also pose risks. Surgical thyroidectomy may be considered as a definitive and safe treatment option in this scenario, provided the patient is an appropriate surgical candidate.

604. Which hormone level would most likely be decreased in a patient with hypopituitarism?
a. Cortisol
b. Insulin
c. Epinephrine
d. Glucagon

Answer: a. Cortisol. Explanation: Hypopituitarism involves decreased secretion of one or more of the pituitary hormones. Cortisol levels would most likely be decreased due to reduced ACTH (adrenocorticotropic hormone) secretion from the pituitary gland, which is necessary for stimulating cortisol production in the adrenal glands.

605. A patient with a history of chronic glucocorticoid use presents with fatigue, hypotension, and hyponatremia after abrupt cessation. What is the most likely diagnosis?
a. Primary adrenal insufficiency

b. Cushing's syndrome
c. Secondary adrenal insufficiency due to glucocorticoid withdrawal
d. Pheochromocytoma

Answer: c. Secondary adrenal insufficiency due to glucocorticoid withdrawal. Explanation: Abrupt cessation of chronic glucocorticoid therapy can lead to secondary adrenal insufficiency, as exogenous steroids suppress the hypothalamic-pituitary-adrenal (HPA) axis, reducing ACTH and consequently cortisol production, leading to symptoms like fatigue, hypotension, and hyponatremia.

606. In evaluating a patient with suspected secondary adrenal insufficiency, which diagnostic test is most appropriate?
a. Serum cortisol level at 8 AM
b. 24-hour urine cortisol
c. ACTH stimulation test
d. Dexamethasone suppression test

Answer: c. ACTH stimulation test. Explanation: The ACTH stimulation test is most appropriate for evaluating secondary adrenal insufficiency. It assesses the adrenal glands' response to synthetic ACTH; a blunted or absent response indicates adrenal insufficiency, which, in the context of pituitary or hypothalamic dysfunction, suggests a secondary cause.

607. A patient with secondary adrenal insufficiency is undergoing surgery. How should their glucocorticoid therapy be managed perioperatively?
a. Continue their usual dose of glucocorticoid.
b. Discontinue glucocorticoids 24 hours before surgery.
c. Administer a stress dose of glucocorticoids.
d. Switch from oral to intravenous glucocorticoids at the same dose.

Answer: c. Administer a stress dose of glucocorticoids. Explanation: Patients with secondary adrenal insufficiency require a stress dose of glucocorticoids perioperatively to mimic the body's normal response to stress, as their HPA axis is suppressed. This helps prevent adrenal crisis during the increased physiological demands of surgery.

608. Which clinical feature is most suggestive of a pituitary adenoma in a patient with secondary adrenal insufficiency?
a. Hyperpigmentation
b. Visual field defects
c. Hyperkalemia
d. Hypertension

Answer: b. Visual field defects. Explanation: Visual field defects, particularly bitemporal hemianopsia, are suggestive of a pituitary adenoma in patients with secondary adrenal insufficiency. The adenoma can compress the optic chiasm, leading to characteristic visual field losses.

609. What is the primary concern with rapid glucocorticoid withdrawal in patients treated for hypothalamic-pituitary disorders?
a. Immediate hypercortisolism
b. Precipitation of thyroid storm
c. Adrenal crisis due to HPA axis suppression
d. Acute renal failure

Answer: c. Adrenal crisis due to HPA axis suppression. Explanation: The primary concern with rapid glucocorticoid withdrawal in patients treated for hypothalamic-pituitary disorders is the risk of adrenal crisis. Long-term glucocorticoid therapy suppresses the HPA axis, and abrupt cessation can lead to acute cortisol deficiency.

610. In secondary adrenal insufficiency, which electrolyte abnormality is less commonly observed compared to primary adrenal insufficiency?
a. Hyponatremia
b. Hyperkalemia
c. Hypocalcemia
d. Hypoglycemia

Answer: b. Hyperkalemia. Explanation: Hyperkalemia is less commonly observed in secondary adrenal insufficiency compared to primary adrenal insufficiency because aldosterone production (which regulates potassium) is typically preserved in secondary adrenal insufficiency, as it is primarily regulated by the renin-angiotensin system rather than ACTH.

611. How does the treatment of secondary adrenal insufficiency differ from the treatment of primary adrenal insufficiency?
a. Secondary does not require glucocorticoid replacement.
b. Secondary requires higher doses of glucocorticoids.
c. Secondary does not typically require mineralocorticoid replacement.
d. Secondary requires additional thyroid hormone supplementation.

Answer: c. Secondary does not typically require mineralocorticoid replacement. Explanation: Treatment of secondary adrenal insufficiency typically involves glucocorticoid replacement without the need for mineralocorticoid replacement, as aldosterone secretion is usually intact due to its primary regulation by the renin-angiotensin system.

612. Following pituitary surgery, a patient develops secondary adrenal insufficiency. What is a key aspect of their long-term management?
a. Lifelong mineralocorticoid replacement
b. Periodic evaluation of pituitary function to adjust hormone replacement therapy

c. High-dose iodine therapy
d. Continuous ACTH replacement therapy

Answer: b.

613. The characteristic hyperpigmentation seen in Addison's disease is primarily due to:
a. Increased melanin synthesis stimulated by high levels of ACTH
b. Direct adrenal hormone effect on the skin
c. Accumulation of bile pigments due to liver involvement
d. Excessive iron deposition in the skin

Answer: a. Increased melanin synthesis stimulated by high levels of ACTH. Explanation: In Addison's disease, the lack of cortisol feedback leads to increased production of ACTH by the pituitary gland. ACTH shares a precursor molecule with melanocyte-stimulating hormone, which can lead to increased melanin production and the characteristic hyperpigmentation.

614. A patient with Addison's disease is most likely to present with:
a. Hypertension and hypernatremia
b. Weight gain and fluid retention
c. Hyperkalemia and hyponatremia
d. Hypoglycemia and polycythemia

Answer: c. Hyperkalemia and hyponatremia. Explanation: Addison's disease, or primary adrenal insufficiency, often presents with electrolyte imbalances such as hyperkalemia (due to decreased aldosterone) and hyponatremia (due to decreased aldosterone leading to sodium loss and water imbalance).

615. In the context of Addison's disease, an adrenal crisis can be precipitated by:
a. Over-replacement with glucocorticoids
b. Prolonged physical exertion without adequate stress dosing of glucocorticoids
c. High intake of potassium-rich foods
d. Starting treatment with a mineralocorticoid

Answer: b. Prolonged physical exertion without adequate stress dosing of glucocorticoids. Explanation: An adrenal crisis in the context of Addison's disease can be precipitated by physical stress, such as illness or exertion, without adequate adjustment (stress dosing) of glucocorticoid medication to mimic the body's normal response to stress.

616. The mainstay of treatment for Addison's disease includes supplementation of:
a. Insulin and oral hypoglycemic agents
b. Glucocorticoids and mineralocorticoids
c. Calcium and vitamin D

d. Potassium binders and saline infusions

Answer: b. Glucocorticoids and mineralocorticoids. Explanation: Treatment for Addison's disease primarily involves hormone replacement with glucocorticoids (such as hydrocortisone) to replace cortisol and mineralocorticoids (such as fludrocortisone) to replace aldosterone, addressing the deficiencies caused by adrenal insufficiency.

617. A key diagnostic test for Addison's disease is the:
a. TSH level assessment
b. ACTH stimulation test
c. 24-hour urine cortisol measurement
d. Serum potassium level evaluation

Answer: b. ACTH stimulation test. Explanation: The ACTH (cosyntropin) stimulation test is a key diagnostic tool for Addison's disease. It measures the adrenal glands' response to ACTH; a lack of cortisol response indicates adrenal insufficiency.

618. In Addison's disease, the autoimmune destruction of the adrenal cortex leads to a deficiency in:
a. Antidiuretic hormone (ADH) and oxytocin
b. Insulin and glucagon
c. Cortisol, aldosterone, and androgens
d. Thyroid hormones T3 and T4

Answer: c. Cortisol, aldosterone, and androgens. Explanation: Addison's disease involves autoimmune destruction of the adrenal cortex, leading to deficiencies in cortisol, aldosterone, and adrenal androgens, which are all produced by the adrenal cortex.

619. Patients with Addison's disease are advised to carry emergency medical identification to indicate:
a. Their need for daily insulin injections
b. Their potential need for emergency glucocorticoid administration
c. The requirement for a low-potassium diet at all times
d. An allergy to iodine-based contrast agents

Answer: b. Their potential need for emergency glucocorticoid administration. Explanation: Patients with Addison's disease are at risk for an adrenal crisis, especially during times of stress or illness. They are advised to carry medical identification to alert healthcare professionals to their condition and the potential need for emergency glucocorticoid administration.

620. A common finding in blood tests for a patient with Addison's disease is:
a. Elevated hemoglobin and hematocrit levels
b. Decreased BUN (blood urea nitrogen) and creatinine levels

c. Elevated eosinophil and lymphocyte counts
d. Decreased liver enzyme levels

Answer: c. Elevated eosinophil and lymphocyte counts. Explanation: Blood tests in Addison's disease may show characteristic findings such as lymphocytosis and eosinophilia due to the increased release of these cells from the bone marrow in response to adrenocortical insufficiency.

621. The dietary advice for a patient with Addison's disease and salt-wasting might include:
a. Strict fluid restriction to manage hyponatremia
b. Increased sodium intake, especially during hot weather or illness
c. High potassium diet to counteract hyperkalemia
d. Calcium supplementation to prevent osteoporosis

Answer: b. Increased sodium intake, especially during hot weather or illness. Explanation: Patients with Addison's disease, particularly those experiencing salt-wasting due to aldosterone deficiency, may be advised to increase their sodium intake to counteract hyponatremia, especially during conditions that promote sodium loss such as hot weather, sweating, or gastrointestinal illness.

622. When educating a patient with Addison's disease about managing their condition, it is important to emphasize:
a. The need to avoid physical stress and exercise
b. The importance of adherence to glucocorticoid and mineralocorticoid replacement therapy
c. That they can stop medication during periods of wellness
d. That Addison's disease can be cured with surgery

Answer: b. The importance of adherence to glucocorticoid and mineralocorticoid replacement therapy. Explanation: Education for patients with Addison's disease should emphasize the critical importance of lifelong adherence to glucocorticoid and mineralocorticoid replacement therapy to manage their condition and prevent adrenal crises.

623. What distinguishes the anemia seen in vitamin B12 deficiency from other forms of anemia?
a. Presence of microcytic red blood cells
b. Elevated mean corpuscular volume (MCV) with megaloblastic changes
c. Decreased reticulocyte count only
d. Hypochromic red blood cells

Answer: b. Elevated mean corpuscular volume (MCV) with megaloblastic changes. Explanation: Vitamin B12 deficiency anemia is characterized by an elevated MCV due to the presence of megaloblastic changes, which are large, immature, and dysfunctional red blood cells. This distinguishes it from other forms of anemia, such as iron deficiency anemia, which typically presents with microcytic (small) red blood cells.

624. Which neurological symptom is commonly associated with vitamin B12 deficiency?

a. Ascending paralysis
b. Sensorimotor peripheral neuropathy
c. Immediate memory loss
d. Seizures

Answer: b. Sensorimotor peripheral neuropathy. Explanation: Vitamin B12 deficiency can lead to sensorimotor peripheral neuropathy, characterized by numbness, tingling, and weakness in the extremities. This occurs due to the essential role of vitamin B12 in the maintenance of the myelin sheath that insulates nerve fibers.

625. In patients with vitamin B12 deficiency, what is a potential consequence of administering folate without vitamin B12 replacement?
a. Exacerbation of neurological symptoms
b. Increased risk of thrombosis
c. Decrease in MCV
d. Resolution of megaloblastic anemia

Answer: a. Exacerbation of neurological symptoms. Explanation: Administering folate without concurrent vitamin B12 replacement in patients with vitamin B12 deficiency can potentially improve hematologic parameters but exacerbate or unmask neurological symptoms due to untreated B12 deficiency, leading to further neurological damage.

626. What is the most reliable marker for diagnosing vitamin B12 deficiency?
a. Serum vitamin B12 level
b. Homocysteine level
c. Methylmalonic acid (MMA) level
d. Folate level

Answer: c. Methylmalonic acid (MMA) level. Explanation: Methylmalonic acid (MMA) levels are a more specific and sensitive marker for vitamin B12 deficiency than serum vitamin B12 levels alone. MMA accumulates in the blood when vitamin B12 levels are insufficient for its role as a cofactor in the metabolism of certain fatty acids and amino acids.

627. For a patient with folate deficiency anemia, what is the recommended initial approach to replacement therapy?
a. High-dose intramuscular vitamin B12 injections
b. Oral folic acid supplementation
c. Intravenous iron supplementation
d. Blood transfusion

Answer: b. Oral folic acid supplementation. Explanation: The recommended initial approach for treating folate deficiency anemia is oral folic acid supplementation. This can effectively restore folate levels, leading to the resolution of megaloblastic anemia associated with folate deficiency.

628. What dietary habit is a common risk factor for vitamin B12 deficiency?
a. High consumption of red meat
b. Strict veganism without supplementation
c. Excessive intake of vitamin C
d. Low intake of carbohydrates

Answer: b. Strict veganism without supplementation. Explanation: Strict veganism without appropriate supplementation is a common risk factor for vitamin B12 deficiency, as vitamin B12 is primarily found in animal products. Vegans are advised to consume B12-fortified foods or take B12 supplements to prevent deficiency.

629. In the context of vitamin B12 deficiency, why is Schilling's test rarely performed in current clinical practice?
a. It is highly invasive and requires a bone marrow biopsy.
b. It has been replaced by more sensitive and specific tests like MMA.
c. It can only diagnose folate deficiency.
d. It requires dietary manipulation for several weeks before testing.

Answer: b. It has been replaced by more sensitive and specific tests like MMA. Explanation: Schilling's test, once used to diagnose vitamin B12 deficiency and its etiology, is rarely performed now because it has been replaced by more sensitive and specific tests, such as serum MMA levels, which do not require radioactive vitamin administration and urine collection.

630. What is the role of intrinsic factor in the absorption of vitamin B12?
a. It binds to vitamin B12 in the stomach, protecting it from degradation.
b. It facilitates the transport of vitamin B12 across the intestinal wall.
c. It is necessary for the renal reabsorption of vitamin B12.
d. It converts vitamin B12 into its active coenzyme form.

Answer: b. It facilitates the transport of vitamin B12 across the intestinal wall. Explanation: Intrinsic factor, produced by the parietal cells of the stomach, binds to vitamin B12 and facilitates its transport across the intestinal wall into the bloodstream. This complex is essential for the absorption of vitamin B12 in the ileum.

631. A patient with a history of gastric bypass surgery is at increased risk for which deficiency?
a. Vitamin C
b. Vitamin A
c. Vitamin B12
d. Vitamin E

Answer: c. Vitamin B12. Explanation: Patients with a history of gastric bypass surgery are at increased risk for vitamin B12 deficiency due to reduced stomach size and decreased production of intrinsic factor, which is essential for the absorption of vitamin B12 in the ileum.

632. What is the recommended management for a patient with neurologic symptoms secondary to vitamin B12 deficiency?
a. Oral cyanocobalamin supplementation
b. High-dose intramuscular vitamin B12 injections
c. Dietary modification to include more vitamin B12-rich foods
d. Intravenous iron supplementation

Answer: b. High-dose intramuscular vitamin B12 injections. Explanation: For patients with vitamin B12 deficiency presenting with neurologic symptoms, the recommended management is high-dose intramuscular vitamin B12 injections. This route ensures rapid correction of the deficiency and can help reverse or stabilize neurologic symptoms.

633. In iron deficiency anemia, the red blood cells are typically described as:
a. Macrocytic and hyperchromic
b. Microcytic and hypochromic
c. Normocytic and normochromic
d. Macrocytic and hypochromic

Answer: b. Microcytic and hypochromic. Explanation: Iron deficiency anemia is characterized by the presence of smaller than normal (microcytic) and paler than normal (hypochromic) red blood cells due to the lack of adequate iron for hemoglobin synthesis, which is crucial for oxygen transport.

634. A key laboratory finding in iron deficiency anemia is:
a. Elevated ferritin levels
b. Low serum iron and low ferritin levels
c. High serum iron with low total iron-binding capacity
d. Elevated B12 and folate levels

Answer: b. Low serum iron and low ferritin levels. Explanation: Iron deficiency anemia is marked by low serum iron levels due to insufficient iron stores and low ferritin levels, as ferritin reflects the body's iron stores. Ferritin decreases in iron deficiency anemia.

635. Oral iron supplementation in the treatment of iron deficiency anemia is best absorbed when taken:
a. With meals to reduce gastrointestinal side effects
b. With a glass of milk to enhance absorption
c. On an empty stomach with vitamin C to enhance absorption
d. Immediately before bedtime to improve bioavailability

Answer: c. On an empty stomach with vitamin C to enhance absorption. Explanation: Iron supplements are best absorbed on an empty stomach to enhance bioavailability, and vitamin C (ascorbic acid) can further increase iron absorption by reducing ferric to ferrous iron, which is more readily absorbed.

636. A common side effect of oral iron therapy that often leads to patient noncompliance is:
a. Hypertension
b. Gastrointestinal discomfort and constipation
c. Insomnia
d. Hyperkalemia

Answer: b. Gastrointestinal discomfort and constipation. Explanation: Oral iron supplementation frequently causes gastrointestinal side effects, including nausea, abdominal discomfort, constipation, and sometimes diarrhea, which can lead to noncompliance with the therapy.

637. In patients with iron deficiency anemia who cannot tolerate oral iron due to gastrointestinal side effects, the alternative treatment is:
a. Increased dietary intake of iron alone
b. Vitamin B12 injections
c. Parenteral iron supplementation
d. Blood transfusion

Answer: c. Parenteral iron supplementation. Explanation: For patients who cannot tolerate oral iron supplements due to gastrointestinal side effects or for those with malabsorption issues, parenteral iron supplementation is an effective alternative to replenish iron stores.

638. The appearance of 'pencil cells' on a peripheral blood smear is characteristic of:
a. Megaloblastic anemia
b. Iron deficiency anemia
c. Hemolytic anemia
d. Aplastic anemia

Answer: b. Iron deficiency anemia. Explanation: 'Pencil cells' or elongated, thin hypochromic red blood cells are a characteristic morphological change seen in the peripheral blood smear of patients with iron deficiency anemia.

639. In assessing a patient for iron deficiency anemia, an important dietary history question is about the intake of:
a. High-fiber foods
b. Dairy products
c. Foods rich in vitamin C
d. Red meat and leafy green vegetables

Answer: d. Red meat and leafy green vegetables. Explanation: Red meat and leafy green vegetables are rich sources of dietary iron. A dietary history that reveals inadequate intake of these foods can support a diagnosis of iron deficiency anemia due to insufficient dietary iron.

640. A patient with chronic kidney disease (CKD) develops iron deficiency anemia. This is primarily due to:
a. Increased iron loss through hemodialysis
b. Reduced erythropoietin production by the kidneys
c. Enhanced iron absorption in the gastrointestinal tract
d. Increased dietary iron intake

Answer: a. Increased iron loss through hemodialysis. Explanation: Patients with CKD often develop iron deficiency anemia due to multiple factors, including increased iron loss through hemodialysis and reduced erythropoietin production, which affects red blood cell production, rather than enhanced absorption or increased intake.

641. In iron deficiency anemia, the total iron-binding capacity (TIBC) is typically:
a. Decreased
b. Normal
c. Increased
d. Not related to iron status

Answer: c. Increased. Explanation: In iron deficiency anemia, the total iron-binding capacity (TIBC), which measures the blood's capacity to bind iron with transferrin, is typically increased due to the body's attempt to maximize iron transport in the face of iron deficiency.

642. A toddler with iron deficiency anemia might exhibit which of the following symptoms?
a. Polycythemia and hypertension
b. Pica and irritability
c. Cyanosis and tachypnea
d. Jaundice and splenomegaly

Answer: b. Pica and irritability. Explanation: In toddlers, iron deficiency anemia can manifest as pica, an unusual craving for non-nutritive substances like dirt or ice, and irritability. These symptoms reflect the systemic effects of inadequate hemoglobin and oxygen delivery to tissues.

643. What is the primary rationale for initiating empiric antibiotic therapy in patients with febrile neutropenia?
a. To target specific identified pathogens
b. To prevent secondary fungal infections
c. To provide broad-spectrum coverage pending culture results
d. To reduce the duration of fever

Answer: c. To provide broad-spectrum coverage pending culture results. Explanation: The primary rationale for initiating empiric antibiotic therapy in patients with febrile neutropenia is to provide broad-spectrum coverage against potential bacterial pathogens while awaiting the results of blood and other relevant cultures, given the high risk of severe infections in this immunocompromised population.

644. When calculating the absolute neutrophil count (ANC) in a patient suspected of having febrile neutropenia, which formula is used?
a. (Total white blood cell count) x (% neutrophils + % bands)
b. (Total white blood cell count) / (% neutrophils + % bands)
c. (Total white blood cell count) x (% lymphocytes + % monocytes)
d. (Total white blood cell count) x (% eosinophils + % basophils)

Answer: a. (Total white blood cell count) x (% neutrophils + % bands). Explanation: The ANC is calculated using the formula: (Total white blood cell count) x (% neutrophils + % bands), where the percentage of neutrophils and bands (immature neutrophils) is expressed as a decimal. This calculation provides a quantitative measure of the patient's neutrophil count, which is crucial in diagnosing neutropenia and assessing the risk of infection.

645. In the management of febrile neutropenia, what is the primary goal of administering granulocyte colony-stimulating factors (G-CSF)?
a. To reduce the need for antibiotic therapy
b. To stimulate the production of red blood cells
c. To enhance the recovery of the neutrophil count
d. To increase platelet production

Answer: c. To enhance the recovery of the neutrophil count. Explanation: The primary goal of administering G-CSF in the management of febrile neutropenia is to stimulate the bone marrow to enhance the production and recovery of neutrophils. This reduces the duration of neutropenia and the associated risk of serious infections.

646. Which clinical sign would most likely prompt an immediate evaluation for febrile neutropenia in a chemotherapy patient?
a. Sudden onset of tachycardia
b. Single oral temperature reading > 38.3°C (101°F)
c. Mild cough without sputum production
d. Presence of petechiae on lower extremities

Answer: b. Single oral temperature reading > 38.3°C (101°F). Explanation: In patients undergoing chemotherapy, a single oral temperature reading > 38.3°C (101°F) is a critical sign that warrants immediate evaluation for febrile neutropenia, given the significant risk of severe infections in this immunocompromised group.

647. When considering empiric antibiotic therapy for febrile neutropenia, what factor primarily influences the choice of antibiotic?
a. The patient's preference

b. The cost of the antibiotic
c. Local antimicrobial resistance patterns
d. The presence of allergies to penicillin

Answer: c. Local antimicrobial resistance patterns. Explanation: The choice of empiric antibiotic therapy for febrile neutropenia is primarily influenced by local antimicrobial resistance patterns, ensuring the selected antibiotic is effective against the most common and resistant pathogens in the specific hospital or geographic area.

648. In a patient with febrile neutropenia, what is a common but serious complication that necessitates urgent medical intervention?
a. Hypertensive crisis
b. Septic shock
c. Hyperglycemic hyperosmolar state
d. Acute coronary syndrome

Answer: b. Septic shock. Explanation: Septic shock is a common and serious complication of febrile neutropenia that requires urgent medical intervention. It is characterized by systemic infection leading to hypotension and organ dysfunction, posing a significant risk of mortality in these patients.

649. For a patient with febrile neutropenia, how is the decision to transition from intravenous to oral antibiotics typically made?
a. Based on the resolution of symptoms and improvement in ANC
b. After a minimum of 14 days of intravenous therapy
c. Once there is a documented clearance of pathogens from the bloodstream
d. When the patient requests to switch to oral therapy

Answer: a. Based on the resolution of symptoms and improvement in ANC. Explanation: The decision to transition from intravenous to oral antibiotics in a patient with febrile neutropenia is usually based on clinical improvement, including the resolution of fever and symptoms of infection, as well as an improvement in the ANC, indicating a reduced risk of severe infection.

650. What is the significance of monitoring liver and kidney function in patients receiving empiric antibiotics for febrile neutropenia?
a. To assess for potential sources of infection
b. To ensure the patient can tolerate increased fluid volumes
c. To detect possible side effects or toxicity from the antibiotics
d. To determine the need for nutritional supplementation

Answer: c. To detect possible side effects or toxicity from the antibiotics. Explanation: Monitoring liver and kidney function in patients receiving empiric antibiotics for febrile neutropenia is crucial to detect any possible side effects or toxicity related to the antibiotic therapy. These organs are key in metabolizing and excreting many antimicrobial agents, and their dysfunction could lead to accumulation and adverse effects.

651. In the setting of febrile neutropenia, what is the threshold for considering antifungal therapy in addition to antibiotics?
a. Persistent fever for more than 48 hours despite broad-spectrum antibiotics
b. Presence of a fungal infection on initial blood cultures
c. Any elevation in white blood cell count
d. Detection of a viral pathogen on serologic tests

Answer: a. Persistent fever for more than 48 hours despite broad-spectrum antibiotics. Explanation: Antifungal therapy is considered in patients with febrile neutropenia who have persistent fever for more than 48 hours despite appropriate broad-spectrum antibiotic therapy, due to the risk of fungal infections in these immunocompromised individuals.

652. In a neutropenic patient with a central venous catheter, what symptom would prompt an evaluation for catheter-related bloodstream infection?
a. Localized erythema and tenderness at the catheter site
b. Isolated headache without other symptoms
c. Sudden onset of dysuria
d. Intermittent claudication

Answer: a. Localized erythema and tenderness at the catheter site. Explanation: In a neutropenic patient with a central venous catheter, localized erythema and tenderness at the catheter insertion site would prompt an evaluation for a possible catheter-related bloodstream infection, a common source of infection in patients with indwelling catheters.

653. The hallmark finding in aplastic anemia, which involves a deficiency of all three blood cell lines, is known as:
a. Hemolysis
b. Leukocytosis
c. Pancytopenia
d. Polycythemia

Answer: c. Pancytopenia. Explanation: Pancytopenia, the reduction or absence of all three types of blood cells (red blood cells, white blood cells, and platelets), is a hallmark finding in aplastic anemia, indicating the bone marrow's failure to produce adequate amounts of blood cells.

654. In the diagnosis of aplastic anemia, a bone marrow biopsy typically shows:
a. Hypercellularity with increased blasts
b. Hypocellularity with increased fat spaces
c. Granulomas and fibrosis
d. Lymphoid aggregates

Answer: b. Hypocellularity with increased fat spaces. Explanation: A bone marrow biopsy in aplastic anemia usually reveals hypocellularity, characterized by a marked reduction in hematopoietic cells and an increase in fat spaces, reflecting the bone marrow's failure to produce blood cells.

655. The first-line treatment for severe aplastic anemia in a young patient without a suitable bone marrow donor is often:
a. High-dose corticosteroids
b. Immunosuppressive therapy with antithymocyte globulin (ATG) and cyclosporine
c. Chemotherapy followed by radiation therapy
d. Supportive care with transfusions only

Answer: b. Immunosuppressive therapy with antithymocyte globulin (ATG) and cyclosporine. Explanation: Immunosuppressive therapy with ATG and cyclosporine is often the first-line treatment for severe aplastic anemia in young patients without a suitable bone marrow donor, aiming to suppress the immune system's activity against the bone marrow.

656. A patient with aplastic anemia presents with fatigue, pallor, and easy bruising. These symptoms are primarily due to:
a. Elevated leukocyte counts causing hyperviscosity
b. Excess iron accumulation in tissues
c. Deficiencies in red cells, white cells, and platelets
d. Overproduction of abnormal plasma cells

Answer: c. Deficiencies in red cells, white cells, and platelets. Explanation: The symptoms of aplastic anemia, such as fatigue (due to anemia), easy bruising (due to thrombocytopenia), and increased susceptibility to infections (due to leukopenia), are directly related to the deficiencies in red cells, white cells, and platelets.

657. In assessing a patient for potential aplastic anemia, it's crucial to inquire about exposure to:
a. High altitudes
b. Sunlight
c. Certain chemicals and drugs, like benzene and chemotherapy agents
d. Allergens such as pollen and dust

Answer: c. Certain chemicals and drugs, like benzene and chemotherapy agents. Explanation: Exposure to certain chemicals (e.g., benzene) and drugs (including some chemotherapy agents and antibiotics) can cause bone marrow suppression, leading to aplastic anemia. A thorough exposure history is critical in the assessment.

658. For a patient diagnosed with aplastic anemia, regular monitoring is crucial to watch for:
a. Rapid increases in hemoglobin levels

b. Signs of congestive heart failure
c. The development of leukocytosis and thrombocytosis
d. Signs of infection, bleeding, and worsening anemia

Answer: d. Signs of infection, bleeding, and worsening anemia. Explanation: Patients with aplastic anemia are at increased risk for infections (due to leukopenia), bleeding episodes (due to thrombocytopenia), and worsening anemia, necessitating regular monitoring for these complications.

659. In aplastic anemia, the use of androgens like oxymetholone may be considered to:
a. Directly stimulate erythropoiesis
b. Increase white blood cell production only
c. Suppress the immune system's attack on the bone marrow
d. Replace deficient clotting factors

Answer: a. Directly stimulate erythropoiesis. Explanation: Androgens like oxymetholone can be used in the treatment of aplastic anemia to stimulate erythropoiesis, thereby increasing the production of red blood cells, although their use may be limited by side effects.

660. A potential complication of long-term immunosuppressive therapy in aplastic anemia is:
a. Development of acute leukemia
b. Rebound hyperplasia of the bone marrow
c. Spontaneous recovery of bone marrow function
d. Increased risk of infections and secondary malignancies

Answer: d. Increased risk of infections and secondary malignancies. Explanation: Long-term immunosuppressive therapy can increase the risk of infections and secondary malignancies due to the suppression of the immune system, which is a significant consideration in the management of aplastic anemia.

661. In a young patient with aplastic anemia and a matched sibling donor, the treatment of choice is:
a. Lifelong erythropoietin injections
b. Bone marrow transplantation
c. Palliative care with periodic blood transfusions
d. Daily oral iron supplementation

Answer: b. Bone marrow transplantation. Explanation: For young patients with severe aplastic anemia who have a matched sibling donor, bone marrow transplantation is often the treatment of choice, offering the potential for a curative outcome by replacing the dysfunctional marrow with healthy donor cells.

662. A 62-year-old male with a history of alcoholic cirrhosis presents with confusion, asterixis, and a serum ammonia level of 150 μmol/L. According to the West Haven criteria, which grade of hepatic encephalopathy does this patient most likely have?
a. grade 1
b. grade 2
c. grade 3
d. grade 4

Answer: c. grade 3. Explanation: The West Haven criteria are a widely used system for grading the severity of hepatic encephalopathy (HE) based on clinical findings. Grade 1 HE is characterized by mild confusion, euphoria or anxiety, and a shortened attention span. Grade 2 HE features lethargy, disorientation, and inappropriate behavior. Grade 3 HE, which this patient most likely has, is characterized by somnolence (but arousable), marked confusion, and asterixis (a flapping tremor). Grade 4 HE is defined by coma and unresponsiveness to verbal or noxious stimuli. The presence of asterixis and a significantly elevated serum ammonia level (normal range: 11-35 μmol/L) further support the diagnosis of grade 3 HE in this patient with known cirrhosis.

663. A 58-year-old female with a history of nonalcoholic steatohepatitis (NASH) cirrhosis presents with personality changes and disorientation. Her caregiver reports that she has been sleeping more during the day and has difficulty with basic arithmetic. Which of the following medications is most appropriate to initiate for this patient's condition?
a. lactulose
b. rifaximin
c. neomycin
d. metronidazole

Answer: a. lactulose. Explanation: The patient's presentation of personality changes, disorientation, daytime somnolence, and difficulty with basic arithmetic is consistent with overt hepatic encephalopathy (HE) in the setting of NASH cirrhosis. The most appropriate initial medication for the treatment of overt HE is lactulose, a nonabsorbable disaccharide that acts as an osmotic laxative and acidifies the colonic lumen, leading to the trapping of ammonia as ammonium and increased excretion in the stool. The typical starting dose of lactulose is 25 mL orally every 1-2 hours until a bowel movement occurs, followed by titration to achieve 2-3 soft stools per day. Rifaximin is an oral nonsystemic antibiotic that is used as an add-on therapy to lactulose for the prevention of overt HE recurrence, but it is not typically used as monotherapy for acute treatment. Neomycin is another oral antibiotic that has been used historically for HE but has fallen out of favor due to the risk of nephrotoxicity and ototoxicity with prolonged use. Metronidazole is not indicated for the treatment of HE and may actually worsen the condition by altering the gut microbiome.

664. A 55-year-old male with a history of hepatitis C cirrhosis and previous episodes of overt hepatic encephalopathy (HE) presents with confusion and asterixis. His wife reports that he has been noncompliant with his lactulose regimen due to diarrhea and abdominal discomfort. In addition to restarting lactulose, which of the following medications should be considered to reduce the risk of future HE episodes?
a. rifaximin
b. neomycin
c. metronidazole
d. vancomycin

Answer: a. rifaximin. Explanation: In patients with a history of overt hepatic encephalopathy (HE) who experience recurrent episodes despite lactulose therapy, rifaximin is the most appropriate add-on medication to reduce the risk of future HE episodes. Rifaximin is a minimally absorbed oral antibiotic that has been shown to reduce the risk of overt HE recurrence by modulating the gut microbiome and reducing the production and absorption of ammonia and other gut-derived toxins. The typical dose of rifaximin for HE prophylaxis is 550 mg orally twice daily. Neomycin is another oral antibiotic that has been used historically for HE but has fallen out of favor due to the risk of nephrotoxicity and ototoxicity with prolonged use. Metronidazole and vancomycin are not indicated for the prevention of HE and may actually worsen the condition by altering the gut microbiome in unfavorable ways. It is important to address the patient's nonadherence to lactulose and consider alternative dosing regimens or formulations (e.g., lactulose packets or enemas) to improve tolerability and compliance.

665. A 60-year-old female with a history of alcohol use disorder and cirrhosis presents with confusion, agitation, and a Glasgow Coma Scale (GCS) score of 10 (E3, V3, M4). Her serum ammonia level is 200 μmol/L, and she has grade 3 asterixis. Which of the following is the most likely precipitating factor for this patient's acute hepatic encephalopathy (HE)?
a. gastrointestinal bleeding
b. spontaneous bacterial peritonitis
c. hypokalemia
d. benzodiazepine use

Answer: a. gastrointestinal bleeding. Explanation: In patients with cirrhosis and a history of alcohol use disorder, gastrointestinal bleeding (e.g., from esophageal varices or peptic ulcer disease) is a common precipitating factor for acute hepatic encephalopathy (HE). Blood in the gastrointestinal tract is digested by gut bacteria, leading to increased production of ammonia and other nitrogenous compounds that are absorbed into the bloodstream and can trigger or worsen HE. The patient's low GCS score, high-grade asterixis, and significantly elevated serum ammonia level are consistent with severe overt HE. Spontaneous bacterial peritonitis (SBP) is another potential precipitating factor for HE in patients with cirrhosis, but it typically presents with abdominal pain, fever, and leukocytosis in addition to encephalopathy. Hypokalemia can cause muscle weakness and paralysis but is not a common trigger for HE. Benzodiazepine use can cause confusion and somnolence but would not typically lead to such severe HE in the absence of other precipitating factors.

666. A 65-year-old male with a history of nonalcoholic fatty liver disease (NAFLD) cirrhosis presents with confusion, sleep disturbances, and difficulty with handwriting. His serum ammonia level is 80 μmol/L, and he has no asterixis. Which of the following is the most appropriate initial management for this patient's condition?
a. initiate lactulose titrated to 2-3 soft stools per day
b. prescribe rifaximin 550 mg orally twice daily
c. recommend a high-protein diet to improve muscle mass
d. advise the patient to avoid driving until symptoms resolve

Answer: d. advise the patient to avoid driving until symptoms resolve. Explanation: The patient's presentation of confusion, sleep disturbances, and difficulty with handwriting is consistent with covert hepatic encephalopathy (HE), a subtle form of neurological dysfunction that occurs in patients with cirrhosis and is characterized by cognitive and psychomotor deficits in the absence of overt neurological signs like asterixis. Covert HE is associated with an increased risk of motor vehicle accidents, falls, and progression to overt HE. The most appropriate initial management for covert HE is to advise the patient to avoid driving and other high-risk activities until the symptoms resolve with treatment. Lactulose and rifaximin are not typically indicated for the initial treatment of covert HE unless the patient has a history of overt HE or fails to respond to conservative measures. A high-protein diet is not recommended for patients with HE, as it can increase the production of ammonia and other nitrogenous compounds that can worsen neurological function. In fact, current guidelines recommend a moderate protein restriction (e.g., 1.2-1.5 g/kg/day) for patients with HE to reduce the nitrogen load while avoiding malnutrition.

667. A 70-year-old male with a history of alcoholic cirrhosis presents with confusion, disorientation, and a Glasgow Coma Scale (GCS) score of 8 (E2, V2, M4). His serum ammonia level is 250 µmol/L, and he has grade 4 asterixis. Despite treatment with lactulose and rifaximin, his mental status continues to deteriorate. Which of the following is the most appropriate next step in management?
a. increase the dose of lactulose to achieve 4-5 soft stools per day
b. switch rifaximin to neomycin 500 mg orally four times daily
c. intubate the patient for airway protection and initiate mechanical ventilation
d. perform an urgent liver transplant evaluation

Answer: c. intubate the patient for airway protection and initiate mechanical ventilation. Explanation: The patient's low GCS score, high-grade asterixis, and significantly elevated serum ammonia level are consistent with severe overt hepatic encephalopathy (HE) that has progressed despite standard medical therapy with lactulose and rifaximin. In patients with advanced HE who are at risk of aspiration or respiratory failure, intubation and mechanical ventilation may be necessary to protect the airway and maintain adequate oxygenation and ventilation. Increasing the dose of lactulose or switching to neomycin are unlikely to provide additional benefit in this setting and may actually worsen the patient's fluid and electrolyte balance. An urgent liver transplant evaluation may be considered for patients with refractory or recurrent HE who have a good prognosis and no contraindications, but it is not the immediate priority in this patient with impending respiratory compromise. After the patient is stabilized, a comprehensive evaluation for liver transplantation should be initiated if appropriate.

668. A 50-year-old female with a history of primary biliary cholangitis (PBC) and cirrhosis presents with confusion, lethargy, and a serum ammonia level of 100 µmol/L. She has no asterixis or other focal neurological deficits. Which of the following is the most appropriate initial treatment for this patient's condition?
a. lactulose 30 mL orally three times daily
b. rifaximin 550 mg orally twice daily
c. neomycin 500 mg orally four times daily
d. metronidazole 500 mg orally three times daily

Answer: a. lactulose 30 mL orally three times daily. Explanation: The patient's presentation of confusion and lethargy in the setting of PBC cirrhosis and an elevated serum ammonia level is consistent with overt hepatic encephalopathy (HE). The most appropriate initial treatment for overt HE is lactulose, a nonabsorbable disaccharide that acts as an osmotic laxative and acidifies the colonic lumen, leading to the trapping of ammonia as ammonium and increased excretion in the stool. The typical starting dose of lactulose for overt HE is 25-45 mL orally three to four times daily, titrated to achieve 2-3 soft stools per day. Rifaximin is an effective add-on therapy for the prevention of HE recurrence but is not typically used as initial monotherapy for acute treatment. Neomycin and metronidazole are not recommended for the routine treatment of HE due to the risk of adverse effects and the availability of safer and more effective alternatives.

669. A 45-year-old male with a history of hepatitis B cirrhosis presents with slurred speech, irritability, and a serum ammonia level of 120 µmol/L. He has grade 2 asterixis and reports taking lactulose 30 mL orally twice daily. Which of the following is the most appropriate next step in management?
a. increase the dose of lactulose to 30 mL orally four times daily
b. add rifaximin 550 mg orally twice daily
c. switch lactulose to polyethylene glycol 17 g orally daily
d. discontinue lactulose and observe for spontaneous improvement

Answer: a. increase the dose of lactulose to 30 mL orally four times daily. Explanation: The patient's presentation of slurred speech, irritability, and asterixis in the setting of hepatitis B cirrhosis and an elevated serum ammonia level is consistent with overt hepatic encephalopathy (HE) that has not been adequately controlled with his current lactulose regimen. The most appropriate next step in management is to increase the frequency and/or dose of lactulose to achieve the goal of 2-3 soft stools per day. In this case, increasing the dose to 30 mL orally four times daily (total daily dose of 120 mL) is a reasonable approach. Adding rifaximin may be considered if the patient continues to have recurrent episodes of overt HE despite optimal lactulose therapy, but it is not typically used as a first-line intervention. Switching lactulose to polyethylene glycol (PEG) is not recommended for the treatment of HE, as PEG has not been extensively studied in this setting and may not have the same ammonia-lowering effects as lactulose. Discontinuing lactulose and observing for spontaneous improvement is not appropriate in this patient with active symptoms and a history of cirrhosis, as untreated HE can progress rapidly and lead to serious complications.

670. A 58-year-old female with a history of nonalcoholic steatohepatitis (NASH) cirrhosis and recurrent overt hepatic encephalopathy (HE) presents with confusion, disorientation, and a serum ammonia level of 150 µmol/L. She is currently taking lactulose 30 mL orally four times daily and rifaximin 550 mg orally twice daily. Which of the following is the most appropriate additional intervention for this patient's refractory HE?
a. add neomycin 500 mg orally four times daily
b. switch rifaximin to vancomycin 125 mg orally four times daily
c. initiate a protein-restricted diet with a target intake of 0.5 g/kg/day
d. perform an urgent liver transplant evaluation

Answer: d. perform an urgent liver transplant evaluation. Explanation: The patient's presentation of confusion and disorientation in the setting of NASH cirrhosis, recurrent overt HE, and a significantly elevated serum ammonia level despite optimal medical therapy with lactulose and rifaximin suggests refractory HE that is unlikely to respond to further adjustments in her current regimen. In patients with recurrent or severe HE who have failed standard medical therapy, liver transplantation may be the only effective long-term treatment option. An urgent liver transplant evaluation is the most appropriate next step for this patient to assess her candidacy and identify any potential contraindications or barriers to transplantation. Adding neomycin or switching rifaximin to vancomycin are not recommended for the treatment of refractory HE due to the lack of evidence for their efficacy and the risk of adverse effects such as nephrotoxicity and ototoxicity. Initiating a protein-restricted diet with a target intake of 0.5 g/kg/day is not appropriate for this patient, as severe protein restriction can lead to malnutrition and may actually worsen HE by promoting muscle wasting and reducing the body's capacity to detoxify ammonia.

671. A 62-year-old male with a history of alcoholic cirrhosis presents with confusion, drowsiness, and a Glasgow Coma Scale (GCS) score of 12 (E3, V4, M5). His serum ammonia level is 180 µmol/L, and he has grade 3 asterixis. Which of the following is the most important prognostic factor for this patient's long-term survival?
a. the severity of his hepatic encephalopathy (HE) at presentation
b. the degree of protein restriction in his diet

c. the presence of comorbid conditions such as diabetes or hypertension
d. his MELD (Model for End-Stage Liver Disease) score

Answer: d. his MELD (Model for End-Stage Liver Disease) score. Explanation: The patient's presentation of confusion, drowsiness, and asterixis in the setting of alcoholic cirrhosis and a significantly elevated serum ammonia level is consistent with severe overt hepatic encephalopathy (HE). While the severity of HE at presentation is an important predictor of short-term mortality and the need for hospitalization, the most important prognostic factor for long-term survival in patients with cirrhosis is the MELD score. The MELD score is a validated predictor of 3-month mortality in patients with end-stage liver disease and is used to prioritize patients for liver transplantation. It is calculated based on three objective variables: serum bilirubin, serum creatinine, and INR (international normalized ratio). A higher MELD score indicates more advanced liver disease and a greater risk of mortality. The degree of protein restriction in the patient's diet is not a significant prognostic factor, as long as malnutrition is avoided. The presence of comorbid conditions such as diabetes or hypertension may impact the patient's overall health and quality of life but is not as strongly predictive of mortality as the MELD score in patients with cirrh

672. Which laboratory finding is typically elevated in disseminated intravascular coagulation (DIC) and is a marker of fibrin degradation?
a. Platelet count
b. Prothrombin time (PT)
c. D-dimer
d. Hemoglobin

Answer: c. D-dimer. Explanation: D-dimer is typically elevated in DIC as it is a marker of fibrin degradation, indicating increased fibrinolysis which is a hallmark of DIC. Elevated D-dimer levels suggest that there is ongoing clot formation and breakdown within the vasculature.

673. In the context of DIC, what is the significance of observing schistocytes on a peripheral blood smear?
a. Indicative of vitamin B12 deficiency
b. Suggestive of active hemolysis due to microangiopathic damage
c. A sign of bone marrow dysplasia
d. Indicative of an acute immune response

Answer: b. Suggestive of active hemolysis due to microangiopathic damage. Explanation: Schistocytes, or fragmented red cells, observed on a peripheral blood smear in the context of DIC suggest active hemolysis due to mechanical damage from microangiopathic processes, including the formation of microthrombi in small vessels.

674. What is the primary initial step in managing a patient with suspected DIC?
a. Immediate administration of unfractionated heparin
b. Transfusion of fresh frozen plasma and platelets
c. Identification and treatment of the underlying cause
d. Administration of vitamin K

Answer: c. Identification and treatment of the underlying cause. Explanation: The primary initial step in managing DIC is the identification and treatment of the underlying cause, as DIC is always secondary to another pathological process. Effective management of the primary condition can often lead to the resolution of DIC.

675. In a patient with sepsis-induced DIC, which clinical intervention is most critical?
a. Broad-spectrum antibiotics
b. Immediate splenectomy
c. High-dose corticosteroid therapy
d. Oral anticoagulants

Answer: a. Broad-spectrum antibiotics. Explanation: In sepsis-induced DIC, the most critical clinical intervention is the administration of broad-spectrum antibiotics to control the underlying infection, as sepsis is a common trigger for DIC through the activation of the coagulation cascade by endotoxins and inflammatory mediators.

676. When considering transfusion support for a patient with DIC, which component is typically administered to correct coagulopathy?
a. Packed red blood cells
b. Fresh frozen plasma (FFP)
c. Cryoprecipitate
d. Both b and c

Answer: d. Both b and c. Explanation: In transfusion support for DIC, both fresh frozen plasma (FFP) and cryoprecipitate are typically administered to correct coagulopathy. FFP provides all coagulation factors, while cryoprecipitate is rich in fibrinogen, factor VIII, and von Willebrand factor, which are often depleted in DIC.

677. What role does anticoagulation therapy play in the management of DIC, particularly in chronic or compensated cases?
a. It is contraindicated due to the risk of bleeding
b. It is the first-line treatment in all cases of DIC
c. It may be used cautiously to prevent further thrombosis
d. It is only used post-splenectomy

Answer: c. It may be used cautiously to prevent further thrombosis. Explanation: In chronic or compensated cases of DIC, where thrombosis is a prominent feature, anticoagulation therapy may be used cautiously to prevent further thrombotic complications, balancing the risks of bleeding with the benefits of reducing thrombotic risk.

678. Which obstetric complication is a well-recognized trigger for the development of DIC?
a. Gestational diabetes
b. Preeclampsia
c. Amniotic fluid embolism
d. Intrauterine growth restriction

Answer: c. Amniotic fluid embolism. Explanation: Amniotic fluid embolism is a well-recognized obstetric complication that can trigger the development of DIC by introducing amniotic fluid components into the maternal circulation, leading to a severe inflammatory and coagulation response.

679. In a trauma patient with DIC, what is a key element of supportive care?
a. Restrictive fluid resuscitation
b. Therapeutic hypothermia
c. Aggressive control of bleeding and resuscitation
d. Immediate limb amputation

Answer: c. Aggressive control of bleeding and resuscitation. Explanation: In a trauma patient with DIC, a key element of supportive care is aggressive control of bleeding and resuscitation to stabilize the patient, correct coagulopathies, and address the underlying traumatic injuries contributing to the DIC.

680. The hallmark clinical presentation of Superior Vena Cava Syndrome includes:
a. Lower extremity edema and deep vein thrombosis
b. Jaundice and pruritus
c. Facial and arm swelling with dyspnea
d. Hematuria and flank pain

Answer: c. Facial and arm swelling with dyspnea. Explanation: Superior Vena Cava Syndrome is characterized by obstruction of the SVC, leading to impaired blood flow from the head, neck, and upper extremities back to the heart, resulting in facial and arm swelling, dyspnea, and visible collateral veins on the chest.

681. First-line management of Tumor Lysis Syndrome involves:
a. Aggressive hydration and allopurinol or rasburicase
b. Immediate chemotherapy to reduce tumor burden
c. High-dose corticosteroids to reduce inflammation
d. Surgical removal of the tumor mass

Answer: a. Aggressive hydration and allopurinol or rasburicase. Explanation: Tumor Lysis Syndrome is characterized by rapid release of intracellular contents from lysed tumor cells, leading to hyperuricemia, hyperkalemia, hyperphosphatemia, and hypocalcemia. First-line management includes aggressive hydration to promote renal excretion of uric acid and electrolytes, along with allopurinol or rasburicase to reduce uric acid levels.

682. Spinal Cord Compression in cancer patients presents with:
a. Acute chest pain and shortness of breath
b. Sudden onset of lower extremity paralysis without pain
c. Back pain, motor/sensory deficits, and bowel/bladder dysfunction

d. Unexplained weight gain and peripheral edema

Answer: c. Back pain, motor/sensory deficits, and bowel/bladder dysfunction. Explanation: Spinal Cord Compression, an oncologic emergency, often presents with progressive back pain, motor and sensory deficits below the level of compression, and bowel/bladder dysfunction, necessitating prompt diagnosis and treatment to prevent permanent damage.

683. In SVC Syndrome, collateral circulation is often visible as:
a. Varicose veins in the lower extremities
b. Engorged veins on the chest and neck
c. Petechiae and ecchymosis on the trunk
d. Spider angiomas on the abdomen

Answer: b. Engorged veins on the chest and neck. Explanation: In SVC Syndrome, the obstruction of blood flow leads to the development of collateral circulation, with visibly engorged veins on the chest, neck, and sometimes face, as the body attempts to reroute blood back to the heart.

684. The definitive diagnostic tool for Spinal Cord Compression is:
a. X-ray of the spine
b. Complete blood count (CBC)
c. Magnetic Resonance Imaging (MRI) of the spine
d. Lumbar puncture

Answer: c. Magnetic Resonance Imaging (MRI) of the spine. Explanation: MRI is the gold standard for diagnosing Spinal Cord Compression, providing detailed images of the spinal cord, vertebrae, and any tumors or masses causing compression, critical for guiding treatment decisions.

685. The electrolyte imbalance most immediately life-threatening in Tumor Lysis Syndrome is:
a. Hyperuricemia
b. Hyperkalemia
c. Hyperphosphatemia
d. Hypocalcemia

Answer: b. Hyperkalemia. Explanation: Hyperkalemia in Tumor Lysis Syndrome can lead to cardiac arrhythmias and cardiac arrest, making it the most immediately life-threatening electrolyte imbalance, requiring urgent management.

686. A key preventive measure in high-risk patients for Tumor Lysis Syndrome is:
a. Prophylactic antibiotics
b. Early initiation of dialysis
c. Prophylactic anticoagulation

d. Initiation of hydration and allopurinol or rasburicase prior to chemotherapy

Answer: d. Initiation of hydration and allopurinol or rasburicase prior to chemotherapy. Explanation: In high-risk patients, prophylactic measures for Tumor Lysis Syndrome include aggressive hydration and administration of allopurinol or rasburicase before starting chemotherapy to prevent the rapid increase in uric acid and electrolyte imbalances.

687. For a patient presenting with acute back pain and suspected Spinal Cord Compression, the immediate treatment should include:
a. Oral nonsteroidal anti-inflammatory drugs (NSAIDs)
b. High-dose corticosteroids
c. Application of a heating pad to the affected area
d. Immediate intensive physical therapy

Answer: b. High-dose corticosteroids. Explanation: High-dose corticosteroids are administered immediately to patients with suspected Spinal Cord Compression to reduce spinal cord edema and inflammation, potentially alleviating symptoms and preventing further neurological damage while further diagnostic and therapeutic measures are planned.

688. A patient with known lung cancer presenting with SVC Syndrome might also exhibit:
a. Hemoptysis and wheezing
b. Cyanosis and facial plethora
c. Ascites and jaundice
d. Pericardial friction rub and chest pain

Answer: b. Cyanosis and facial plethora. Explanation: In SVC Syndrome, particularly in patients with lung cancer, obstruction of the SVC can lead to facial plethora (reddening) and cyanosis due to impaired venous return from the head and upper extremities, along with possible dyspnea and swelling of the face, neck, and arms.

689. In managing a patient with aplastic anemia and concurrent infection, a critical consideration is:
a. Immediate initiation of erythropoietin therapy
b. Aggressive chemotherapy to eliminate malignant cells
c. Administration of broad-spectrum antibiotics and supportive care
d. Rapid blood transfusions to restore normal cell counts

Answer: c. Administration of broad-spectrum antibiotics and supportive care. Explanation: In aplastic anemia, especially with concurrent infection, the administration of broad-spectrum antibiotics is critical due to the increased risk of infection from neutropenia. Supportive care, including transfusions and growth factors, may also be necessary to manage anemia and thrombocytopenia.

690. Which first-line medication is recommended for the initial treatment of status epilepticus?
a. Phenytoin
b. Carbamazepine
c. Lorazepam
d. Levetiracetam

Answer: c. Lorazepam. Explanation: Lorazepam is commonly recommended as a first-line medication for the initial treatment of status epilepticus due to its rapid onset of action and effectiveness in stopping continuous seizure activity. Benzodiazepines like lorazepam enhance the effect of the neurotransmitter GABA, which is inhibitory and helps to stop seizure activity.

691. During a generalized tonic-clonic seizure, what is the typical sequence of motor activity?
a. Initial myoclonic jerks followed by sustained muscle contraction and then rhythmic jerking
b. Sustained muscle contraction (tonic phase) followed by rhythmic jerking (clonic phase)
c. Immediate loss of consciousness without motor activity followed by gradual recovery
d. Rhythmic jerking without a preceding tonic phase

Answer: b. Sustained muscle contraction (tonic phase) followed by rhythmic jerking (clonic phase). Explanation: In a generalized tonic-clonic seizure, the typical sequence starts with a tonic phase, where there is sustained muscle contraction causing the body to stiffen, followed by a clonic phase, where there is rhythmic jerking of the limbs.

692. What is a key feature distinguishing absence seizures from brief moments of inattention?
a. Presence of aura before the seizure
b. Sudden onset and cessation without postictal confusion
c. Accompanying headache and nausea
d. Progressive increase in intensity before cessation

Answer: b. Sudden onset and cessation without postictal confusion. Explanation: Absence seizures are characterized by a sudden onset and cessation of seizure activity, typically lasting only a few seconds, without any postictal confusion. This differentiates them from mere inattention or daydreaming episodes.

693. In a patient experiencing a complex partial seizure, what is a common symptom?
a. Sudden, unexplained feelings of joy or fear
b. Bilateral, symmetrical muscle twitching
c. Complete loss of muscle tone
d. Aura of flashing lights

Answer: a. Sudden, unexplained feelings of joy or fear. Explanation: Complex partial seizures often involve alterations in consciousness and can manifest with sudden, unexplained emotional experiences such as fear, joy, or deja vu, among other complex sensory or psychological phenomena.

694. When considering the use of antiepileptic drugs (AEDs), what is an important consideration for women of childbearing age?
a. AEDs are contraindicated during pregnancy
b. Some AEDs have teratogenic risks and may require additional folic acid supplementation
c. AEDs enhance fertility and require contraceptive measures
d. All AEDs are safe during pregnancy without additional precautions

Answer: b. Some AEDs have teratogenic risks and may require additional folic acid supplementation. Explanation: In women of childbearing age who require antiepileptic drugs, an important consideration is the teratogenic risk associated with some AEDs. Such patients may require additional folic acid supplementation to mitigate these risks and careful selection of AEDs to balance seizure control with safety during pregnancy.

695. For a patient with epilepsy, what is an important lifestyle modification to reduce the risk of seizure recurrence?
a. Complete avoidance of physical activity
b. Strict ketogenic diet for all patients
c. Regular sleep patterns and avoiding sleep deprivation
d. High caffeine intake to maintain alertness

Answer: c. Regular sleep patterns and avoiding sleep deprivation. Explanation: Maintaining regular sleep patterns and avoiding sleep deprivation are important lifestyle modifications for patients with epilepsy, as sleep deprivation can lower the seizure threshold and increase the risk of seizure recurrence.

696. In the management of myoclonic seizures, which medication is commonly used due to its efficacy in treating this seizure type?
a. Gabapentin
b. Valproic acid
c. Topiramate
d. Oxcarbazepine

Answer: b. Valproic acid. Explanation: Valproic acid is commonly used in the management of myoclonic seizures due to its broad-spectrum efficacy in treating various seizure types, including myoclonic seizures. It works by increasing the availability of GABA in the brain, contributing to its anticonvulsant properties.

697. What is the significance of identifying an aura in a patient with seizures?
a. It indicates an imminent risk of status epilepticus
b. It suggests a primary psychiatric disorder rather than epilepsy
c. It can help localize the seizure focus in partial seizures
d. It confirms the diagnosis of absence seizures

Answer: c. It can help localize the seizure focus in partial seizures. Explanation: Identifying an aura, which is a perceptual disturbance experienced by some patients before a seizure, can help localize the seizure focus, especially in partial seizures. Auras can provide clues about the region of the brain from which the seizure originates.

698. In assessing a patient after a seizure, what finding is characteristic of the postictal state?
a. Immediate full recovery of consciousness
b. Sudden onset of repetitive seizures without recovery
c. Transient confusion and somnolence
d. Persistent neurological deficits lasting several days

Answer: c. Transient confusion and somnolence. Explanation: The postictal state following a seizure is characterized by transient confusion, somnolence, and disorientation, which gradually resolves over minutes to hours. This period reflects the brain's recovery after the seizure activity.

699. The National Institutes of Health Stroke Scale (NIHSS) is used in the assessment of a stroke patient to:
a. Determine the size of the cerebral infarct on imaging
b. Measure the patient's blood pressure and heart rate
c. Evaluate the severity of neurological deficits
d. Decide on the necessity for surgical intervention

Answer: c. Evaluate the severity of neurological deficits. Explanation: The NIHSS is a systematic assessment tool that provides a quantitative measure of stroke-related neurological deficit. It evaluates various aspects of neurologic function, including consciousness, vision, motor function, and speech, aiding in determining the severity of the stroke.

700. In the management of acute ischemic stroke, tPA (tissue Plasminogen Activator) administration is indicated within:
a. 24 hours of symptom onset
b. 3-4.5 hours of symptom onset, with specific criteria
c. Immediately after a CT scan, regardless of the time frame
d. The first week of stroke symptoms to enhance recovery

Answer: b. 3-4.5 hours of symptom onset, with specific criteria. Explanation: tPA is a thrombolytic agent used to dissolve the clot causing an ischemic stroke. It's most effective when administered within 3-4.5 hours of symptom onset, following specific eligibility criteria to minimize the risk of hemorrhagic complications.

701. Mechanical thrombectomy in ischemic stroke is recommended for patients with:
a. Small vessel occlusion
b. Large artery occlusions in the anterior circulation
c. Hemorrhagic stroke as a first-line treatment
d. Any stroke symptom lasting less than 1 hour

Answer: b. Large artery occlusions in the anterior circulation. Explanation: Mechanical thrombectomy is recommended for patients with acute ischemic stroke due to large artery occlusions in the anterior circulation, typically within 6-24 hours of symptom onset, depending on specific criteria and imaging findings.

702. In the context of hemorrhagic stroke, aggressive blood pressure control is initiated to prevent:
a. Further ischemic damage
b. Expansion of the hematoma
c. Immediate seizure activity
d. Rapid resolution of symptoms

Answer: b. Expansion of the hematoma. Explanation: In hemorrhagic stroke, controlling high blood pressure is crucial to prevent the expansion of the hematoma and secondary damage to brain tissue. Tight blood pressure management can reduce the risk of ongoing bleeding.

703. The most common initial symptom of a subarachnoid hemorrhage is:
a. Gradual onset of headache over several days
b. "Thunderclap" headache - sudden and severe
c. Progressive visual loss
d. Isolated aphasia without headache

Answer: b. "Thunderclap" headache - sudden and severe. Explanation: A subarachnoid hemorrhage often presents with a sudden, severe "thunderclap" headache, frequently described as the "worst headache of my life," often accompanied by nausea, vomiting, and possibly altered consciousness.

704. For ischemic stroke, the window for mechanical thrombectomy has been extended up to:
a. 1 hour post-onset
b. 6 hours post-onset
c. 12 hours post-onset
d. 24 hours for select patients based on imaging criteria

Answer: d. 24 hours for select patients based on imaging criteria. Explanation: Recent guidelines and studies have shown that mechanical thrombectomy can be beneficial up to 24 hours post-onset for select patients with ischemic stroke, particularly those with salvageable brain tissue as demonstrated by advanced neuroimaging.

705. Intracerebral hemorrhage management may include all the following EXCEPT:
a. Immediate anticoagulant therapy
b. Blood pressure management
c. Surgical evacuation of the hematoma in select cases
d. Supportive care and monitoring for neurological changes

Answer: a. Immediate anticoagulant therapy. Explanation: Immediate anticoagulant therapy is generally contraindicated in the acute management of intracerebral hemorrhage, as it can exacerbate bleeding. Instead, the focus is on blood pressure control, possible surgical intervention, and supportive care.

706. Identification and management of risk factors for stroke include all the following EXCEPT:
a. Smoking cessation
b. Regular exercise and maintaining a healthy diet
c. Routine use of anticoagulants in the general population
d. Control of hypertension, diabetes, and hyperlipidemia

Answer: c. Routine use of anticoagulants in the general population. Explanation: While anticoagulants are crucial for specific conditions like atrial fibrillation, they are not routinely used in the general population for stroke prevention due to the risk of bleeding. Instead, modifiable risk factors such as smoking, diet, exercise, and control of medical conditions are targeted.

707. The differentiation between ischemic and hemorrhagic stroke in an acute setting is primarily made by:
a. Clinical symptoms and physical examination alone
b. Immediate initiation of tPA
c. Non-contrast head CT scan or MRI
d. Electroencephalogram (EEG) findings

Answer: c. Non-contrast head CT scan or MRI. Explanation: A non-contrast head CT scan or MRI is essential in the acute setting to differentiate between ischemic and hemorrhagic stroke, as the treatment approaches differ significantly. This imaging helps identify the presence of blood or signs of ischemia.

708. A patient presenting with back pain, motor deficits, and bladder dysfunction may be experiencing:
a. Migraine with aura
b. Spinal cord compression
c. Peripheral neuropathy
d. Classic lacunar stroke

Answer: b. Spinal cord compression. Explanation: Back pain combined with motor deficits and bowel/bladder dysfunction raises concern for spinal cord compression, a neurological emergency that requires prompt diagnosis and treatment to prevent permanent damage.

709. Which component is not included in the systemic inflammatory response syndrome (SIRS) criteria?
a. Temperature >38°C or <36°C
b. Heart rate >90 beats/min
c. White blood cell count >12,000/μL or <4,000/μL, or >10% immature (band) forms
d. Blood urea nitrogen (BUN) >20 mg/dL

Answer: d. Blood urea nitrogen (BUN) >20 mg/dL. Explanation: The SIRS criteria include temperature, heart rate, respiratory rate, and white blood cell count abnormalities, but do not include BUN levels. BUN is more relevant to renal function and is not a marker of systemic inflammation.

710. In the context of sepsis management, what is the primary goal of early goal-directed therapy (EGDT)?
a. To maintain hemodynamic stability through fluid resuscitation and vasopressors
b. To achieve rapid surgical source control within the first hour
c. To complete a full course of antibiotics within the first 24 hours
d. To normalize white blood cell count

Answer: a. To maintain hemodynamic stability through fluid resuscitation and vasopressors. Explanation: The primary goal of EGDT in sepsis management is to maintain hemodynamic stability and adequate tissue perfusion through timely fluid resuscitation, vasopressor support, and other interventions based on monitored parameters such as central venous pressure, mean arterial pressure, and central venous (or mixed venous) oxygen saturation.

711. What is the significance of altered mental status in the quick Sequential (Sepsis-related) Organ Failure Assessment (qSOFA) score?
a. It is used to diagnose sepsis definitively
b. It indicates the need for immediate intubation
c. It serves as a marker for increased risk of mortality in patients with suspected infection outside the ICU
d. It is a criterion for initiating renal replacement therapy

Answer: c. It serves as a marker for increased risk of mortality in patients with suspected infection outside the ICU. Explanation: Altered mental status in the qSOFA score serves as a clinical marker indicating that a patient with suspected infection outside the ICU is at increased risk of mortality, and it helps clinicians identify patients who may need more aggressive monitoring and management.

712. Which pathophysiological mechanism is primarily involved in septic shock?
a. Cardiac tamponade leading to decreased cardiac output
b. Massive blood loss causing hypovolemia
c. Widespread vasodilation and increased capillary permeability leading to hypotension
d. Acute respiratory distress syndrome (ARDS) causing hypoxia

Answer: c. Widespread vasodilation and increased capillary permeability leading to hypotension. Explanation: The primary mechanism involved in septic shock is widespread vasodilation and increased capillary permeability due to the systemic inflammatory response, leading to profound hypotension that is not fully responsive to fluid resuscitation, and associated with organ dysfunction.

713. What is the rationale for using broad-spectrum antibiotics in the initial management of sepsis?
a. To target specific pathogens identified in blood cultures

b. To provide prophylaxis against hospital-acquired infections
c. To cover a wide range of potential pathogens until specific organisms are identified
d. To reduce the development of antibiotic resistance

Answer: c. To cover a wide range of potential pathogens until specific organisms are identified. Explanation: The use of broad-spectrum antibiotics in the initial management of sepsis aims to cover a wide range of potential pathogens, providing effective empirical therapy until specific organisms are identified through cultures, at which point antibiotic therapy can be de-escalated based on sensitivity patterns.

714. In a patient with sepsis, what is the significance of a lactate level >2 mmol/L?
a. It is a direct indicator of bacterial load in the bloodstream
b. It suggests increased risk of progression to severe sepsis and septic shock
c. It indicates an immediate need for antifungal therapy
d. It confirms the diagnosis of viral sepsis

Answer: b. It suggests increased risk of progression to severe sepsis and septic shock. Explanation: An elevated lactate level (>2 mmol/L) in a patient with sepsis is a marker of tissue hypoperfusion and aerobic metabolism, suggesting an increased risk of progression to severe sepsis and septic shock, and is associated with higher mortality rates.

715. For septic patients, why is source control (e.g., drainage of abscess, removal of infected devices) critical in management?
a. It provides definitive evidence for the diagnosis of sepsis
b. It directly reduces the systemic inflammatory response
c. It eliminates the source of infection, reducing the ongoing inflammatory response and microbial load
d. It increases the effectiveness of antiviral therapies

Answer: c. It eliminates the source of infection, reducing the ongoing inflammatory response and microbial load. Explanation: Source control is critical in the management of sepsis because it directly addresses and eliminates the source of infection, thereby reducing the ongoing inflammatory response, microbial load, and toxin production, which are central to the pathophysiology of sepsis.

716. In the treatment of sepsis, why is timely antibiotic administration within the first hour of recognizing sepsis crucial?
a. It ensures compliance with healthcare regulations
b. It minimizes the risk of antibiotic-associated diarrhea
c. It is associated with reduced mortality and improved outcomes
d. It allows for easier transition to oral antibiotics

Answer: c. It is associated with reduced mortality and improved outcomes. Explanation: Timely antibiotic administration within the first hour of recognizing sepsis is crucial because early empirical antibiotic therapy is associated with reduced mortality and improved outcomes in septic patients, as it promptly targets and reduces the microbial load contributing to the septic process.

717. A key predisposing factor for developing delirium in hospitalized patients is:
a. Previous athletic ability
b. High educational level
c. Advanced age and cognitive impairment
d. Consumption of a vegetarian diet

Answer: c. Advanced age and cognitive impairment. Explanation: Advanced age and pre-existing cognitive impairment, such as dementia, significantly increase the risk for developing delirium in hospitalized patients due to the decreased cognitive reserve and vulnerability of the brain.

718. In managing delirium, the first step should involve:
a. Immediate administration of high-dose antipsychotics
b. Identification and treatment of the underlying cause
c. Physical restraints to prevent harm
d. Scheduled benzodiazepines for sedation

Answer: b. Identification and treatment of the underlying cause. Explanation: The management of delirium begins with identifying and treating the underlying cause, such as infections, electrolyte imbalances, or drug side effects, to address the root of the delirium.

719. Nonpharmacologic interventions for delirium prevention and management include all the following EXCEPT:
a. Frequent reorientation and cognitive stimulation
b. Ensuring adequate hydration and nutrition
c. Use of blindfolds and earplugs at all times to reduce sensory overload
d. Maintaining a regular sleep-wake cycle and providing a calm environment

Answer: c. Use of blindfolds and earplugs at all times to reduce sensory overload. Explanation: While reducing sensory overload can be beneficial, the continuous use of blindfolds and earplugs is not recommended as it can exacerbate confusion and disorientation. Instead, tailored sensory input and maintaining a connection with the environment are encouraged.

720. In the context of delirium, haloperidol may be considered for:
a. First-line treatment for all patients with delirium
b. Patients with severe agitation posing an immediate risk to themselves or others, when nonpharmacologic measures have failed
c. Routine prophylaxis in all elderly hospitalized patients
d. Enhancing sleep quality in delirious patients

Answer: b. Patients with severe agitation posing an immediate risk to themselves or others, when nonpharmacologic measures have failed. Explanation: Haloperidol, an antipsychotic, may be used judiciously in cases of severe agitation or psychosis in delirium where there's a risk of harm, and nonpharmacologic measures are insufficient.

721. A common precipitating factor for delirium in postoperative patients is:
a. Participation in preoperative physical therapy
b. Elective surgery
c. Administration of general anesthesia
d. Adequate postoperative pain control

Answer: c. Administration of general anesthesia. Explanation: General anesthesia can be a precipitating factor for delirium, particularly in vulnerable populations such as the elderly or those with pre-existing cognitive impairment, due to its profound effects on brain function.

722. Polypharmacy, particularly in the elderly, increases the risk of delirium due to:
a. The synergistic effect of medications promoting cognitive clarity
b. Enhanced renal clearance of drugs
c. Potential drug-drug interactions and anticholinergic burden
d. Increased physical activity stimulated by multiple medications

Answer: c. Potential drug-drug interactions and anticholinergic burden. Explanation: Polypharmacy increases the risk of delirium due to potential drug-drug interactions and the cumulative anticholinergic effects of multiple medications, which can impair cognitive function.

723. A critical aspect of delirium management in the ICU involves:
a. Limiting family visits to reduce confusion
b. Continuous deep sedation to reduce agitation
c. Early mobilization and orientation interventions
d. Exclusive use of visual cues without verbal reorientation

Answer: c. Early mobilization and orientation interventions. Explanation: In the ICU, nonpharmacologic strategies like early mobilization, reorientation, and environmental modifications play a crucial role in managing and preventing delirium.

724. When considering the use of quetiapine in delirium management, it is important to:
a. Start with the highest possible dose for immediate effect
b. Use as a first-line agent in all cases of delirium for rapid sedation
c. Monitor for potential side effects, such as orthostatic hypotension and sedation
d. Reserve for exclusive treatment of insomnia associated with delirium

Answer: c. Monitor for potential side effects, such as orthostatic hypotension and sedation. Explanation: Quetiapine, an atypical antipsychotic, can be used in delirium management, particularly when there are contraindications to haloperidol. It's essential to monitor for side effects like orthostatic hypotension, sedation, and others.

725. Sensory deficits in the elderly, such as hearing and vision impairment, contribute to delirium risk by:
a. Enhancing the ability to interpret the environment accurately
b. Decreasing reliance on healthcare staff for orientation
c. Increasing confusion and disorientation due to misinterpretation of the environment
d. Improving cognitive reserve and resilience to stressors

Answer: c. Increasing confusion and disorientation due to misinterpretation of the environment. Explanation: Sensory deficits like hearing and vision impairments can contribute to the risk of delirium by increasing confusion and disorientation, as they impair the patient's ability to accurately interpret and interact with their environment.

726. What is the first-line antibiotic choice for uncomplicated cystitis in women without any contraindications?
a. Ciprofloxacin
b. Nitrofurantoin
c. Vancomycin
d. Amoxicillin

Answer: b. Nitrofurantoin. Explanation: Nitrofurantoin is often the first-line antibiotic choice for uncomplicated cystitis, particularly in women, due to its effectiveness against common urinary pathogens and low resistance rates, as well as its minimal impact on the gut flora.

727. Which symptom is least likely associated with uncomplicated cystitis?
a. Hematuria
b. Fever
c. Urinary urgency
d. Dysuria

Answer: b. Fever. Explanation: Fever is least likely associated with uncomplicated cystitis and may indicate a more severe infection like pyelonephritis. Symptoms of uncomplicated cystitis typically include dysuria, urinary urgency, and frequency, sometimes with hematuria, but not systemic symptoms like fever.

728. In the treatment of pyelonephritis, why is a longer course of antibiotics often required compared to uncomplicated cystitis?
a. To ensure complete eradication of biofilm
b. Due to the higher likelihood of resistant pathogens
c. Because of the greater severity and potential for renal involvement
d. To prevent the spread of infection to the bloodstream

Answer: c. Because of the greater severity and potential for renal involvement. Explanation: A longer course of antibiotics is often required for pyelonephritis due to the infection's greater severity and potential for renal involvement, necessitating a more extended treatment duration to ensure complete eradication of the infection and prevent complications.

729. For a patient with a catheter-associated urinary tract infection (CAUTI), what is an essential step in management?
a. Increasing fluid intake to flush out bacteria
b. Immediate removal or change of the indwelling catheter
c. Administration of intravenous antibiotics only
d. Bladder irrigation with antiseptic solutions

Answer: b. Immediate removal or change of the indwelling catheter. Explanation: An essential step in managing a catheter-associated urinary tract infection (CAUTI) is the immediate removal or change of the indwelling catheter when possible, as this eliminates the primary source of infection and can significantly reduce bacterial load.

730. What role do biofilms play in catheter-associated urinary tract infections?
a. They enhance antibiotic penetration to the bacteria
b. They protect bacteria from the host immune response and antibiotics
c. They decrease the adherence of bacteria to the catheter surface
d. They facilitate the rapid clearance of bacteria from the urinary tract

Answer: b. They protect bacteria from the host immune response and antibiotics. Explanation: Biofilms in catheter-associated urinary tract infections protect bacteria from the host's immune response and antibiotics. This protection makes it more challenging to eradicate the bacteria and contributes to the persistence and recurrence of CAUTIs.

731. In patients with recurrent UTIs, what preventative measure is commonly recommended?
a. Long-term corticosteroid therapy
b. Prophylactic antibiotics
c. High-dose vitamin C supplementation
d. Routine catheterization

Answer: b. Prophylactic antibiotics. Explanation: In patients with recurrent UTIs, prophylactic antibiotics are commonly recommended as a preventative measure, especially in cases where UTIs are frequent and significantly impact the patient's quality of life. This approach aims to reduce the incidence of infections.

732. Why is flank pain a concerning symptom in the context of a urinary tract infection?
a. It suggests the possible development of renal calculi
b. It is a common symptom of uncomplicated cystitis
c. It may indicate the infection has ascended to the kidneys (pyelonephritis)

d. It is indicative of bladder overdistension

Answer: c. It may indicate the infection has ascended to the kidneys (pyelonephritis). Explanation: Flank pain is a concerning symptom in the context of a urinary tract infection because it may indicate that the infection has ascended to the kidneys, leading to pyelonephritis. This condition is more severe than uncomplicated cystitis and requires prompt and effective treatment.

733. What is the significance of costovertebral angle (CVA) tenderness in patients with suspected UTIs?
a. It is a diagnostic criterion for interstitial cystitis
b. It typically indicates lower urinary tract involvement
c. It is a sign of pyelonephritis, suggesting upper urinary tract involvement
d. It confirms the presence of a urinary tract obstruction

Answer: c. It is a sign of pyelonephritis, suggesting upper urinary tract involvement. Explanation: Costovertebral angle (CVA) tenderness is significant in patients with suspected UTIs as it is a sign of pyelonephritis. CVA tenderness suggests the involvement of the kidney and upper urinary tract, requiring a more aggressive treatment approach than lower tract infections.

734. In the context of UTIs, how does dysuria primarily manifest, and what does it indicate?
a. As lower abdominal pain, indicating bladder inflammation
b. As pain or burning during urination, indicating urethral or bladder inflammation
c. As back pain, indicating kidney involvement
d. As cloudy urine, indicating the presence of bacteria or pus

Answer: b. As pain or burning during urination, indicating urethral or bladder inflammation. Explanation: Dysuria primarily manifests as pain or burning during urination and indicates inflammation of the urethra or bladder, which is commonly seen in urinary tract infections, especially in cases of uncomplicated cystitis.

735. What is the primary reason for using short-course antibiotics in the treatment of uncomplicated cystitis?
a. To prevent the development of acute kidney injury
b. To reduce the risk of antibiotic resistance and adverse effects
c. Because longer courses improve patient compliance
d. To quickly escalate to more potent antibiotics if needed

Answer: b. To reduce the risk of antibiotic resistance and adverse effects. Explanation: The primary reason for using short-course antibiotics in the treatment of uncomplicated cystitis is to reduce the risk of antibiotic resistance and minimize adverse effects associated with longer antibiotic courses, while still effectively treating the infection.

736. The CURB-65 score, a tool used to assess the severity of community-acquired pneumonia, includes all the following criteria EXCEPT:

a. Confusion of new onset
b. Urea level
c. Respiratory rate of 30 breaths per minute or more
d. Blood pressure below 90/60 mmHg

Answer: d. Blood pressure below 90/60 mmHg. Explanation: The CURB-65 score for assessing the severity of community-acquired pneumonia includes Confusion, Urea >7 mmol/L, Respiratory rate ≥30/min, Blood pressure (systolic <90 mmHg or diastolic ≤60 mmHg), and age ≥65 years. Hypotension is defined as systolic <90 mmHg or diastolic ≤60 mmHg, not specifically below 90/60 mmHg.

737. Empiric antibiotic therapy for community-acquired pneumonia in an otherwise healthy adult without recent antibiotic use typically includes:
a. A combination of vancomycin and piperacillin-tazobactam
b. A macrolide or doxycycline as monotherapy
c. Broad-spectrum beta-lactams alone
d. Antiviral agents as first-line therapy

Answer: b. A macrolide or doxycycline as monotherapy. Explanation: For otherwise healthy adults with community-acquired pneumonia and no recent antibiotic use, empiric therapy typically includes a macrolide (e.g., azithromycin, clarithromycin) or doxycycline as monotherapy, based on local susceptibility patterns.

738. A major risk factor for hospital-acquired pneumonia (HAP) and ventilator-associated pneumonia (VAP) is:
a. Outdoor air pollution
b. Use of inhaled corticosteroids for asthma
c. Prolonged mechanical ventilation
d. High altitude

Answer: c. Prolonged mechanical ventilation. Explanation: Prolonged mechanical ventilation is a significant risk factor for developing ventilator-associated pneumonia (VAP), due to the increased opportunity for pathogenic organisms to enter the lower respiratory tract and the potential for biofilm formation on the endotracheal tube.

739. In the treatment of pneumonia caused by multi-drug resistant organisms in a hospital setting, an important consideration is:
a. Minimizing the use of antibiotics to reduce resistance
b. Utilizing narrow-spectrum antibiotics as first-line therapy
c. Tailoring antibiotic therapy based on culture and sensitivity results
d. Exclusive use of oral antibiotics for ease of administration

Answer: c. Tailoring antibiotic therapy based on culture and sensitivity results. Explanation: For pneumonia caused by multi-drug resistant organisms, it's crucial to tailor antibiotic therapy based on culture and sensitivity results to ensure effectiveness and minimize further resistance development.

740. A patient with community-acquired pneumonia presents with a CURB-65 score of 3. The appropriate management for this patient would be:
a. Outpatient treatment with oral antibiotics
b. Admission to the general medical ward for intravenous antibiotics
c. Immediate intubation and mechanical ventilation
d. Palliative care only

Answer: b. Admission to the general medical ward for intravenous antibiotics. Explanation: A CURB-65 score of 3 indicates a severe pneumonia with a higher risk of mortality, warranting admission to the hospital for close monitoring and treatment with intravenous antibiotics.

741. The presence of "rust-colored" sputum in a patient with pneumonia is classically associated with infection by:
a. Pseudomonas aeruginosa
b. Mycoplasma pneumoniae
c. Streptococcus pneumoniae
d. Legionella pneumophila

Answer: c. Streptococcus pneumoniae. Explanation: "Rust-colored" sputum is classically associated with pneumonia caused by Streptococcus pneumoniae, reflecting the presence of blood in the sputum due to lung tissue damage and inflammation.

742. For a patient with suspected ventilator-associated pneumonia, the initial diagnostic step should include:
a. Immediate discontinuation of the ventilator
b. Administration of empirical broad-spectrum antibiotics
c. Obtaining respiratory secretions for culture before antibiotic initiation
d. Performing a bronchoscopy on all patients

Answer: c. Obtaining respiratory secretions for culture before antibiotic initiation. Explanation: Obtaining lower respiratory tract secretions for culture before starting antibiotics is critical in managing suspected ventilator-associated pneumonia to guide appropriate and targeted antibiotic therapy.

743. A nonpharmacologic intervention to reduce the risk of hospital-acquired pneumonia in at-risk patients includes:
a. Routine prophylactic antibiotics for all hospitalized patients
b. Elevating the head of the bed to 30-45 degrees
c. Daily sedation vacations for all patients on mechanical ventilation
d. Implementing a strict NPO (nothing by mouth) status for all ICU patients

Answer: b. Elevating the head of the bed to 30-45 degrees. Explanation: Elevating the head of the bed to 30-45 degrees is a nonpharmacologic intervention that can help reduce the risk of aspiration and subsequent development of hospital-acquired pneumonia in at-risk patients.

744. In evaluating a patient with pneumonia, the finding of dullness to percussion over the affected lung area suggests:
a. Pneumothorax
b. Pleural effusion
c. Asthma exacerbation
d. Simple bronchitis

Answer: b. Pleural effusion. Explanation: Dullness to percussion over an area of the lung in a patient with pneumonia suggests the presence of a pleural effusion, which is an accumulation of fluid in the pleural space, often complicating pneumonia.

745. A 68-year-old female with a history of chronic lymphocytic leukemia (CLL) presents with fever, chills, and a productive cough. Her absolute neutrophil count (ANC) is 400 cells/μL. Blood cultures are pending. Which of the following is the most appropriate initial antibiotic regimen for this patient?
a. ceftriaxone and azithromycin
b. vancomycin and cefepime
c. piperacillin-tazobactam and levofloxacin
d. meropenem and vancomycin

Answer: d. meropenem and vancomycin. Explanation: The patient's presentation of fever, chills, and productive cough in the setting of CLL and severe neutropenia (ANC < 500 cells/μL) is consistent with febrile neutropenia, a life-threatening complication of cancer and its treatment that requires prompt initiation of empiric broad-spectrum antibiotics. The most appropriate initial antibiotic regimen for patients with febrile neutropenia is a combination of an anti-pseudomonal beta-lactam (e.g., cefepime, piperacillin-tazobactam, or meropenem) and vancomycin to cover both gram-negative and gram-positive pathogens, including Pseudomonas aeruginosa and methicillin-resistant Staphylococcus aureus (MRSA). Meropenem is a carbapenem antibiotic that provides the broadest coverage against gram-negative bacteria, including extended-spectrum beta-lactamase (ESBL) producers and multidrug-resistant (MDR) strains. Ceftriaxone and azithromycin are appropriate for community-acquired pneumonia but do not provide adequate coverage for neutropenic fever. Vancomycin and cefepime or piperacillin-tazobactam and levofloxacin are also acceptable regimens for febrile neutropenia but may not be as effective as meropenem and vancomycin in patients with a high risk of MDR infections.

746. A 55-year-old male with a history of multiple myeloma presents with new-onset back pain and weakness in his lower extremities. MRI of the spine reveals a compression fracture at T12 with spinal cord compression. Which of the following is the most appropriate initial management for this patient's condition?
a. intravenous bisphosphonates
b. radiation therapy to the affected area
c. high-dose systemic corticosteroids
d. emergent surgical decompression

Answer: d. emergent surgical decompression. Explanation: The patient's presentation of back pain and lower extremity weakness in the setting of multiple myeloma and MRI findings of a compression fracture with spinal cord compression is consistent with malignant spinal cord compression (MSCC), a medical emergency that requires prompt intervention to prevent permanent neurological deficits. The most appropriate initial management for patients with MSCC and neurological symptoms is emergent surgical decompression to relieve pressure on the spinal cord and preserve neurological function. Radiation therapy is an effective adjunctive treatment for MSCC but is not sufficient as a sole intervention in patients with acute neurological deficits. High-dose systemic corticosteroids (e.g., dexamethasone) can help to reduce edema and inflammation around the spinal cord but should be used in conjunction with, not instead of, surgical decompression. Intravenous bisphosphonates are used to prevent and treat skeletal-related events in patients with multiple myeloma but are not effective for the acute management of MSCC.

747. A 62-year-old female with a history of breast cancer presents with progressive fatigue, dyspnea, and a hemoglobin level of 7.5 g/dL. Her reticulocyte count is 0.5%, and her serum erythropoietin level is 500 mU/mL (normal range: 4-24 mU/mL). Which of the following is the most likely cause of this patient's anemia?
a. iron deficiency
b. chemotherapy-induced myelosuppression
c. tumor infiltration of the bone marrow
d. anemia of chronic disease

Answer: d. anemia of chronic disease. Explanation: The patient's presentation of progressive fatigue and dyspnea in the setting of breast cancer and a low hemoglobin level is consistent with cancer-related anemia. The most likely cause of anemia in this patient is anemia of chronic disease (ACD), also known as anemia of inflammation, which is a common complication of cancer and other chronic inflammatory conditions. ACD is characterized by a normocytic, normochromic anemia with a low reticulocyte count and an elevated serum erythropoietin level, reflecting the body's attempt to compensate for the anemia. The pathogenesis of ACD involves a complex interplay of inflammatory cytokines, hepcidin-mediated iron sequestration, and impaired erythropoiesis. Iron deficiency is less likely in this patient given the low reticulocyte count and high erythropoietin level, which would be unusual in iron deficiency anemia. Chemotherapy-induced myelosuppression can cause anemia but would typically be associated with a more profound and acute drop in hemoglobin level and other cytopenias (e.g., neutropenia, thrombocytopenia). Tumor infiltration of the bone marrow can also cause anemia but would usually be accompanied by other signs and symptoms of advanced disease, such as bone pain, hypercalcemia, and leukoerythroblastic changes on peripheral blood smear.

748. A 48-year-old male with a history of acute myeloid leukemia (AML) presents with fever, shortness of breath, and a non-productive cough. His white blood cell count is 500 cells/µL, and his absolute neutrophil count (ANC) is 0 cells/µL. Chest X-ray reveals diffuse bilateral infiltrates. Which of the following is the most likely cause of this patient's pulmonary infiltrates?
a. bacterial pneumonia
b. invasive aspergillosis
c. Pneumocystis jirovecii pneumonia (PCP)
d. leukemic infiltration of the lungs

Answer: b. invasive aspergillosis. Explanation: The patient's presentation of fever, shortness of breath, and non-productive cough in the setting of AML and profound neutropenia (ANC = 0 cells/µL) is consistent with an opportunistic pulmonary infection. The most likely cause of diffuse bilateral pulmonary infiltrates in this patient is invasive aspergillosis, a life-threatening fungal infection that occurs almost exclusively in severely immunocompromised hosts, such as patients with hematologic malignancies and prolonged neutropenia. Aspergillus species are ubiquitous environmental molds that can cause invasive disease when inhaled by susceptible individuals. The diagnosis of invasive aspergillosis is challenging and often requires a combination of clinical, radiographic, and microbiological findings. Bacterial pneumonia is a common cause of pulmonary infiltrates in patients with cancer and neutropenia but would typically present with a more acute onset and focal or lobar consolidation on chest imaging. Pneumocystis jirovecii pneumonia (PCP) is another opportunistic infection that can cause diffuse pulmonary infiltrates in immunocompromised patients but is more commonly associated with cellular immune deficiencies (e.g., AIDS) than with neutropenia. Leukemic infiltration of the lungs can cause respiratory symptoms and radiographic abnormalities but would be unusual in a patient with such profound neutropenia and is more likely to present with nodular or mass-like lesions than with diffuse bilateral infiltrates.

749. A 60-year-old female with a history of non-Hodgkin lymphoma presents with new-onset seizures and altered mental status. MRI of the brain reveals multiple enhancing lesions with surrounding edema. Lumbar puncture is performed, and cerebrospinal fluid (CSF) analysis shows a white blood cell count of 20 cells/µL with 90% lymphocytes, a protein level of 80 mg/dL, and a glucose level of 40 mg/dL. Which of the following is the most likely diagnosis?
a. primary central nervous system lymphoma (PCNSL)
b. metastatic solid tumor
c. bacterial meningitis
d. herpes simplex virus (HSV) encephalitis

Answer: a. primary central nervous system lymphoma (PCNSL). Explanation: The patient's presentation of new-onset seizures and altered mental status in the setting of non-Hodgkin lymphoma and MRI findings of multiple enhancing brain lesions with edema is highly suggestive of primary central nervous system lymphoma (PCNSL), a rare and aggressive form of extranodal non-Hodgkin lymphoma that arises within the brain, spinal cord, or leptomeninges. PCNSL is more common in immunocompromised individuals, such as patients with HIV/AIDS or those who have undergone solid organ transplantation, but can also occur in immunocompetent patients with a history of systemic lymphoma. The CSF analysis in this patient, showing a lymphocytic pleocytosis with elevated protein and low glucose levels, is consistent with leptomeningeal involvement by PCNSL. Metastatic solid tumors can also cause multiple brain lesions with edema but would be unlikely to present with such a prominent CSF lymphocytosis. Bacterial meningitis and HSV encephalitis can cause altered mental status and CSF abnormalities but would typically present with more acute symptoms, higher CSF white blood cell counts with a neutrophilic predominance, and more pronounced CSF glucose hypoglycorrhachia.

750. A 72-year-old male with a history of chronic lymphocytic leukemia (CLL) presents with fatigue, weight loss, and progressive cervical lymphadenopathy. His white blood cell count is 150,000 cells/µL with 90% lymphocytes, and his hemoglobin level is 8.5 g/dL. Which of the following is the most appropriate initial treatment for this patient's CLL?
a. oral ibrutinib
b. intravenous fludarabine, cyclophosphamide, and rituximab (FCR)
c. oral chlorambucil and obinutuzumab
d. allogeneic stem cell transplantation

Answer: a. oral ibrutinib. Explanation: The patient's presentation of fatigue, weight loss, and progressive lymphadenopathy in the setting of CLL with a high white blood cell count and anemia is consistent with symptomatic, active disease that requires treatment. The most appropriate initial treatment for this patient is oral ibrutinib, a Bruton's tyrosine kinase (BTK) inhibitor that has revolutionized the management of CLL in recent years. Ibrutinib is a targeted therapy that inhibits B-cell receptor signaling and has been shown to produce durable responses and improve overall survival in patients with CLL, including those with high-risk genetic features such as del(17p) or TP53 mutations. Intravenous fludarabine, cyclophosphamide, and rituximab (FCR) is a chemoimmunotherapy regimen that was previously considered the standard of care for fit patients with CLL but has largely been replaced by ibrutinib and other novel agents due to their superior efficacy and more favorable toxicity profile. Oral chlorambucil and obinutuzumab is another chemoimmunotherapy option that may be considered for older or frail patients with CLL who are not candidates for ibrutinib or FCR, but it is not the preferred first-line therapy for most patients. Allogeneic stem cell transplantation is a potentially curative option for younger, fit patients with high-risk or refractory CLL but is not typically used as initial therapy due to the associated morbidity and mortality.

751. A 58-year-old female with a history of metastatic breast cancer presents with severe back pain and lower extremity weakness. MRI of the spine reveals multiple vertebral metastases with epidural extension and spinal cord compression at T8. Which of the following is the most appropriate initial management for this patient's condition?
a. intravenous bisphosphonates and radiation therapy
b. high-dose systemic corticosteroids and chemotherapy
c. emergent surgical decompression and stabilization
d. intrathecal chemotherapy and radiation therapy

Answer: c. emergent surgical decompression and stabilization. Explanation: The patient's presentation of severe back pain and lower extremity weakness in the setting of metastatic breast cancer and MRI findings of vertebral metastases with epidural extension and spinal cord compression is consistent with malignant spinal cord compression (MSCC), a medical emergency that requires prompt intervention to prevent permanent neurological deficits. The most appropriate initial management for this patient is emergent surgical decompression and stabilization to relieve pressure on the spinal cord, restore neurological function, and prevent further progression of the disease. Surgical intervention is particularly indicated in patients with MSCC who have spinal instability, rapidly progressive neurological deficits, or a radioresistant tumor such as breast cancer. Intravenous bisphosphonates and radiation therapy are important adjunctive treatments for patients with MSCC but are not sufficient as sole interventions in the setting of acute spinal cord compression. High-dose systemic corticosteroids (e.g., dexamethasone) can help to reduce edema and inflammation around the spinal cord but should be used in conjunction with, not instead of, surgical decompression. Intrathecal chemotherapy and radiation therapy are not typically used for the initial management of MSCC and may be associated with a higher risk of complications compared to systemic therapy.

752. A 65-year-old male with a history of chronic myeloid leukemia (CML) presents with fatigue, weight loss, and splenomegaly. His white blood cell count is 250,000 cells/μL with 80% myeloblasts, and his platelet count is 50,000 cells/μL. Bone marrow biopsy reveals 70% myeloblasts with cytogenetic evidence of t(9;22) translocation. Which of the following is the most likely diagnosis?
a. chronic phase CML
b. accelerated phase CML
c. blast phase CML
d. acute myeloid leukemia (AML)

Answer: c. blast phase CML. Explanation: The patient's presentation of fatigue, weight loss, and splenomegaly in the setting of CML with a high white blood cell count, thrombocytopenia, and increased myeloblasts in the peripheral blood and bone marrow is consistent with blast phase (BP) CML, also known as blast crisis. BP-CML is an advanced stage of the disease characterized by the rapid proliferation and accumulation of immature myeloid or lymphoid blast cells, typically defined as ≥20% blasts in the blood or bone marrow. The presence of t(9;22) translocation, also known as the Philadelphia chromosome, is a hallmark of CML and confirms the diagnosis. Chronic phase CML is the initial stage of the disease and is characterized by a marked leukocytosis with predominance of mature myeloid cells, splenomegaly, and absent or minimal symptoms. Accelerated phase CML is an intermediate stage between chronic and blast phases and is defined by the presence of 10-19% blasts in the blood or bone marrow, basophilia, persistent thrombocytopenia or thrombocytosis, and clonal cytogenetic evolution. Acute myeloid leukemia (AML) is a separate entity from CML and is characterized by the proliferation of immature myeloid blast cells with distinct genetic and molecular abnormalities. While BP-CML can resemble AML morphologically, the presence of t(9;22) translocation and a history of CML favor the diagnosis of BP-CML over de novo AML.

753. A 70-year-old female with a history of multiple myeloma presents with severe anemia and acute renal failure. Her hemoglobin level is 6.5 g/dL, and her serum creatinine is 4.5 mg/dL (baseline 1.0 mg/dL). Peripheral blood smear reveals numerous red blood cell fragments and schistocytes. Which of the following is the most likely cause of this patient's presentation?
a. chemotherapy-induced myelosuppression
b. myeloma kidney (cast nephropathy)
c. hyperviscosity syndrome
d. thrombotic microangiopathy

Answer: d. thrombotic microangiopathy. Explanation: The patient's presentation of severe anemia and acute renal failure in the setting of multiple myeloma, along with the presence of red blood cell fragments and schistocytes on peripheral blood smear, is highly suggestive of a thrombotic microangiopathy (TMA), such as thrombotic thrombocytopenic purpura (TTP) or atypical hemolytic uremic syndrome (aHUS). TMAs are rare but life-threatening complications of multiple myeloma that are characterized by microangiopathic hemolytic anemia (MAHA), thrombocytopenia, and end-organ damage, particularly acute kidney injury. The pathogenesis of TMAs in multiple myeloma is complex and may involve direct endothelial damage by monoclonal proteins, immune-mediated mechanisms, and acquired deficiencies of ADAMTS13 (a metalloprotease that cleaves von Willebrand factor).

754. What aspect of the PQRSTU method helps to understand the triggers or relieving factors of a patient's pain?
a. Provocation/Palliation
b. Quality
c. Region/Radiation
d. Timing

Answer: a. Provocation/Palliation. Explanation: The "P" in PQRSTU stands for Provocation/Palliation, which involves understanding what activities, movements, or external factors provoke the pain or make it worse, as well as what actions or treatments alleviate it, providing valuable insights into the nature and potential causes of the pain.

755. Which pain assessment tool is most suitable for non-verbal patients?
a. Numeric Rating Scale (NRS)
b. Visual Analog Scale (VAS)
c. FACES scale
d. PQRSTU method

Answer: c. FACES scale. Explanation: The FACES scale, which utilizes a series of facial expressions to represent levels of pain, is particularly suitable for non-verbal patients, including children or those who are unable to communicate their pain verbally, allowing them to indicate their pain intensity by pointing to the face that best represents their pain.

756. In the context of pain management, what does the "Quality" component of the PQRSTU method refer to?
a. The intensity of the pain
b. The physical location of the pain
c. The descriptive characteristics of the pain (sharp, dull, burning, etc.)
d. The duration of the pain episodes

Answer: c. The descriptive characteristics of the pain (sharp, dull, burning, etc.). Explanation: The "Quality" component of the PQRSTU method refers to the descriptive characteristics of the pain, such as whether it is sharp, dull, throbbing, burning, or shooting. This helps to further define the nature of the pain and can provide clues to its etiology.

757. How does the Numeric Rating Scale (NRS) quantify pain?
a. By using a series of images depicting different levels of discomfort
b. Through patient selection of a number from 0 (no pain) to 10 (worst pain imaginable)
c. By measuring the physical response to pain stimuli
d. Through detailed patient descriptions of the pain experience

Answer: b. Through patient selection of a number from 0 (no pain) to 10 (worst pain imaginable). Explanation: The Numeric Rating Scale (NRS) quantifies pain by asking the patient to select a number from 0, representing no pain, to 10, representing the worst pain imaginable. This provides a simple and straightforward way to gauge pain intensity.

758. What does the "Timing" component in the PQRSTU assessment help to determine about a patient's pain?
a. The effectiveness of pain medication over time
b. The frequency and duration of pain episodes
c. The patient's emotional response to pain
d. The anatomical pathway of pain transmission

Answer: b. The frequency and duration of pain episodes. Explanation: The "Timing" component of the PQRSTU assessment is concerned with understanding the frequency and duration of pain episodes, including when the pain occurs, how long it lasts, and if there is any pattern, which can be critical for diagnosing and managing pain effectively.

759. In which scenario would the Visual Analog Scale (VAS) be preferred over the Numeric Rating Scale (NRS) for pain assessment?
a. When the patient has a cognitive impairment
b. In research settings where visual representation of pain intensity is required
c. For patients who are unable to understand numerical values
d. In emergency situations where quick assessment is necessary

Answer: b. In research settings where visual representation of pain intensity is required. Explanation: The Visual Analog Scale (VAS), which typically involves a line marked from "no pain" to "worst pain imaginable," can be particularly useful in research settings where a visual representation of pain intensity changes over time is required, as it allows for more nuanced distinctions in pain levels.

760. What role does the "U=You" component play in the PQRSTU pain assessment method?
a. It assesses the patient's understanding of their pain condition
b. It evaluates the impact of pain on the patient's daily function and quality of life
c. It determines the patient's personal pain threshold
d. It gauges the patient's willingness to undergo pain treatment

Answer: b. It evaluates the impact of pain on the patient's daily function and quality of life. Explanation: The "U=You" component of the PQRSTU method focuses on understanding the impact of pain on the patient's daily activities, function, and overall quality of life, emphasizing the personal and subjective experience of pain and its broader implications.

761. When using the FACES scale for pediatric patients, what is a critical consideration for accurate pain assessment?
a. Ensuring the child is accompanied by a parent
b. Choosing the appropriate version of the scale for the child's age and developmental level
c. Administering an analgesic before assessment to observe changes
d. Using the scale only for acute pain conditions

Answer: b. Choosing the appropriate version of the scale for the child's age and developmental level. Explanation: When using the FACES scale for pediatric patients, it's critical to choose the appropriate version of the scale that matches the child's age and developmental level to ensure they can accurately associate their pain with the depicted expressions, facilitating more accurate pain assessment.

762. In managing a patient with chronic pain, how does the "Region/Radiation" aspect of the PQRSTU assessment inform treatment planning?
a. By identifying potential areas for surgical intervention
b. By pinpointing the source of pain for targeted physical therapy
c. Through highlighting areas at risk of developing pressure ulcers
d. By determining the need for regional anesthesia

Answer: b. By pinpointing the source of pain for targeted physical therapy. Explanation: The "Region/Radiation" aspect of the PQRSTU assessment helps in pinpointing the specific location of the pain and any areas to which the pain may radiate. This information is crucial for targeted interventions such as physical therapy, where treatments can be directed specifically to the affected areas to alleviate pain and improve function.

763. A key risk factor for Clostridium difficile Infection (CDI) includes:
a. Recent use of antacids
b. Use of broad-spectrum antibiotics
c. Consumption of probiotic foods
d. Use of topical antibiotics

Answer: b. Use of broad-spectrum antibiotics. Explanation: The use of broad-spectrum antibiotics disrupts normal gut flora, creating an environment conducive to Clostridium difficile overgrowth and toxin production, leading to CDI.

764. The gold standard for diagnosing CDI is:
a. Stool culture for Clostridium difficile
b. PCR testing for Clostridium difficile toxin genes
c. Serology testing for Clostridium difficile antibodies
d. Complete blood count showing leukocytosis

Answer: b. PCR testing for Clostridium difficile toxin genes. Explanation: PCR testing for C. difficile toxin genes is highly sensitive and specific, making it a preferred diagnostic method for detecting the presence of toxin-producing C. difficile strains in stool samples.

765. In the management of CDI, the first step should be:
a. Administration of oral metronidazole
b. Discontinuation of the inciting antibiotic, if possible
c. Immediate colectomy to prevent complications
d. Initiation of probiotics

Answer: b. Discontinuation of the inciting antibiotic, if possible. Explanation: Discontinuing the inciting antibiotic can often lead to resolution of mild CDI cases and is a critical first step in management before initiating specific CDI treatment.

766. For a patient with severe CDI, the recommended treatment is:
a. Oral vancomycin or fidaxomicin
b. Intravenous immunoglobulin therapy
c. High-dose intravenous metronidazole
d. Loperamide to control diarrhea

Answer: a. Oral vancomycin or fidaxomicin. Explanation: For severe CDI cases, oral vancomycin or fidaxomicin is recommended due to their efficacy in targeting C. difficile in the colon, where the infection resides.

767. A hallmark finding on colonoscopy for a patient with CDI is:
a. Transmural inflammation

b. Granulomas
c. Pseudomembranous colitis
d. Diverticulosis

Answer: c. Pseudomembranous colitis. Explanation: Pseudomembranous colitis, characterized by raised yellow plaques (pseudomembranes) visible on colonoscopy, is a hallmark finding in CDI and provides direct visual evidence of the infection.

768. In recurrent CDI cases, a recommended treatment approach is:
a. Repeated courses of the same antibiotic used initially
b. Fecal microbiota transplantation (FMT)
c. Lifetime administration of oral vancomycin
d. Permanent discontinuation of all antibiotics

Answer: b. Fecal microbiota transplantation (FMT). Explanation: Fecal microbiota transplantation (FMT) has emerged as an effective treatment for recurrent CDI by restoring healthy gut flora, thereby outcompeting C. difficile.

769. For a patient with CDI and renal insufficiency, caution should be exercised when prescribing:
a. Oral vancomycin
b. Oral fidaxomicin
c. Intravenous metronidazole
d. Oral metronidazole

Answer: d. Oral metronidazole. Explanation: In patients with renal insufficiency, caution is advised with oral metronidazole due to potential neurotoxicity; oral vancomycin or fidaxomicin may be safer alternatives as they are minimally absorbed systemically.

770. A nonpharmacologic intervention to prevent the spread of CDI in healthcare settings includes:
a. Handwashing with alcohol-based hand rubs exclusively
b. Use of private rooms for all patients
c. Strict contact precautions and hand hygiene with soap and water
d. Mandatory antibiotic prophylaxis for all admitted patients

Answer: c. Strict contact precautions and hand hygiene with soap and water. Explanation: Strict contact precautions, including the use of gloves and gowns and handwashing with soap and water (since alcohol-based hand rubs are not effective against C. difficile spores), are critical to prevent the spread of CDI in healthcare settings.

771. Advanced age is a risk factor for CDI due to:
a. Increased use of antacids in this population
b. More frequent exposure to hospital environments and antibiotic use

c. Higher consumption of probiotics
d. Decreased mobility leading to prolonged hospital stays

Answer: b. More frequent exposure to hospital environments and antibiotic use. Explanation: Advanced age is associated with increased healthcare exposure, including hospitalizations and antibiotic use, both of which are significant risk factors for CDI.

772. In a patient with CDI, the presence of leukocytosis and acute kidney injury indicates:
a. A mild form of CDI that can be managed with dietary changes
b. Severe CDI, warranting aggressive treatment and close monitoring
c. An unrelated comorbidity that should be addressed separately
d. A false-positive result for CDI necessitating retesting

Answer: b. Severe CDI, warranting aggressive treatment and close monitoring. Explanation: Leukocytosis and acute kidney injury in the context of CDI are indicative of a severe infection, necessitating aggressive management with appropriate antibiotics and close clinical monitoring to prevent complications.

773. What is the maximum recommended daily dose of acetaminophen for an adult to avoid the risk of hepatotoxicity?
a. 2 grams
b. 3 grams
c. 4 grams
d. 5 grams

Answer: c. 4 grams. Explanation: The maximum recommended daily dose of acetaminophen for an adult is 4 grams to avoid the risk of hepatotoxicity. Exceeding this amount can lead to liver damage due to the accumulation of toxic metabolites.

774. Which of the following is a characteristic adverse effect associated with non-selective NSAIDs due to COX-1 inhibition?
a. Hypertension
b. Gastrointestinal bleeding
c. Bronchospasm
d. Sedation

Answer: b. Gastrointestinal bleeding. Explanation: Non-selective NSAIDs inhibit both COX-1 and COX-2 enzymes. COX-1 inhibition can lead to reduced protection of the gastric mucosa, increasing the risk of gastrointestinal bleeding.

775. For a patient with a history of renal insufficiency, which class of non-opioid analgesics should be used with caution due to the potential for worsening renal function?

a. Acetaminophen
b. NSAIDs
c. Antidepressants
d. Anticonvulsants

Answer: b. NSAIDs. Explanation: NSAIDs should be used with caution in patients with renal insufficiency because they can reduce renal blood flow by inhibiting prostaglandins that dilate afferent arterioles, potentially worsening renal function.

776. Which COX-2 inhibitor is known for its analgesic and anti-inflammatory effects with a lower risk of gastrointestinal side effects compared to non-selective NSAIDs?
a. Ibuprofen
b. Naproxen
c. Celecoxib
d. Acetaminophen

Answer: c. Celecoxib. Explanation: Celecoxib is a COX-2 inhibitor that provides analgesic and anti-inflammatory effects similar to non-selective NSAIDs but with a lower risk of gastrointestinal side effects due to its selective inhibition of COX-2, which is less involved in the protection of the gastrointestinal mucosa.

777. In managing pain for a patient at risk of cardiovascular events, why might a physician prefer acetaminophen over NSAIDs?
a. Acetaminophen has antiplatelet effects
b. NSAIDs can increase the risk of cardiovascular events
c. Acetaminophen is a stronger anti-inflammatory agent
d. NSAIDs can lower blood pressure

Answer: b. NSAIDs can increase the risk of cardiovascular events. Explanation: A physician might prefer acetaminophen over NSAIDs for pain management in patients at risk of cardiovascular events because some NSAIDs have been associated with an increased risk of cardiovascular events such as heart attack and stroke.

778. What is a common strategy to mitigate the risk of gastrointestinal complications when prescribing NSAIDs for long-term pain management?
a. Co-prescription of a proton pump inhibitor (PPI)
b. Increasing the NSAID dose gradually
c. Switching to a high-dose acetaminophen regimen
d. Administering NSAIDs on an empty stomach

Answer: a. Co-prescription of a proton pump inhibitor (PPI). Explanation: Co-prescribing a proton pump inhibitor (PPI) is a common strategy to mitigate the risk of gastrointestinal complications associated with long-term NSAID use, as PPIs can help protect the gastric mucosa from the erosive effects of NSAIDs.

779. Which of the following patients would be most at risk for developing NSAID-induced nephrotoxicity?
a. A young adult with no prior medical history
b. An elderly patient with congestive heart failure
c. A patient with a recent history of viral infection
d. A patient taking low-dose aspirin for cardioprotection

Answer: b. An elderly patient with congestive heart failure. Explanation: An elderly patient with congestive heart failure would be most at risk for developing NSAID-induced nephrotoxicity due to compromised renal perfusion and the reliance on prostaglandin-mediated renal blood flow, which can be inhibited by NSAIDs.

780. In the context of NSAID therapy, what is the primary therapeutic action of COX-2 inhibition?
a. Decreased platelet aggregation
b. Reduction of fever
c. Relief of pain and inflammation
d. Protection of the gastric mucosa

Answer: c. Relief of pain and inflammation. Explanation: The primary therapeutic action of COX-2 inhibition in the context of NSAID therapy is the relief of pain and inflammation. COX-2 is predominantly involved in the synthesis of prostaglandins that mediate inflammation and pain.

781. Why might a patient with asthma need to avoid certain NSAIDs?
a. NSAIDs can cause bronchospasm in sensitive individuals
b. NSAIDs directly increase mucus production in the airways
c. NSAIDs decrease the effectiveness of asthma medications
d. NSAIDs can lead to the development of allergic rhinitis

Answer: a. NSAIDs can cause bronchospasm in sensitive individuals. Explanation: Certain NSAIDs can cause bronchospasm in individuals with asthma due to their ability to shift arachidonic acid metabolism from prostaglandin synthesis to leukotriene synthesis, which can exacerbate asthma symptoms.

782. A common adverse effect of opioid analgesics like morphine and hydromorphone is:
a. Diuresis
b. Hypertension
c. Respiratory depression
d. Tachycardia

Answer: c. Respiratory depression. Explanation: Respiratory depression is a well-known and potentially serious adverse effect of opioid analgesics, resulting from their action on the brainstem respiratory centers.

783. In converting from oral morphine to transdermal fentanyl, it is important to consider:
a. Transdermal fentanyl is 100 times more potent than oral morphine
b. Oral morphine has a longer half-life than transdermal fentanyl
c. Transdermal fentanyl should be applied twice daily
d. Oral morphine is more potent on a milligram-for-milligram basis

Answer: a. Transdermal fentanyl is 100 times more potent than oral morphine. Explanation: When converting from oral morphine to transdermal fentanyl, the increased potency of fentanyl must be accounted for to avoid overdose; fentanyl is approximately 100 times more potent than morphine.

784. A Patient-Controlled Analgesia (PCA) pump setting for morphine might include a demand dose of 1 mg with a lockout interval of:
a. 2 minutes
b. 6 minutes
c. 15 minutes
d. 30 minutes

Answer: b. 6 minutes. Explanation: A typical lockout interval for a PCA pump using morphine is often set around 5-10 minutes to prevent overdosing while allowing adequate pain control, making 6 minutes a reasonable choice.

785. The basal rate in a PCA pump refers to:
a. The maximum dose allowed per hour
b. A continuous infusion rate of the analgesic
c. The minimum dose required to prevent withdrawal
d. The time between demand doses

Answer: b. A continuous infusion rate of the analgesic. Explanation: The basal rate on a PCA pump is a continuous infusion rate that provides a steady level of analgesic to maintain baseline pain control, in addition to the on-demand doses controlled by the patient.

786. Hydromorphone is preferred over morphine in patients with renal impairment because:
a. It has a longer duration of action
b. It is less likely to accumulate active metabolites
c. It provides better gastrointestinal motility
d. It has a lower risk of causing allergies

Answer: b. It is less likely to accumulate active metabolites. Explanation: Hydromorphone is often preferred in patients with renal impairment because it is less likely to accumulate neurotoxic metabolites compared to morphine, which has metabolites that can accumulate in renal failure and exacerbate side effects.

787. The equianalgesic dose conversion is most important when:
a. Switching between different routes of administration for the same opioid
b. Increasing the dose of the same opioid and route of administration
c. Adding a non-opioid analgesic to the regimen
d. Applying topical analgesics in addition to oral opioids

Answer: a. Switching between different routes of administration for the same opioid. Explanation: Equianalgesic dose conversion is crucial when switching opioids or changing routes of administration to ensure equivalent pain control and minimize the risk of overdose.

788. One reason for opioid rotation in pain management is to:
a. Increase the analgesic effect without increasing the dose
b. Minimize the risk of addiction
c. Reduce the development of tolerance and manage side effects
d. Simplify the medication regimen

Answer: c. Reduce the development of tolerance and manage side effects. Explanation: Opioid rotation, or switching from one opioid to another, can help manage opioid tolerance and side effects, improving pain control by exploiting differences in opioid receptor interactions.

789. For a patient with a history of substance abuse, opioid management may require:
a. Avoiding opioids altogether, regardless of pain severity
b. Utilizing a multimodal pain management approach and close monitoring
c. Doubling the standard opioid dose for efficacy
d. Restricting pain management to non-pharmacological methods only

Answer: b. Utilizing a multimodal pain management approach and close monitoring. Explanation: In patients with a history of substance abuse, a careful, multimodal approach to pain management, including non-opioid analgesics, non-pharmacological methods, and close monitoring of opioid use, is essential to balance effective pain control with the risk of relapse.

790. The use of a PCA pump allows for:
a. Unlimited access to opioids for the patient
b. Enhanced patient mobility and independence in pain management
c. The patient to bypass set dosing schedules completely
d. Healthcare providers to administer higher doses of opioids safely

Answer: b. Enhanced patient mobility and independence in pain management. Explanation: PCA pumps empower patients by allowing them to self-administer pain medication within preset limits, enhancing their control over pain management and potentially improving pain control and satisfaction.

791. When initiating opioid therapy for chronic pain, it's essential to:
a. Start with the highest effective dose to ensure immediate relief
b. Combine multiple opioids to enhance analgesic effect
c. Establish goals for pain management and functionality
d. Disregard non-opioid therapies as they are generally ineffective

Answer: c. Establish goals for pain management and functionality. Explanation: When starting opioid therapy for chronic pain, it's crucial to establish clear goals for pain management and functionality, ensuring that the benefits of opioid use outweigh the risks while considering the patient's overall quality of life.

792. An appropriate indication for spinal cord stimulation (SCS) is:
a. Acute postoperative pain
b. Chronic neuropathic pain unresponsive to conventional treatments
c. Generalized anxiety disorder
d. Acute muscle strain

Answer: b. Chronic neuropathic pain unresponsive to conventional treatments. Explanation: Spinal cord stimulation is indicated for chronic neuropathic pain conditions that have not responded to conventional medical management, including medications, physical therapy, and less invasive pain management techniques.

793. The trial period for spinal cord stimulation typically involves:
a. Permanent implantation without a trial
b. A 1-year trial period with an external device
c. A short-term (5-7 days) evaluation with a temporary electrode
d. A 6-month trial with daily hospital visits

Answer: c. A short-term (5-7 days) evaluation with a temporary electrode. Explanation: Before permanent SCS implantation, a trial period with a temporary electrode is conducted to assess the effectiveness of the therapy. This usually lasts about 5-7 days and allows the patient and clinician to determine if significant pain relief is achieved.

794. Epidural nerve blocks are commonly used for pain relief in:
a. Chronic back pain with radiculopathy
b. Headaches and migraines
c. Post-herpetic neuralgia
d. Diabetic neuropathy

Answer: a. Chronic back pain with radiculopathy. Explanation: Epidural nerve blocks, involving the injection of steroids or anesthetics into the epidural space of the spine, are often used to manage chronic back pain, particularly when associated with radiculopathy or sciatica.

795. A contraindication for the use of sympathetic nerve blocks is:
a. Complex regional pain syndrome (CRPS)
b. Coagulopathy or use of anticoagulant therapy
c. Post-surgical pain
d. Cancer-related pain

Answer: b. Coagulopathy or use of anticoagulant therapy. Explanation: Sympathetic nerve blocks should be used cautiously or avoided in patients with coagulopathies or those on anticoagulant therapy due to the increased risk of bleeding complications.

796. Peripheral nerve blocks are particularly beneficial for:
a. Generalized fibromyalgia pain
b. Targeted pain relief in a specific nerve distribution
c. Widespread chronic pain conditions
d. Central pain syndromes

Answer: b. Targeted pain relief in a specific nerve distribution. Explanation: Peripheral nerve blocks involve the injection of anesthetic near a specific nerve or nerve group to provide targeted pain relief in the area supplied by that nerve, making it suitable for conditions with localized pain.

797. The main advantage of patient-controlled analgesia (PCA) in pain management is:
a. It allows for continuous, high-dose opioid administration
b. Patients can self-administer pain medication as needed, enhancing pain control and patient satisfaction
c. It eliminates the need for oral pain medications
d. It is suitable for all patient populations, including those with cognitive impairments

Answer: b. Patients can self-administer pain medication as needed, enhancing pain control and patient satisfaction. Explanation: PCA enables patients to self-administer a predetermined dose of pain medication when needed, within safe limits, providing more personalized pain control and increasing patient satisfaction by allowing them to manage their own pain relief.

798. The basal rate in a PCA device refers to:
a. The maximum dose a patient can administer in one hour
b. A continuous infusion rate of the analgesic, independent of patient demand doses
c. The total amount of medication used in 24 hours
d. The minimum interval between doses

Answer: b. A continuous infusion rate of the analgesic, independent of patient demand doses. Explanation: The basal rate in PCA refers to a continuous, low-level infusion of pain medication provided by the device, alongside the ability for patients to self-administer additional doses as needed (demand doses).

799. In interventional pain management, the lockout interval in PCA is designed to:
a. Allow unlimited access to pain medication for the patient
b. Prevent overdose by limiting the frequency at which a patient can self-administer additional doses
c. Increase the basal rate automatically based on patient usage
d. Lock the device after a set number of uses

Answer: b. Prevent overdose by limiting the frequency at which a patient can self-administer additional doses. Explanation: The lockout interval is a safety feature in PCA devices that prevents patients from administering additional doses of medication too frequently, thereby reducing the risk of overdose.

800. When considering a patient for spinal cord stimulation, it's important to:
a. Ensure the patient has tried and failed at least one surgery for pain relief
b. Confirm the absence of psychological factors contributing to the pain
c. Assess for the presence of an active infection, which would contraindicate the procedure
d. Determine if the patient prefers not to take oral pain medications

Answer: c. Assess for the presence of an active infection, which would contraindicate the procedure. Explanation: An active infection is a contraindication for spinal cord stimulation due to the risk of spreading the infection through the implanted device. Patients must be screened carefully for infections before proceeding with SCS.

801. What is the primary purpose of the Beers Criteria in geriatric medicine?
a. To identify high-cost medications for budgeting purposes
b. To list preferred medications for common geriatric conditions
c. To outline potentially inappropriate medications for older adults
d. To provide a comprehensive list of all medications safe for geriatric use

Answer: c. To outline potentially inappropriate medications for older adults. Explanation: The Beers Criteria serves to outline potentially inappropriate medications (PIMs) for older adults, aiming to improve medication selection and reduce adverse drug events in the geriatric population by highlighting drugs with a higher risk of causing harm.

802. During medication reconciliation, what is the significance of obtaining a Best Possible Medication History (BPMH)?
a. It ensures the patient's medication costs are minimized
b. It helps in identifying discrepancies between prescribed and actual medication use
c. It provides a list of medications the patient is allergic to
d. It is used to prescribe new medications during hospital admission

Answer: b. It helps in identifying discrepancies between prescribed and actual medication use. Explanation: The Best Possible Medication History (BPMH) is a comprehensive and accurate account of a patient's medication regimen, obtained through a structured process. It helps in identifying discrepancies between what the patient should be taking (as per medical records) and what they are actually taking, which is critical for ensuring medication safety and efficacy.

803. In the context of polypharmacy in older adults, why is it important to regularly review a patient's medication regimen?
a. To switch all medications to generic versions
b. To ensure compliance with the latest clinical guidelines
c. To identify and minimize the use of unnecessary or harmful medications
d. To continually increase dosages to meet changing health needs

Answer: c. To identify and minimize the use of unnecessary or harmful medications. Explanation: Regularly reviewing a patient's medication regimen in the context of polypharmacy is important to identify and minimize the use of unnecessary or potentially harmful medications, thereby reducing the risk of adverse drug events, interactions, and improving overall patient care in older adults.

804. What role does patient education play in managing polypharmacy in the geriatric population?
a. It ensures that patients will self-prescribe additional medications
b. It helps patients understand the purpose and potential side effects of their medications, promoting adherence and safe use
c. It encourages patients to rely solely on non-pharmacological treatments
d. It prepares patients to conduct their own medication reconciliation

Answer: b. It helps patients understand the purpose and potential side effects of their medications, promoting adherence and safe use. Explanation: Patient education is crucial in managing polypharmacy among the elderly, as it helps them understand the rationale, benefits, and potential side effects of their medications. Informed patients are more likely to adhere to their prescribed regimens and communicate about any issues, contributing to safer medication use.

805. How can healthcare providers reduce the risk of adverse drug reactions in older adults with multiple comorbidities?
a. By prescribing the maximum doses recommended for each condition
b. Through the use of as many medications as possible to address all symptoms
c. By prioritizing medications for the most life-threatening conditions only
d. Through careful selection, dosing, and monitoring of medications to avoid interactions and side effects

Answer: d. Through careful selection, dosing, and monitoring of medications to avoid interactions and side effects. Explanation: In older adults with multiple comorbidities, the risk of adverse drug reactions can be reduced through careful medication selection, appropriate dosing, and diligent monitoring. This approach helps to minimize drug-drug and drug-disease interactions and mitigate side effects, particularly important in this vulnerable population.

806. What is a common challenge in the medication reconciliation process for geriatric patients upon hospital admission?
a. Determining the brand names of all medications the patient is taking
b. Ensuring all medications are available in the hospital formulary
c. Obtaining an accurate and complete list of home medications, including over-the-counter drugs and supplements
d. Converting all oral medications to their injectable equivalents

Answer: c. Obtaining an accurate and complete list of home medications, including over-the-counter drugs and supplements. Explanation: A common challenge in the medication reconciliation process for geriatric patients upon hospital admission is obtaining an accurate and complete list of all medications the patient is taking at home, including prescription drugs, over-the-counter medications, and supplements, which is essential for preventing adverse drug events and ensuring continuity of care.

807. In managing an older adult patient's medication regimen, why is it important to consider the pharmacokinetic changes that occur with aging?
a. Older adults metabolize medications more quickly, requiring higher doses
b. Aging can affect drug absorption, distribution, metabolism, and excretion, impacting drug effectiveness and risk of side effects
c. All older adults require the same dose adjustments based on age alone
d. Pharmacokinetic changes lead to a decreased need for medications in older age

Answer: b. Aging can affect drug absorption, distribution, metabolism, and excretion, impacting drug effectiveness and risk of side effects. Explanation: Considering pharmacokinetic changes with aging is crucial because these changes can affect how drugs are absorbed, distributed, metabolized, and excreted in the body, thereby impacting their effectiveness and increasing the risk of side effects and toxicity in older adults.

808. When might a healthcare provider choose to deprescribe a medication in an older adult patient?
a. When the medication is no longer effective for its intended use
b. As soon as any side effect is reported, regardless of severity
c. Only at the patient's request, without clinical justification
d. When the medication is a non-prescription, over-the-counter drug

Answer: a. When the medication is no longer effective for its intended use. Explanation: Deprescribing may be chosen when a medication is no longer effective for its intended use or when its risks outweigh the benefits, especially in the context of the patient's overall health status, goals of care, and life expectancy. This process involves careful evaluation and shared decision-making with the patient.

809. What is an essential aspect of the Best Possible Medication History (BPMH) process in older adults?
a. Relying solely on the patient's memory for medication information
b. Including only those medications prescribed within the last month

c. Involving a detailed review of all medications, including how they are actually being taken, using multiple sources of information
d. Assuming that the current medication list in the electronic health record is accurate and complete

Answer: c. Involving a detailed review of all medications, including how they are actually being taken, using multiple sources of information. Explanation: An essential aspect of the BPMH process is conducting a detailed review of all medications the older adult is taking, including prescription drugs, over-the-counter medications, and supplements, and understanding how they are actually being taken. This often involves using multiple sources of information, such as patient interviews, pharmacy records, and family input, to ensure accuracy and completeness.

810. One major modifiable risk factor for falls in the elderly is:
a. Genetic predisposition
b. Use of multiple medications, especially sedatives and antihypertensives
c. Age over 65 years
d. Gender

Answer: b. Use of multiple medications, especially sedatives and antihypertensives. Explanation: Polypharmacy, particularly the use of medications like sedatives and antihypertensives, can increase the risk of falls due to their effects on balance, coordination, and blood pressure, making them a significant modifiable risk factor.

811. An effective environmental modification to prevent falls in the home includes:
a. Lowering the temperature in living spaces
b. Installation of grab bars in the bathroom
c. Dim lighting to reduce glare
d. Use of high-pile carpets for soft landing

Answer: b. Installation of grab bars in the bathroom. Explanation: Installing grab bars in key areas like the bathroom provides support and stability, significantly reducing the risk of falls, particularly in individuals with mobility or balance issues.

812. A history of previous falls is considered:
a. Only relevant if injuries were sustained
b. A strong predictor of future falls
c. Less important than other risk factors like age
d. Unrelated to future fall risk

Answer: b. A strong predictor of future falls. Explanation: A history of previous falls is a significant predictor of future falls, as it often indicates underlying balance, strength, or cognitive impairments that increase fall risk.

813. Regular exercise recommended to reduce fall risk primarily focuses on:

a. High-intensity cardiovascular workouts
b. Strength training and balance exercises
c. Flexibility training only
d. Passive range-of-motion exercises

Answer: b. Strength training and balance exercises. Explanation: Strength and balance exercises, such as tai chi or supervised physical therapy programs, are particularly effective in reducing fall risk by improving muscle strength, coordination, and stability.

814. Vitamin D supplementation is recommended for fall prevention because it:
a. Directly improves balance and coordination
b. Enhances mood and cognitive function
c. Contributes to bone health and may reduce fall-induced injuries
d. Increases muscle mass rapidly

Answer: c. Contributes to bone health and may reduce fall-induced injuries. Explanation: Vitamin D plays a crucial role in calcium absorption and bone health; adequate levels can help maintain bone strength and reduce the risk of fractures in the event of a fall.

815. In assessing fall risk, gait and balance impairment can be evaluated using:
a. Comprehensive genetic testing
b. The Timed Up and Go (TUG) test
c. Daily temperature monitoring
d. Continuous heart rate monitoring

Answer: b. The Timed Up and Go (TUG) test. Explanation: The Timed Up and Go (TUG) test is a simple and quick assessment used to evaluate a person's mobility and balance by timing how long it takes to stand up from a seated position, walk a short distance, turn around, walk back, and sit down.

816. Environmental assessments for fall prevention in older adults should include:
a. Checking for adequate social support networks
b. Ensuring there is minimal furniture to navigate around
c. Reviewing personal medication regimes
d. Ensuring floors are clutter-free and well-lit pathways are available

Answer: d. Ensuring floors are clutter-free and well-lit pathways are available. Explanation: Reducing environmental hazards such as clutter and ensuring adequate lighting, especially along pathways and stairs, are critical steps in minimizing fall risks in the home.

817. The role of assistive devices in fall prevention is to:

a. Completely replace the need for personal mobility
b. Provide support and stability during movement
c. Serve as a long-term solution for gait abnormalities
d. Enhance the aesthetic of home environments

Answer: b. Provide support and stability during movement. Explanation: Assistive devices like canes or walkers provide additional support and stability for individuals with mobility or balance issues, aiding in safer ambulation and reducing the risk of falls.

818. A comprehensive fall prevention program for older adults should NOT include:
a. Regular vision and hearing checks
b. Scheduled napping to prevent fatigue
c. Assessment and modification of home hazards
d. Education on the risks of sedentary behavior

Answer: b. Scheduled napping to prevent fatigue. Explanation: While adequate rest is important, scheduled napping is not typically a component of fall prevention programs. Focus is rather on physical activity, environmental safety, and health assessments.

819. For a patient with a fear of falling due to a previous fall, an effective intervention is:
a. Limiting physical activity to reduce the risk of falls
b. Cognitive-behavioral therapy to address fear and build confidence
c. Immediate use of a wheelchair for all mobility
d. Avoiding leaving the home to minimize fall risk

Answer: b. Cognitive-behavioral therapy to address fear and build confidence. Explanation: Cognitive-behavioral therapy can be effective for patients with a fear of falling, as it addresses the psychological aspects of fear, helps build confidence in mobility, and encourages safe, gradual increases in physical activity.

820. Which stage of the NPUAP classification system describes a pressure injury with full-thickness skin loss, where adipose is visible, and granulation tissue and epibole (rolled wound edges) may be present?
a. Stage 1
b. Stage 2
c. Stage 3
d. Stage 4

Answer: c. Stage 3. Explanation: Stage 3 of the NPUAP classification system describes a pressure injury with full-thickness skin loss, where adipose tissue is visible but bone, tendon, and muscle are not exposed. Granulation tissue and epibole (rolled wound edges) may also be present in this stage.

821. In the Braden Scale for predicting pressure sore risk, which factor is not assessed?
a. Nutritional status
b. Cognitive function
c. Moisture
d. Activity level

Answer: b. Cognitive function. Explanation: The Braden Scale assesses risk factors including sensory perception, moisture, activity, mobility, nutrition, and friction/shear. Cognitive function is not directly assessed by the Braden Scale, although it may indirectly affect other assessed factors.

822. What is the primary goal of using pressure redistribution devices in the prevention of pressure injuries?
a. To completely eliminate the need for patient repositioning
b. To increase tissue perfusion by enhancing vasodilation
c. To reduce or eliminate pressure on vulnerable areas
d. To absorb excess moisture and prevent maceration

Answer: c. To reduce or eliminate pressure on vulnerable areas. Explanation: The primary goal of using pressure redistribution devices, such as specialized mattresses or cushions, is to reduce or eliminate pressure on vulnerable areas, thereby preventing the development or worsening of pressure injuries.

823. Which stage of the NPUAP classification system includes intact skin with non-blanchable redness?
a. Stage 1
b. Stage 2
c. Stage 3
d. Unstageable

Answer: a. Stage 1. Explanation: Stage 1 of the NPUAP classification system is characterized by intact skin with a localized area of non-blanchable erythema, which may appear differently in darkly pigmented skin. This stage indicates the earliest signs of pressure injury development.

824. A pressure injury described as "unstageable" by the NPUAP classification system is primarily characterized by:
a. Partial-thickness loss of dermis
b. Full-thickness skin and tissue loss
c. Obscured full-thickness skin and tissue loss due to slough or eschar
d. Non-blanchable erythema of intact skin

Answer: c. Obscured full-thickness skin and tissue loss due to slough or eschar. Explanation: An unstageable pressure injury is one in which the true depth of the injury cannot be determined because it is obscured by slough (yellow, tan, gray, green, or brown) or eschar (tan, brown, or black) in the wound bed.

825. Which component of the Braden Scale assesses the effect of shear forces on the skin?
a. Moisture
b. Activity
c. Mobility
d. Friction and shear

Answer: d. Friction and shear. Explanation: The "Friction and Shear" component of the Braden Scale specifically assesses the effect of shear forces on the skin, which can contribute to the development of pressure injuries by causing displacement and damage to skin and subcutaneous tissues.

826. For a patient with a stage 2 pressure injury, what type of dressing is generally recommended to facilitate a moist wound healing environment?
a. Dry gauze dressing
b. Hydrocolloid dressing
c. Alginate dressing
d. Silver sulfadiazine cream

Answer: b. Hydrocolloid dressing. Explanation: For a stage 2 pressure injury, which involves partial-thickness loss of dermis, a hydrocolloid dressing is generally recommended to facilitate a moist wound healing environment. Hydrocolloid dressings help maintain optimal moisture while protecting the wound from contamination.

827. When considering the risk of developing pressure injuries, which patient factor contributes significantly to reduced mobility?
a. Hypertension
b. Age over 65
c. Spinal cord injury
d. Diabetes mellitus

Answer: c. Spinal cord injury. Explanation: A spinal cord injury contributes significantly to reduced mobility, one of the key risk factors for the development of pressure injuries, due to paralysis or weakness, limiting the patient's ability to change positions independently.

828. In the context of pressure injury prevention, what is the significance of managing moisture?
a. Moisture enhances the natural barrier function of the skin
b. Moisture can lead to maceration and increase the risk of skin breakdown
c. Moisture is essential for the activation of topical medications
d. Moisture reduces the friction between the skin and support surfaces

Answer: b. Moisture can lead to maceration and increase the risk of skin breakdown. Explanation: Managing moisture is significant in pressure injury prevention because excessive moisture can lead to maceration of the skin, weakening its integrity and increasing the risk of breakdown and injury, especially in areas under pressure.

829. What is a key consideration when selecting a pressure redistribution device for a patient at high risk for pressure injuries?
a. The device should only be used during the night
b. The device must eliminate the need for turning and repositioning
c. The device should be chosen based on the patient's specific risk factors and needs
d. All pressure redistribution devices offer the same level of protection

Answer: c. The device should be chosen based on the patient's specific risk factors and needs. Explanation: When selecting a pressure redistribution device for a patient at high risk for pressure injuries, it is crucial to choose based on the patient's specific risk factors, such as their level of mobility, body weight, and the presence of existing pressure injuries, to ensure the most effective prevention and management strategy.

830. A 25-year-old female presents with sudden onset of fever, headache, neck stiffness, and photophobia. Lumbar puncture reveals a cerebrospinal fluid (CSF) white blood cell count of 2,500 cells/μL with 90% neutrophils, a protein level of 200 mg/dL, and a glucose level of 20 mg/dL. Which of the following is the most appropriate initial antibiotic regimen for this patient?
a. vancomycin and ceftriaxone
b. ampicillin and gentamicin
c. trimethoprim-sulfamethoxazole and fluconazole
d. acyclovir and dexamethasone

Answer: a. vancomycin and ceftriaxone. Explanation: The patient's presentation of fever, headache, neck stiffness, and photophobia, along with the CSF findings of a neutrophilic pleocytosis, elevated protein, and low glucose, is highly suggestive of acute bacterial meningitis. The most common causative organisms of community-acquired bacterial meningitis in adults are Streptococcus pneumoniae and Neisseria meningitidis. Empiric antibiotic therapy for suspected bacterial meningitis should cover these pathogens and should be initiated promptly, ideally within 1 hour of presentation, to reduce the risk of neurologic sequelae and death. The recommended empiric regimen for adults with suspected bacterial meningitis is vancomycin plus a third-generation cephalosporin such as ceftriaxone. Vancomycin provides coverage against penicillin-resistant S. pneumoniae, while ceftriaxone covers both S. pneumoniae and N. meningitidis. Ampicillin and gentamicin may be considered in patients over 50 years old or immunocompromised to cover Listeria monocytogenes but are not necessary for initial empiric therapy in most adults. Trimethoprim-sulfamethoxazole and fluconazole are used for the treatment of fungal meningitis, such as cryptococcal meningitis, but are not appropriate for empiric therapy of bacterial meningitis. Acyclovir is used for the treatment of viral meningitis caused by herpes simplex virus (HSV) but is not effective against bacteria.

831. A 40-year-old male with a history of HIV/AIDS presents with fever, headache, and altered mental status. Lumbar puncture reveals a cerebrospinal fluid (CSF) white blood cell count of 50 cells/μL with 80% lymphocytes, a protein level of 80 mg/dL, and a glucose level of 30 mg/dL. CSF cryptococcal antigen is positive. Which of the following is the most appropriate initial treatment for this patient's condition?
a. intravenous acyclovir
b. intravenous amphotericin B and oral flucytosine
c. oral fluconazole
d. intravenous penicillin G

Answer: b. intravenous amphotericin B and oral flucytosine. Explanation: The patient's presentation of fever, headache, and altered mental status in the setting of HIV/AIDS, along with the CSF findings of a lymphocytic pleocytosis, elevated protein, low glucose, and positive cryptococcal antigen, is diagnostic of cryptococcal meningitis. Cryptococcal meningitis is a life-threatening opportunistic infection that occurs primarily in immunocompromised individuals, particularly those with advanced HIV/AIDS. The most appropriate initial treatment for cryptococcal meningitis is a combination of intravenous amphotericin B and oral flucytosine for at least 2 weeks, followed by oral fluconazole for consolidation and maintenance therapy. Amphotericin B is a fungicidal agent that is the backbone of induction therapy for cryptococcal meningitis, while flucytosine enhances the efficacy of amphotericin B and helps to clear the infection more rapidly. Oral fluconazole monotherapy is not recommended for induction therapy of cryptococcal meningitis due to the risk of treatment failure and the development of resistance. Intravenous acyclovir is used for the treatment of viral meningitis caused by herpes simplex virus (HSV) but is not effective against fungi. Intravenous penicillin G is used for the treatment of bacterial meningitis caused by susceptible organisms, such as Streptococcus pneumoniae or Neisseria meningitidis, but is not active against Cryptococcus.

832. A 65-year-old female with a history of chronic sinusitis presents with fever, headache, and progressive confusion. MRI of the brain reveals multiple enhancing lesions with surrounding edema. Lumbar puncture reveals a cerebrospinal fluid (CSF) white blood cell count of 500 cells/μL with 70% neutrophils, a protein level of 100 mg/dL, and a glucose level of 40 mg/dL. CSF cultures grow Aspergillus fumigatus. Which of the following is the most likely predisposing factor for this patient's condition?
a. HIV/AIDS
b. immunosuppressive therapy
c. diabetes mellitus
d. intravenous drug use

Answer: b. immunosuppressive therapy. Explanation: The patient's presentation of fever, headache, and progressive confusion, along with the MRI findings of multiple enhancing brain lesions and the CSF findings of a neutrophilic pleocytosis, elevated protein, low glucose, and growth of Aspergillus fumigatus, is consistent with central nervous system (CNS) aspergillosis, a rare and often fatal invasive fungal infection. Aspergillus species are ubiquitous environmental molds that can cause invasive disease in immunocompromised hosts, particularly those with prolonged neutropenia, hematopoietic stem cell transplantation, solid organ transplantation, or chronic corticosteroid use. The most common route of CNS invasion by Aspergillus is through direct extension from the sinuses or lungs, although hematogenous dissemination can also occur. In this patient with a history of chronic sinusitis, the most likely predisposing factor for CNS aspergillosis is immunosuppressive therapy, such as chronic corticosteroid use or other immunomodulatory agents, which can impair the host's ability to contain the fungal infection. HIV/AIDS is a risk factor for other opportunistic CNS infections, such as cryptococcal meningitis or toxoplasmosis, but is not a common predisposing condition for invasive aspergillosis. Diabetes mellitus can increase the risk of certain bacterial infections but is not a major risk factor for CNS aspergillosis. Intravenous drug use is a risk factor for bacterial meningitis and brain abscesses but is not typically associated with fungal infections of the CNS.

833. A 20-year-old male presents with fever, severe headache, and a petechial rash on his trunk and extremities. Lumbar puncture reveals a cerebrospinal fluid (CSF) white blood cell count of 10,000 cells/μL with 95% neutrophils, a protein level of 500 mg/dL, and a glucose level of 10 mg/dL. Gram stain of the CSF shows gram-negative diplococci. Which of the following is the most likely causative organism of this patient's condition?
a. Streptococcus pneumoniae
b. Neisseria meningitidis
c. Listeria monocytogenes

d. Haemophilus influenzae

Answer: b. Neisseria meningitidis. Explanation: The patient's presentation of fever, severe headache, and a petechial rash, along with the CSF findings of a markedly elevated white blood cell count with neutrophilic predominance, high protein, very low glucose, and gram-negative diplococci on Gram stain, is highly suggestive of meningococcal meningitis caused by Neisseria meningitidis. N. meningitidis is a gram-negative diplococcus that is a common cause of bacterial meningitis in children and young adults. It is known for its ability to cause rapidly progressive, fulminant infections with high morbidity and mortality rates. The presence of a petechial or purpuric rash is a classic clinical finding in meningococcal meningitis and is caused by the release of endotoxin and the activation of the coagulation cascade, leading to thrombosis and hemorrhage in small blood vessels. Streptococcus pneumoniae is another common cause of bacterial meningitis but typically presents with a less fulminant course and is not associated with a petechial rash. Listeria monocytogenes is a gram-positive rod that can cause meningitis in neonates, elderly, and immunocompromised individuals but is not typically associated with such high CSF white blood cell counts or a petechial rash. Haemophilus influenzae type b (Hib) was a common cause of bacterial meningitis in young children prior to the introduction of the Hib vaccine but is now rare in vaccinated populations.

834. A 45-year-old female with a history of systemic lupus erythematosus (SLE) presents with fever, headache, and transient neurologic deficits. Lumbar puncture reveals a cerebrospinal fluid (CSF) white blood cell count of 100 cells/μL with 80% lymphocytes, a protein level of 150 mg/dL, and a glucose level of 50 mg/dL. CSF cultures are negative. Which of the following is the most appropriate next step in the management of this patient?
a. Initiate intravenous acyclovir
b. Start intravenous vancomycin and ceftriaxone
c. Perform brain MRI with gadolinium contrast
d. Administer high-dose intravenous methylprednisolone

Answer: c. Perform brain MRI with gadolinium contrast. Explanation: The patient's presentation of fever, headache, and transient neurologic deficits in the setting of SLE, along with the CSF findings of a lymphocytic pleocytosis, elevated protein, and normal glucose, raises concern for central nervous system (CNS) lupus, a serious neuropsychiatric manifestation of SLE that can cause a wide range of symptoms, including cognitive dysfunction, seizures, stroke, and meningitis. The most appropriate next step in the management of this patient is to perform a brain MRI with gadolinium contrast to evaluate for evidence of CNS inflammation, ischemia, or demyelination. MRI is the imaging modality of choice for assessing CNS involvement in SLE and can help to guide treatment decisions. If the MRI shows evidence of active CNS lupus, high-dose intravenous corticosteroids (e.g., methylprednisolone) may be indicated to suppress the inflammatory response and prevent further neurologic damage. Intravenous acyclovir is used for the treatment of herpes simplex virus (HSV) encephalitis but is not indicated in this patient with negative CSF cultures and a clinical picture suggestive of CNS lupus. Intravenous vancomycin and ceftriaxone are used for the empiric treatment of bacterial meningitis but are not necessary in this patient with negative CSF cultures and a lymphocytic pleocytosis suggestive of a non-bacterial etiology.

835. A 70-year-old male with a history of chronic obstructive pulmonary disease (COPD) presents with fever, cough, and altered mental status. Chest X-ray shows a right lower lobe infiltrate. Lumbar puncture reveals a cerebrospinal fluid (CSF) white blood cell count of 1,000 cells/μL with 90% neutrophils, a protein level of 200 mg/dL, and a glucose level of 30 mg/dL. Which of the following is the most likely causative organism of this patient's condition?
a. Streptococcus pneumoniae
b. Neisseria meningitidis
c. Listeria monocytogenes

d. Haemophilus influenzae


Answer: a. Streptococcus pneumoniae. Explanation: The patient's presentation of fever, cough, and altered mental status in the setting of COPD and a right lower lobe infiltrate on chest X-ray, along with the CSF findings of a neutrophilic pleocytosis, elevated protein, and low glucose, is highly suggestive of pneumococcal meningitis secondary to a pulmonary infection. Streptococcus pneumoniae is the most common cause of community-acquired bacterial meningitis in adults and is particularly prevalent in older individuals and those with chronic underlying diseases such as COPD. S. pneumoniae is also a common cause of pneumonia, and the presence of a concomitant pulmonary infiltrate in this patient further supports the diagnosis of pneumococcal meningitis. Neisseria meningitidis is another common cause of bacterial meningitis but is more typically seen in children and young adults and is not usually associated with pneumonia. Listeria monocytogenes is a gram-positive rod that can cause meningitis in elderly and immunocompromised individuals but is not a common cause of pneumonia. Haemophilus influenzae type b (Hib) was a common cause of bacterial meningitis in young children prior to the introduction of the Hib vaccine but is now rare in vaccinated populations and is not a significant pathogen in adults.


836. A 25-year-old female presents with fever, headache, and neck stiffness. Lumbar puncture reveals a cerebrospinal fluid (CSF) white blood cell count of 200 cells/μL with 80% lymphocytes, a protein level of 100 mg/dL, and a normal glucose level. CSF Gram stain and cultures are negative. Which of the following is the most likely etiology of this patient's condition?
a. Bacterial meningitis
b. Viral meningitis
c. Fungal meningitis
d. Tuberculous meningitis


Answer: b. Viral meningitis. Explanation: The patient's presentation of fever, headache, and neck stiffness, along with the CSF findings of a lymphocytic pleocytosis, mildly elevated protein, and normal glucose, in the absence of positive Gram stain or cultures, is most consistent with viral meningitis. Viral meningitis is the most common cause of aseptic meningitis in immunocompetent adults and is typically caused by enteroviruses, such as coxsackievirus and echovirus. Other viral etiologies include herpes simplex virus (HSV), varicella-zoster virus (VZV), and human immunodeficiency virus (HIV). The CSF profile in viral meningitis typically shows a mild to moderate lymphocytic pleocytosis (usually < 500 cells/μL), a mildly elevated protein level (< 150 mg/dL), and a normal glucose level. Bacterial meningitis, in contrast, typically presents with a more severe clinical picture and CSF findings of a neutrophilic pleocytosis, markedly elevated protein, and low glucose, along with positive Gram stain or cultures. Fungal meningitis, such as cryptococcal meningitis, can present with a lymphocytic pleocytosis but is usually associated with a low glucose level and positive fungal stains or cultures. Tuberculous meningitis, caused by Mycobacterium tuberculosis, can also present with a lymphocytic pleocytosis and low glucose but typically evolves over a more subacute to chronic course and may show acid-fast bacilli on CSF stains or cultures.


837. A 60-year-old male with a history of alcoholism presents with fever, headache, and confusion. Lumbar puncture reveals a cerebrospinal fluid (CSF) white blood cell count of 500 cells/μL with 60% lymphocytes, a protein level of 80 mg/dL, and a glucose level of 40 mg/dL. CSF Gram stain shows gram-positive rods. Which of the following is the most appropriate antibiotic to add to this patient's regimen?
a. Vancomycin
b. Ceftriaxone
c. Ampicillin
d. Trimethoprim-sulfamethoxazole

Answer: c. Ampicillin. Explanation: The patient's presentation of fever, headache, and confusion in the setting of alcoholism, along with the CSF findings of a mixed neutrophilic and lymphocytic pleocytosis, mildly elevated protein, low glucose, and gram-positive rods on Gram stain, raises concern for Listeria monocytogenes meningitis. L. monocytogenes is a facultative intracellular gram-positive rod that can cause meningitis, encephalitis, and sepsis in immunocompromised individuals, particularly those with cell-mediated immune deficiencies such as alcoholics, elderly, pregnant women, and neonates. The CSF profile in Listeria meningitis often shows a mixed pleocytosis with a predominance of lymphocytes, a mildly elevated protein level, and a low glucose level, which can mimic viral or tuberculous meningitis. However, the presence of gram-positive rods on Gram stain is highly suggestive of Listeria and warrants prompt initiation of appropriate antibiotic therapy.

838. Assessment of ADLs is crucial for determining:
a. The need for specialized medical equipment only
b. A patient's ability to perform basic self-care tasks
c. Cognitive function exclusively
d. Social interaction skills

Answer: b. A patient's ability to perform basic self-care tasks. Explanation: ADLs assessment focuses on a patient's ability to independently perform basic self-care tasks such as bathing, dressing, toileting, transferring, maintaining continence, and feeding, which are fundamental for personal care and independence.

839. In evaluating IADLs, difficulty with medication management can indicate:
a. An immediate need for surgery
b. Challenges with complex cognitive and organizational skills
c. A lack of social support
d. Ineffective pain management

Answer: b. Challenges with complex cognitive and organizational skills. Explanation: Difficulty with medication management, an IADL, often reflects challenges with more complex cognitive tasks such as organization, memory, and the ability to understand and follow medical instructions, which are crucial for maintaining health and managing chronic conditions.

840. A comprehensive assessment of functional status in the elderly includes both ADLs and IADLs because:
a. IADLs are less important than ADLs
b. ADLs do not provide a complete picture of an individual's functional capabilities
c. Only ADLs are related to physical health
d. IADLs are solely concerned with social activities

Answer: b. ADLs do not provide a complete picture of an individual's functional capabilities. Explanation: Including both ADLs and IADLs in a functional assessment provides a holistic view of an individual's ability to live independently.

ADLs assess basic self-care tasks, while IADLs evaluate the ability to perform more complex activities necessary for independent living, such as shopping, cooking, and managing finances.

841. A decline in the ability to perform IADLs might first manifest as difficulty in:
a. Walking short distances
b. Preparing complex meals and managing finances
c. Basic grooming activities
d. Short-term memory recall

Answer: b. Preparing complex meals and managing finances. Explanation: Difficulties with IADLs such as preparing meals and managing finances often precede issues with ADLs, as IADLs require higher cognitive function and organizational skills.

842. The Katz Index of Independence in Activities of Daily Living is used to:
a. Diagnose specific types of dementia
b. Assess a patient's functional ability in six basic ADLs
c. Predict life expectancy
d. Evaluate professional skills for job placement

Answer: b. Assess a patient's functional ability in six basic ADLs. Explanation: The Katz Index measures a person's independence in six basic ADLs (bathing, dressing, toileting, transferring, continence, and feeding), providing a standardized way to evaluate a patient's functional status and need for assistance.

843. An occupational therapist might recommend environmental modifications for a patient with IADL limitations, such as:
a. Installing advanced security systems
b. Lowering kitchen countertops for a wheelchair-bound individual
c. Increasing daily protein intake
d. Implementing a strict exercise regimen

Answer: b. Lowering kitchen countertops for a wheelchair-bound individual. Explanation: For patients with mobility issues affecting IADLs like cooking, occupational therapists might recommend practical home modifications such as lowering countertops to enhance independence and safety in the kitchen.

844. When assessing a patient's ability to perform ADLs, a significant focus is on:
a. Educational background and achievements
b. Physical and cognitive abilities affecting self-care
c. Previous employment history
d. Leisure activities and hobbies

Answer: b. Physical and cognitive abilities affecting self-care. Explanation: The assessment of ADLs centers on understanding the physical and cognitive abilities that influence an individual's capacity to perform basic self-care tasks, highlighting areas where assistance or intervention might be necessary.

845. For elderly patients, regular review of IADL capabilities is important because:
a. Changes can indicate alterations in cognitive status
b. Only IADLs are covered by insurance
c. IADLs are not as critical as ADLs
d. They solely relate to legal competency

Answer: a. Changes can indicate alterations in cognitive status. Explanation: Regularly reviewing IADL capabilities in elderly patients is crucial as changes can signify shifts in cognitive function, necessitating adjustments in care plans to support independence and safety.

846. A patient's difficulty in transferring, such as moving from bed to chair, directly impacts their ability to perform:
a. Complex meal preparation
b. Basic ADLs, particularly mobility-related tasks
c. Professional tasks and responsibilities
d. Engaging in social activities outside the home

Answer: b. Basic ADLs, particularly mobility-related tasks. Explanation: Difficulty in transferring affects basic ADLs by limiting the individual's mobility and independence in performing self-care tasks, necessitating interventions like physical therapy or assistive devices to enhance mobility and safety.

847. What component of the Mini-Cog test is used to assess executive function and visuospatial abilities?
a. 3-item recall
b. Clock drawing test
c. Orientation to time and place
d. Verbal fluency

Answer: b. Clock drawing test. Explanation: The clock drawing test, a component of the Mini-Cog, is used to assess executive function and visuospatial abilities by requiring the patient to draw a clock and set a specific time, which evaluates planning, execution, and the ability to visualize and spatially organize objects.

848. In the Montreal Cognitive Assessment (MoCA), which task is specifically designed to evaluate language abilities?
a. Naming animals within a minute
b. Repeating two syntactically complex sentences
c. Identifying three-dimensional shapes
d. Subtracting serial 7s from 100

Answer: b. Repeating two syntactically complex sentences. Explanation: In the MoCA, repeating two syntactically complex sentences is a task specifically designed to evaluate language abilities, focusing on the patient's ability to process complex language structures and articulate them accurately.

849. Which domain is not directly assessed by the Mini-Cog test?
a. Attention
b. Memory
c. Language
d. Executive function

Answer: c. Language. Explanation: The Mini-Cog test, consisting of a 3-item recall and a clock drawing test, directly assesses memory and executive function but does not include a specific component for evaluating language abilities.

850. How does the 3-item recall component of the Mini-Cog test assess cognitive function?
a. By evaluating short-term memory retention and recall
b. Through assessing the patient's orientation to time and place
c. By measuring the patient's ability to perform complex calculations
d. Through evaluating verbal fluency and language comprehension

Answer: a. By evaluating short-term memory retention and recall. Explanation: The 3-item recall component of the Mini-Cog test assesses cognitive function by evaluating short-term memory retention and recall, requiring the patient to remember and repeat three unrelated words after a brief distraction, such as the clock drawing test.

851. In the MoCA, what does the visuospatial/executive domain assess?
a. The ability to recognize and name familiar objects
b. The ability to sustain attention and concentrate
c. The capacity for abstract thinking and symbol interpretation
d. Skills related to understanding spatial relationships and planning

Answer: d. Skills related to understanding spatial relationships and planning. Explanation: The visuospatial/executive domain in the MoCA assesses skills related to understanding spatial relationships and planning, which includes tasks such as drawing a cube, clock, or identifying how patterns continue in a sequence, evaluating the patient's executive function and visuospatial abilities.

852. What is the significance of the orientation section in cognitive assessments like the MoCA?
a. It assesses the patient's ability to learn new information
b. It evaluates the patient's awareness of their own cognitive deficits
c. It tests the patient's awareness of time, place, and personal information
d. It measures the patient's visual-spatial orientation only

Answer: c. It tests the patient's awareness of time, place, and personal information. Explanation: The orientation section in cognitive assessments like the MoCA evaluates the patient's awareness of time, place, and personal information, providing insight into their level of consciousness and connection with their environment, which is crucial for assessing cognitive impairment.

853. Why is medication reconciliation (BPMH) essential in the context of cognitive assessments?
a. It identifies medications that may impair cognitive function
b. It ensures that the patient is compliant with their medication regimen
c. It assesses the patient's ability to manage their own medications
d. It provides a list of medications for potential pharmacological interventions

Answer: a. It identifies medications that may impair cognitive function. Explanation: Medication reconciliation (Best Possible Medication History) is essential in the context of cognitive assessments because it helps identify medications that may impair cognitive function, allowing clinicians to differentiate between drug-induced cognitive changes and underlying cognitive disorders.

854. In the context of geriatric cognitive assessment, why are potentially inappropriate medications (PIMs) according to the Beers Criteria significant?
a. They can cause or exacerbate cognitive impairment
b. They are the most effective treatment for cognitive decline
c. They are specifically designed for geriatric patients
d. They have no adverse side effects in older adults

Answer: a. They can cause or exacerbate cognitive impairment. Explanation: Potentially inappropriate medications (PIMs) according to the Beers Criteria are significant in geriatric cognitive assessment because they can cause or exacerbate cognitive impairment in older adults, necessitating careful review and adjustment of medication regimens to optimize cognitive function.

855. How does the delayed recall section of the MoCA contribute to assessing memory function?
a. By testing the patient's immediate memory span
b. By evaluating the patient's ability to retain and recall information after a delay
c. By assessing procedural memory through task repetition
d. By measuring semantic memory through category fluency tasks

Answer: b. By evaluating the patient's ability to retain and recall information after a delay. Explanation: The delayed recall section of the MoCA assesses memory function by evaluating the patient's ability to retain and recall information after a delay, providing insights into their short-term and working memory capabilities, which are often affected in cognitive disorders.

856. What role does abstraction play in cognitive assessments like the MoCA?
a. It evaluates the patient's fine motor skills
b. It assesses the patient's ability to understand and differentiate concepts

c. It measures the patient's spatial awareness and balance
d. It tests the patient's knowledge of factual information

Answer: b. It assesses the patient's ability to understand and differentiate concepts. Explanation: Abstraction in cognitive assessments like the MoCA plays a role in evaluating the patient's ability to understand, differentiate, and make connections between concepts, often involving tasks that require the patient to identify the relationship between different words or objects, reflecting higher-level cognitive processing and executive function.

857. A 65-year-old female with a history of diabetic neuropathy presents with burning pain and numbness in her feet. She has been taking acetaminophen with minimal relief. Which of the following adjuvant medications is most appropriate to consider adding to her regimen?
a. amitriptyline
b. duloxetine
c. gabapentin
d. lidocaine patch

Answer: c. gabapentin. Explanation: Gabapentin is an anticonvulsant medication that is commonly used as an adjuvant agent for the treatment of neuropathic pain, particularly in patients with diabetic neuropathy. Gabapentin works by binding to the α2δ subunit of voltage-gated calcium channels in the central nervous system, reducing the release of excitatory neurotransmitters and modulating pain signaling. Numerous randomized controlled trials have demonstrated the efficacy of gabapentin in reducing neuropathic pain and improving quality of life in patients with diabetic neuropathy. Amitriptyline is a tricyclic antidepressant (TCA) that can be used for neuropathic pain but is associated with more anticholinergic side effects and is generally reserved for patients who have failed other therapies. Duloxetine is a serotonin-norepinephrine reuptake inhibitor (SNRI) that is also effective for diabetic neuropathy but may be less well-tolerated than gabapentin due to side effects such as nausea and somnolence. Lidocaine patches provide localized analgesia and are useful for focal neuropathic pain but are not typically used as first-line therapy for generalized neuropathic pain syndromes like diabetic neuropathy.

858. A 58-year-old male with a history of postherpetic neuralgia presents with persistent burning pain and allodynia over his left chest wall. He has been taking gabapentin 300 mg three times daily with partial relief. Which of the following is the most appropriate next step in managing his neuropathic pain?
a. Switch gabapentin to pregabalin
b. Add amitriptyline 25 mg at bedtime
c. Apply lidocaine 5% patch to the affected area
d. Initiate tramadol 50 mg every 6 hours as needed

Answer: c. Apply lidocaine 5% patch to the affected area. Explanation: Postherpetic neuralgia (PHN) is a chronic neuropathic pain syndrome that can occur following an outbreak of herpes zoster (shingles). PHN is characterized by persistent burning, shooting, or electric-like pain and allodynia (pain triggered by normally non-painful stimuli) in the affected dermatome. Lidocaine 5% patches are a topical adjuvant therapy that can provide localized analgesia and reduce allodynia in patients with PHN. The lidocaine patch works by stabilizing neuronal membranes and reducing ectopic discharges in damaged peripheral nerves. In this patient who is already taking gabapentin, adding a lidocaine patch to the affected area is a reasonable next step to optimize neuropathic pain control. Switching gabapentin to pregabalin, another gabapentinoid anticonvulsant, may provide additional relief but is not necessarily superior to optimizing the gabapentin dosage or adding a topical agent. Adding a low-dose TCA like amitriptyline can be considered if the patient fails to respond to gabapentin and lidocaine, but TCAs are associated with more side effects and are not typically used as first- or second-line therapies. Tramadol is an opioid agonist that can be used for neuropathic pain but is not recommended as a first-line agent due to the risk of dependence and side effects.


859. A 72-year-old female with a history of chronic low back pain presents with worsening pain and difficulty sleeping. She has been taking ibuprofen 400 mg three times daily and oxycodone 5 mg every 6 hours as needed with minimal relief. Which of the following adjuvant medications is most appropriate to consider for this patient?
a. amitriptyline 25 mg at bedtime
b. duloxetine 30 mg daily
c. gabapentin 100 mg three times daily
d. pregabalin 50 mg twice daily


Answer: b. duloxetine 30 mg daily. Explanation: Chronic low back pain is a complex condition that often involves a combination of nociceptive and neuropathic pain mechanisms. In older adults with chronic low back pain who have not responded adequately to traditional analgesics like NSAIDs and opioids, adjuvant medications targeting neuropathic pain pathways can be helpful. Duloxetine is a serotonin-norepinephrine reuptake inhibitor (SNRI) that has been shown to be effective for the treatment of chronic musculoskeletal pain, including low back pain. Duloxetine works by increasing the levels of serotonin and norepinephrine in the central nervous system, which modulates descending pain inhibitory pathways and reduces pain perception. Compared to TCAs like amitriptyline, duloxetine has a more favorable side effect profile and is less likely to cause anticholinergic effects or sedation. Gabapentin and pregabalin are anticonvulsants that can be used for neuropathic pain but are not necessarily the best choice for this patient with chronic musculoskeletal pain and no clear evidence of radiculopathy or neuropathy. Additionally, gabapentin and pregabalin can cause sedation and dizziness, which may be problematic in an older adult.


860. A 45-year-old male with a history of fibromyalgia presents with diffuse muscle pain, fatigue, and sleep disturbances. He has tried acetaminophen, ibuprofen, and cyclobenzaprine with minimal relief. Which of the following adjuvant medications is most appropriate to consider for this patient?
a. amitriptyline 10 mg at bedtime
b. duloxetine 60 mg daily
c. gabapentin 300 mg three times daily
d. pregabalin 75 mg twice daily


Answer: d. pregabalin 75 mg twice daily. Explanation: Fibromyalgia is a chronic pain disorder characterized by widespread musculoskeletal pain, fatigue, sleep disturbances, and cognitive symptoms. The exact pathophysiology of fibromyalgia is not fully understood but is thought to involve central sensitization and abnormalities in pain processing. Pregabalin is an anticonvulsant medication that has been FDA-approved for the treatment of fibromyalgia. Pregabalin works by binding to the α2δ subunit of voltage-gated calcium channels in the central nervous system, reducing the release of excitatory neurotransmitters and modulating pain signaling. Several randomized controlled trials have demonstrated the efficacy of pregabalin in reducing pain, improving sleep, and enhancing quality of life in patients with fibromyalgia. Duloxetine is an SNRI that is also FDA-approved for fibromyalgia but may be less effective than pregabalin for pain relief. Amitriptyline is a TCA that can be used for fibromyalgia but is associated with more side effects and is generally reserved for patients who have failed other therapies. Gabapentin is another anticonvulsant that can be used for fibromyalgia but may be less effective than pregabalin and is not FDA-approved for this indication.

861. A 52-year-old female with a history of chronic pelvic pain presents with worsening pain and dyspareunia. She has been taking naproxen 500 mg twice daily with minimal relief. Pelvic exam reveals diffuse tenderness and no obvious pathology. Which of the following adjuvant medications is most appropriate to consider for this patient?
a. amitriptyline 50 mg at bedtime
b. duloxetine 60 mg daily
c. gabapentin 600 mg three times daily
d. pregabalin 150 mg twice daily

Answer: a. amitriptyline 50 mg at bedtime. Explanation: Chronic pelvic pain is a complex condition that can involve a combination of nociceptive, neuropathic, and central sensitization mechanisms. In women with chronic pelvic pain who have not responded adequately to traditional analgesics like NSAIDs, adjuvant medications targeting neuropathic pain and central sensitization can be helpful. Amitriptyline is a tricyclic antidepressant (TCA) that has been shown to be effective for the treatment of chronic pelvic pain, particularly in women with comorbid depression, anxiety, or sleep disturbances. Amitriptyline works by increasing the levels of serotonin and norepinephrine in the central nervous system, which modulates descending pain inhibitory pathways and reduces pain perception. Additionally, amitriptyline has anticholinergic effects that can help to reduce bladder spasms and improve sleep. The dosage of 50 mg at bedtime is a reasonable starting point for this patient, with titration up to 150 mg as tolerated. Duloxetine is an SNRI that can be used for chronic pain but has not been extensively studied in chronic pelvic pain specifically. Gabapentin and pregabalin are anticonvulsants that can be used for neuropathic pain but may be less effective for chronic pelvic pain and are associated with more side effects than low-dose TCAs.

862. A 68-year-old male with a history of painful diabetic neuropathy presents with worsening burning pain and paresthesias in his feet. He has been taking gabapentin 600 mg three times daily with partial relief. Which of the following adjuvant medications is most appropriate to add to his regimen?
a. amitriptyline 25 mg at bedtime
b. capsaicin 0.075% cream applied to the feet
c. duloxetine 60 mg daily
d. lidocaine 5% patch applied to the feet

Answer: c. duloxetine 60 mg daily. Explanation: Painful diabetic neuropathy is a common complication of diabetes mellitus that involves damage to peripheral nerves, leading to burning pain, paresthesias, and allodynia in the affected extremities. Gabapentin is a first-line adjuvant medication for painful diabetic neuropathy, but some patients may require additional therapies for optimal pain control. Duloxetine is a serotonin-norepinephrine reuptake inhibitor (SNRI) that has been FDA-approved for the treatment of painful diabetic neuropathy. Duloxetine works by increasing the levels of serotonin and norepinephrine in the central nervous system, which modulates descending pain inhibitory pathways and reduces pain perception. Several randomized controlled trials have demonstrated the efficacy of duloxetine in reducing pain and improving quality of life in patients with painful diabetic neuropathy, with a number needed to treat (NNT) of about 6. Amitriptyline is a TCA that can be used for neuropathic pain but is associated with more side effects and is generally reserved for patients who have failed other therapies. Capsaicin cream and lidocaine patches are topical agents that can provide localized analgesia for neuropathic pain but are not typically used as systemic adjuvants to oral medications like gabapentin. Additionally, capsaicin cream can cause burning and irritation of the skin, which may limit its use in patients with sensory neuropathy.

863. A 55-year-old female with a history of chronic headaches presents with daily tension-type headaches that are not relieved by acetaminophen or ibuprofen. She reports difficulty sleeping and frequent stress at work. Which of the following adjuvant medications is most appropriate to consider for this patient?
a. amitriptyline 25 mg at bedtime
b. duloxetine 30 mg daily
c. gabapentin 100 mg three times daily
d. pregabalin 50 mg twice daily

Answer: a. amitriptyline 25 mg at bedtime. Explanation: Chronic tension-type headaches are a common type of headache disorder characterized by bilateral, pressure-like pain that is often associated with stress, anxiety, and sleep disturbances. In patients with chronic tension-type headaches who have not responded adequately to over-the-counter analgesics like acetaminophen and ibuprofen, adjuvant medications targeting the underlying psychophysiological mechanisms can be helpful. Amitriptyline is a tricyclic antidepressant (TCA) that has been widely studied and used for the prevention of chronic tension-type headaches. Amitriptyline works by increasing the levels of serotonin and norepinephrine in the central nervous system, which modulates pain perception, improves sleep, and reduces anxiety and depression. The dosage of 25 mg at bedtime is a reasonable starting point for this patient, with titration up to 100 mg as tolerated. Duloxetine is an SNRI that can be used for chronic pain but has not been extensively studied in chronic tension-type headaches specifically. Gabapentin and pregabalin are anticonvulsants that are not typically used for tension-type headaches and may cause more side effects than low-dose TCAs. Non-pharmacologic therapies like stress management, relaxation techniques, and cognitive-behavioral therapy can also be valuable adjuncts in the management of chronic tension-type headaches.

864. A 62-year-old male with a history of chronic neck pain presents with worsening pain and stiffness after a recent motor vehicle accident. He has been taking oxycodone 10 mg every 6 hours with minimal relief. MRI of the cervical spine reveals multilevel degenerative changes and foraminal stenosis. Which of the following adjuvant medications is most appropriate to consider for this patient?
a. amitriptyline 10 mg at bedtime
b. cyclobenzaprine 5 mg three times daily
c. duloxetine 30 mg daily
d. gabapentin 100 mg three times daily

Answer: d. gabapentin 100 mg three times daily. Explanation: Chronic neck pain is a common condition that can involve a combination of nociceptive and neuropathic pain mechanisms, particularly in the setting of cervical degenerative disease and neural foraminal stenosis. In patients with chronic neck pain who have not responded adequately to opioid analgesics, adjuvant medications targeting neuropathic pain pathways can be helpful. Gabapentin is an anticonvulsant medication that has been widely used for the treatment of neuropathic pain, including radicular pain from cervical spine disorders. Gabapentin works by binding to the α2δ subunit of voltage-gated calcium channels in the central nervous system, reducing the release of excitatory neurotransmitters and modulating pain signaling. The dosage of 100 mg three times daily is a reasonable starting point for this patient, with titration up to 1800-3600 mg daily as tolerated. Amitriptyline is a TCA that can be used for neuropathic pain but is associated with more side effects and may not be the best choice for this patient with a history of trauma and potential for increased fall risk. Cyclobenzaprine is a muscle relaxant that can be used for acute musculoskeletal pain but is not typically used as a long-term adjuvant for chronic neuropathic pain. Duloxetine is an SNRI that can be used for chronic pain but may be less effective than gabapentin for radicular neuropathic pain.

865. A 48-year-old female with a history of fibromyalgia and generalized anxiety disorder presents with worsening widespread pain and sleep disturbances. She has been taking pregabalin 150 mg twice daily and zolpidem 10 mg at bedtime with partial relief. Which of the following adjuvant medications is most appropriate to add to her regimen?
a. amitriptyline 25 mg at bedtime
b. duloxetine 30 mg daily
c. gabapentin 300 mg three times daily
d. tramadol 50 mg every 6 hours as needed

Answer: b. duloxetine 30 mg daily. Explanation: Fibromyalgia is a chronic pain disorder that often coexists with psychiatric conditions like anxiety and depression. In patients with fibromyalgia who have not achieved adequate pain relief with one adjuvant medication, combining agents with different mechanisms of action can be helpful. This patient is already taking pregabalin, an anticonvulsant that modulates calcium channels and reduces excitatory neurotransmission. Adding duloxetine, a serotonin-norepinephrine reuptake inhibitor (SNRI), can provide additional pain relief and improve symptoms of anxiety and depression. Duloxetine works by increasing the levels of serotonin and norepinephrine in the central nervous system, which modulates descending pain inhibitory pathways and regulates mood and sleep. Several studies have demonstrated the efficacy of duloxetine in reducing pain, fatigue, and sleep disturbances in patients with fibromyalgia, with a number needed to treat (NNT) of about 8. The dosage of 30 mg daily is a reasonable starting point for this patient, with titration up to 60 mg as tolerated. Amitriptyline is a TCA that can be used for fibromyalgia but may cause more side effects and sedation when combined with pregabalin and zolpidem

Made in the USA
Middletown, DE
24 August 2024